BUDDHISM

BUDDHISM,

IN ITS CONNEXION WITH BRAHMANISM AND HINDUISM,

AND

IN ITS CONTRAST WITH CHRISTIANITY

SIR MONIER MONIER- WILLIAMS, K. C. I. E.

GYAN

Published by

GYAN

Gyan Publishing House
5, Ansari Road
Daryaganj, New Delhi-110002
Phone: 011-47034999, 9811692060
E-mail: books@gyanbooks.com

Distribution Network
gyanbooks.com
India, USA, Canada, UK, Australia, France

ISBN: 978-81-212-9071-5 (PB)
First Published, 1889

2nd Impression 2023

Printed at: Gyan Press, Delhi.

BUDDHISM
AUTHOR: SIR MONIER MONIER - WILLIAMS

BUDDHISM.

BRASS IMAGE OF GAUTAMA BUDDHA FROM CEYLON.

He is seated on the Mućalinda Serpent (see p. 480), in an attitude of profound meditation, with eyes half closed, and five rays of light emerging from the crown of his head.

[*Frontispiece.*

BUDDHISM,

IN ITS CONNEXION WITH BRĀHMANISM AND HINDŪISM,

AND

IN ITS CONTRAST WITH CHRISTIANITY,

BY

SIR MONIER MONIER-WILLIAMS, K.C.I.E.,

M.A., HON. D.C.L. OF THE UNIVERSITY OF OXFORD, HON. LL.D. OF THE UNIVERSITY OF CALCUTTA, HON. PH.D. OF THE UNIVERSITY OF GÖTTINGEN, HON. MEMBER OF THE ASIATIC SOCIETIES OF BENGAL AND BOMBAY, AND OF THE ORIENTAL AND PHILOSOPHICAL SOCIETIES OF AMERICA, BODEN PROFESSOR OF SANSKṚIT, AND LATE FELLOW OF BALLIOL COLLEGE, OXFORD, ETC.

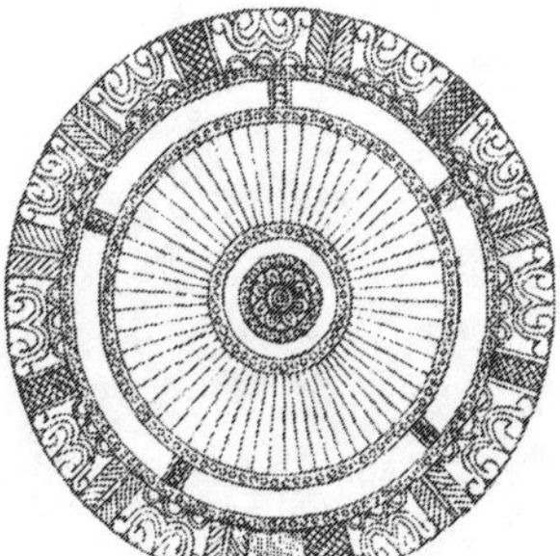

LONDON:
JOHN MURRAY, ALBEMARLE STREET.
1889.

PREFACE.

The 'Duff Lectures' for 1888 were delivered by me at Edinburgh in the month of March. In introducing my subject, I spoke to the following effect :—

'I wish to express my deep sense of the responsibility which the writing of these Lectures has laid upon me, and my earnest desire that they may, by their usefulness, prove in some degree worthy of the great missionary whose name they bear.

'Dr. Duff was a man of power, who left his own foot-print so deeply impressed on the soil of Bengal, that its traces are never likely to be effaced, and still serve to encourage less ardent spirits, who are striving to imitate his example in the same field of labour.

'But not only is the impress of his vigorous personality still fresh in Bengal. He has earned an enduring reputation throughout India and the United Kingdom, as the prince of educational missionaries. He was in all that he undertook an enthusiastic and indefatigable workman, of whom, if of any human being, it might be truly said, that, when called upon to quit the sphere of his labours, "he needed not to be ashamed." No one can have travelled much in India without having observed how wonderfully the results of his indomitable energy and fervid eloquence in the cause of Truth wait on the memory of his work everywhere. Monuments may be erected and lectureships founded to perpetuate his name and testify to his victories over difficulties which few other men could have overcome, but better than these will be the living testimony of successive generations of Hindū men and women, whose growth and progress in true enlightenment will be due to the seed which he planted, and to which God has given the increase.'

I said a few more words expressive of my hope that the 'Life of Dr. Duff'[1] would be read and pondered by every student destined for work of any kind in our Indian empire, and to that biography I refer all who are unacquainted with the particulars of the labours of a man to whom Scotland has assigned a place in the foremost rank of her most eminent Evangelists.

I now proceed to explain the process by which these Lectures have gradually outgrown the limits required by the Duff Trustees.

When I addressed myself to the carrying out of their wishes—communicated to me by Mr. W. Pirie Duff—I had no intention of undertaking more than a concise account of a subject which I had been studying for many years. I conceived it possible to compress into

[1] 'Life of Alexander Duff, D.D., LL.D., by George Smith, C.I.E., LL.D.' London: Hodder and Stoughton; published first in 1879, and a popular edition in 1881.

six Lectures a scholarly sketch of what may be called true Buddhism,—that is, the Buddhism of the Piṭakas or Pāli texts which are now being edited by the Pāli Text Society, and some of which have been translated in the 'Sacred Books of the East.' It soon, however, became apparent to me that to write an account of Buddhism which would be worthy of the great Indian missionary, I ought to exhibit it in its connexion with Brāhmanism and Hindūism and even with Jainism, and in its contrast with Christianity. Then, as I proceeded, I began to feel that to do justice to my subject I should be compelled to enlarge the range of my researches, so as to embrace some of the later phases and modern developments of Buddhism. This led me to undertake a more careful study of Koeppen's Lamaismus than I had before thought necessary. Furthermore, I felt it my duty to study attentively numerous treatises on Northern Buddhism, which I had before read in a cursory manner. I even thought it incumbent on me to look a little into the Tibetan language, of which I was before wholly ignorant.

I need scarcely explain further the process of expansion through which the present work has passed. A conviction took possession of my mind, that any endeavour to give even an outline of the whole subject of Buddhism in six Lectures, would be rather like the effort of a foolish man trying to paint a panorama of London on a sheet of note-paper. Hence the expansion of six Lectures into eighteen, and it will be seen at once that many of these eighteen are far too long to have been delivered *in extenso.* In point of fact, by an arrangement with the Trustees, only a certain portion of any Lecture was delivered orally. The present work is rather a treatise on Buddhism printed and published in memory of Dr. Duff.

I need not encumber the Preface with a re-statement of the reasons which have made the elucidation of an intricate subject almost hopelessly difficult. They have been stated in the Introductory Lecture (pp. 13, 14).

Moreover the plan of the present volume has been there set forth (see p. 17).

I may possibly be asked by weary readers why I have ventured to add another tributary to the too swollen stream of treatises on Buddhism? or some may employ another metaphor and inquire why I have troubled myself to toil and plod over a path already well travelled over and trodden down? My reply is that I think I can claim for my own work an individuality which separates it from that of others—an individuality which may probably commend it to thoughtful students of Buddhism as helping to clear a thorny road, and introduce some little order and coherence into the chaotic confusion of Buddhistic ideas.

At any rate I request permission to draw attention to the following points, which, I think, may invest my researches with a distinctive character of their own.

In the first place I have been able to avail myself of

the latest publications of the Pāli Text Society, and to consult many recent works which previous writers on Buddhism have not had at their command.

Secondly, I have striven to combine scientific accuracy with a popular exposition sufficiently readable to satisfy the wants of the cultured English-speaking world—a world crowded with intelligent readers who take an increasing interest in Buddhism, and yet know nothing of Sanskṛit, Pāli, and Tibetan.

Thirdly, I have aimed at effecting what no other English Orientalist has, to my knowledge, ever accomplished. I have endeavoured to deal with a complex subject as a whole, and to present in one volume a comprehensive survey of the entire range of Buddhism, from its earliest origin in India to its latest modern developments in other Asiatic countries.

Fourthly, I have brought to the study of Buddhism and its sacred language Pāli, a life-long preparatory study of Brāhmanism and its sacred language Sanskṛit.

Fifthly, I have on three occasions travelled through the sacred land of Buddhism (p. 21), and have carried on my investigations personally in the place of its origin, as well as in Ceylon and on the borders of Tibet.

Lastly, I have depicted Buddhism from the standpoint of a believer in Christianity, who has shown, by his other works on Eastern religions, an earnest desire to give them credit for all the good they contain.

In regard to this last point, I shall probably be told

by some enthusiastic admirers of Buddhism, that my prepossessions and predilections—inherited with my Christianity—have, in spite of my desire to be just, distorted my view of a system with which I have no sympathy. To this I can only reply, that my consciousness of my own prepossessions has made me the more sensitively anxious to exhibit Buddhism under its best aspects, as well as under its worst. An attentive perusal of my last Lecture (see p. 537) will, I hope, make it evident that I have at least done everything in my power to dismiss all prejudice from my mind, and to assume and maintain the attitude of an impartial judge. And to this end I have taken nothing on trust, or at second hand. I have studied Pāli, as I have the other Indian Prākṛits, on my own account, and independently. I have not accepted unreservedly any man's interpretation of the original Buddhist texts, and have endeavoured to verify for myself all doubtful statements and translations which occur in existing treatises. Of course I owe much to modern Pāli scholars, and writers on Buddhism, and to the translators of the 'Sacred Books of the East;' but I have frequently felt compelled to form an independent opinion of my own.

The translations given in the 'Sacred Books of the East'—good as they generally are—have seemed to me occasionally misleading. I may mention as an instance the constant employment by the translators of the word 'Ordination' for the ceremonies of admission to the Buddhist monkhood (see pp. 76–80 of the present volume). I have ventured in such instances to give what has appeared to me a more suitable equivalent for the Pāli. On the same principle I have avoided all needless employment of Christian terminology and Bible-language to express Buddhist ideas.

For example, I have in most cases excluded such words as 'sin,' 'holiness,' 'faith,' 'trinity,' 'priest' from my explanations of the Buddhist creed, as wholly unsuitable.

I regret that want of space has compelled me to curtail my observations on Jainism—the present representative of Buddhistic doctrines in India (see p. 529.) I hope to enter more fully on this subject hereafter.

The names of authors to whom students of Buddhism are indebted are given in my first Lecture (pp. 14, 15). We all owe much to Childers. My own thanks are specially due to General Sir Alexander Cunningham, to Professor E. B. Cowell of Cambridge, Professor Rhys Davids, Dr. Oldenberg, Dr. Rost, Dr. Morris, Dr. Wenzel, who have aided me with their opinions, whenever I have thought it right to consult them. Dr. Rost, C.I.E., of the India Office, is also entitled to my warmest acknowledgments for having placed at my disposal various subsidiary works bearing on Buddhism, some of which belong to his own Library.

My obligations to Mr. Hoey's translation of Dr. Oldenberg's 'Buddha,' to the translations of the travels of the Chinese pilgrims by Professor Legge, Mr. Beal, M. Abel Rémusat, and M. Stanislas Julien, to M. Huc's travels, and to Mr. Scott's 'Burman,' will be evident, and have been generally acknowledged in my notes. I am particularly grateful to Mr. Sarat Chandra Dās, C.I.E., for the information contained in his Report and for the instruction which I received from him personally while prosecuting my inquiries at Dārjīling.

I have felt compelled to abbreviate nearly all my quotations, and therefore occasionally to alter the phraseology. Hence I have thought it right to mark them by a different type without inverted commas.

With regard to transliteration I must refer the student to the rules for pronunciation given at p. xxxi. They conform to the rules given in my Sanskṛit Grammar and Dictionary. Like Dr. Oldenberg, I have preferred to substitute Sanskṛit terminations in *a* for the Pāli *o*. In Tibetan I have constantly consulted Jäschke, but have not followed his system of transliteration.

In conclusion, I may fitly draw attention to the engravings of objects, some of which were brought by myself from Buddhist countries. They are described in the list of illustrations (see p. xxix), and will, I trust, give value to the present volume. It has seemed to me a duty to make use of every available appliance for throwing light on the obscurities of a difficult subject; and, as these Lectures embrace the whole range of Buddhism, I have adopted as a frontispiece a portrait of Buddha which exhibits Buddhism in its receptivity and in its readiness to adopt serpent-worship, or any other superstition of the races which it strove to convert.

On the other hand, the Wheel, with the Tri-ratna and the Lotus (pp. 521, 522), is engraved on the title-page as the best representative symbol of early Buddhism. It is taken from a Buddhist sculpture at Amarāvatī engraved for Mr. Fergusson's 'Tree and Serpent-worship' (p. 237).

The portrait which faces page 74 is well worthy of attention as illustrating the connexion[1] between Bud-

---

[1] A reference to pages 74, 226, 232 of the following Lectures will make the connexion which I wish to illustrate clearer. In many images of the Buddha the robe is drawn over both shoulders, as in the portrait of the living Sannyāsī. Then mark other particulars in the portrait:—e.g. the Rudrāksha rosary round the neck (see 'Brāhmanism and Hindūism,' p. 67). Then in front of the raised seat of the Sannyāsī are certain ceremonial implements. First, observe the Kamaṇḍalu, or water-gourd, near the right hand corner of the seat. Next, in front of the seat, on the right hand of the figure, is the Upa-pātra—a subsidiary vessel to be used with the Kamaṇḍalu. Then, in the middle, is the Tāmra-pātra or copper vessel, and on the left the Pañća-pātra with the Āćamanī (see 'Brāhmanism and Hindūism,' pp. 401, 402). Near the left hand corner of the seat are the wooden clogs. Finally, there is the Daṇḍa or staff held in the left hand, and used by a Sannyāsī as a defence against evil spirits, much as the Dorje (or Vajra) is used by Northern Buddhist monks (see p. 323 of the present volume). This mystical staff is a bambu with six knots, possibly symbolical of six ways (Gati) or states of life, through which it is believed that every being may have to migrate—a belief common to both Brāhmanism and Buddhism (see p. 122 of this volume). The staff is called Su-darśana (a name for Vishṇu's Ćakra), and is daily worshipped for the preservation of its mysterious powers. The mystic white roll which begins just above the left hand and ends before the left knot is called the Lakshmī-vastra, or auspicious covering. The projecting piece of cloth folded in the form of an axe (Paraśu) represents the weapon of Paraśu-Rāma, one of the incarnations of Vishṇu (see pp. 110, 270 of 'Brāhmanism and Hindūism') with which he subdued the enemies of the Brāhmans. With this so-called axe may be contrasted the Buddhist weapon for keeping off the powers of evil (engraved at p. 352).

dhism and Brāhmanism. It is from a recently-taken photograph of Mr. Gaurī-Śaṅkar Uday-Śaṅkar, C.S.I. —a well-known and distinguished Brāhman of Bhaunagar—who (with Mr. Percival) administered the State during the minority of the present enlightened Mahārāja. Like the Buddha of old, he has renounced the world—that is, he has become a Sannyāsī, and is chiefly engaged in meditation. He has consequently dropped the title C.S.I., and taken the religious title—Svāmī Śrī Saććidānanda-Sarasvatī. His son, Mr. Vijay-Śaṅkar Gaurī-Śaṅkar, kindly sent me the photograph, and with his permission I have had it engraved.

It will be easily understood that, as a great portion of the following pages had to be delivered in the form of Lectures, occasional repetitions and recapitulations were unavoidable, but I trust I shall not be amenable to the charge of repeating anything for the sake of 'padding.' I shall, with more justice, be accused of 'cramming,' in the sense of attempting to force too much information into a single volume.

January 1, 1889.

POSTSCRIPT.

Since writing the foregoing prefatory remarks, I have observed with much concern that a prevalent error, in regard to Buddhism, is still persistently propagated.

It is categorically stated in a newspaper report of a quite recent lecture, that out of the world's population of about 1500 millions at least 500 millions are Buddhists, and that Buddhism numbers more adherents than any other religion on the surface of the globe.

Almost every European writer on Buddhism, of late years, has assisted in giving currency to this utterly erroneous calculation, and it is high time that an attempt should be made to dissipate a serious misconception.

It is forgotten that mere sympathizers with Buddhism, who occasionally conform to Buddhistic practices, are not true Buddhists. In China the great majority are first of all Confucianists and then either Tāoists or Buddhists or both. In Japan Confucianism and Shintoism co-exist with Buddhism. In some other Buddhist countries a kind of Shamanism is practically dominant. The best authorities (including the Oxford Professor of Chinese, as stated in the Introduction to his excellent work 'The Travels of Fā-hien') are of opinion that there are not more than 100 millions of real Buddhists in the world, and that Christianity with its 430 to 450 millions of adherents has now the numerical preponderance over all other religions. I am entirely of the same opinion. I hold that the Buddhism, described in the following pages, contained within itself, from the earliest times, the germs of disease, decay, and death (see p. 557), and that its present condition is one of rapidly increasing disintegration and decline.

We must not forget that Buddhism has disappeared from India proper, although it dominates in Ceylon and Burma, and although a few Buddhist travellers find their way back to the land of its origin and sojourn there.

Indeed, if I were called upon to give a rough comparative numerical estimate of the six chief religious systems of the world, I should be inclined, on the whole, to regard Confucianism as constituting, next to Christianity, the most numerically prevalent creed. We have to bear in mind the immense populations, both in China and Japan, whose chief creed is Confucianism.

Professor Legge informs me that Dr. Happer—an American Presbyterian Missionary of about 45 years standing, who has gone carefully into the statistics of Buddhism—reckons only 20 millions of Buddhists in China, and not more than 72½ millions in the whole of Asia. Dr. Happer states that, if the Chinese were required to class themselves as Confucianists or Buddhists or Tāoists, $\frac{19}{20}$ths, if not $\frac{99}{100}$ths, of them would, in his opinion, claim to be designated as Confucianists.

In all probability his estimate of the number of Buddhists in China is too low, but the Chinese ambassador Liū, with whom Professor Legge once had a conversation on this subject, ridiculed the view that they were as numerous as the Confucianists.

Undeniably, as it seems to me, the next place after Christianity and Confucianism should be given to Brāhmanism and Hindūism, which are not really two systems but practically one; the latter being merely an expansion of the former, modified by contact with Buddhism.

Brāhmanism, as I have elsewhere shown, is nothing but spiritual Pantheism; that is, a belief in the universal diffusion of an impersonal Spirit (called Brăhmăn or Brăhmă)—as the only really existing Essence—and in its manifesting itself in Mind and in countless material forces and forms, including gods, demons, men, and animals, which, after fulfilling their course, must ultimately be re-absorbed into the one impersonal Essence and be again evolved in endless evolution and dissolution.

Hindūism, with its worship of Vishṇu and Śiva, is based on this pantheistic doctrine, but the majority of the Hindūs are merely observers of Brāhmanical institutions with their accompanying Hindū caste usages. If, however, we employ the term Hindū in its widest acceptation (omitting only all Islāmized Hindūs) we may safely affirm that the adherents of Hindūism have reached an aggregate of nearly 200 millions. In the opinion of Sir William Wilson Hunter, they are still rapidly increasing, both by excess of births over deaths and by accretions from more backward systems of belief.

Probably Buddhism has a right to the fourth place in the scale of numerical comparison. At any rate the number of Buddhists can scarcely be calculated at less than 100 millions.

In regard to Muhammadanism, this creed should not, I think, be placed higher than fifth in the enumeration. In its purest form it ought to be called

Islām, and in that form it is a mere distorted copy of Judaism.

The Empress of India, as is well known, rules over more Muhammadans than any other potentate in the world. Probably the Musalmān population of the whole of India now numbers 55 millions.

As to the number of Muhammadans in the Turkish empire, there are no very trustworthy data to guide us, but the aggregate is believed to be about 14 millions; while Africa can scarcely reckon more than that number, even if Egypt be included.

The sixth system, Tāoism (the system of Lāo-tsze), according to Professor Legge, should rank numerically after both Muhammadanism and Buddhism.

Of course Jainism (p. 529) and Zoroastrianism (the religion of the Pārsīs) are too numerically insignificant to occupy places in the above comparison.

It is possible that a careful census might result in a more favourable estimate of the number of Buddhists in the world, than I have here submitted; but at all events it may safely be alleged that, even as a form of popular religion, Buddhism is gradually losing its vitality—gradually loosening its hold on the vast populations once loyal to its rule; nay, that the time is rapidly approaching when its capacity for resistance must give way before the mighty forces which are destined in the end to sweep it from the earth.

88 ONSLOW GARDENS, LONDON. M. M.-W.
January 15, 1889.

CONTENTS.

LECTURE III.

The Dharma or Law and Scriptures of Buddhism.

LECTURE IV.

The Saṅgha or Buddhist Order of Monks.

LECTURE V.

The Philosophical Doctrines of Buddhism.

LECTURE VI.

THE MORALITY OF BUDDHISM AND ITS CHIEF AIM—ARHATSHIP OR NIRVĀṆA.

LECTURE VII.

CHANGES IN BUDDHISM AND ITS DISAPPEARANCE FROM INDIA.

LECTURE X.

Mystical Buddhism in its connexion with the Yoga Philosophy.

LECTURE XI.

Hierarchical Buddhism, especially as developed in Tibet and Mongolia.

LECTURE XVIII.

BUDDHISM CONTRASTED WITH CHRISTIANITY.

OBSERVE.

The prevalent error in regard to the number of Buddhists at present existing in the world is pointed out in the Postscript at the end of the Preface (p. xiv).

LIST OF ILLUSTRATIONS

WITH DESCRIPTIONS.

RULES FOR PRONUNCIATION.

VOWELS.

A, *a*, pronounced as in rur*a*l, or the last *a* in Americ*a*; *Ā*, *ā*, as in t*a*r, f*a*ther; *I*, *i*, as in f*i*ll; *Ī*, *ī*, as in pol*i*ce; *U*, *u*, as in b*u*ll; *Ū*, *ū*, as in r*u*de; *Ṛi*, *ṛi*, as in me*rri*ly; *Ṛī*, *ṛī*, as in ma*ri*ne; *E*, *e*, as in pr*e*y; *Ai*, *ai*, as in *ai*sle; *O*, *o*, as in g*o*; *Au*, *au*, as in H*au*s (pronounced as in German).

CONSONANTS.

K, *k*, pronounced as in *k*ill, see*k*; *Kh*, *kh*, as in in*kh*orn; *G*, *g*, as in *g*un, do*g*; *Gh*, *gh*, as in lo*gh*ut; *Ṅ*, *ṅ*, as *ng* in si*ng* (siṅ).

Ć, *ć*, as in dolce (in music),=English *ch* in *ch*ur*ch*, lur*ch* (lurć); *Ćh*, *ćh*, as in chur*chh*ill (ćurćhill); *J*, *j*, as in *j*et; *Jh*, *jh*, as in he*dge*-*h*og (he*jh*og); *Ñ*, *ñ*, as in si*nge* (siñj).

Ṭ, *ṭ*, as in *t*rue (ṭru); *Ṭh*, *ṭh*, as in an*th*ill (anṭhill); *Ḍ*, *ḍ*, as in *d*rum (ḍrum); *Ḍh*, *ḍh*, as in re*dh*aired (reḍhaired); *Ṇ*, *ṇ*, as in *none* (ṇuṇ).

T, *t*, as in wa*t*er (as pronounced in Ireland); *Th*, *th*, as nu*t*-*h*ook (but more dental); *D*, *d*, as in *d*ice (more like *th* in *th*is); *Dh*, *dh*, as in a*dh*ere (more dental); *N*, *n*, as in *n*ot, i*n*.

P, *p*, as in *p*ut, si*p*; *Ph*, *ph*, as in u*ph*ill; *B*, *b*, as in *b*ear, ru*b*; *Bh*, *bh*, as in a*bh*or; *M*, *m*, as in *m*ap, ja*m*.

Y, *y*, as in *y*et; *R*, *r*, as in *r*ed, yea*r*; *L*, *l*, as in *l*ie; *V*, *v*, as in *v*ie (but like *w* after consonants, as in t*w*ice).

Ś, *ś*, as in *s*ure, se*ss*ion; *Sh*, *sh*, as in *sh*un, hu*sh*; *S*, *s*, as in *s*ir, his*s*. *H*, *h*, as in *h*it.

In Tibetan the vowels, including even *e* and *o*, have generally the short sound, but accentuated vowels are comparatively long. I have marked such words as Lāma with a long mark to denote this, but Koeppen and Jäschke write Lama. Jäschke says that the Tibetan alphabet was adapted from the Lañćha form of the Indian letters by Thumi (Thonmi) Sambhoṭa (see p. 270) about the year 632.

OBSERVE.

It is common to hear English-speakers mispronounce the words Buddha and Buddhism. But any one who studies the rules on the preceding page will see that the *u* in *Bud*dha, must not be pronounced like the *u* in the English word '*bud*,' but like the *u* in b*u*ll.

Indeed, for the sake of the general reader, it might be better to write Booddha and Booddhism, provided the *oo* be pronounced as in the words 'wood,' 'good.'

ADDENDA AND CORRIGENDA.

Page 21, line 15. One hundred is given as a round number. The actual distance is about one hundred and twenty miles.

Page 138, line 16. It must not be inferred that the episode of the Bhagavad-gītā is of great antiquity. This point I have made clear in 'Brāhmanism and Hindūism' (p. 63) as well as in 'Indian Wisdom.' My object at p. 138 is simply to show that Nirvāṇa is an expression common to Buddhism, Brāhmanism, and Hindūism.

Page 161, line 2. Sang Yun is properly written Sung Yun or Sung-Yun.

Page 178, line 16. Probably all the images of Dharma are meant to be female, as described in the note on the same page, and at p. 485.

Page 296, line 2. 'Cloven-headed' seems a misprint for eleven-headed; but the account of the creation of Avalokiteśvara at p. 487 of this volume justifies 'cloven-headed.'

Page 440, line 10 from bottom, *for* Lhāsta *read* Lhāssa.

It is feared that the long-mark over the letter A may have been omitted in one or two cases or may have broken off in printing.

PREFACE TO THE SECOND EDITION.

THIS edition will be found to possess the advantage of a full index.

Not a few improvements, too, will be observed in the body of the work. These, however, are chiefly verbal, and occur in the first 224 pages. They are such as have suggested themselves to my own mind in my efforts to express my meaning with the greatest possible lucidity.

For indeed I have been disappointed in my hope that in the interval between the publication of the First Edition of 'Buddhism,' in February last, and the putting forth of this Second Edition, some really helpful criticisms would have appeared, written by fellow-students of Buddhism and fellow-labourers in the field of Oriental Research, whose animadversions, even if severe, I should have welcomed, or whose suggestions, even if held by me to be inadmissible, would have received my careful and respectful consideration.

It is true that numerous notices and reviews have been published in various journals, both in this country and in America, but the majority have been written by professional journalistic critics, whose duty compels them to produce reviews on all subjects, and who are unable to do more than skim the pages of works like 'Buddhism,' which no one is competent to praise or censure without either special knowledge, or attentive and continuous perusal.

It is on this account that some of those who have dipped here and there into my book for purposes of criticism have taken me to task for omitting what I have not omitted, or for asserting what I have not meant to assert, and could not have been represented as asserting if every passage had been taken with its context, and the book had been carefully read throughout.

A few critics have blamed me for unfairness in my method of contrasting Buddhism with Christianity, and have almost accused me of intentionally warping Buddhism to suit the conditions of the 'Duff Lectureship.'

Such critics belong to a class who are quite unconscious that their exaggerated estimate of the excellence of Buddhism is derived from highly-coloured and one-sided views of a many-sided system, and from forgetfulness of the fundamental and really distinctive features of Christian doctrine.

One of these critics has also accused me of want of fairness in my numerical comparison of the world's religions (see Postcript, p. xv).

It is possible that I may have over-estimated the number of Confucianists, but I find that Dr. Edkins—

the well-known Chinese scholar, long resident at Peking —states in the 'Indian Antiquary' (for November, 1888) that the books of Confucius are held sacred by 200 millions of people.

Any candid and attentive reader will at once perceive that the expressions 'true' and 'real' Buddhists used by me are meant to apply to those who, if questioned as to their religious belief, would profess to be exclusively or primarily Buddhists, and not equally Confucianists or Tāoists.

Of reviews written by fellow-labourers in the field of Oriental Research, only two or three, so far as I have been able to ascertain, have as yet appeared.

One of these was published in the 'Nonconformist' of April 4, 1889, and is evidently written by an expert who knows what Buddhism is by personal experience and by residence in Buddhist countries.

From that thoughtful and generally laudatory review, I make the following extract (with a few abbreviations):—

'We welcome the appearance of this exhaustive treatise on Buddhism. It forms a natural supplement to the Professor's former work on "Brāhmanism and Hinduism." There are more English people, probably, who know a little about Buddha and his system than there are Europeans who profess anything worth calling knowledge about Brāhmanism which has much stronger claims on the attention and interest of Englishmen from the fact that it retains its hold upon nearly 200 millions of our Indian fellow-subjects. We will not stay to enquire into the cause of this preference beyond remarking that there is an attractive simplicity in a system that can be attributed to one founder, and consists of principles definitely connected with his teaching, over a system of uncertain origin and equally uncertain doctrine. It is this that has made it possible for people calling themselves "Theosophists" to obtain a hearing for their ideas which they call "Esoteric Buddhism," or the "Secret Doctrine," and attempt to pass off upon the public as the true wisdom of the East.'

Further on in his review the writer finds fault with me for dealing 'far too leniently' with the Theosophists in my chapter on mystical Buddhism (p. 223).

A reviewer in the 'Saturday Review' also intimates that I ought to have expressed myself more decidedly in condemnation of 'Esoteric Buddhism.'

It seems to me that I could scarcely have used more decided language than that at p. 249 of my volume. Nevertheless it may be well to add here that the printed report of the Psychical Research Society's Transactions, for December, 1885, gives a full account of the exposure by their Delegate, Mr. Richard Hodgson, of the alleged supernatural phenomena which took place at Madras.

Whether I have been sufficiently out-spoken on this subject or not, it is certain that the Theosophists themselves are generally indignant at my statements, and in their literary organs do not hesitate to pour contempt on my knowledge of the whole subject.

Another review by an expert appeared in the 'Ceylon Literary Register' (for May 31, 1889), and is extremely valuable as coming from one who must have had special advantages for forming a right judgment.

I have been much encouraged by this reviewer's warm approval of my work, and only wish that his criticisms had been more numerous.

He justly points out that I ought to have made it clearer, at p. 504, that the word Dāgaba is a Sinhalese corruption of the Pāli Dhātu-gabbha.

With regard, however, to the derivation of the word Pagoda, I still hold to my expressed opinion, and any one who studies Sir Henry Yule's article in 'Hobson-Jobson,' will, I think, arrive at the conclusion that the conjectural derivation given by me is as deserving of acceptance as any of the others which the author of the article has carefully enumerated and ably discussed.

As to Csoma de Körös, I find that my statement at p. 326, 1. is borne out by Dr. Duka's Life of this celebrated Hungarian traveller (in Trübner's Oriental Series, p. 6). It is there alleged 'that Csoma and two of his fellow-pupils had made a vow to undertake a scientific journey with the object of discovering some trace of the origin of their nation.'

In regard to American criticisms only a small proportion of the many critical notices published in America have reached me, and most of these have been favourable, and even laudatory—notably, a well-written Review by President Warren, of Boston University.

Doubtless some few adverse criticisms have appeared, but I have only been made aware of the existence of these through letters addressed to me, and through interesting articles written by Mr. W. Emmette Coleman, of San Francisco.

Moreover, the Bishop of Long Island—one of the ablest Bishops of the American Episcopal Church—has adverted to the contradictory character of the American criticisms in a letter from which, with his permission, I give the following extract :—

SEE HOUSE, GARDEN CITY,
June 29, 1889.

'The book ("Buddhism") has greatly interested me, and has filled me with gratitude, because of the telling use made of its learning in favour of the distinctive and essential superiority of Christianity over the Religion which has created the latest *craze* [underlined by the Bishop] among avowed free-thinkers of every name[1]. I have watched the criticisms on this side of the water. Some of them have been written by persons more or less deeply affected by the *craze*, and those, of course, have not been favourable. Others have been penned by strong men who are in sympathy with the Gospel of the Son of God. All such have been most appreciative, praising alike the erudition and the spirit of the book.'

Although my descriptions of Southern Buddhism are entirely founded on the recently published Pāli texts of the Southern Canon—the only true Canon of the Buddhist sacred scriptures—and on recent translations made by the best authorities; and although all my quotations have been carefully compared with the original Pāli, and the actual Pāli is often given in parentheses, still it is clear that much of what I have

[1] The strange partiality for Buddhism now prevalent in America is illustrated by an account (given in the *Times* of Sept. 28, 1889) of the reception of an American gentleman named Powell into the Buddhist community. The ceremony took place under the direction of the 'Buddhist high-priest' at Colombo, 'assisted by eleven yellow-robed monks.' The convert 'knelt before them and intimated his desire to be admitted to the Buddhist church.' The high priest then 'catechized him' and gave him the Pan-sil (Pañćasīla, see p. 126 of this volume), which the convert repeated with joined hands.

written is calculated to give umbrage to the Buddhists of Ceylon.

I find, as a matter of fact, that I have incurred the displeasure of the learned Sumaṅgala (mentioned at p. 256 of this volume). This, of course, was only to be expected. What I did not expect was that he should have imperilled his claim to be ranked among the true followers of the great Teacher, whom he calls his 'Lord,' by personal allusions wholly inconsistent with that Teacher's inculcation of fairness, impartiality, and truthfulness.

I must remind Sumaṅgala, that our short colloquy at Colombo, took place, not as he states, 'a few years ago,' but nearly thirteen years ago, on January 16, 1877, at a time when I did not profess anything more than an elementary knowledge of Pāli, and that our conversation was chiefly in English, interspersed, it is true, with occasional Sanskṛit words, but only so far as it was necessary to make that language—pronounced in many respects differently, and not used colloquially by European scholars—a medium of communication between us.

M. M.-W.

88, Onslow Gardens, London.
December, 1889.

RULES FOR PRONUNCIATION.

The *u* in Buddha must not be pronounced like the *u* in the English word *bud* but like the *u* in '*bull.*'

A, a, pronounced as in rur*a*l, or the last *a* in Americ*a*; *Ā, ā,* as in t*a*r, f*a*ther; *I, i,* as in f*i*ll; *Ī, ī,* as in pol*i*ce; *U, u,* as in b*u*ll; *Ū, ū,* as in r*u*de; *Ṛi, ṛi,* as in me*rri*ly; *Ṛī, ṛī,* as in ma*ri*ne; *E, e,* as in pr*e*y; *Ai, ai,* as in *ai*sle; *O, o,* as in g*o*; *Au, au,* as in H*au*s (pronounced as in German); *n* or *ṃ* for the Anusvāra, as *n* in French mo*n*, or as the nasal of a following consonant; *ḥ* for Visarga.

K, k, pronounced as in *k*ill, see*k*; *Kh, kh,* as in in*kh*orn; *G, g,* as in *g*un, do*g*; *Gh, gh,* as in lo*gh*ut; *Ṅ, ṅ,* as *ng* in si*ng* (siṅ).

Ć, ć, as in dolce (in music),=English *ch* in *ch*ur*ch*, lur*ch* (lur*ć*); *Ćh, ćh,* as in chur*chh*ill (ćur*ćh*ill); *J, j,* as in *j*et; *Jh, jh,* as in hed*ge-h*og (he*jh*og); *Ñ, ñ,* as in si*n*ge (si*ñj*).

Ṭ, ṭ, as in *t*rue (*ṭ*ru); *Ṭh, ṭh,* as in an*th*ill (an*ṭh*ill); *Ḍ, ḍ,* as in *d*rum (*ḍ*rum); *Ḍh, ḍh,* as in re*dh*aired (re*ḍh*aired); *Ṇ, ṇ,* as in *n*o*n*e (*ṇ*u*ṇ*).

T, t, as in wa*t*er (as pronounced in Ireland); *Th, th,* as nu*t-h*ook (but more dental); *D, d,* as in *d*ice (more like *th* in *th*is); *Dh, dh,* as in a*dh*ere (more dental); *N, n,* as in *n*ot, i*n*.

P, p, as in *p*ut, si*p*; *Ph, ph,* as in u*ph*ill; *B, b,* as in *b*ear, ru*b*; *Bh, bh,* as in a*bh*or; *M, m,* as in *m*ap, ja*m*.

Y, y, as in *y*et; *R, r,* as in *r*ed, yea*r*; *L, l,* as in *l*ie; *V, v,* as in *v*ie (but like *w* after consonants, as in t*w*ice).

Ś, ś, as in *s*ure, se*ss*ion; *Sh, sh,* as in *sh*un, hu*sh*; *S, s,* as in *s*ir, hi*ss*. *H, h,* as in *h*it.

In Tibetan the vowels, including even *e* and *o*, have generally the short sound, but accentuated vowels are comparatively long. I have marked such words as Lāma with a long mark to denote this, but Koeppen and Jäschke write Lama. Jäschke says that the Tibetan alphabet was adapted from the Lañćha form of the Indian letters by Thumi (Thonmi) Sambhoṭa (see p. 270) about the year 632.

CORRECTIONS.

Page 296, line 2, 'Cloven-headed' would be better 'eleven-headed,' but see p. 487.

Page 440, line 10 from bottom, *for* Lhāsta *read* Lhāssa.

BUDDHISM.

LECTURE I.

Introductory. Relation of Buddhism to Brāhmanism.

In my recent work[1] on Brāhmanism I have traced the progress of Indian religious thought through three successive stages—called by me Vedism, Brāhmanism, and Hindūism—the last including the three subdivisions of Śaivism, Vaishṇavism, and Śāktism. Furthermore I have attempted to prove that these systems are not really separated by sharp lines, but that each almost imperceptibly shades off into the other.

I have striven also to show that a true Hindū of the orthodox school is able quite conscientiously to accept all these developments of religious belief. He holds that they have their authoritative exponents in the successive bibles of the Hindū religion, namely, (1) the four Vedas—Ṛig-veda, Yajur-veda, Sāma-veda, Atharva-veda—and the Brāhmaṇas; (2) the Upanishads; (3) the Law-books—especially that of Manu; (4) the Bhakti-śāstras, including the Rāmāyaṇa, the Mahā-bhārata, the Purāṇas—especially the Bhāgavata-purāṇa—and the Bhagavad-gītā; (5) the Tantras.

---

[1] 'Brāhmanism and Hindūism.' Third Edition. John Murray, Albemarle Street.

The chief works under these five heads represent the principal periods of religious development through which the Hindū mind has passed.

Thus, in the first place, the hymns of the Vedas and the ritualism of the Brāhmaṇas represent physiolatry or the worship of the personified forces of nature—a form of religion which ultimately became saturated with sacrificial ideas and with ceremonialism and asceticism. Secondly, the Upanishads represent the pantheistic conceptions which terminated in philosophical Brāhmanism. Thirdly, the Law-books represent caste-rules and domestic usages. Fourthly, the Rāmāyaṇa, Mahā-bhārata, and Purāṇas represent the principle of personal devotion to the personal gods, Śiva, Vishṇu, and their manifestations; and fifthly, the Tantras represent the perversion of the principle of love to polluting and degrading practices disguised under the name of religious rites. Of these five phases of the Hindū religion probably the first three only prevailed when Buddhism arose; but I shall try to make clear hereafter that Buddhism, as it developed, accommodated itself to the fourth and even ultimately to the fifth phase, admitting the Hindū gods into its own creed, while Hindūism also received ideas from Buddhism.

At any rate it is clear that the so-called orthodox Brāhman admits all five series of works as progressive exponents of the Hindū system—although he scarcely likes to confess openly to any adoption of the fifth. Hence his opinions are of necessity Protean and multiform.

The root ideas of his creed are of course Pantheistic, in the sense of being grounded on the identification of the whole external world—which he believes to be a mere illusory appearance—with one eternal, impersonal, spiritual Essence; but his religion is capable of presenting so many phases, according to the stand-point from which it is viewed, that its pantheism appears to be continually sliding into forms of monotheism and polytheism, and even into the lowest types of animism and fetishism.

We must not, moreover, forget—as I have pointed out in my recent work—that a large body of the Hindūs are unorthodox in respect of their interpretation of the leading doctrine of true Brāhmanism.

Such unorthodox persons may be described as sectarians or dissenters. That is to say, they dissent from the orthodox pantheistic doctrine that all gods and men, all divine and human souls, and all material appearances are mere illusory manifestations of one impersonal spiritual Entity—called Ātman or Purusha or Brahman—and they believe in one supreme personal god—either Śiva or Vishṇu or Kṛishṇa or Rāma—who is not liable (as orthodox Brāhmans say he is) to lose his personality by subjection to the universal law of dissolution and re-absorption into the one eternal impersonal Essence, but exists in a heaven of his own, to the bliss of which his worshippers are admitted[1].

And it must be borne in mind that these sectarians are very far from resting their belief on the Vedas, the Brāhmaṇas, and Upanishads.

Their creed is based entirely on the Bhakti-śāstras

[1] The heaven of Śiva is Kailāsa, of Vishṇu is Vaikuṇṭha, of Kṛishṇa is Goloka.

—that is, on the Rāmāyaṇa, Mahā-bhārata, and Purāṇas (especially on the Bhāgavata-purāṇa) and the Bhagavad-gītā, to the exclusion of the other scriptures of Hindūism.

Then again it must always be borne in mind that the terms 'orthodox' and 'unorthodox' have really little or no application to the great majority of the inhabitants of India, who in truth are wholly innocent of any theological opinions at all, and are far too apathetic to trouble themselves about any form of religion other than that which has belonged for centuries to their families and to the localities in which they live, and far too ignorant and dull of intellect to be capable of inquiring for themselves whether that religion is likely to be true or false.

To classify the masses under any one definite denomination, either as Pantheists or Polytheists or Monotheists, or as simple idol-worshippers, or fetish-worshippers, would be wholly misleading.

Their faculties are so enfeebled by the debilitating effect of early marriages, and so deadened by the drudgery of daily toil and the dire necessity of keeping body and soul together, that they can scarcely be said to be capable of holding any definite theological creed at all.

It would be nearer the truth to say that the religion of an ordinary Hindū consists in observing caste-customs, local usages, and family observances, in holding what may be called the Folk-legends of his neighbourhood, in propitiating evil spirits and in worshipping the image and superscription of the Empress of India, impressed on the current coin of the country.

As a rule such a man gives himself no uneasiness

whatever about his prospects of happiness or misery in the world to come.

He is quite content to commit his interests in a future life to the care and custody of the Brāhmans; while, if he thinks about the nature of a Supreme Being at all, he assumes His benevolence and expects His good will as a matter of course.

What he really troubles himself about is the necessity for securing the present favour of the inhabitants of the unseen world, supposed to occupy the atmosphere everywhere around him—of the good and evil demons and spirits of the soil—generally represented by rude and grotesque images, and artfully identified by village priests and Brāhmans with alleged forms of Vishṇu or Śiva.

It follows that the mind of the ordinary Hindū, though indifferent about all definite dogmatic religion, is steeped in the kind of religiousness best expressed by the word *δεισιδαιμονία*. He lives in perpetual dread of invisible beings who are thought to be exerting their mysterious influences above, below, around, in the immediate vicinity of his own dwelling. The very winds which sweep across his homestead are believed to swarm with spirits, who, unless duly propitiated, will blight the produce of his fields, or bring down upon him injury, disease, and death.

Then again, besides the orthodox and besides the sectarian Hindū and besides the great demon-worshipping, idolatrous, and superstitious majority, another class of the Indian community must also be taken into account—the class of rationalists and free-thinkers.

These have been common in India from the earliest times.

First came a class of conscientious doubters, who strove to solve the riddle of life by microscopic self-introspection and sincere searchings after truth, and these did their best not to break with the Veda, Vedic revelation, and the authority of the Brāhmans.

Earnestly and reverently such men applied themselves to the difficult task of trying to answer such questions as—What am I? Whence have I come? Whither am I going? How can I explain my consciousness of personal existence? Have I an immaterial spirit distinct from, and independent of, my material frame? Of what nature is the world in which I find myself? Did an all-powerful Being create it out of nothing? or did it evolve itself out of an eternal protoplasmic germ? or did it come together by a combination of eternal atoms? or is it a mere illusion? If created by a Being of infinite wisdom and love, how can I account for the co-existence in it of good and evil, happiness and misery? Has such a Creator form, or is He formless? Has He qualities and affections, or has He none?

It was in the effort to solve such insoluble enigmas by their own unaided intuitions and in a manner not too subversive of traditional dogma, that the systems of philosophy founded on the Upanishads originated.

These have been described in my book on Brāhmanism. They were gradually excogitated by independent thinkers, who claimed to be Brāhmans or twice-born men, and nominally accepted the Veda with its Brāhmaṇas or at least abstained from denouncing it as absolutely untrue, while they covertly attacked it. Such men tacitly submitted to traditional authority, though they really propounded a way of salvation based entirely on self-evolved knowledge, and quite independent of all Vedic sacrifices and sacrificing priests. The most noteworthy and orthodox of the systems propounded by them was the Vedānta[1], which, as I have shown, was simply spiritual Pantheism, and asserted that the one Spirit was the only real Being in the Universe.

But the origin of the more unorthodox systems, which denied the authority of both the Veda and the Brāhmans, must also be traced to the influence of the Upanishads. For it is undeniable that a spirit of atheistic infidelity grew up in India almost *pari passu* with dogmatic Brāhmanism, and has always been prevalent there. In fact it would be easy to show that periodical outbursts of unbelief and agnosticism have taken place in India very much in the same way as in Europe; but the tendency to run into extremes has always been greater on Indian soil and beneath the glow and glamour of Eastern skies. On the one side, a far more unthinking respect than in any other country has been paid to the authority of priests, who have declared their supernatural revelation to be the very breath of God, sacrificial rites to be the sole instruments of salvation,

---

[1] The Sāṅkhya system, as I have shown, was closely connected with the Vedānta, though it recognized the separate existence of countless individual Purushas or spirits instead of the one (called Ātman). Both had much in common with Buddhism, though the latter substituted *Śūnya* 'a void' for Purusha and Ātman.

and themselves the sole mediators between earth and heaven; on the other, far greater latitude than in any other country has been conceded to infidels and atheists who have poured contempt on all sacerdotal dogmas, have denied all supernatural revelation, have made no secret of their disbelief in a personal God, and have maintained that even if a Supreme Being and a spiritual world exist they are unknowable by man and beyond the cognizance of his faculties.

We learn indeed from certain passages of the Veda (Ṛig-veda II. 12. 5; VIII. 100. 3, 4) that even in the Vedic age some denied the existence of the god Indra.

We know, too, that Yāska, the well-known Vedic commentator, who is believed to have lived before the grammarian Pāṇini (probably in the fourth century B.C.), found himself obliged to refute the sceptical arguments of Kautsa and others who pronounced the Veda a tissue of nonsense (Nirukta I. 15, 16).

Again, Manu—whose law-book, according to Dr. Bühler, was composed between the second century B.C. and the second A.D., and, in my opinion, earlier—has the following remark directed against sceptics:—

'The twice-born man who depending on rationalistic treatises (hetu-śāstra) contemns the two roots of law (śruti and smṛiti), is to be excommunicated (vahish-kāryaḥ) by the righteous as an atheist (nāstika) and despiser of the Veda' (Manu II. 11).

Furthermore, the Mahā-bhārata, a poem which contains many ancient legends quite as ancient as those of early Buddhism, relates (Śānti-parvan 1410, etc.) the story of the infidel Ćārvāka, who in the disguise of a mendicant Brāhman uttered sentiments dangerously heretical.

This Ćārvāka was the supposed founder of a materialistic school of thought called Lokāyata. Rejecting all instruments of knowledge (pramāṇa) except perception by the senses (pratyaksha), he affirmed that the soul did not exist separately from the body, and that all the phenomena of the world were spontaneously produced.

The following abbreviation of a passage in the Sarva-darśana-saṅgraha [1] will give some idea of this school's infidel doctrines, the very name of which (Lokāyata, 'generally current in the world') is an evidence of the popularity they enjoyed :—

> No heaven exists, no final liberation,
> No soul, no other world, no rites of caste,
> No recompense for acts; let life be spent,
> In merriment [2]; let a man borrow money
> And live at ease and feast on melted butter.
> How can this body when reduced to dust
> Revisit earth? and if a ghost can pass
> To other worlds, why does not strong affection
> For those he leaves behind attract him back?
> Oblations, funeral rites, and sacrifices
> Are a mere means of livelihood devised
> By sacerdotal cunning—nothing more.
> The three composers of the triple Veda
> Were rogues, or evil spirits, or buffoons.
> The recitation of mysterious words
> And jabber of the priests is simple nonsense.

Then again, the continued prevalence of sceptical opinions may be shown by extracts from other portions

---

[1] Freely translated by me in 'Indian Wisdom,' p. 133, and literally translated by Prof. E. B. Cowell.

[2] 'Let us eat and drink for to-morrow we die.' 1 Cor. xv. 32.

of the later literature. For example, in the Rāmāyaṇa (II. 108) the infidel Brāhman Jāvāli gives utterance to similar sentiments thus:—

'The books composed by theologians, in which men are enjoined to worship, give gifts, offer sacrifice, practise austerities, abandon the world, are mere artifices to draw forth donations. Make up your mind that no one exists hereafter. Have regard only to what is visible and perceptible by the senses (pratyaksham). Cast everything beyond this behind your back.'

Furthermore, in a parallel passage from the Vishṇu-purāṇa, it is declared that the great Deceiver, practising illusion, beguiled other demon-like beings to embrace many sorts of heresy; some reviling the Vedas, others the gods, others the ceremonial of sacrifice, and others the Brāhmans [1]. These were called Nāstikas.

Such extracts prove that the worst forms of scepticism prevailed in both early and mediæval times. But all phases and varieties of heretical thought were not equally offensive, and it would certainly be unfair and misleading to place Buddhism and Jainism on the same level with the reckless Pyrrhonism of the Ćārvākas who had no code of morality.

And indeed it was for this very reason, that when Buddhism and Jainism began to make their presence felt in the fifth century B.C. they became far more formidable than any other phase of scepticism.

Whether, however, Buddhism or Jainism be entitled to chronological precedence is still an open question,

[1] See Dr. John Muir's Article on Indian Materialists, 'Journal of Royal Asiatic Society,' N. S. xix, p. 302.

about which opinions may reasonably differ. Some hold that they were always quite distinct from each other, and were the products of inquiry originated by two independent thinkers, and many scholars now consider that the weight of evidence is in favour of Jainism being a little antecedent to Buddhism. Possibly the two systems resulted from the splitting up of one sect into two divisions. The subject of Jainism has been elucidated by the labours of Weber, Bühler, Jacobi, Leumann, and others, but is still somewhat obscure.

One point at least is certain, that notwithstanding much community of thought between Buddhism and Jainism, Buddhism ended in gaining for itself by far the more important position of the two. For although Jainism has shown more tenacity of life in India, and has lingered on there till the present day, it never gained any hold on the masses of the population; whereas its rival, Buddhism, radiating from a central point in Hindūstān, spread itself first over the whole of India and then over nearly all Eastern Asia, and has played an important rôle in the history of the world.

To Buddhism, therefore, we have now to direct our attention, and at the very threshold of our inquiries we are confronted with this difficulty, that its great popularity and its wide diffusion among many peoples have made it most difficult to answer the question:—What is Buddhism? If it were possible to reply to the inquiry in one word, one might perhaps say that true Buddhism, theoretically stated, is Humanitarianism, meaning by that term something very like the gospel of humanity preached by the Positivist, whose doctrine is the elevation of man through man—that is, through human intellect, human intuitions, human teaching, human experiences, and accumulated human efforts—to the highest ideal of perfection; and yet something very different. For the Buddhist ideal differs toto cælo from the Positivist's, and consists in the renunciation of all personal existence, even to the extinction of humanity itself. The Buddhist's perfection is destruction (p. 123).

But such a reply would have only reference to the truest and earliest form of Buddhism. It would cover a very minute portion of the vast area of a subject which, as it grew, became multiform, multilateral, and almost infinite in its ramifications.

Innumerable writers, indeed, during the past thirty years have been attracted by the great interest of the inquiry, and have vied with each other in their efforts to give a satisfactory account of a system whose developments have varied in every country; while lecturers, essayists, and the authors of magazine articles are constantly adding their contributions to the mass of floating ideas, and too often propagate crude and erroneous conceptions on a subject, the depths of which they have never thoroughly fathomed.

It is to be hoped that the annexation of Upper Burma, while giving an impulse to Pāli and Buddhistic studies, may help to throw light on some obscure points.

Certainly Buddhism continues to be little understood by the great majority of educated persons. Nor can any misunderstanding on such a subject be matter of surprise, when writers of high character colour their descriptions of it from an examination of one part of the system only, without due regard to its other phases, and in this way either exalt it to a far higher position than it deserves, or depreciate it unfairly.

And Buddhism is a subject which must continue for a long time to present the student with a boundless field of investigation. No one can bring a proper capacity of mind to such a study, much less write about it clearly, who has not studied the original documents in Pāli, Sanskṛit, and Tibetan, after a long course of preparation in the study of Vedism, Brāhmanism, and Hindūism. It is a system which resembles these other forms of Indian religious thought in the great variety of its aspects. Starting from a very simple proposition, which can only be described as an exaggerated truism —the truism, I mean, that all life involves sorrow, and that all sorrow results from indulging desires which ought to be suppressed—it has branched out into a vast number of complicated and self-contradictory propositions and allegations. Its teaching has become both negative and positive, agnostic and gnostic. It passes from apparent atheism and materialism to theism, polytheism, and spiritualism. It is under one aspect mere pessimism; under another, pure philanthropy; under another, monastic communism; under another, high morality; under another, a variety of materialistic philosophy; under another, simple demonology; under another, a mere farrago of superstitions, including necromancy, witchcraft, idolatry, and fetishism. In some form or other it may be held with almost any religion, and embraces something from almost every creed. It is founded on philosophical Brāhmanism, has much in common with Sāṅkhya and Vedānta ideas, is closely connected with Vaishṇavism, and in some of its phases with both Śaivism and Śāktism, and yet is, properly speaking, opposed to every one of these systems. It has in its moral code much common ground with Christianity, and in its mediæval and modern developments presents examples of forms, ceremonies, litanies, monastic communities, and hierarchical organizations, scarcely distinguishable from those of Roman Catholicism; and yet a greater contrast than that presented by the essential doctrines of Buddhism and of Christianity can scarcely be imagined. Strangest of all, Buddhism—with no God higher than the perfect man—has no pretensions to be called a religion in the true sense of the word, and is wholly destitute of the vivifying forces necessary to give vitality to the dry bones of its own morality; and yet it once existed as a real power over at least a third of the human race, and even at the present moment claims a vast number of adherents in Asia, and not a few sympathisers in Europe and America.

Evidently, then, any Orientalist who undertakes to give a clear and concise account of Buddhism in the compass of a few lectures, must find himself engaged in a very venturesome and difficult task.

Happily we are gaining acquaintance with the Southern or purest form of Buddhism through editions and translations of the texts of the Pāli Canon by Fausböll, Childers, Rhys Davids, Oldenberg, Morris, Trenckner, L. Feer, etc. We owe much, too, to the works of Turnour, Hardy, Clough, Gogerly, D'Alwis,

Burnouf, Lassen, Spiegel, Weber, Koeppen, Minayeff, Bigandet, Max Müller, Kern, Ed. Müller, E. Kuhn, Pischel, etc., and to the decipherment of Buddhist inscriptions by Cunningham, Bühler, Kielhorn, Senart, Fleet, and others.

But the case is different when we turn to the Northern Buddhist Scriptures, written generally in tolerably correct Sanskṛit (with Tibetan translations). These continue to be little studied, notwithstanding the materials placed at our command and the good work done by that distinguished 'founder of the study of Buddhism,' Brian Hodgson, and by Burnouf, Wassiljew, Cowell, Senart, Kern, Beal, Legge, Foucaux, etc. In fact, the moment we pass from the Buddhism of India, Ceylon, Burma, and Siam, to that of Nepāl, Kashmīr, Tibet, Bhutān, Sikkim, China, Mongolia, Manchuria, Corea, and Japan, we seem to have entered a labyrinth.

Nor is it possible to classify the varying and often conflicting systems in these latter countries, under the one general title of Northern Buddhism.

For indeed the changes which religious systems undergo, even in countries adjacent to each other, not unfrequently amount to an entire reversal of their whole character. We may illustrate these changes by the variations of words derived from one and the same root in neighbouring countries. Take, for example, the German words selig, 'blessed,' and knabe, 'a boy,' which in England are represented by 'silly' and 'knave.'

A similar law appears to hold good in the case of religious ideas. Their whole character seems to change by a change of latitude and longitude. This is even true of Christianity. Can it be maintained, for instance, that the Christianity of modern Greece and Rome has much in common with early Christianity, and would any casual observer believe that the inhabitants of St. Petersburg, Berlin, Edinburgh, London, and Paris were followers of the same religion?

It cannot therefore surprise us if Buddhism developed into apparently contradictory systems in different countries and under varying climatic conditions. In no two countries did it preserve the same features. Even in India, the land of its birth, it had greatly changed during the first ten centuries of its prevalence. So much so that had it been possible for its founder to reappear upon earth in the fifth century after Christ, he would have failed to recognize his own child, and would have found that his own teaching had not escaped the operation of a law which experience proves to be universal and inevitable.

It is easy, therefore, to understand how difficult it will be to give any semblance of unity to my present subject. It will be impossible for me to treat as a consistent whole a system having a perpetually varying front and no settled form. I can only give a series of somewhat rough, though, I hope, trustworthy outlines, as far as possible in methodical succession.

And in the carrying out of such a design, the three objects that will at first naturally present themselves for delineation will be three which constitute the well-known triad of Buddhism—that is to say, the Buddha himself, his Law and his Fraternity of Monks.

Hence my aim will be, in the first place, to give such

a historical account of the Buddha and of his earliest teaching as may be gathered from his legendary biography, and from the most trustworthy parts of the Buddhist canonical scriptures. Secondly, I shall give a brief description of the origin and composition of those scriptures as containing the Buddha's 'Law' (Dharma); and thirdly, I shall endeavour to explain the early constitution of the Buddha's Fraternity of Monks (Saṅgha). After treating of these three preliminary topics, I shall next describe the Law; that is, the philosophical doctrines of Buddhism, its code of morality and theory of perfection, terminating in Nirvāṇa. Lastly, I shall attempt to trace out the confused outlines of theistic, mystical, and hierarchical Buddhism, as developed in Northern countries, adding an account of sacred places and objects, and contrasting the chief doctrines of Christianity. And in treating of Northern Buddhism, I shall continually refer to Koeppen and to the travels of Huc, as well as to those of Indian explorers and to the translations from Chinese works made by our own scholars; but I shall also give the result of my own researches during my travels through the districts bordering on Tibet.

And here I ought to state that my explanations and descriptions will, I fear, be wholly deficient in picturesqueness. My simple aim will be to convey clear and correct information in unembellished language; and in doing this, I shall often be compelled to expose myself to the reproach contained in the expressions, *ćarvita-ćarvaṇam*, 'chewing the chewed,' and *pishṭa-peshaṇam*, 'grinding the ground.' I shall constantly be obliged to tread on ground already well trodden.

LECTURE II.

The Buddha as a personal Teacher.

It is much to be regretted that among all the sacred books that constitute the Canon of the Southern Buddhists (see p. 61)—the only true Canon of Buddhism—there is no trustworthy biography of its Founder.

For Buddhism is nothing without Buddha, just as Zoroastrianism is nothing without Zoroaster, Confucianism nothing without Confucius, Muhammadanism nothing without Muhammad, and I may add with all reverence, Christianity nothing without Christ.

Indeed, no religion or religious system which has not emanated from some one heroic central personality, or in other words, which has not had a founder whose strongly marked personal character constituted the very life and soul of his teaching and the chief factor in its effectiveness, has ever had any chance of achieving world-wide acceptance, or ever spread far beyond the place of its origin.

Hence the barest outline of primitive Buddhism must be incomplete without some sketch of the life and character of Gautama Buddha himself. Yet it is difficult to find any sure basis of fact on which we may construct a fairly credible biography.

In all likelihood legendary histories of the Founder of

Buddhism were current in Nepāl and Tibet in the early centuries of our era; but unhappily his too enthusiastic and imaginative admirers have thought it right to testify their admiration by interweaving with the probable facts of Gautama Buddha's life, fables so extravagant that some modern critical scholars have despaired of attempting to sift truth from fiction, and have even gone to the extreme of doubting that Gautama Buddha ever lived at all.

To believe nothing that has been recorded about him, is as unreasonable as to accept with unquestioning faith all the miraculous circumstances which are made to encircle him as with a halo of divine glory.

We must bear in mind that when Gautama Buddha lived—about the fifth century B.C.—the art of writing was not common in India[1]. We may point out, too, that in all countries, European as well as Asiatic—notably in Greece (witness, for example, the familiar instance of Socrates)—men have thought more of preserving the sayings of their teachers than of recording the facts of their lives.

And we must not forget that in India—where the imaginative faculties have always been too active, and anything like real history is unknown—any plain matter-of-fact biography of the most heroic personage would have few charms for any one, and little chance of gaining acceptance anywhere.

Hence it has happened that the ballads (gāthā) and legends current about Gautama among Northern

---

[1] It is difficult to accept the theory of those who maintain that writing had not been invented.

Buddhists, bristle with the wildest fancies and the most absurd exaggèrations.

Yet it is not impossible to detect a few scattered historical facts beneath stories, however childish, and legends, however extravagant. We shall not at least be far wrong, if, in attempting an outline of the Buddha's life, we begin by asserting that intense individuality, fervid earnestness, and severe simplicity of character, combined with singular beauty of countenance, calm dignity of bearing, and above all, almost superhuman persuasiveness of speech, were conspicuous in the great Teacher.

The earliest authorities, however, never claim for him anything extraordinary or superhuman in regard to external form. It was only in later times that Buddhist writers pandered to the superstitions of the people, by describing the Buddha as possessed of various miraculous characteristics of mind and body. He is said to have been of immense stature—according to some, eighteen feet high—and to have had on his body thirty-two chief auspicious marks (mahā-vyañjana), regarded as indications of a Supreme Lord and Universal Ruler, eighty secondary marks (anu-vyañjana), besides one hundred and eight symbols on the sole of each foot, and a halo extending for six feet round his person.

All that can be said with any degree of probability about his personal appearance is, that he was endowed with certain qualities, which acted like a spell, or with a kind of irresistible magnetism, on his hearers. These must have formed, so to speak, the foundation-stone on which the superstructure of his vast influence rested.

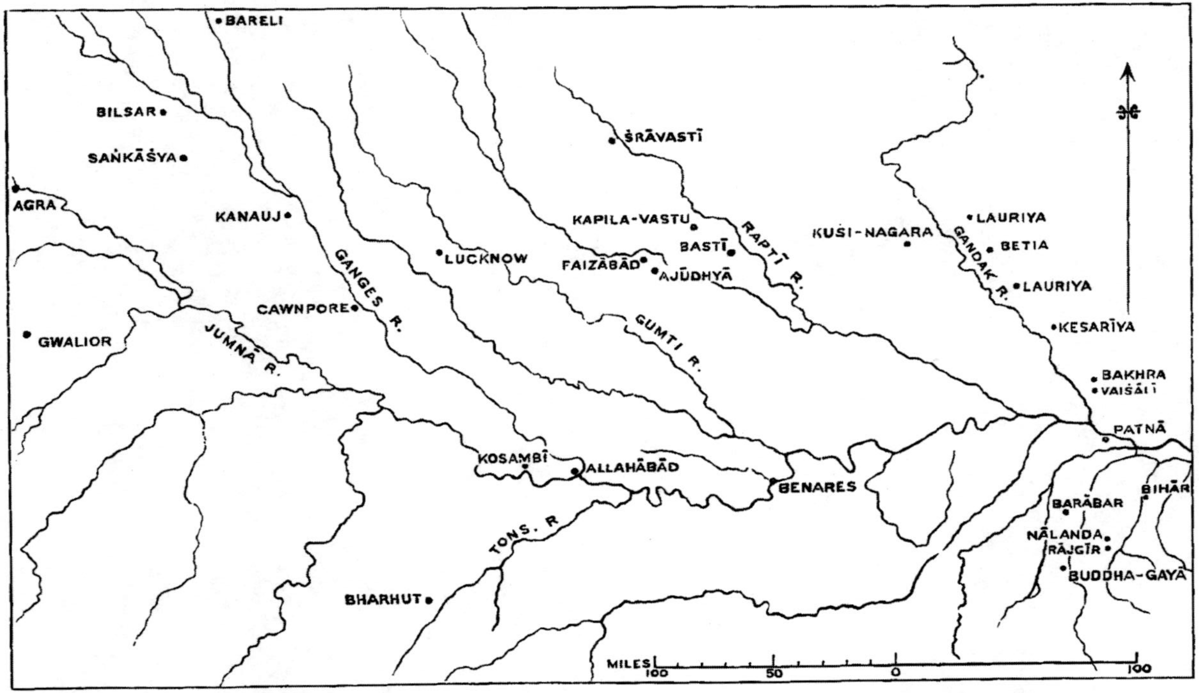

SACRED LAND OF BUDDHISM, AND SCENE OF THE BUDDHA'S ITINERATION AND PREACHING FOR FORTY-FIVE YEARS.

[*To face page* 21.

Unhappily, no authoritative Buddhist scripture gives any trustworthy clue to the exact year of the Buddha's birth. The traditions which refer back his *death* to a date corresponding to 543 B.C. are now rejected by modern European scholars. Nor can we as yet accept as infallible the results of the latest researches, which making use of various other data, such as the inscriptions on coins, rocks, and columns, place his death more than a century later. We shall not, however, be far wrong if we assert that he was born about the year 500 B.C. at Kapila-vastu (now Bhūila)—a town situated about half-way between Bastī and Ajūdhyā (Ayodhyā) in the territory of Kosala (the modern Oudh, see pp. 29, 48), about sixty miles from its capital city Śrāvasti (a favourite residence of Gautama), and about one hundred miles north-west of Benares, and near the borders of the kingdom of Magadha (now Behār or Bihār).

His father, named Śuddhodana, was a land-owner of the tribe of the Śākyas (a name possibly connected with the Sanskṛit root Śak, 'to be powerful'), whose territory in the Gorakh-pur district extended from the lower Nepālese mountains to the river Raptī in Oudh. It has been conjectured that the Śākyas may have been originally a non-Āryan tribe, connected perhaps with certain nomad immigrants from Tibet or Northern Asia, who may have immigrated into India at various periods; but even if this could be proved, it would have to be admitted that the Śākyas had become Āryanized. It is said that the chief families claimed to be Rājputs, tracing back their origin to Ikshvāku, the first of the Solar race. It appears, too, that though belonging to the

Kshatriya caste, they were agriculturists, and mainly engaged in the cultivation of rice. It is also asserted that Śākya families were in the habit of taking the name of the family of the Brāhmans who were their spiritual guides and performed religious offices for them, and that the family of Śuddhodana took the name Gautama, that is, descendant of the sage Gotama. It does not, however, seem necessary to account for the name in this manner. It was an auspicious name, which in ancient times might have been given to the child of any great land-owner as a proof of orthodoxy, or with the view, perhaps, of pleasing the Brāhmans and securing their prayers and good wishes on its behalf.

The father of the Founder of Buddhism was simply a chief of the Śākya tribe—certainly not a king in our sense of the term—but rather a great Zamīndār or landlord, whose territory was not so large in area as Yorkshire. His name Śuddhodana, 'one possessed of pure rice,' probably indicated the occupation and ordinary food of the peasantry inhabiting the district belonging to him and subject to his authority. Those who have travelled much in India must often have met great land-owners of the Śuddhodana type—men to whom the title Mahā-rāja is given much as 'Lord' is to our aristocracy. For example, the Mahā-rāja of Darbhanga is probably a more important personage than Gautama's father ever was, and his territory larger than that of Śuddhodana ever was.

The name Gautama (in Pāli spelt Gotama) was the personal name corresponding to that given to all children at the name-giving ceremony. It was not till his supposed attainment of perfect wisdom that Gautama assumed the title of Buddha, or 'the enlightened one.' But from that time forward this became his recognized title. Every other name besides Gautama (or Gotama), and every other title except Buddha (or together, Gautama Buddha), are simply epithets; for example, Śākya-muni, 'sage of the tribe of the Śākyas;' Śākya-siṉha, 'lion of the Śākyas;' Śramaṇa (Samaṇa), 'the ascetic;' Siddhārtha, 'one who has fulfilled the object (of his coming);' Sugata, 'whose coming is auspicious;' Tathāgata, 'who comes and goes as his predecessors;' Bhagavān (Bhagavā), 'the blessed lord;' Śāstā (Satthā), 'the Teacher;' Aśaraṇa-śaraṇa, 'Refuge of the refugeless;' Āditya-bandhu, 'kinsman of the Sun;' Jina, 'conqueror;' Mahā-vīra, 'great hero;' Mahā-purusha, 'great man;' Ćakravartī, 'universal monarch.' Devout Buddhists call him 'Lord of the World,' 'the Lord,' 'World-honoured One,' 'King of the Law,' 'the Jewel,' etc.; and prefer to use the titles rather than the personal name Gautama, which is thought too familiar.

The names of previous Buddhas, supposed to have existed in previous ages, are given at p. 136.

Little of the story of the miraculous birth of Buddha is worthy of repetition. Since, however, a white elephant is reckoned among the sacred objects of Buddhism, as something rare and precious, it is worth while mentioning the fable, that when the time came for the Bodhi-sattva (p. 98) to leave the Tushita heaven (p. 207) and be born as Gautama Buddha, he descended into the womb of his mother in the form of a white elephant. He was born under a Śāl tree and the god Brahmā received him from his mother's side. (See illustration opposite p. 477.) His mother, Māyā, died seven days afterwards, and the infant was committed to her sister (Mahā-prajāpatī), a second wife of Śuddhodana.

It is not related of Gautama that, as he grew up, any efforts were made to imbue him with sacred learning; though, as a Kshatriya, he was privileged to receive instruction in certain portions of the Veda.

Nor are we told of him that as a Kshatriya he was trained to the profession of a soldier. It is more probable, that his love of contemplation developed itself very early, and that from a desire to humour this not uncommon Oriental propensity, he was allowed to pass most of his time in the open air.

There is a well-known legend, which relates how Gautama's relations came in a body to his father and complained that the youth's deficiency in martial and athletic exercises would incapacitate him, on reaching manhood, from taking part in warlike expeditions. This might be reckoned among the few trustworthy historical incidents, were the story not marred by the legendary addition, that on a day of trial being fixed, the youth, without any previous practice, and of course to the surprise of all present, proved his superiority in archery and in 'the twelve arts.'

One statement may certainly be accepted without much qualification. It is said that Gautama was made to marry early, according to the universal custom throughout India in the present day. No son of any respectable person in modern times could remain unmarried at the age of sixteen or seventeen, without, so to speak, tarnishing the family escutcheon, and exposing the youth himself to a serious social stigma, likely to cling to him in after-life. In ancient times marriage was equally universal, and there is no reason to suppose that among Kshatriyas it was delayed to a much later period of life.

No doubt, therefore, the future Buddha had at least one wife (whose name was Yaśodharā, though often called Rāhula-mātā, 'Rāhula's mother'), and probably at least one son, named Rāhula. It is said that this son was not born till his father was twenty-nine years of age, or not till the time when a sense of the vanity of all human aims, and a resolution to abandon all worldly ties, and a longing to enter upon a monastic life had begun to take possession of his father's mind.

The story of the four visions, which led to his final renunciation of the world, is profusely overlaid with fanciful hyperbole, but, however slight the basis of fact on which it may reasonably be held to rest, it is too picturesque and interesting to be passed over without notice. I therefore here abridge the account given in Mr. Beal's translation of the Chinese version of the Abhinishkramaṇa-sūtra, varying (for the sake of brevity) the phraseology, but retaining the expression 'prince':—

Gautama's father, warned of his son's tendencies, had kept him strictly secluded. One day, however, Gautama drove through the town to some gardens.

Then there appeared before his eyes in one of the streets the form of a decrepid old man, his skin shrivelled, his head bald, his teeth gone, his body infirm and bent. A staff supported his tottering limbs, as he stood right across the path of the prince's advancing chariot.

Seeing this aged person, Siddhārtha inquired of his charioteer :—'What human form is this, so miserable and so distressing, the like of which I have never seen before?'

The charioteer replied :—'This is what is called an old man.'

The prince again inquired :—'And what is the exact meaning of this expression "old"?'

The charioteer answered :—'Old age implies the loss of bodily power, decay of the vital functions, and failure of mind and memory. This poor man before you is old and approaching his end.'

Then asked the prince :—'Is this law universal?'

'Yes,' he replied, 'this is the common lot of all living creatures. All that is born must die.'

Soon afterwards another strange sight presented itself—a sick man, worn by disease and suffering, pale and miserable, scarcely able to draw his breath, was seen tottering on the road.

Then the prince inquired of his charioteer :—'Who is this unhappy being?'

The charioteer replied :—'This is a sick man, and such sickness is common to all.'

Soon afterwards there passed before them a corpse, borne on a bier.

Then asked the prince :—'Who is this borne onwards on his bed, covered with strangely-coloured garments, surrounded by people weeping and lamenting?'

'This,' replied the charioteer, 'is called a dead body; he has ended his life; he has no further beauty of form, and no desires of any kind; he is one with the stones and the felled tree; he is like a ruined wall, or fallen leaf; no more shall he see his father or mother, brother or sister, or other relatives; his body is dead, and your body also must come to this.'

Next day on his going out by a different gate there appeared advancing with measured steps a man with a shaven crown and monk's robe—his right shoulder bare, a religious staff in his right hand, and a mendicant's alms-bowl in his left.

'Who is this,' the prince inquired, 'proceeding with slow and dignified steps, looking neither to the right hand nor to the left, absorbed in thought, with shaven head and garments of reddish colour?'

'This man,' said the charioteer, 'devotes himself to charity, and restrains his appetites and his bodily desires. He hurts nobody, but does good to all, and is full of sympathy for all.'

Then the prince asked the man himself to give an account of his own condition.

He answered:—'I am called a homeless ascetic; I have forsaken the world, relatives, and friends; I seek deliverance for myself and desire the salvation of all creatures, and I do harm to none.'

After hearing these words, the prince went to his father and said, 'I wish to become a wandering ascetic (parivrājika) and to seek Nirvāṇa; all worldly things, O king! are changeable and transitory.'

Such is an epitome of the legendary story of the 'four visionary appearances,' so called because they are supposed to have been divine visions or appearances, miraculously produced. The remainder of the legendary life of Gautama Buddha is interesting and here and there not without some historical value, and portions of it I now add in an abridged form.

Very shortly after the occurrences just described, Gautama receives intelligence of the birth of his son Rāhula. This is the first momentous crisis of his life, and Gautama remains for a long time lost in profound thought. He sees in his child the strongest of all fetters, binding him to family and home. But his mind is made up. He must fly at once, or be for ever held in bondage. Around him gather the beautiful women of his father's household, striving by their blandishments to divert him from his purpose; but in vain. He seeks the chamber of his wife, and finds her asleep with her hand on the head of his infant son. He longs for a last embrace; but fearing to arouse her suspicions hurries away. Outside, his favourite horse is waiting to aid his flight. He accomplishes the first stage of what Buddhists call with pride the Mahābhinishkramaṇa, 'the great going forth from home;' but not without overcoming other still more formidable trials. For Māra, the evil deity who tempts men to indulge their passions (see p. 208), makes himself visible, and promises the prince all the glories of empire if he will return to the pleasures of worldly life.

Finding all his allurements disregarded, Māra alters his method of attack; he fills the air with mighty thunderings, and creates on the road before the youthful fugitive's eyes apparitions of torrents, lofty mountains, and blazing conflagrations. But nothing alarms or deters him. 'I would rather,' he exclaims, 'be torn to pieces limb by limb, or be burnt in a fiery furnace, or be ground to pieces by a falling mountain than forego my fixed purpose for one single instant.'

Arrived at a safe distance from his father's territory, he exchanges garments with a passing beggar, cuts off his own hair with a sword, and assumes the outward aspect and character of a wandering ascetic. The hair does not fall to the ground but is taken up to the Trayastriṉśas heaven (p. 207), and worshipped by the gods.

His first halting-place is Rāja-gṛiha (now Rāj-gīr), the chief city of Magadha, which, with Kosala (Oudh, pp. 21, 48), afterwards became the holy land of Buddhism. There he attaches himself as a disciple to two Brāhmans named Āḷāra (in Sanskṛit Ārāḍa, with epithet Kālāpa or Kālāma) and Uddaka (Udraka, also written Rudraka, and called Rāma-putta, Mahā-vagga I. 6. 3), who imbue him with their own philosophical tenets and theory of salvation. Sufficient evidence exists to warrant a belief in this part of the story.

No place in India abounds in more interesting Buddhistic remains than Rāja-gṛiha (about 40 miles south-east of Patnā), proving that it was one of the most sacred places of Buddhism, consecrated by some of its most cherished associations. Its Pāli name is Rājagaha. It may be conjectured that the connexion between the doctrines of Buddhism and those of Brāhmanism was due to Gautama's intercourse with the Brāhmans of this district, and to the ideas he thus imbibed at the earliest stage of his career.

But to resume our story. Gautama fails to find in

Brāhmanical pantheistic philosophy that rest and peace for which his soul was craving when he left his home.

Still there was another way of emancipation and union with the Universal Soul, taught by the Brāhmans. This was the way of Tapas[1], or self-inflicted bodily pain and austerity.

From the earliest times a favourite doctrine of Brāhmanism has been, that self-inflicted bodily suffering is before all things efficacious for the accumulation of religious merit, for the acquirement of supernatural powers, and for the spirit's release from the bondage of transmigration and its re-absorption into the One Universal Spirit.

Among other forms of self-inflicted pain, religious devotees (Tapasvīs) sometimes went through the process of sitting all day long unmoved during the hottest months on a prepared platform or plot of ground, surrounded by five fires, or by four blazing fires, with the burning sun above their heads as a fifth[2]. Even gods (and notably Śiva) are described as mortifying themselves by bodily austerities (*tapas*), so as not to be outdone by men; for according to the theory of Hindūism, the gods themselves might be supplanted and even ousted from their rank and position as

---

[1] Tapas is a Sanskṛit word, derived from the root tap, 'to burn, torment.' It is connected with Lat. tepeo, Greek θάπτω, which last originally denoted 'to burn,' not 'to bury' dead bodies. Tapas ought not to be translated by 'penance,' unless that word is restricted to the sense poena, 'pain.'

[2] Such men are called Pañća-tapās (Manu VI. 23). A good representation of this form of Tapas may be seen in the Museum of the Indian Institute, Oxford.

divinities by human devotees or saints who had become omnipotent through protracted endurance of severe bodily suffering.

Hence we are not surprised to find it recorded of Gautama Buddha, that seeking in vain for rest in the teaching of Brāhmanical philosophy, and eager to try the effect of a course of self-mortification, he wandered forth from Rāja-gṛiha to a wood in the district of Gayā, called Uruvilvā (or Uruvelā).

There, in company with five other ascetics, he began his celebrated sexennial fast. Sitting down with his legs folded under him on a raised seat in a place unsheltered from sun, wind, rain, dew, and cold, he gradually reduced his daily allowance of food to a single grain of rice. Then holding his breath, he harassed and macerated his body, but all in vain. No peace of mind came, and no divine enlightenment. He became convinced of his own folly in resorting to bodily austerity as a means of attaining supreme enlightenment, and delivering himself from the evils and sufferings of life.

Rousing himself, as if from a troubled dream, he took food and nourishment in a natural way, thereby incurring the temporary disapproval of his five companions in self-mortification. Then, when sufficiently refreshed, he moved away to another spot in the same district. There, under the shelter of a sacred fig-tree (Aśvattha, *Ficus religiosa*, known as the Pippala or Pīpal), in a village, afterwards called Buddha-Gayā, he gave himself up to higher and higher forms of meditation (Jhāna = Dhyāna). In this he merely conformed to the Hindū Yoga,—a method of attaining mystic union with the Deity, which although not then formulated into a system, was already in vogue among the Brāhmans (p. 226). There can be little doubt that the Dhāraṇā, Dhyāna (p. 209), and Samādhi of the Yoga were resorted to, even in Gautama's time, as a means for the attainment of perfect spiritual illumination, as well as of final absorption in the Deity.

In Manu VI. 72 it is said:—'Let him purge himself from all taints (doshān) by suppression of breath, from sin by restraints of thought (dhāraṇābhiḥ), from sensual attachments by control, and from unspiritual qualities by meditation (dhyānena).'

In the later work called Bhagavad-gītā (see p. 95 of this volume) it is declared:—'holding his body, head, and neck quite immovable, seated on a firm seat in a pure spot with Kuśa grass around, the devotee (Yogī) should look only at the tip of his nose, and should meditate on the Supreme Being' (VI. 11, 12). Further on he is directed to meditate so profoundly as to think about nothing whatever (VI. 25).

The very Gāyatrī or ancient Vedic prayer (Ṛig-veda III. 62. 10, see p. 78 of this volume)—which is to Hindūs what the Lord's Prayer is to Christians, and is still repeated by millions of our Indian fellow-subjects at their daily devotions—was originally an act of meditation, performed with the very object Gautama had in view. The prayer is as follows:—'Let us meditate (Dhīmahi, root *dhyai*) on the excellent glory of the divine vivifying Sun, may he enlighten our understandings.' Even the selection of a seat under an Aśvattha tree was in keeping with Brāhmanical ideas (see 'Brāhmanism and Hindūism,' p. 335).

The first result, however, of his engaging in abstract meditation, was that he seemed to himself to be as far as ever from the emancipation which was the one aim of his great renunciation. Why not then return to the world? Why not indulge again in the pleasures of sense? Why not go back to home, wife, and child? Thoughts of this kind passed through his mind, while all his old affections and feelings seemed to revive with tenfold intensity. Then on one particular night, during this mental struggle, Māra, the Destroyer and personification of carnal desire, seized his opportunity. The spirit of evil had bided his time; had waited to assail the sage at the right moment, when protracted self-mortification had done its work—when with exhausted strength he had little power of resistance.

It is certainly remarkable that a great struggle between good and evil, right and wrong, truth and error, knowledge and ignorance, light and darkness, is recognized in all religious systems, however false. (See a notable allusion to this in Śaṅkara's Commentary to Ćhāndogya Upanishad, p. 26, ll. 2–8.)

The legendary description of the Buddha's temptation, and of the assault made upon him by Māra (the deadly inciter to sensuous desire[1]), and by all his troop of attendants, is so interesting and curious, notwithstanding its extravagance, that I here abridge it:—

Fiends and demons swarmed about him in the form

[1] According to Dr. Oldenberg, the Mṛityu of the Kaṭhopanishad.

of awful monsters, furies, vampires, hobgoblins, armed to the teeth with every implement of destruction. Their million faces were frightful to behold, their limbs encircled by myriads of serpents, their heads enveloped in a blaze of fire. They surrounded the saint and assailed him in a thousand different ways. Missiles of all kinds were hurled against him; poison and fire were showered over him—but the poison changed into flowers, the fire formed a halo round his head.

The baffled evil One now shifted his ground. He summoned his enchanting daughters, and sent them to display their charms in the presence of the youthful saint (see engraving opposite p. 477). But the resolute young ascetic was not to be lured by their wiles. He remained calm and impassive, and with a stern face rebuked the maidens for their boldness, forcing them to retire discomfited and disgraced.

Other forms of temptation followed, and the debilitated ascetic's strength seemed to be giving way. But this was merely the crisis. After rising to higher and higher stages of meditation (p. 233) at the end of a long night he shook off his foe. The victory was won, and the light of true knowledge broke upon his mind. A legend relates that in the first night-watch he gained a knowledge of all his previous existences; in the second—of all present states of being; in the third—of the chain of causes and effects (p. 102); and at the dawn of day he knew all things.

The dawn on which this remarkable struggle terminated was the birthday of Buddhism. Gautama was at that time about thirty-five years of age. It was then, and not till then, that his Bodhi-sattvaship (see p. 135) ended and he gained a right to the title Buddha, 'the Enlightened.' No wonder that the tree under which he sat became celebrated as 'the tree of knowledge and enlightenment.' It is remarkable, too, that just as the night on which the Buddha attained perfect enlightenment is the most sacred night with Buddhists, so the Bodhi-tree (in familiar language, Bo-tree) is their most sacred symbol—a symbol as dear to Buddhists as the Cross is to Christians (p. 517).

And what was this true knowledge, evolved out of a mind sublimated by intense meditation?

This is, perhaps, the strangest point of all in this strange story. It was after all a mere partial one-sided truth—the outcome of a single line of thought, dwelt upon with morbid intensity, to the exclusion of every other line of thought which might have modified and balanced it. It was an ultra-pessimistic view of the miseries of life, and a determination to ignore all its counterbalancing joys. It was the doctrine that this present life is only one link in a chain of countless transmigrations—that existence of all kinds involves suffering, and that such suffering can only be got rid of by self-restraint and the extinction of desires, especially of the desire for continuity of personal existence.

For let it be made clear at the outset, that whatever may be said of the Christian-like self-renunciation enjoined by the Buddhist code of morality, the only self it aims at renouncing is the self of personality, and the chief self-love it deprecates is the self-love which consists in craving for continuous individual life.

To those who have never travelled or resided much in the East, indulgence in such a morbid form of pessimism, under glowing skies and amid bright surroundings, may seem almost an impossibility. But those who know India by personal experience are aware that its climate is not conducive to optimistic views of life, and that even in the present day men of the Buddha type, who seek in various ways to impress their pessimistic theories of existence on their fellow-men, are not uncommon.

In the course of my travels I frequently met ascetics who had given up family and friends, and were leading a life of morose seclusion, and pretended meditation, undergoing long courses of bodily mortification. Nay, I have even seen men who, to prove their utter contempt for the pleasures of worldly existence, and to render themselves fit for the extinction of all personality by absorption into the Universal Soul, have sat in one posture, or held up one arm for years, or allowed themselves no bed but a bed of spikes, no shelter but the foliage of trees [1]. Gautama's course of protracted cogitation therefore had in it nothing peculiar or original.

Nor need we doubt that certain historical facts underlie the legendary narrative. We cannot admit with the learned Senart and Kern that the life of Gautama was based on a mere solar myth. To us it is more difficult not to believe than to believe that there lived in the fifth century B. C. the youthful son of a petty Rāja or land-owner in Oudh, distinguished from ordinary

[1] In the same way the Cistercian monks of Fountain's Abbey lived under certain trees while the Abbey was building.

men by many remarkable qualities of mind and body—notably by a thoughtful and contemplative disposition; that he became impressed with a sense of the vanity of all earthly aims, and of the suffering caused by disease and death; that he often said to himself, 'Life is but a troubled dream, an incubus, a nightmare,' or, like the Jewish sage of old, 'All the days of man are sorrow,' 'Man walketh in a vain shadow and disquieteth himself in vain;' and that like many other of the world's philosophers, instead of acquiescing in the state of things around him, and striving to make the best of them, or to improve them, he took refuge from the troubles of life in abandoning all its ties, renouncing all its joys, and suppressing all its affections and desires.

And again, it is more difficult not to believe than to believe that in such a man introspection and abstinence, protracted for many years, induced a condition of mind favourable to ecstatic visions, which were easily mistaken for flashes of inner enlightenment.

We know, indeed, that eleven centuries later another great thinker arose among the Semitic races in Western Asia, who went through the same kind of mental struggle, and that Muhammad, like Gautama, having by his long fasts and austerities brought himself into a highly wrought condition of the nervous system, became a fanatical believer in the reality of his own delusions and in his own divine commission as a teacher.

But the parallel between the Buddha and Muhammad cannot be carried on much further. And indeed, in point of fact, no two characters could be more different. For the Buddha never claimed to be the channel of a supernatural revelation; never represented the knowledge that burst on his mind as springing from any but an internal source; never taught that a divine force operating from without compelled him to communicate that knowledge to mankind; never dreamed of propagating that knowledge to others by compulsion, much less by the sword. On the contrary, he always maintained that the only revelation he had received was an illumination from within—due entirely to his own intuitions, assisted by his reasoning powers and by severe purgatorial discipline protracted through countless previous births in every variety of bodily form.

But how did this internal self-enlightenment[1]—the great distinguishing feature of Buddhism—first find expression? It is said that the first words uttered by the Buddha at the momentous crisis when true knowledge burst upon him, were to the following effect:—

'Through countless births have I wandered, seeking but not discovering (anibbisan) the maker of this my mortal dwelling-house (gaha-kāraka), and still again and again have birth and life and pain returned. But now at length art thou discovered, thou builder of this house (of flesh). No longer shalt thou rear a house for me. Rafters and beams are shattered and with destruction of *Desire* (Taṉhā) deliverance from repeated life is gained at last' (Dhamma-pada 153, 154, Sumaṅgala 46, p. 43 of this volume).

---

[1] The Bhagavad-gītā (V. 28) asserts:—'The saint (Yogī) who is internally happy, internally at peace, and internally illumined, attains extinction in Brahmā.' This is pure Buddhism if we substitute Cessation of individual existence for Brahmā.

Contrast with these first utterances of Gautama Buddha the first words of Jesus Christ:—

'Wist ye not that I must be about My Father's business?' (St. Luke ii. 49.)

The Buddha's first exclamations, as well as the account of his subsequent sayings and doings, are the more worthy of credit as taken from the Southern Canon.

The Mahā-vagga (I. 1) tells us that after attaining complete intelligence, the Buddha sat cross-legged on the ground under the Bodhi-tree for seven days, absorbed in meditation and enjoying the bliss of enlightenment. At the end of that period, during the first three watches of the night, he fixed his mind on the causes of existence. Then having thought out the law of causation (p. 102), he exclaimed: 'When the laws of being become manifest to the earnest thinker, his doubts vanish, and, like the Sun, he dispels the hosts of Māra.'

Next he meditated for another seven days under a banyan tree, called the tree of goat-herds (aja-pāla). It was there that a haughty Brāhman accosted him with the question, 'Who is a true Brāhman?' and was told, 'One free from evil and pride; self-restrained, learned, and pure.'

Then he meditated under another tree for a third period of seven days. There the serpent (Nāga) Mućalinda (see frontispiece) coiled his body round the Buddha, and formed a canopy to protect him from the raging of a storm—this being one of the trials he had to go through. When it was over the Buddha exclaimed, 'Happy is the seclusion of the satisfied man (tushṭa) who has learned and seen the truth.'

A fourth period of meditation was passed under the tree Rājāyatana, making four times seven days. May not these symbolize the four stages of meditation (p. 209)? Later legends, however, reckon seven times seven days.

During the whole of the interval between the first acquisition of knowledge and the setting forth to proclaim it, the Buddha fasted, being too elated to seek food, and only once receiving it from two merchants, named Tapussa (Trapusha) and Bhallika. These became his first lay-reverers (p. 89) by repeating the *double* formula of reverence for the Buddha and for his doctrine (the Saṅgha not being then instituted, Mahā-v° I. 4. 5). A later legend relates that they received in return eight of his hairs which they preserved as relics.

In connexion with the legend of a forty-nine days' fast, I may mention that an ancient carving of Gautama was pointed out to me at Buddha-Gayā, which represents him as holding a bowl of rice-milk divided into forty-nine portions, one for each day.

With these legends we may contrast the simple Gospel narrative of Christ's forty days' fast in the wilderness.

The Buddha's first resolution to come forth from his seclusion and proclaim his gospel to mankind is of course a great epoch with all Buddhists.

And here it should be observed, that, strictly, according to Gautama's own teaching he ought to have ceased from all action on arriving at perfect enlightenment. For had he not attained the great object of his ambition —the end of all his struggles—the goal of all his efforts —carried on through hundreds of existences? He had, therefore, no more lives to lead, no more misery to undergo. In short he had achieved the summum bonum of all true Buddhists—the extinction of the fires of passions and desires—and had only to enjoy the well-earned peace (nirvṛiti) of complete Nirvāṇa. Yet the love of his fellow-men impelled him to action (pravṛitti). In fact it was characteristic of a supreme Buddha that he should belie, by his own activity and compassionate feelings, the utter apathy and indifference to which his own doctrines logically led (p. 128).

But he did not carry out his benevolent design without going through further temptations—temptations which it is usual to compare with the temptation of Christ. Evil thoughts arose in his mind, and these were suggested, according to later legends, by Māra (p. 33), thus:—'With great pains, blessed one, hast thou acquired this doctrine (dharma). Why proclaim it? Beings lost in desires and lusts will not understand it. Remain in quietude. Enjoy Nirvāṇa' (Mahā-v° I. 5. 3).

To counteract these malevolent suggestions, the god Brahmā Sahāmpati (Pāli Sahămpati, p. 210) presented himself and exclaimed:—'Arise, O spotless one, open the gate of Nirvāṇa. Arise, look down on the world lost in suffering. Arise, wander forth, preach the doctrine.'

First the Buddha thought of his two teachers, Āḷāra and Uddaka (p. 29), but found they were dead. Next he thought of going to the five ascetics whom he had offended by his abandonment of the method of gaining knowledge through painful austerities. They were at that time prosecuting their bodily mortifications at Benares in the Deer-park called Isipatana. It was only natural that the Buddha should think of wending his way in the first instance to Benares, even if special considerations had not drawn him there; for that city was the great centre of Eastern thought and life, the Indian Athens, where all peculiar doctrines were most likely to gain a hearing.

On his way thither, Upaka, a member of the Ājīvaka sect of naked ascetics, met him and inquired why his countenance was so bright (pariśuddha)? He replied, 'I am the all-subduer, the all-wise, the stainless, the highest teacher, the conqueror (p. 135); I go to Benares to dissipate the world's darkness' (Mahā-vagga I. 6. 7).

The five ascetics (Kauṇḍinya = Koṇḍañño, Aśvajit = Assaji, Vāshpa, Mahānāma, and Bhadrika) were soon converted by his words, and by merely repeating the triple formula were admitted at once to his Order of monks. They constituted, with Gautama, the first six members of the Saṅgha, or fraternity of men seeking release from the misery of existence by cœnobitic monasticism.

And of what nature were Gautama Buddha's first didactic utterances? His first sermon, delivered in the Deer-park at Benares, is held in as much reverence by Buddhists as the first words of Christ are by Christians. It is called Dhamma-ćakka-ppavattana-sutta, or in Sanskṛit Dharma-ćakra-pravartana-sūtra, 'the discourse which set in motion the wheel of the law,' or 'of the universal dominance of the true belief.'

The following is the substance of it, as given in the Mahā-vagga (I. 6. 17). It is important to note that the Buddha spoke in the vernacular of Magadha (now called Pāli), and not to men generally, but to the first five would-be members of his Order of monks :—

'There are two extremes (antā), O monks (Bhikkhus), to be avoided by one who has given up the world—a life devoted to sensual pleasures (kāma), which is degrading, common, vulgar, ignoble, profitless; and a life given to self-mortification (ātma-klamatha)—painful, ignoble, profitless. There is a middle path, avoiding both extremes—the noble eightfold path discovered by the Buddha (Tathāgata)—which leads to insight, to wisdom, to quietude (upaśama), to knowledge, to perfect enlightenment (sambodhi), to final extinction of desire and suffering (Nirvāṇa).'

So far there is nothing very explicit in the discourse. Doubtless such precepts as 'virtue is a mean' and that 'medio tutissimus ibis' are useful, though trite, truths; but the difficulty is to prove that the Buddha's eightfold path is really a middle course of the kind described; for the most fanatical enthusiasts will always regard their own creed, however extravagant, as moderate.

The Buddha, therefore, goes on to propound what he calls the four noble truths (ariya-saććāni = ārya-satyāni) and the eightfold path, which are the key to his whole doctrine. They may be stated thus:—

1. All existence—that is, existence in any form, whether on earth or in heavenly spheres—necessarily involves pain and suffering (dukkha). 2. All suffering is caused by lust (rāga) or craving or desire (taṉhā = tṛishṇā, 'thirst') of three kinds—for sensual pleasure (kāma), for wealth (vibhava), and for existence (bhava). 3. Cessation of suffering is simultaneous with extinction of lust, craving, and desire (p. 139). 4. Extinction of lust, craving, and desire, and cessation of suffering are

accomplished by perseverance in the noble eightfold path (ariyo aṭṭhaṅgiko maggo), viz. right belief or views (sammā diṭṭhi), right resolve (saṅkappo), right speech, right work (kammanto), right livelihood (ājīvo), right exercise or training (vāyāmo = vyāyāma), right mindfulness (sati, p. 50), right mental concentration (samādhi).

And how is all life mere suffering (I. 6. 19)?—

'Birth is suffering. Decay is suffering. Illness is suffering. Death is suffering. Association with (samprayogo) objects we hate is suffering. Separation from objects we love is suffering. Not to obtain what we desire is suffering. Clinging (upādāna) to the five elements (p. 109) of existence is suffering. Complete cessation of thirst (taṉhā) and desires is cessation of suffering. This is the noble truth of suffering.'

This sermon (called in Ceylon the first Baṇa = Bhāṇa, 'recitation,' p. 70) was addressed to monks, and however unfavourably it must compare with that of Christ (St. Luke iv. 18), addressed not to monks but to suffering sinners—and however obvious may be the idea that pain must result from giving way to lust and the desire for life through countless existences—is of great interest because it embodies the first teaching of one, who, if not worthy to be called 'the Light of Asia,' and certainly unworthy of comparison with the 'Light of the World,' was at least one of the world's most successful teachers.

Bear in mind that, as the result of his earliest meditation (pp. 39, 56, 102), the Buddha made ignorance precede lust as the primary cause of life's misery.

Observe, moreover, that the force of the whole sermon depends on the interpretation of the word 'right' (sammā = samyak) in describing the eightfold path, and the plain explanation is that 'right belief' means believing in the Buddha and his doctrine; 'right resolve' means abandoning one's wife and family as the best method of extinguishing the fires of the passions; right speech is recitation of the Buddha's doctrine; right work (Karmānta) is that of a monk; right livelihood is living by alms as a monk does; right exercise is suppression of the individual self; right mindfulness (Smṛiti) is keeping in mind the impurities and impermanence of the body; right mental concentration is trance-like quietude.

Mark, too, that in describing the misery of life, association with loved objects is not mentioned as compensating for the pain of connexion with hateful objects.

The Buddha's early disciples were not poor men; for the sixth to be admitted to the Saṅgha was a high-born youth named Yasa. Then this youth's father, a rich merchant, became the first lay-disciple by repeating the *triple* formula (pp. 40, 78), and his mother and wife became the first lay-sisters. Next, four high-born friends of Yasa, and subsequently fifty more became monks. Thus, not long after the first sermon, Gautama had sixty enrolled monks; all from the upper classes.

In sending forth these sixty monks to proclaim his own gospel of deliverance, he addressed them thus:—

'I am delivered from all fetters (p. 127), human and divine. You too, O monks, are freed from the same fetters. Go forth and wander everywhere, out of compassion for the world and for the welfare of gods and men. Go forth, one by one, in different directions. Preach the doctrine (Dharmam), salutary (kalyāṇa) in its beginning, middle, and end, in its spirit (artha) and in its letter (vyañjana). Proclaim a life of perfect restraint, chastity, and celibacy (brahmaćariyam). I will go also to preach this doctrine' (Mahā-vagga I. 11. 1).

When his monk-missionaries had departed, Gautama himself followed, though not till Māra (p. 41) had again tempted him. Quitting Benares he journeyed back to Uruvelā, near Gayā. There he first converted thirty rich young men and then one thousand orthodox Brāhmans, led by Kāśyapa and his two brothers, who maintained a sacred fire ('Brāhmanism,' p. 364). The fire-chamber was haunted by a fiery snake-demon; so Buddha asked to occupy the room for a night, fought the serpent and confined him in his own alms-bowl. Next he worked other miracles (said to have been 3500 in number), such as causing water to recede, fire-wood to split, fire-vessels to appear at his word. Then Kāśyapa and his brothers, convinced of his miraculous powers, were admitted with the other Brāhmans to the Saṅgha. Thus Buddha gathered round him about a thousand monks.

To them on a hill Gayāsīsa (Brahma-yoni), near Gayā, he preached his 'burning' fire-sermon (Mahā-v° I. 21): 'Everything, O monks, is burning (ādittam = ādīptam). The eye is burning; visible things are burning. The sensation produced by contact with visible things is burning—burning with the fire of lust (desire), enmity and delusion (rāgagginā dosagginā mohagginā), with birth, decay (jarayā), death, grief, lamentation, pain, dejection (domanassehi), and despair (upāyāsehi). The ear is burning; sounds are burning; the nose is burning, odours are burning; the tongue is burning, tastes are burning; the body is burning, objects of sense are burning. The mind is burning;

thoughts are burning. All are burning with the fire of passions and lusts. Observing this, O monks, a wise and noble disciple becomes weary of (or disgusted with) the eye, weary of visible things, weary of the ear, weary of sounds, weary of odours, weary of tastes, weary of the body, weary of the mind. Becoming weary, he frees himself from passions and lusts. When free, he realizes that his object is accomplished, that he has lived a life of restraint and chastity (brahma-ćariyam), that re-birth is ended.'

It is said that this 'fire-sermon'—which is a key to the meaning of Nirvāṇa—was suggested by the sight of a conflagration. It was Gautama's custom to impress ideas on his hearers by pointing to visible objects. He compares all life to a flame; and the gist of the discourse is the duty of extinguishing the fire of lusts, and with it the fire of all existence, and the importance of monkhood and celibacy for the attainment of this end.

Contrast in Christ's Sermon on the Mount the words addressed to the multitude (not to monks), 'Blessed are the pure in heart, for they shall see God.'

The Buddha and his followers next proceeded to Rājagṛiha. Among them were two, afterwards called 'chief disciples' (Agra-śrāvakas), Sāriputta and Moggallāna (or Maudgalyāyana), who died before the Buddha, and sixteen leaders among the so-called eighty '*great* disciples' (Mahā-śrāvakas); the chief of these being Kāśyapa (or Mahā-kāśyapa), Upāli, and Ānanda (a cousin), besides Ánuruddha (another cousin), and Kātyāyana. Of course among the eighty are reckoned the five original Benares converts. At a later time two chief female disciples

(Agra-śrāvikās) named Khemā and Uppala-vaṇṇā (Utpala-varṇā) were added (see p. 86). Each leading disciple was afterwards called Sthavira, 'an elder,' or Mahā-sthavira, 'great elder' (Pāli Thera, Mahāthera; fem. Therī). Mark, too, that Bimbi-sāra, king of Magadha, and Prasenajit (Pasenadi), king of Kosala, were Gautama's lay-disciples and constant patrons.

It was not long before the Buddha's followers were more formally incorporated into a monastic Order (Saṅgha), and rules of discipline drawn up (see pp. 61, 72, 73, 83). And doubtless the success of Buddhism was due to the carrying out of this idea of establishing a brotherhood offering a haven of rest to all.

About forty-five years elapsed between Gautama's attainment of Buddhahood and his death. During that period he continued teaching and itinerating with his disciples; only going 'into retreat' during the rains. A list of 45 places of residence is given. He seems to have resided oftenest at Śrāvastī (see map, p. 21) in the monastery Jetavana given by Anātha-piṇḍika; but the whole region between Śrāvastī and Rāja-gṛiha (p. 29), for nearly 300 miles, was the scene of his itineration. Favourite resorts near Rāja-gṛiha were the 'Vulture-peak' and Bambu-grove (Veḷu-vana). Continual itineration was one chief means of propagating Buddhism.

It is said that his death occurred at Kuśi-nagara[1] (Kusinārā), a town about eighty miles east of Kapila-

[1] Or Kuśa-nagara, identified by Gen. Sir A. Cunningham with Kasia, thirty-five miles east of Gorakh-pore on an old channel of the Chota Gandak.

vastu—the place of his birth—when he was eighty years of age, and probably about the year 420 B.C.[1]

The story is that Gautama died from eating too much pork (or dried boar's flesh [2]). As this is somewhat derogatory to his dignity it is not likely to have been fabricated. A fabrication, too, would scarcely make him guilty of the inconsistency of saying 'Kill no living thing,' and yet setting an example of eating flesh-meat.

These were his words when he felt his end near:—

'O Ānanda, I am now grown old, and full of years, and my journey is drawing to its close; I have reached eighty years—my sum of days—and just as a worn-out cart can only with much care be made to move along, so my body can only be kept going with difficulty. It is only when I become plunged in meditation that my body is at ease. In future be ye to yourselves your own light, your own refuge; seek no other refuge. Hold fast to the truth as your lamp. Hold fast to the truth as your refuge; look not to any one but yourselves as a refuge' (Mahā-parinibbāna-sutta II. 32, 33).

Afterwards he enumerated every monk's duties, thus:—'Which then are the truths (the 7 jewels or 37 steps to Nirvāṇa, p. 127) it behoves you to spread abroad, out of pity for the world, for the good of gods and men? They are: 1. the four earnest reflections (Smṛiti, Sati-paṭṭhāna, on the body's impurities, on the impermanence of the sensations, of the thoughts, of

---

[1] I give 420 as a round number. Rhys Davids has good reasons for fixing the date of Gautama's death about B.C. 412, Oldenberg about 480, Cunningham 478, Kern 388. The old date is 543.

[2] See 'Book of the great Decease,' translated by Rhys Davids, p. 72.

the conditions of existence, p. 127); 2. the four right exertions (Sammappadhāna, viz. to prevent demerit from arising, get rid of it when arisen, produce merit, increase it); 3. the four steps to supernatural power (Iddhi-pāda, viz. will, effort, thought, intense thought); 4. the five forces (Pañća-bala, viz. faith, energy, recollection, self-concentration, reason); 5. the five right senses (indriyāṇi); 6. the seven "limbs" of knowledge (Bodhy-aṅga, viz. recollection, investigation, energy, joy, serenity, concentration of mind, equanimity); 7. the noble eightfold path' (p. 44). See Mahā-parinibbāna III. 65.

Then shortly before his decease, he said, 'It may be, Āṇanda, that in some of you this thought may arise:—The words of our Teacher are ended; we have lost our Master. But it is not thus. The truths and the rules of the Order, which I have taught and preached, let these be your teacher, when I am gone' (VI. 1).

'Behold now, O monks, I exhort you:—Everything that cometh into being passeth away; work out your own perfection with diligence' (III. 66).

Not long after his last utterances the Buddha, who had before, through intense meditation, attained Nirvāṇa or extinction of the fire of desires, passed through the four stages of meditation (p. 209) till the moment came for his Pari-nirvāṇa, whereby the fire of life also was extinguished. A couch had been placed for him between two Śāl trees (p. 23), with the head towards the north. In sculptures he is represented as lying on his right side at death, and such images of him are highly venerated (see top figure of the engraving opposite p. 477).

The chief men of Kuśi-nagara burnt his body with

the ceremonies usual at the death of a Ćakravartin or Universal Ruler, which the Buddha claimed to be.

Then his ashes were distributed among eight princes, who built Stūpas over them (p. 499; Buddha-vaṇsa 28).

A legend states that when the Buddha died there was an earthquake. Then the gods Brahmā and Indra appeared and the latter exclaimed: 'Transient are all the elements of being; birth and decay are their nature; they are born and dissolved; then only is happiness when they have ceased to be' (Mahā-p° VI. 16).

Contrast with Buddha's last words the last words of Christ: 'Father, into Thy hands I commend my Spirit.'

A greater contrast than that presented by the account of the Buddha's death and the Gospel narrative of the death of Christ can scarcely be imagined.

Of course as a result of discourses during forty-five years, a large number were gathered into Gautama's monastic Order. His first aim was the founding of this Order, and his chief sermons were to his monks; but he accepted all men and ultimately multitudes attached themselves to him as lay-brethren (p. 87).

In fact Gautama's doctrine of a universal brotherhood, open to all, constituted the corner-stone of his popularity. He spoke to them in their own provincial dialect, which could not have differed much from the Pāli of the texts—and he enforced his words by dialogues, parables, fables, reiterations, and repetitions. Probably he was the first introducer of real preaching into India, and by his practical method he seemed to bring down knowledge from the clouds to every man's door.

The following (and p. 144) are examples: 'As the

peasant sows the seed but cannot say: "the grain shall swell to-day, to-morrow germinate"—so also it is with the disciple. He must obey the precepts, practise meditation, study the doctrine. He cannot say: "to-day or to-morrow, I shall be delivered." Again: as when a herd of deer lives in a forest a man comes who opens for them a false path and the deer suffer hurt; and another comes who opens a safe path and the deer thrive; so when men live among pleasures the evil one comes and opens the false eightfold path. Then comes the perfect one and opens the safe eightfold path of right belief, etc.' (p. 44, Oldenberg, 191, 192).

Six rival heretical teachers are alluded to. His chief opponent was his cousin Devadatta, who set up a school of his own, and is said to have plotted against the Buddha's life. His efforts failed (Ćulla-vagga VII), and he himself came to an untimely end. Possibly he may have belonged to the rival Jaina sect (Nigaṇṭha) of naked ascetics, of which the leader was Varďhamāna Mahāvīra Nāta-putta (Jñāti-putra). See p. 529.

Gautama's teaching gained the day. It claimed universality, and was aptly symbolized by a wheel rolling among all alike. Yet at first it had no attractions for the poor and the child-like.

By degrees, a fuller system, adapted in an ascending scale to laymen, novices, monks, nuns, and Arhats, was developed—a system which had its abstruse doctrines suited to men of philosophical minds, as well as its plain practical side (see pp. 93, 125). This constituted the Buddhist Dharma, which was ultimately collected in certain sacred books to be next described.

LECTURE III.

The Law (Dharma) and Sacred Scriptures of Buddhism.

PROBABLY most educated persons are aware that Buddhists have their own sacred scriptures, like Hindūs, Pārsīs, Confucianists, Muhammadans, Jews, and Christians. It is not, however, so generally known that in one important particular these Buddhist scriptures, constituting the Tri-piṭaka (p. 61), differ wholly from other sacred books. They lay no claim to supernatural inspiration. They contain the doctrines of Buddhism, but these are believed to be purely human—that is, they are held to be the product of man's own natural faculties working naturally.

The Tri-piṭaka was never like the Veda of the Brāhmans, believed to be the very 'breath of God'[1]; the same care, therefore, was not taken to preserve every sound; and when at last it was written down the result was a more scholastic production than the Veda.

Moreover, it was not composed in the Sanskṛit of the Veda and Śāstras—in the sacred language, the very

---

[1] The Śatapatha-brāhmaṇa (p. 1064) and the Bṛihad-āraṇyaka Upanishad (p. 455) affirm that the Ṛig- Yajur- Sāma- and Atharva-veda, the Upanishads, Itihāsas, and Purāṇas were all the breath (niḥśvasitāni) of the Supreme Being. And Sāyaṇa, the well-known Indian Commentator on the Ṛig-veda, speaking of the Supreme Being in his Introduction, says, Yasya niḥśvasitaṃ Vedāḥ, 'whose breath the Vedas were.'

grammar and alphabet of which were supposed to come from heaven—but in the vernacular of the part of India in which Buddhism flourished. Indeed, it is a significant fact that while the great sages of Sanskṛit literature and philosophy, such as Vyāsa, Kumārila, and Śaṅkara, in all probability spoke and taught in Sanskṛit[1], the Founder of Buddhism preferred to communicate his precepts to the people in their own vernacular, afterwards called Pāli. Nevertheless, he never composed a single book of his own. In all probability he never wrote down any of his own precepts; for if writing was then invented, it was little practised, through the absence of suitable materials. This is the more remarkable as Buddhism ultimately became an instrument for introducing literary culture among uncivilized races.

All that Gautama did was to preach his Dharma, 'Law,' during forty-five years of itineration, and oral teaching. It was not till some time after his death that his sayings were collected (p. 97), and still longer before they were written down. Itineration, recitation of the Law, and preaching were the chief instruments for the propagation of Buddhism.

At present the Buddhist Canon is about as extensive as the Brāhmanical[2], and in both cases we are left in

---

[1] How else can we account for Pāṇini's applying the term Bhāshā to colloquial Sanskṛit? Professor E. B. Cowell holds that Pāṇini's standard is the Brāhmaṇa language as opposed to the Saṃhitā of the Veda and to Loka or ordinary usage.

[2] According to Professor Rhys Davids, the Pāli text of the whole Tri-piṭaka, or true Canon of Buddhist Scripture, contains about twice as many words as our Bible; but he calculates that an English translation, if all repetitions were given, would be about four times as

doubt as to the date when the books were composed. How, then, did their composition take place?

All that can be said is that at three successive epochs after the Buddha's death, three gatherings of his followers were held for the purpose of collecting his sayings and settling the true Canon, and that a fourth assembly took place much later in the North.

The first of these assemblages can scarcely with any fitness be called a Council. Nor can the fact of its meeting together in any formal manner be established on any trustworthy historical basis. It is said that a number of monks (about five hundred, called Mahā-sthavirāḥ, 'the great elders,' Pāli Mahā-therā) assembled in a cave called Sattapaṇṇi, near the then capital city of Magadha—Rāja-gṛiha, now Rāj-gīr—under the sanction of king Ajāta-śatru, during the rainy season immediately succeeding the death of Gautama, to think over, put together, and arrange the sayings of their Master, but not, so far as we know, to write them down.

There, in all likelihood, they made the first step towards a methodical arrangement. But even then it is doubtful whether any systematic collections were composed. The assembled monks chose Kāśyapa (or Mahā-kāśyapa, p. 47), the most esteemed of all the Buddha's surviving disciples, as their leader, and chanted the Thera-vāda (Sthavira-v°), 'words of the elders,' or precepts of their Founder preserved in the memory of the older men; the rules of discipline (Vinaya) being

---

long. I should state here that in this chapter Koeppen, Childers, Rhys Davids, Oldenberg and others have been consulted, though I have not failed to examine the original Pāli documents myself.

recited by Upāli[1], and the ethical precepts (Sūtra), which constituted at first the principal Dharma[2] (*par excellence*, in contradistinction to the Vinaya), being imparted by Gautama's favourite, Ānanda (p. 47); while the philosophical doctrines—then undeveloped—were communicated by the president, Kāśyapa. If any arrangement was then made it was probably in two collections—the Vinaya and Dharma (say about 400 B.C.).

In regard to the Dharma, two main lines were, in all likelihood, laid down as the basis of all early teaching. The first consisted of the four sublime verities, as they are called—that is, of the four fundamental truths originally taught by the Founder of Buddhism, namely, the inevitable inherence of suffering in every form of life, the connexion of all suffering with indulgence of desires, especially with craving for continuity of existence, the possibility of the cessation of suffering by restraining lusts and desires, and the eightfold course leading to that cessation (see p. 44).

The second line of doctrine probably consisted of an outline of the twelve-linked chain of causality (nidāna), which traced back all suffering to a still deeper origin than mere lusts and desires—namely, to ignorance (p. 103).

It is not, however, at all likely that any philosophical

---

[1] Upāli is said to have been originally the family barber of the Śākyas. Professor Oldenberg rightly remarks that this did not make him a man of low position, though he was probably the lowest in rank of all the early disciples of Gautama.

[2] Professor Oldenberg, in his preface to his edition of the Mahāvagga, shows that in early times there were only two divisions of the Piṭaka, one called Vinaya and the other Dharma (Dhamma), which were often contrasted.

or metaphysical doctrines were clearly and methodically formulated at the earliest assembly which took place soon after Gautama's death. It is far more probable that the first outcome of the gathering together of the Buddha's disciples was the collecting of his precepts and the enforcing of rules of discipline for the monks, and this may have taken place soon after 400 B.C.

After a time, certain relaxations of these rules or unauthorized departures from them (ten in number, such as reception of *money-gifts*, eating a second meal in the afternoon, drinking stimulating beverages, if pure as water in appearance[1]), began to be common. The question as to whether liberty should be allowed in these points, *especially in the first*, shook the very foundations of the community. In fact the whole society became split up into two contending parties, the strict and the lax, and a second Council became necessary for the restoration of order. All ten points were discussed at this Council, said to have consisted of 700 monks and held at Vaiśālī (Vesālī, now Besārh), 27 miles north of Patnā, about 380 B.C.[2] The discussions were protracted for eight months, and all the ten unlawful relaxations were finally prohibited.

[1] The ten usually enumerated are the three above-named and seven others, viz. power of admitting to the Order and confession in private houses, the use of comfortable seats, relaxation of monastic rules in remote country places, power of obtaining a dispensation from the Order *after* the infringement of a rule, drinking whey, putting salt aside for future use, power of citing the example of others as a valid excuse for relaxing discipline.

[2] According to Professor Oldenberg's calculation. The date is doubtful. A round number (say 350 B.C.) might be given.

It has been observed that this second Council stands in a relation to Buddhism very similar to that which the Council of Nicæa bears to Christianity.

The exact date, however, of either the first or second assemblies cannot be determined with precision.

Not long afterwards occurred the political revolution caused by the well-known Ćandra-gupta (= Sandrakottus)—sometimes called the first Aśoka (or disparagingly, Kālāśoka). This man, who was a low-born Śūdra, usurped the throne and founded the Maurya dynasty, after killing king Nanda and taking possession of Pāṭaliputra (or Palibothra, now Patnā, the then metropolis of Magadha or Behār), about 315 B.C. He extended the kingdom of Magadha over all Hindūstān, and became so powerful that when Alexander's successor, Seleukos Nikator (whose reign commenced about 312 B.C.), invaded India from his kingdom of Bactria, so effectual was the resistance offered by Ćandra-gupta, that the Greek thought it politic to form an alliance with the Hindū king, and sent his own countryman, Megasthenes, as an ambassador to reside at his court.

To this circumstance we owe the earliest authentic account of Indian customs and usages, by an intelligent observer who was not a native; and Megasthenes' narrative, preserved by Strabo, furnishes a basis on which a fair inference may be founded that Brāhmanism and Buddhism existed side by side in India on amicable terms in the fourth and third centuries B.C. There is even ground for believing that king Ćandragupta himself favoured the Buddhists, though outwardly he never renounced his faith in Brāhmanism.

Ćandra-gupta's reign is thought to have lasted until 291 B.C., and that of his son and successor, Vindusāra, from 291 to (say) about 260 B.C. Then came Ćandra-gupta's grandson, the celebrated Aśoka (sometimes called Dharmāśoka), who, though of Śūdra origin, was perhaps the greatest Hindū monarch of India.

It was about this period that Gautama Buddha's followers began to develope his doctrines, and to make additions to them in such a way that the Abhi-dharma or 'further Dharma' had to be added to the Sūtra which constituted the original Dharma (p. 56). Even in Gautama's time there were great dissensions. Afterwards differences of opinion increased, so that before long eighteen schools of schismatic thought (p. 158) were established. The resulting controversies were very disturbing, and a third Council became necessary. It consisted of a thousand oldest members of the Order, and was held in the 16th or 17th year of Aśoka's reign at Patnā (Pāṭali-putra), about 244–242 B.C.

This third Council was, perhaps, the most important; for through its deliberations the decision was arrived at to propagate Buddhism by missions. Hence missionaries, supported by king Aśoka (see p. 66), were sent in all directions; the first being Mahinda (Mahendra), the king's son, who carried the doctrine into Ceylon.

Dr. Oldenberg has shown that in a part of the Tri-piṭaka now extant, the first and second Councils are mentioned but not the third. The plain inference is that the portion of the Buddhist Canon in which the second Council is described cannot be older than that Council. Yet in all likelihood a great part of the Vinaya (including the Pātimokkha and the Khandhaka, p. 62) was composed before the second Council—possibly as early as about 400 B.C.—and the rest of the Canon during the succeeding century and a half before the third Council—that is, from 400 to 250 B.C. It was composed in the then vernacular language of Magadha (Māgadhī), where all three Councils were held.

It seems, however, probable that in each district to which Buddhism spread the doctrine of its founder was taught in the peculiar dialect understood by the inhabitants. It even appears likely that when Gautama himself lived in Kosala (Oudh) he preached in the dialect of that province just as he taught in Māgadhī when he resided in Magadha. The Ćullavagga (V. 33. 1) makes him direct that his precepts should be learnt by every convert in the provincial dialect, which doubtless varied slightly everywhere. In time it became necessary to give fixity to the sacred texts, and the form they finally assumed may have represented the prevalent dialect of the time, and not necessarily the original Māgadhī dialect[1]. This final form of the language was called Pāli[2] (or Tanti). It

---

[1] Professor Oldenberg places the locality of the Pāli on the eastern coast of Southern India in the northern part of Kaliṅga (Purī in Orissa), and would therefore make it an old form of Uriya. That country he thinks had most frequent communications with Ceylon.

[2] Professor Childers thought that Pāli merely meant the language of the line or series of texts, the word pāli like tanti meaning 'line.' Pāli varies from the Prākṛit of the Inscriptions, and from that of the dramas, and from that of the Jainas (which is still later and called Ardha-māgadhī) by its retention of some consonants and infusion of Sanskṛit. The Gāthā dialect of the northern books is again different.

developed variations from the earlier Aśoka inscription dialect, and from Māgadhī Prākṛit as now known.

Some think that the Pāli resulted from an artificial infusion of Sanskṛit. It is said that nearly two-fifths of the Pāli vocabulary consists of unmodified Sanskṛit.

At any rate, it was in this language that the Buddhist Law was carried (probably by Mahendra) into Ceylon, and the whole Canon is thought by some to have been handed down orally till it was written down there about 85 B.C. Oral transmission, we know, was common in India, but if edicts were written by Aśoka (p. 67), why should not the Law have been written down also?

As, however, Pāli was not spoken in Ceylon, the Pāli commentaries brought by Mahendra were translated by him into Sinhalese, and the Pāli originals being lost, were not retranslated into Pāli till about the beginning of the fifth century of our era.

Turning next to the final arrangement of the Pāli Canon, we find that it resolved itself into three collections (called Tri-piṭaka, Pāli Tipiṭaka, 'Three baskets,' the word piṭaka, however, not occurring in the early texts), namely: 1. Vinaya, 'discipline' for the Order; 2. Sūtra (Pāli Sutta), 'precepts,' which at first constituted the principal Dharma, or moral Law (p. 56); 3. Abhi-dharma (Abhi-dhamma), 'further Dharma,' or additional precepts relative to the law and philosophy.

This division was not logical, as each collection may treat of the subjects belonging to the others.

Taking, then, in the first place, the Vinaya or discipline portion of the Buddhist bible, we ought to observe that a portion of it (the Pātimokkha) is not only the oldest, but also the most important in its bearing on the whole theory of Buddhism. For, as we shall point out more fully hereafter, the Buddha's paramount aim was to convince others that to get rid of ignorance, gain knowledge, practise morality, and obtain deliverance, it was incumbent on a wise man to renounce married life and become a member of a monastic Order.

Pure Buddhism, in fact, was pure monachism—implying celibacy, poverty, and mendicancy—and this could not be maintained without rules for discipline and outward conduct, which, as adopted by the Buddha, were simply a modification of the rules for the two religious orders of the Brahma-ćārī and Sannyāsī, already existing in Brāhmanism.

With regard to the classification of the Vinaya rules, they were divided into three sets: *a.* the Khandhaka, in two collections called Mahā-vagga (Mahā-varga), 'great section,' and Ćulla-vagga, 'minor section' (vagga = varga); *b.* the Vibhaṅga (including the two works called Pārājika and Paćittiya), or a systematic arrangement and explanation of certain ancient 'release-precepts' (pratimoksha-sūtra, Pāli Pātimokkha) for setting free, through penances, any who had offended against the Order; *c.* Parivāra-pāṭha, or a comparatively modern summary of the above two divisions.

Mark, however, that the Vinaya abounds in details of the life and teaching of Gautama.

The second Piṭaka, called Sutta (Sūtra), 'precepts,' contains the ethical doctrines which at first constituted the whole Buddhist Law. It consists of five Nikāyas, or collections, viz. *a.* the Dīgha, or collection of 34 long suttas, among which is the Mahā-parinibbāna-sutta (one of the oldest parts of the Canon after the Pātimokkha); *b.* the Majjhima, or collection of 152 suttas of middling length; *c.* the Saṃyutta, or collection of 55 groups of joined suttas, some of them very short; *d.* the Aṅguttara, or miscellaneous suttas in divisions, which go on increasing by one (aṅga); *e.* the Khuddaka, or minor collection, consisting of fifteen works.

According to one school, this fifth Nikāya is more correctly referred to the Abhi-dhamma Piṭaka. In character, however, it conforms more to the Sutta. Of its fifteen works, perhaps the most important are the following six:—

The Khuddaka-pāṭha, 'short readings;' the Dhamma-pada, 'precepts of the Law' (or 'steps of the Law,' in twenty-six sections); the Jātaka (with their commentaries), a series of stories relating to about 550[1] previous births of the Buddha (p. 111), which have formed the basis of many stories in the Pañća-tantra, fables of Æsop, etc.; the Sutta-nipāta, 'collection of discourses;' the Thera-gāthā (= Sthavira-g°), 'verses or stanzas by elder monks;' Therī-gāthā, 'verses by elder nuns.'

The other nine are the Udāna, containing 82 short suttas and joyous utterances of the Buddha at crises of his life; the Itivuttaka, 'thus it was said' (= ity ukta), 110 sayings of the Buddha; the Vimāna-vatthu, on the mansions of the gods (which move about at will and sometimes descend on earth); the Peta-vatthu (= Preta-vastu, Peta standing for Preta and Pitṛi),

---

[1] 550 is a round number. The text of the Jātakas has been edited by Fausböll and translated by Rhys Davids and others. See a specimen at p. 112.

on departed spirits; the Niddesa, a commentary on the Sutta-nipāta; the Paṭi-sambhidā, on the supernatural knowledge of Arhaṭs; the Apadāna (Sanskṛit Avadāna), 'stories about the achievements' of Arhats; the Buddha-vaṉsa, or history of the 24 preceding Buddhas (the Dīgha mentions only six) and of Gautama; the Ćariyā-piṭaka, 'treasury of acts,' giving stories based on the Jātakas, describing Gautama's acquisition of the ten transcendent virtues (p. 128) in former births.

The works included in this Sutta-piṭaka frequently take the form of conversations on doctrine and morality, between Gautama, or one of his chief disciples, and some inquirer. As constituting the ethical Dharma, they are the most interesting portion of the Canon.

With regard to the third Piṭaka, called Abhi-dhamma (Abbhi-dharma, 'further dharma'), which is held by modern scholars to be of later origin and supplementary to the Sutta (p. 62), it contains seven prose works[1]. Moreover, it was once thought to relate entirely to metaphysics and philosophy; but this is now held to be an error, for all seven works treat of a great variety of subjects, including discipline and ethics. Metaphysical discussions occur, but it is probable that originally Buddha kept clear of metaphysics (see p. 98).

Besides the numerous works we have thus described as constituting the Tri-piṭaka or three collections of

---

[1] The seven are called: 1. Dhamma-saṅgaṇi, 'enumeration of conditions of existence,' edited by Dr. E. Müller; 2. Vibhaṅga, 'explanations;' 3. Kathā-vatthu, 'discussions on one thousand controverted points;' 4. Puggala-paññatti, 'explanation of personality;' 5. Dhātu-kathā, 'account of elements;' 6. Yamaka, 'pairs;' 7. Paṭṭhāna, 'causes.'

works of the Southern Buddhists, there are the Pāli commentaries called Aṭṭha-kathā (Artha-kathā, 'telling of meanings[1]'), which were translated into Sinhalese, according to tradition, by Mahendra himself. Afterwards the original Pāli text was lost and some of the commentaries were retranslated into Pāli by Buddha-ghosha, 'he who had the very voice of Buddha,' at the end of the fourth and beginning of the fifth century of our era.

The Mahā-vaṉśa or 'history of the great families of Ceylon,' a well-known work (written in Pāli by a monk named Mahā-nāma in the fifth century and translated by Turnour), gives an account of this writer[2]. It says that a Brāhman youth, born near Buddha-Gayā in Magadha, had achieved great celebrity as a disputant in Brāhmanical philosophy. This youth was converted by a Buddhist sage in India, and induced to enter the Buddhist monastic Order. He soon became renowned for his eloquence, and was on that account called Buddha-ghosha. He wrote a commentary, called Aṭṭha-sālinī, on the Dhamma-saṅgani, a work belonging to the Abhi-dharma. He also wrote a most valuable Pāli compendium of Buddhist doctrine called Visuddhi-magga, 'path of purity,' and a commentary on the Dharma-pada containing many parables. He went to Ceylon about A.D. 430 for the purpose of retranslating the Sinhalese commentaries into Pāli. His literary reputation stands very high in that island, and he was instrumental in spreading Buddhism throughout Burma.

---

[1] A list of these is given in Childers' Dictionary.

[2] See Introduction to Buddha-ghosha's Parables, by Professor Max Müller; Turnour's Mahā-vaṉśa, pp. 250–253.

It may be noted that the two important Pāli works, Mahā-vaṉśa and Dīpa-vaṉśa (Dvīpa-vaṉśa), perhaps the oldest extant histories of Ceylon, are also fairly authentic sources for Buddhistic history before Christ.

Turn we now to the Mahāyāna or 'Great Vehicle.' This cannot be said to possess any true Canon distinct from the Tri-piṭaka, though certain Nepālese Sanskṛit works, composed in later times, are held to be canonical by Northern Buddhists.

To understand this part of the subject we must revert to the great king Aśoka. It is usual to call this second and more celebrated Aśoka the Constantine of Buddhism. Being of Śūdra origin he was the more inclined to favour the popular teaching of Gautama, and, as he was the first king who adopted Buddhism openly (about 257 B.C.) he doubtless did for Buddhism very much what Constantine did for Christianity.

The Buddhist system then spread over the whole kingdom of Aśoka, and thence over other portions of India, and even to some outlying countries. For gradually during this period most of the petty princes of India, from Peshāwar and Kashmīr to the river Kistna, and from Surat to Bengal and Orissa, if not actually brought under subjection to the king of Magadha, were compelled to acknowledge his paramount authority.

This is proved by Aśoka's edicts, which are inscribed on rocks and stone pillars[1] (the earliest dating from

---

[1] They are in two quite distinct kinds of writing. That at Kapurdagarhi—sometimes called Northern Aśoka or Ariano-Pāli—is clearly Semitic, and traceable to a Phœnician source, being written from right to left. That at Girnār, commonly called Southern Aśoka or

about 251 B.C.), and are found in frontier districts separated from each other by enormous distances.

These inscriptions are of the greatest interest and value, as furnishing the first authentic records of Indian history. They are written in a more ancient language than the Pāli of Ceylon, and in at least three different dialects. Ten of the most important are found on six rocks and five pillars (Lāṭs), though numerous other monuments are scattered over Northern India, from the Indian Ocean to the Bay of Bengal, from the Vindhya range on the south to the Khaibar Pass on the north [1].

Indo-Pāli, is read from left to right, and is not so clearly traceable. If it came from the west it probably came through a Pahlavī channel, and gave rise to Devanāgarī. General Cunningham and others believe this latter character to have originated independently in India. James Prinsep was the first to decipher the inscription character.

[1] See Dr. R. N. Cust's article in the 'Journal of the National Indian Association' for June, 1879, and one of his Selected Essays, and General Sir A. Cunningham's great work, 'The Corpus Inscriptionum Indicarum.' The General reckons thirteen rock inscriptions, seventeen cave inscriptions, and six inscribed pillars.

The eight most important rock inscriptions are those on (1) the Rock of Kapurda-garhi (at Shāhbāz-garhi), in British Afghānistān, forty miles east-north-east of Peshāwar—this is in the Ariano-Pāli character; (2) the Rock of Khālsi, situated on the bank of the river Jumnā, just where it leaves the Himālaya mountains, fifteen miles west of the hill-station of Mussourie; (3) the Rock of Girnār, half-a-mile to the east of the city of Junagarh, in Kāthiāwār; (4) the Rock of Dhauli, in Kuttack (properly Kaṭak), twenty miles north of Jagan-nāth; (5) the Rock of Jaugada, in a large old fort eighteen miles west-north-west of Ganjam in Madras; (6) Bairāt; (7) Rūpnāth, at the foot of the Kaimur range; (8) Sahasarām, at the north-east end of the Kaimur. The second Bairāt inscription is most important as the only one which mentions Buddha by name.

The five most important pillars are: (1) the Pillar at Delhi known

In these proclamations and edicts (one of which was addressed to the third Buddhist Council), king Aśoka, who calls himself Priya-darśī (Pāli Piya-dassī), issues various orders. He prohibits the slaughter of animals for food or sacrifice, gives directions for what may be called the first hospitals, i. e. for treating men and even animals medically, appoints missionaries for the propagation of Buddhist doctrines, inculcates peace and mercy, charity and toleration, morality and self-denial, and what is still more remarkable, enjoins quinquennial periods of national humiliation and confession of sins by all classes, accompanied by a re-proclamation of the Buddha's precepts. Aśoka, in fact, became so zealous a friend of Buddhism, that he is said to have maintained 64,000 Buddhist monks in and around the country of Magadha, which was on that account called the land of monasteries (Vihāra = the modern Bihār or Behār).

No doubt it was Aśoka's propagation of Buddhism by missions in various countries—where it came in contact with and partly adopted various already existing indigenous faiths and superstitions—that led to the ultimate separation of the Buddhist system into the two great divisions of Southern and Northern.

Indeed, the formation of a Northern School, as distinct from a Southern, became inevitable after the conversion of Kanishka, the Indo-Scythian king of Kashmīr, who

---

as Firoz Shāh's Lāṭ; (2) another Pillar at Delhi, which was removed to Calcutta, but has recently been restored; (3) the Pillar at Allāhābād, a single shaft without capital, of polished sandstone, thirty-five feet in height; (4) the Pillar at Lauriya, near Bettiah, in Bengal; (5) the Pillar at another Lauriya, seventy-seven miles north-west of Patnā.

came from the North, and became a zealous Buddhist. He probably reigned in the second half of the first century (A.D.), and extended his dominions as far as Gujarāt, Sindh, and even Mathurā (see p. 167, note 2).

It was during Kanishka's reign that a fourth Council[1] was held at Jālandhara in Kashmīr, under Pārśva and Vasu-mitra. It consisted of 500 monks, who composed three Sanskṛit works of the nature of commentaries (Upadeśa, Vinaya-vibhāshā, Abhidharma-vibhāshā) on the three Pāli Piṭakas. These were the earliest books of the Mahā-yāna or Northern School, which afterwards formulated its more developed doctrines on the Indus, while the Pāli Canon of the South represented the true doctrine promulgated on the Ganges.

Kashmīr was a centre of Sanskṛit learning, and Kanishka, who was a patron of it, became to Northern Buddhism what Aśoka had been to Southern. Hence in process of time other Northern Buddhist books were written in Sanskṛit, with occasional Gāthās or stanzas in an irregular dialect, half Sanskṛit, half Prākṛit.

It is usual to enumerate nine Nepālese canonical scriptures (Dharmas):—1. Prajñā pāramitā, 'transcendent knowledge,' or an abstract of metaphysical and mystic philosophy; 2. Gaṇḍa-vyūha; 3. Daśa-bhūmīśvara (describing the ten stages leading to Buddhahood); 4. Samādhi-rāja; 5. Laṅkāvatāra; 6. Saddharma-puṇḍarīka, 'Lotus of the True Law;' 7. Tathāgata-guhyaka (containing the secret Tantric doctrines); 8. Lalita-vistara (giving a legendary life of Buddha);

[1] Hiouen Thsang states that the three commentaries were engraved on sheets of copper and buried in a Stūpa. Beal, I. 152–156.

9. Suvarṇa-prabhāsa. The eighth is probably as old as the 2nd century of our era, and next comes the sixth. Tibetan translations were made of all of them. These extend to 100 volumes and are collectively called Kanjur (strictly Ka-gyur or Kan-gyur). We owe our knowledge of these to the indefatigable Hungarian traveller, Alexander Csoma de Körös (see p. 326, 1).

Copies of the Sanskṛit works were brought to England by Mr. B. H. Hodgson. The sixth has been translated by Burnouf and recently by H. Kern. Dr. Rājendra-lāla-mitra has edited the eighth. As to the non-canonical works M. Senart has edited part of the Mahāvastu, and Professor E. B. Cowell and Mr. R. A. Neil, the Divyāvadāna. They contain interesting old legends —some about the achievements of Aśoka, some about Buddha himself, some perhaps from lost Vinaya books.

As to the Pāli written character, it is a question whether that current in the holy land of Buddhism, or in Ceylon, or in Siam (Kambodia), or in Burma—that is, Devanāgarī, Sinhalese, Kambodian, or Burmese—should be used. Many think Burmese most suited to it, and in Europe the Roman character is preferred.

It should be added that the recitation (Bhāṇa, Sanskṛit root Bhaṇ, 'to speak;' in Sinhalese spelt Baṇa) of the Law is one of the principal duties of monks, the reciter being called Bhāṇaka. A peculiar mode of intoning is called Sara-bhañña (sara = svara). The Buddha, they say, is not extinct, for he lives in the Dharma and in the Saṅgha, in the Law and in the Brotherhood of monks who recite it. Hence the importance of recitation in the Buddhist system (p. 84).

LECTURE IV.

The Saṅgha or Buddhist Order of Monks.

PERHAPS the first point made clear by the study of the Buddhist Scriptures is, that the Buddha never seriously thought of founding a new system in direct opposition to Brāhmanism and caste. Even his Order or fraternity of Monks, which attained a world-wide celebrity and spread through a great part of Asia, was a mere imitation of an institution already established in India. He himself was a Hindū of the Hindūs, and he remained a Hindū to the end. His very name, Gautama, connected him with one of the most celebrated Hindū sages, and was significant of his original connexion with orthodox Brāhmanism. It is true he was a determined opponent of all Brāhmanical sacerdotalism and ceremonialism, and of all theories about the supernatural character of the Vedas (see p. 53); but, being himself a Hindū, he never required his adherents to make any formal renunciation of Hindūism, as if they had been converted to an entirely new faith; just as, if I may say so with all reverence, the Founder of the Christian Church, being Himself a Jew, never required His followers to give up every Jewish usage.

Nor had the Buddha any idea of courting popularity as a champion of social equality and denouncer of all distinctions of rank and ancient traditions—

a kind of Tribune of the people, whose mission was to protect them from the tyranny of the upper classes.

There was, no doubt, at one time a prevalent opinion among scholars that Gautama aimed at becoming a great social reformer. It was generally supposed that he began by posing before his fellow-countrymen as a popular leader whose mission was to deliver them from the tyranny of caste [1]. But such an opinion is now known to be based on mistaken assumptions. What ought rather to be claimed for him is that he was the first to establish a universal brotherhood (Saṅgha) of cœnobite monks, open to all persons of all ranks. In other words, he was the first founder of what may be called a kind of universal monastic communism (for Buddhist monks never, as a rule, lived alone), and the first to affirm that true enlightenment—the knowledge of the highest path leading to saintship—was not confined to the Brāhmans, but open to all the members of all castes. This was the only sense in which he abolished caste. His true followers, however, constituted a caste of their own, distinguished from the laity. From the want of a more suitable term we are forced to call them 'monks [2].'

And this Order of monks was not a hierarchy. It had no ecclesiastical organization under any centralized authority. Its first Head, Gautama, appointed no successor. It was not the depository of theological learning. Nor was it a mediatorial caste of priests, claiming to

---

[1] I plead guilty to having stated this myself in former days.

[2] Our word *monk* (derived from *μοναχός*, 'one who lives alone') must be taken to mean 'one who withdraws from worldly life.' Friar (i. e. frère, 'a brother') would in some respects be better; but see p. 75.

mediate between earth and heaven. It ought not to be called a Church, and it had no rite of ordination in the true sense. It was a *brotherhood*, in which all were under certain obligations of celibacy, moral restraint, fasting, poverty, itineration and confession to each other—all were dominated by one idea, and pledged to the propagation of the one doctrine, that all life was in itself misery, and to be got rid of by a long course of discipline, as not worth living, whether on earth or in heaven, whether in present or future bodies. The founding of a monastic brotherhood of this kind which made personal extinction its final aim, and might be co-extensive with the whole world, was the Buddha's principal object.

In point of fact, the so-called enlightenment of mind which entitled him to Buddhahood, led him at the early stage of his career into no abstruse or transcendental region of thought, but took a very practical direction. It led him to see that an association of monks offering equality of condition to high and low, rich and poor, and a haven of refuge to all oppressed by the troubles of life, would soon become popular. His Order started with first ten, then fifty, then sixty original members (see p. 45), but its growth soon surpassed all anticipations, and its ramifications extended to distant countries, where, like the branches of the Indian fig-tree, they sent down roots to form vigorous independent plants, even after the decay of the parent stem. On this account it was called the fraternity of the four quarters (Ćātuddisa, Mahā-vagga VIII. 27. 5) of the globe.

In brief, a carefully regulated monastic brotherhood, which opened its arms to all comers of all ranks, and enforced on its members the duty of extending its boundaries by itinerancy, and by constantly rolling onward the wheel of the true doctrine (Law), constituted in its earliest days the very essence, the very backbone of Buddhism, without which it could never have been propagated, nor even have held its own.

But we repeat that in this, his main design, Gautama was after all no innovator; no introducer of novel ideas.

Monachism had always been a favourite adjunct of the Brāhmanical system, and respect for monastic life had taken deep root among the people. Thus we find it laid down in its most authoritative exponent, Manu's Law-book (Book VI), that every twice-born man was bound to be first an unmarried student (Brahma-ćārī); secondly, a married householder (Gṛihastha); thirdly, a liver in retirement (Vānaprastha); and fourthly a Sannyāsī, 'world-renouncer.' Kshatriyas—like Gautama—as well as Brāhmans, were subject to this law; and it is through these very states that Brāhmans, even in the present day, are theoretically bound to pass (see illustration opposite).

Hence monks of various kinds were common in Buddha's time. They belonged to different sects, and took vows of self-torture, of silence, of fasting, of poverty, of mendicancy, of celibacy, of abandoning caste, rank, wife and family. Accordingly they had various names. The Brāhman became a Sannyāsī, 'one who gives up the world.' Others were called Vairāgī, 'free from affections;' Yogī, 'seeking mystic union with the Deity;' Dig-ambara, 'sky-clothed,' 'naked;' Tapasvī, 'practising austerities;' Yati, 'restraining desires;' Jitendriya,

PORTRAIT OF MR. GAURĪ-ŚAṄKAR UDAY-ŚAṄKAR, C.S.I.
NOW SVĀMĪ ŚRĪ SAĆĆIDĀNANDA-SARASVATĪ.

Seated, as a Brāhman Sannyāsī, in meditation (described at p. xiii of the Preface).

[*To face page* 74.

'conquering passions;' Śramaṇa, 'undergoing discipline;' Bhikshu, 'living by alms;' Nirgrantha, 'without ties.' Such names prove that asceticism was an ancient institution. The peculiarity about Gautama's teaching in regard to monachism was that he discouraged[1] solitary asceticism, severe austerities, and irrevocable vows, though he enjoined moral restraint in celibate fraternities, conformity to rules of discipline, upright conduct, and confession to each other.

His usual mode of designating his monks was by the old term Bhikshu (Pāli Bhikkhu), 'living by alms,' to indicate their poverty. They were also called Śrāmaṇera and Śramaṇa (Pāli Sāmaṇera, Samaṇa), as subject to monastic discipline[2]. Those who entered the stream leading to Arhatship (p. 132) were called Ārya.

The term Śrāvaka, 'hearers,' seems to have been used in the Hīna-yāna system to denote gręat disciples only, and especially those 'great disciples' (p. 47) of Gautama who heard the Law from his own lips, and were afterwards called Sthaviras and became Arhats (p. 133). They had also the title Āyushmat, 'possessing life.'

We perceive again the close connexion between Brāhmanism and Buddhism; for clearly the Brahmaćārī and Sannyāsī of the one became the Śrāmaṇera or junior monk, and Śramaṇa or senior monk of the other.

As to the name Śramaṇa (from root Śram, 'to toil'),

---

[1] Although he discouraged, he did not prohibit monks from living solitary lives. See p. 132 as to the Pratyeka-Buddha, and note, p. 72.

[2] Some prefer to derive the Pāli Samaṇa (Samaṇo) from the Sanskṛit root Śam, 'to be quiet.' Śmāśānika, 'frequenting burning grounds,' is a later name, life being to monks a kind of graveyard.

bear in mind that, although Buddhism has acquired the credit of being the easiest religious system in the world, and its monks are among the idlest of men—as having no laborious ceremonies and no work to do for a livelihood—yet in reality the carrying out of the great object of extinguishing lusts, and so getting rid of the burden of repeated existences, was no sinecure if earnestly undertaken. Nor was it possible for men to lead sedentary lives, whose only mode of avoiding starvation was by house to house itinerancy.

As to the form of admission, there was no great strictness in early times, when all applicants were admitted without inquiry. It was only when the Order increased that murderers, robbers, debtors, soldiers and others in the King's service, lepers, cripples, blind, one-eyed, deaf and dumb, and consumptive persons, and all subject to fits were rejected[1].

Originally it was enough for the Buddha to have said, 'Come, be my disciple.' This alone conferred discipleship. In time, however, he commissioned those he had himself admitted to admit others. Then the form of admission to the brotherhood was divided into two stages, marked by two ceremonies, which have been very unsuitably compared to our ordination services for deacon and priest. At any rate the term 'ordination' is wholly misleading, if any idea of a priestly commission or gift of spiritual powers be implied.

The youthful layman who desired admission to the first degree, or that of a novice, had to be at least

[1] In the Mṛiććhakaṭi, 'Clay-Cart,' a Sanskṛit drama written in an early century of our era, a gambler becomes a Buddhist monk.

fifteen years old[1] (Mahā-v° I. 50); and such novices had to be at least twenty (from conception) before the second rite or admission to the full monkhood.

The first rite was called pravrajyā (pabbajjā), 'going forth from home' (Mahā-v° I. 12). Persons admitted to this first degree of monkhood were called Śrāmaṇera (Sāmaṇera), 'novices,' though they were also called 'new' or 'junior monks' (Navako Bhikkhu). They might be admitted by a senior monk without appearing before any formal conclave; but not without the consent of their parents, and not without attaching themselves to a religious teacher (upādhyāya) after their admission. It is said that Gautama was urged by his father Śuddhodana to require the sanction of parents, in rather touching and remarkable words, to the following effect:—

'The love for a son cuts into the cuticle (ćhavi); having cut into the cuticle, it cuts into the inner skin (ćamma); having cut into the inner skin, it cuts into the flesh; having cut into the flesh, it cuts into the tendons (nhāru or nahāru); having cut into the tendons, it cuts into the bones; having cut into the bones, it reaches the marrow (aṭṭhi-miñjā), and abides in the marrow. Let not Pabbajjā, therefore, be performed by a son without his father's and mother's permission' (Mahā-vagga I. 54).

The admission ceremony of a novice was extremely

---

[1] I hear from Dr. Oldenberg that the mention in his 'Buddha' of twelve years as the minimum is a mistake. The age of eight mentioned by Prof. Rhys Davids as the minimum, must be a modern rule peculiar to Ceylon, if it be admissible at all.

simple, and confined to certain acts and words on the part of the candidate, witnessed by any competent monk. The Saṅgha, as a body, took no part in it. The novice first cut off his hair, put on three yellow ragged garments (tri-ćīvara), adjusted the upper robe so as to leave the right shoulder bare, and then before a monk repeated three times the three-refuge formula:

'I go for refuge to the Buddha (Buddhaṃ śaraṇaṃ gaććhāmi).'
'I go for refuge to the Law (Dharmaṃ śaraṇaṃ gaććhāmi).'
'I go for refuge to the Order (Saṅghaṃ śaraṇaṃ gaććhāmi).'

Very remarkably, this, the only prayer of true Buddhism, resembled the Gāyatrī or sacred prayer of the Veda (repeated by the Brahma-ćārī) in consisting of three times eight syllables. But if the Buddhist novice had a right to the Brahma-ćārī's sacred cord (upavīta), this was probably abandoned on admission. He was then instructed in the Ten Precepts (Dasa-sīla or sikkhā-pada, compare p. 126) or ten prohibitions (Mahā-vagga I. 56), requiring ten abstinences (veramaṇī):—

1. from destroying life (pāṇātipato = prāṇātipāta); 2. from taking anything not given (adinnādāna); 3. from unchastity (abrahmaćariyā); 4. from speaking falsely (musā-vāda = mṛishā-vāda); 5. from drinking strong drinks (surā); 6. from eating at forbidden times (vikāla-bhojana); 7. from dancing, singing, music, and worldly spectacles (visūka); 8. from garlands, scents, unguents or ornaments; 9. from the use of a high or broad bed; 10. from receiving gold or silver. The prohibition not to receive money, even in return for religious teaching or any supposed spiritual benefits conferred, was held to be most important, and was for a

long time obeyed, though in the end monasteries became owners of large property and landed estates.

Of course the Upasampadā, or admission to full brotherhood (described Mahā-vagga I. 76), was a more formal ceremony. A conclave (Saṅgha) of at least ten monks was required. The candidate had to appear before them, but was first instructed by some competent and learned monk as to the nature of the rite and the questions he would have to answer. This instructor also directed him to choose some other monk competent to act as his Upādhyāya (upajjhāya) or teacher for five years after his admission, and made him provide himself with an alms-bowl and with the usual yellow monkish vestments. Then his first instructor presented himself before the conclave and informed them that the candidate was ready to be admitted. Thereupon the novice came forward, adjusted his upper garment so as to cover the left shoulder, bowed down before the feet of the assembled monks, seated himself on the ground, and, raising his joined hands, asked three times for admission to the full monkhood, thus:—'I entreat the Saṅgha for admission to full monkhood (Upasampadā), have compassion on me and uproot me (ullumpatu mām) from the world,' repeated thrice.

Thereupon he was questioned [not, as in our Ordination Service: 'Are you inwardly moved by the Holy Spirit to take upon you this office?' Not: 'Will you apply all your diligence to frame and fashion your own life and that of your family so as to be wholesome examples?' but] thus:—Are you free from leprosy, boils, consumption, fits, etc.? Are you a male? Are you a free man and not in the royal service? Are you free from debts? Have you the consent of your parents? Are you full twenty years old? Have you an alms-bowl and vestments? What is your name? What is your teacher's name?

If the answers were satisfactory the candidate was admitted. After admission no prayer was pronounced [such as in our Ordination Service: 'We beseech Thee, merciful Father, send on Thy servant Thy heavenly blessing that he may be clothed with righteousness'[1]; but he was informed that he was to trust to only four Resources (nissaya), and to abstain from four chief forbidden acts (akaraṇīyāni). These four Resources and four Prohibitions were then communicated to him thus:—

First the four Resources as follow:—(1) Broken morsels given in alms for food; (2) Rags from a dust-heap for clothes; (3) Roots of trees for an abode; (4) Liquid putrefying excreta of cows for medicine. Note, however, that, in practice, indulgences (atirekha-lābha) were in all four cases allowed; such as, better food when it happened to be given, or when invited to dinner by rich laymen; linen, cotton, or woollen garments, if dyed yellow and in three pieces (but only one change was allowed); houses, huts, or caves to dwell in, when not itinerating; ghee, honey, or molasses when out of health (Mahā-v° I. 30. 4).

Next the four chief Prohibitions (compare the Ten Prohibitions, p. 78), viz.:—(1) Unchastity and sexual acts

[1] I give these quotations to show the unsuitableness of the term 'Ordination' applied to Pabbajjā and Upasampadā in the S. B. E.

of any kind; (2) Taking anything not given, even a blade of grass; (3) Killing any living thing, even an ant, or worm, or plant; (4) Falsely claiming the extraordinary powers of a perfected saint (uttarimanussa-dhamma. Mahā-v° I. 78. 2).

Clearly there were great temptations to gain celebrity by claiming such powers, or else this fourth prohibition would not have terminated the ceremony.

So soon as a man was admitted to full monkhood, he went through a five years' course of instruction in the entire doctrine and discipline, under the preceptor (Upādhyāya, Āćārya) who had been previously chosen and was required to be of at least ten years' standing.

This was a modification of the Brāhmanical rule that a student (Brahma-ćārī) should study under his preceptor for thirty-six years, or less, until he knew the Veda.

The full Buddhist monk had in theory to dwell under trees or in huts formed of leaves (pāṇ-sālā = paṇṇa-sāla = parṇa-śālā); but practically he resided in collections of simple mud or brick tenements, in cells, or in rows of caves hewn out of rocky hills. At any rate, collections of monastic dwellings, called Vihāras[1], were his usual abode during Vassa (or the rainy season, see p. 82); and at such times he had fellow-monks (saddhivihārika) living in companies around him, or in the same monastery.

Strict discipline was supposed to be enforced, and yet

[1] In Mahā-vagga I. 30. 4, five kinds of dwellings are named besides trees, viz. Vihāras, Aḍḍhayogas (a kind of house shaped like Garuḍa), storied dwellings (prāsāda), mansions (harmya), and caves (guhā).

there was no central authority, no Chief Hierarch, no Archbishop whom he was bound 'reverently to obey.'

Offences against the four forbidden acts were called Pārājikā āpatti, 'offences meriting expulsion from the community of monks (Saṅgha).'

Then there were thirteen Saṅghādisesā āpatti, as well as certain Dukkata or less serious offences, requiring only confession before the Saṅgha, and dealt with by a Saṅgha-kamma, or act of a conclave of monks imposing some penance. There were penances (Prāyaśćitta) for lying, prevarication, abusive language, destroying vegetable or animal life, etc. (see Pātimokkha, Pāćittiyā dhammā, and pp. 62, 84). The following practices were also incumbent on all monks:—

(1) The wearing vestments given by laymen (not purchased) and consisting of three lengths of yellow-coloured rags; or, if entire lengths of cotton cloths were given, the saleable value had to be destroyed by tearing them into at least three pieces, and then sewing them together; (2) The owning no possessions except the three cloths, a girdle, bowl, razor, needle, and water-strainer to prevent the swallowing of animalculæ; ( ) The living only on food collected in a wooden bowl by daily going from house to house, but without ever asking for it; (4) The eating at mid-day the one meal so collected and at no other time; (5) The fasting on four prescribed days; (6) The abiding in one spot for three or four months during Vassa, 'the rains' (from middle of June to middle of October), when itineration would involve trampling on vegetable and insect life; (7) The refraining from a recumbent posture under all

circumstances; (8) The visiting cremation-grounds for meditation on the corruption of the body.

In truth it might almost be said that in every movement and action, in waking and sleeping, in dressing and undressing, in standing and sitting, in going out and coming in, in fasting and eating, in speaking and not speaking, the Buddhist monk had to submit to the most stringent regulations.

It was a noteworthy feature in Buddhist monachism that monks were never allowed to appear in public in a state of even semi-nudity. 'Properly clad,' says the Sekhiyā dhammā (4), 'must the monk itinerate.' 'Not nakedness,' says the Dhamma-pada (141), 'can purify a mortal who has not overcome desires.' The monk's three garments (tićīvara = tri-ćīvara) were an inner one (antara-vāsaka), another wound about the thighs (saṅghāṭī) and an upper robe (uttarāsaṅga) worn loosely and brought round over the left shoulder. This constituted an important distinction between the Buddhist monks and the Jaina and other naked ascetics whose want of decency the Buddha condemned.

The Buddhist monk's daily life probably began by meditation and by his reciting or intoning (Bhāṇa, Sarabhañña) portions of the Law, or by hearing it recited, followed perhaps by lessons in doctrine, or by discussions or by confessions. Next came itineration for food, followed by the one noon-day meal. Then came rest and further meditation and recitation, while possibly the senior monks preached to laymen. Such preaching took place especially during Vassa. In later times the daily duties were of a more varied kind, and included the teaching of boy pupils and many tedious ceremonial and ritualistic practices (see pp. 311–339).

The efficacy of recitation of the Law was believed to be immense (see p. 318 and note story at p. 558). Although the laity took no part in these recitations, except as listeners, yet they had their ceremonies and rites and prayer-formularies (see pp. 340–386).

Doubtless quarrels and faults of omission and commission occurred among the monks, especially during their residence together in Vassa (miscalled the Buddhist Lent). We read of six monks named Ćhabbaggiya who were constantly committing offences. Hence a day called Pavāraṇā (Pravāraṇā), 'invitation,' was kept at the end of Vassa, when all were invited to assemble for confession and for felicitation and rejoicing, if harmony had been preserved.

An important part of every monk's duties was confession on Uposatha (Upavasatha) or fast-days (miscalled the Buddhist sabbaths)—which were kept at first on two days in each month, at full and new moon (corresponding to the Darśa and Paurṇamāsa days of Brāhmanism), and afterwards also at the intermediate days of quarter-moon. On these four Uposatha days the Pātimokkha or general confession (p. 62) was recited. The confession was by monks to each other, not by laymen to monks, though the four days were also observed by laymen, and we know that Aśoka enjoined periodical ceremonies, and expression of sorrow for sins on the part of all his subjects. Such confession did not cause remission of sin or absolution in our sense, but only release from evil consequences by penances (p. 62).

We have learnt, then, that Buddhist monks were not under irrevocable vows. They undertook to obey rules of discipline, but took no actual vows—not even of obedience to a superior. Buddhist monkhood was purely voluntary, so that all were free to come and go. It had nothing hereditary about it like the rank of a Brāhman.

We have also learnt, that the term 'priest' is not suitably applied to Buddhist monks. For true Buddhism has no ecclesiastical hierarchy, no clergy, no priestly ordination; no divine revelation, no ceremonial rites, no prayer, no worship in the proper sense of these terms. Each man was a priest to himself in so far as he depended on himself alone for internal sanctification.

Evidently, too, all Buddhist monks were integral parts of one organic whole. It is true that in the end they were collected in various monasteries, each of which practically became an independent Saṅgha (each under one Head). But in theory all were parts of one and the same brotherhood, which was republican and communistic in its constitution. And this word Saṅgha cannot be correctly rendered by 'church,' if by that term is meant an ecclesiastical body with legislative functions, embracing clergy and *laity* united in a common faith and under one Head; for as founded by the Buddha, it was not this. It was simply a vast fraternity intended to embrace all monks of the four quarters (ćaturdiśa) of the world, from the Buddha himself and the perfected Arhat (p. 133), to every monk of the lowest degree, but not a single layman. Indeed in its highest sense the Saṅgha comprised only true Nirvāṇa-seeking monks who had entered the paths of true sanctification (p. 132).

And here observe that, notwithstanding the stigma attached to unmarried women in India, Gautama in the end permitted an Order of Nuns (Pāli Bhikkhunī) and female novices (Sāmaṇerī, p. 47). The Ćulla-vagga (X. 1. 3) relates how women were indebted to the intercession of a monk, Gautama's cousin Ānanda, for permission to form an Order, and how Mahā-prajāpatī, the Buddha's nurse (p. 24), became the first nun; yet when Ānanda first asked: 'How are we monks to behave when we see women?' Gautama replied: 'Don't see them.' 'But if we should see them, what are we to do?' 'Don't speak to them.' 'But if they speak to us, what then?' 'Let your thoughts be fixed in deep meditation' (Sati upaṭṭhāpetabbā. Mahā-parin° V. 23).

Clearly the Buddha was originally a misogynist as well as a misogamist, and wished his followers to be misogynists also. Even when he had been induced to admit the justice of the plea for women's rights, he placed his nuns under the direction of monks. They could only be admitted by monks, and were subject to the male Order in all matters of discipline. They were under eight special obligations, one of which was to rise up in the presence of a monk, even if a novice.

The Buddha's exhortation to the first nun is noteworthy:—'Whatsoever, O Gotamī (Mahā-prajāpatī), conduces to absence of passion, to absence of pride, to wishing for little and not for much, to seclusion and not to love of society, to earnest effort and not to indolence, to contentment and not to querulousness, verily that is the true doctrine' (Ćulla-v° X. 5).

It was certainly a great gain for a woman when she

was permitted to become a nun (or a Therī); for, as a nun, she could even attain Arhatship. This is clearly laid down in Ćulla-vagga X. 1. 3. 4. No woman, however, could attain to Buddhahood without being born as a man, so that it could scarcely be said that in Buddha there is 'neither male nor female.'

Such, then, was the monachism which constituted the very pith and marrow of Buddhism. All truly enlightened disciples of Buddha were monks or nuns.

Let us not forget, however, that in practice Buddhism admitted lay-brothers, lay-sisters, married householders and working-men, as necessary adjuncts.

Yet they were only appendages. Of course the Buddha knew very well that it was not possible to enforce celibacy on all his followers. He knew that having prohibited his monks from making or taking money or holding property, they would have to depend on lay-associates and householders for food, clothing, and habitation, and that, if every layman were to become a monk, there would be no work done, no food produced, no children born, and in time no humanity—nay, no Buddhism—left.

Universal monkhood, in short, might have been a consummation to be aimed at in some Utopia; but was practically unattainable. In fact Gautama had to take the world as he found it, and the very idea of a world perpetuating itself—according to his own theory of a constant succession of birth, decay, and reproduction—implied that a youth, on reaching manhood, married, had children, worked and earned a livelihood for their support. No man could impose this burden on others.

Besides, the generality of people were in Gautama's day what they are in India now-a-days—bent on early marriage, and resolute in working hard for a livelihood. Even Manu only enjoined celibacy on young religious students and on old men, though there were occasional cases of perpetual (naishṭhika) Brahma-ćārins.

Without doubt, celibacy in instances of extraordinary sanctity has always commanded respect in India; but in no country of the world has married life been so universally honoured. It is not very likely, then, that the following sentiments, enunciated by the Buddha, could have met with general approval:—

'A wise man should avoid married life (abrahma-ćariyam) as if it were a burning pit of live coals' (Dhammika-Sutta 21).

'Full of hindrances is married life, defiled by passion. How can one who dwells at home live the higher life in all its purity?' (Tevijja-Sutta 47).

And in reality Buddha's anti-matrimonial doctrines *did* excite opposition. The people murmured and said, 'He is come to bring childlessness among us, and widowhood, and destruction of family-life.' Indeed, the two facts—first, that the foundations of Buddhism were not laid (as those of Christianity notably are), on the hallowed hearth of home and on the sacred rock of family-life with its daily round of honest work; and—secondly, that the precept enjoining monkhood and abstinence from marriage was not combined with any organized ecclesiastical hierarchy under a central government, are sufficient to account for the circumstance that Buddhism never gained any real stability in India.

No doubt lay-brethren were always welcomed; but they were bound to Buddhism by very slender ties in regard to dogma, and were only expected to conform to the simplest possible code of morality.

Probably the only form of admission for a layman was the repetition of the 24 syllables of the three-refuge (tri-śaraṇa) formula:—'I go for refuge to the Buddha, his Law and his Order' (p. 78). He was of course required to obey the five chief rules of conduct (pañća-sīla, p. 126), but he was already bound to do so by the rules of Hindū caste and family-religion. The chief test of his Buddhism was his readiness to serve the monks. It was for this reason, I think, that lay-adherents were not called, as might have been expected, Śrāvakas, 'Hearers,' but simply Upāsakas, 'Servers,' and in the case of women Upāsikās. They could not be called disciples of Buddha in the *truest sense*, unless they entered his monastic Order.

Of course the majority of Buddhist householders never cared to do this. Their chief religion consisted in giving food and clothing, earned by daily toil, to the monks[1]. If they failed in this, there was only one punishment. They were forbidden the privilege of giving at all, and so of accumulating a store of merit. No monk was allowed to ask them for a single thing. Of course, too, the majority of Buddhist householders

---

[1] To compare Western with Eastern Monachism would require a volume. The chief duty of the lay-brethren of the Cistercian monastery at Fountain's Abbey was to wait upon the monks, procure food and cook it for them. We learn from the *Times* of December 24, 1885, that the same duty devolved on the Carthusian lay-brothers.

were worldly-minded; they were no believers in ultra-pessimistic views of life. They looked for a life in some heaven, not Nirvāṇa. Yet in theory all laymen might enter the paths of sanctification (p. 132), and thousands of earnest men are said to have done so [1].

A layman's progress, however, towards Arhatship, except through monkhood and abandoning the world, was almost hopelessly barred. At page 264 of the Milinda-pañha it is implied that an earnest layman might become an Arhat, even while still a layman, but he had either to enter monkhood or else to pass away in Pari-nirvāṇa (p. 140) at the moment of becoming so.

The best proof of the truth of this view of the matter is, that after a layman had attached himself to the Buddha, the Law, and the Order, he was not required to undergo any ritual ceremony, like baptism, or to receive any stamp of membership, or to assume a peculiar dress, or to give up all belief in his family religion, or caste-customs. In short, he did not as a lay-brother break entirely with Hindūism.

That universal tolerance was of the very essence of Buddhism is indicated by Aśoka's twelfth edict:—'The beloved of the gods honours all forms of religious faith—there ought to be reverence for one's own faith and no reviling of that of others.' Compare p. 126.

Nor did Gautama himself ever set an example of intolerance. He never railed at the Brāhmans. He treated them with respect, and taught others to do so;

---

[1] The Chronicles of Ceylon state that 80,000 laymen entered the paths in Kashmīr. Compare Divyāvadāna, p. 166, line 12; p. 271, 12.

and even adopted the title Brāhmaṇa for his own saints and Arhats (Dhamma-pada 383–423).

What he opposed was priestcraft and superstition, not Brāhmanism; as indeed other reformers had done before him. Probably the great receptivity of Buddhism was one of the causes that led to its decay in India.

Yet Gautama's victory over one of the most inveterate propensities in human nature—the tendency to seek salvation through a mediatorial caste of priests—was a wonderful achievement. This is proved by the fact that his followers in other countries became re-entangled in a network of priestcraft, even more enslaving than that out of which he had rescued them.

It will be hereafter shown (pp. 278, 279, 339 of this volume) that the Buddhism of Tibet, with its Pope-like grand Lāmas—its cardinals and abbots, monks and mendicant friars, nuns and novices, canonized saints and angelic hosts, temples and costly shrines, monasteries and nunneries, images and pictures, altars and relics, robes and mitres, rosaries and consecrated water, litanies and chants, processions and pilgrimages, confessions and penances, bell-ringing and incense—is in everything, except doctrine, almost a counterpart of the Romish system. How little could the Buddha have foreseen such a development of his brotherhood of monks, whose chief duties were meditation and itineration!

And what is to be said of the present condition of the Buddhist monkhood? Do we see anywhere evidences of that enlightenment of mind which Buddhism claims as its chief characteristic?

When I was travelling in Ceylon, I met a few learned

and many intelligent monks (see pp. 256–258), but not a few seemed to me idle and indifferent.

In Burma the monks are called Pungīs (Phongies), and are a little more active. Every youth in Burma is supposed for a time to inhabit a monastery.

In Tibet the monks are called Lāmas (a lower title being Gelong) and constitute a large proportion of the population. They are slaves to gross superstitions. Some are mere devil-charmers, a belief in the power of evil spirits being the chief religion of the people.

In China the monks are called Ho-shang (or Ho-sang). They constitute the chief section of the population who call themselves Buddhists, though, after all, they are not Buddhists in the true sense. Professor Legge informs me that he has known a few learned men among them, and learned works have been written by them. But the general testimony of Europeans in China is that the mass of the monks there are simply drones, or aimless dreamers, who go through their repetitions by rote. Almost all are conspicuous for apathy, inertness, and a vacant idiotic expression of countenance.

Clearly we have in their condition an example of the fact that even moral restraint, if carried to the extreme of extinguishing all the natural affections and desires, must inevitably be followed by a Nemesis. Surely we have in these monkish fraternities an illustration of the truth that any transgression of the laws of nature, common-sense, and reason—any suppression of the primary instincts of humanity, must in the end incur the penalty attached to every violation of the eternal ordinances of God.

LECTURE V.

The Philosophical Doctrines of Buddhism.

One of the most noteworthy points in the early history of Buddhistic thought is that while Gautama Buddha denied the existence of Brahmā as a personal Creator, and repudiated the Veda and all Vedic sacrifices and ceremonial observances, he at the same time made the philosophical teaching of the Brāhmans the point of departure for his own peculiar philosophical teaching.

Another noteworthy point is that while Buddhism was undoubtedly a modification of philosophical Brāhmanism, the latter was also modified by an interchange with Buddhistic ideas.

It may certainly be questioned whether Gautama himself, in the early stages of his career, ever caused much offence to the most orthodox Brāhmans by the free expression of his opinions. He did not spare either his criticism or sarcasm, but it is well known that the Brāhmans were not only tolerant of criticism; they were equally critical themselves, and delighted in controversial discussions, as they do to this day.

In the Tevijja-Sutta an account is given of a discussion in which, though Gautama expressed himself strongly, he does not seem to have excited any wrath in his opponent—a Brāhman named Vāsettha.

The argument attributed to the Buddha is so remarkable that a portion of it may be given here :—

'Then you say, Vāsettha, that not one of the Brāhmans, or of their teachers, or of their pupils, even up to the seventh generation, has ever seen Brahman (the God of the Brāhmans) face to face. And that even the Ṛishis of old, the utterers of the ancient verses, which the Brāhmans of to-day so carefully intone and recite precisely as they have been handed down—even they did not pretend to know or to have seen where or whence or whither Brahman is. So that the Brāhmans versed in the three Vedas have forsooth said thus: "To a state of union with that which we know not and have not seen, we can show the way and can say: 'This is the straight path, this is the direct way which leads him who acts according to it, into a state of union with Brahman[1].'"

'Now what think you, Vāsettha? Does it not follow, this being so, that the talk of the Brāhmans, versed though they be in the three Vedas, is foolish talk?

'Verily, Vāsettha, that Brāhmans versed in the three Vedas should be able to show the way to a state of union with that which they do not know, neither have seen—such a condition of things has no existence.

'As when a string of blind men are clinging one to the other, neither can the foremost see, nor can the middle one see, nor can the hindmost see, just so is the talk of the Brāhmans versed in the three Vedas[1].'

These no doubt were trenchant words, but it might easily be shown that the Brāhmans themselves did not

---

[1] See Tevijja-Sutta, S. B. E. §§ 14, 15.

scruple to use almost as strong language against their own revelation. For instance, the Ćhāndogya Upanishad (p. 473) speaks of the Veda as 'mere name' (nāma eva). The Bṛihadāraṇyaka Upanishad declares that when a man is in a condition of knowledge, 'the gods are no gods to him, and the Veda no Veda;' and the Muṇḍaka describes the sacrificial Veda as inferior to Brahma-vidyā.

And in truth every Hindū was allowed to choose one of three ways of securing his own salvation.

The first was 'the way of works' (Karma-mārga), that is to say, of sacrifices (Yajña), of ceremonial rites, of lustral washings, penances and pilgrimages, as enjoined in the Mantra and Brāhmaṇa portion of the Veda, in Manu, the Law-books and parts of the Purāṇas.

The second was 'the way of faith' (bhakti), meaning by that term devotion to one or other of certain commonly worshipped personal deities,—a way leading in later times to the worship of Śiva and Vishṇu (unfolded in the Purāṇas), and involving merely heart-devotion, without sacrificial or ceremonial acts.

The third was 'the way of knowledge' (Jñāna), as set forth in the Upanishads.

The mediæval Brāhman Kumārila—a really historical teacher—advocated the first way; another teacher of less note, Śāṇḍilya, advocated the second; another celebrated historical teacher, Śaṅkara, advocated the third.

Even in Gautama's time any one of these ways or all three together might be chosen, so long as the authority of the Brāhmans was not impugned.

This, at least, is the general teaching of the Bhagavad-gītā—an eclectic work which is the most popular exponent of the Hindū creed[1].

Yet even the Author of the Bhagavad-gītā had a preference for the way of knowledge. In one passage (II. 42) he describes the Veda as 'mere flowery doctrine' (pushpitā vāć), and is careful to point out that works must be performed as acts of devotion leading to absorption into the Supreme (Brahma-nirvāṇam).

Indeed there can be no doubt that it was generally held by the Brāhmans of Buddha's time that the way of knowledge was the highest way. But this way was not open to all. It was reserved for the privileged few—for the more intellectual and philosophically-minded Brāhmans. The generality of men had to content themselves with the first and second ways.

What the Buddha then did was this:—First he stretched out the right hand of brotherhood to all mankind by inviting all without exception to join his fraternity of celibate monks, which he wished to be co-extensive with the world itself. Then he abolished the first and second ways of salvation (p. 95), that is, Yajña, 'sacrifices,' and Bhakti, 'devotion to personal gods,' and substituted for these meditation and moral conduct as the only road to true knowledge and emancipation. And then, lastly, he threw open this highest way

[1] The venerable Svāmī Śrī Saććidānanda Sarasvatī, in sending me a copy of the Bhagavad-gītā with a metrical commentary, says, 'It is the best of all books on the Hindū religion, and contains the essence of all kinds of religious philosophy.' I find in the Madras *Times* for October 29, 1886, the following: 'At a meeting of the "Society for the Propagation of True Religion," at 6 p.m. to-day, the Bhagavad-gītā will be read and explained.'

of true knowledge to all who wished to enter it, of whatever rank or caste or mental calibre they might be, not excepting the most degraded.

Without doubt the distinguishing feature in the Buddha's gospel was that no living being, not even the lowest, was to be shut out from true enlightenment.

And here it will be necessary to inquire more closely into the nature of that knowledge which the Buddha thus made accessible to every creature in the universe.

Was it some deep mystery? Some occult doctrine of physical or metaphysical science? Some startling revelation of a law of nature never before imparted to the world? Was the Buddha's open way very different from the old, well fenced-off Brāhmanical way?

Of one point we may be certain. He was too sensible to cast aside all ancient traditions. Nor was he a mere enthusiast claiming to be the sole possessor of a new secret for regenerating society.

Unhappily, however, we are here met by a difficulty. The Buddha never, like Muhammad, wrote a book, or, so far as we know, a line. He was the Socrates of India, and we are obliged to trust to the record of his sayings (see p. 38). Still we have no reason to doubt the genuineness of what was for some time handed down orally in regard to the doctrines he taught, and we are struck with the fact that Gautama called his own knowledge *Bodhi* (from *budh*, 'to understand'), and not *Veda* (from *vid*, 'to know'). Probably by doing so he wished to imply that his own knowledge was attainable by all through their own intuitions, inner consciousness, and self-enlightening intellect, and was to be distinguished from *Veda* or knowledge obtainable through the Brāhmans alone, and by them through supernatural revelation only. Hence, too, every being destined to become a Buddha received the title Bodhisattva (Bodhi-satta), 'one having knowledge *derived from self-enlightening intellect* for his essence.'

But it should be noted, that even in the choice of a name derived from the Sanskṛit root *budh*, the Buddha only adopted the phraseology of the Sāṅkhya philosophy and of the Brāhmaṇas. The Sāṅkhya system made Buddhi, 'intellect,' its great principle (Mahat), and the Śatapatha-brāhmaṇa called a man who had attained to perfect knowledge of Self prati-buddha[1]. It may be pointed out, too, that Manu (IV. 204) uses the same root when he calls his wise man Budha.

Moreover, the doctrines which grew out of his own special knowledge Gautama still called *Dharma* (Dhamma), 'law,' using the very same term employed by the Brāhmans—a term expressive of law in its most comprehensive sense, as comprising under it the physical laws of the Universe, as well as moral and social duties.

In what, then, did the Buddha's Dharma differ from that of the Brāhmans? One distinction was that it contained no esoteric (rahasya) metaphysical doctrines—in regard to the difference between matter and spirit—reserved for the privileged few; yet some of its root-ideas were after all mere modifications of the Sāṅkhya, Yoga, and Vedānta systems of philosophy. His way of knowledge, though it developed into many paths, had

---

[1] XIV. 7. 2. 17. This was first pointed out by Professor A. Weber.

the same point of departure. It was a knowledge of the truth, that all life was merely one link in a series of successive existences, and inseparably bound up with misery. Moreover as there were two causes of that misery—lust and ignorance—so there were two cures.

The first cure was *the suppression of lust and desire,* especially of all desire for continuity of existence.

The second cure was *the removal of ignorance.* Indeed Ignorance was, according to Gautama, the first factor in the misery of life, and stands first in his chain of causation (p. 102). Not, however, the Vedāntist's ignorance—not ignorance of the fact that man and the universe are identical with God, but ignorance of the four truths of Buddhism (p. 43):—ignorance that all life is misery, and that the misery of life is caused by indulging lusts, and will cease by suppressing them.

It would be easy to show how all Indian philosophy was a mere scheme for getting rid of the bugbear of metempsychosis, and how common was the doctrine that everything is for the worst in the worst of all possible worlds. This was taught by the Brāhmans five centuries B.C., and continued to be a thoroughly Hindū idea long after the disappearance of Buddhism. Witness the following from the Maitrāyaṇi Upanishad:—

In this weak body, ever liable
To wrath, ambition, avarice, illusion,
To fear, grief, envy, hatred, separation
From those we hold most dear, association
With those we hate; continually exposed
To hunger, thirst, disease, decrepitude,
Emaciation, growth, decline and death,
What relish can there be for true enjoyment?

Also the following, from Manu (VI. 77):—

This body, like a house composed of the (five) elements, with bones for its rafters, tendons for its connecting links, flesh and blood for its mortar, skin for its covering; this house filled with impurities, infested by sorrow and old age, the seat of disease, full of pain and passion, and not lasting—a man ought certainly to abandon.

Also Bhartṛi-hari (Vairāgya-śataka III. 32. 50):—

Enjoyments are alloyed by fear of sickness,
High rank may have a fall, abundant wealth
Is subject to exactions, dignity
Encounters risk of insult, strength is ever
In danger of enfeeblement by foes,
A handsome form is jeoparded by women,
Scripture is open to assaults of critics,
Merit incurs the spite of wicked men,
The body lives in constant dread of death—
One course alone is proof against alarm,
Renounce the world, and safety may be won.

One hundred years[1] is the appointed span
Of human life, one half of this goes by
In sleep and night; one half the other half
In childhood and old age; the rest is passed
In sickness, separation, pain, and service—
How can a human being find delight
In such a life, vain as a watery bubble?

No doubt this kind of pessimism has always found advocates in all ages, and among all nations in Europe as well as in Asia. It was a favourite idea with the Stoics, and it has found favour with Schopenhauer, Von Hartmann, and other modern philosophers; and Shakespeare makes Hamlet give expression to it.

---

[1] Centenarians (Śatāyus, Śata-varsha) seem to have been rather common in India in ancient times, if we may judge by the allusions to them in Manu and other works. See Manu III. 186; II. 135, 137.

Happily the general tone of European philosophical thought is in another key, and the admirers of Aristotle still constitute a majority in Europe. The great Stagirite described God as 'Energy,' and in dealing with Solon's dictum that 'no man can be called happy while he lives,' gave expression to a different belief. A good man's virtuous energies, he asserted, are in this present life a genuine source of happiness to him; misfortunes cannot shake his well-balanced character; he surmounts the worst sufferings by generous magnanimity[1].

Even in the East a greater than Aristotle and no less an Authority than the true 'Light of the world'—bade men rejoice and leap for joy under the most trying circumstances of life, and prize His gift of Eternal Life as their highest good.

In India, on the contrary, the Upanishads and systems of philosophy which followed on them, all harped on the same string. They all dwelt on the same minor keynote. Their real object was not to investigate truth, but to devise a scheme for removing the misery believed to result from repeated bodily existence and from all action, good or bad, in the present, previous, and future births.

The Sāṅkhya (I. 1) defines the chief aim of man to be deliverance from the pain incident to bodily life and energy; or according to the Nyāya (I. 2), from the pain resulting from birth, actions, and false knowledge;

[1] I here merely give the substance of what may be found fully stated in Aristotle's Ethics, I. 1 and IV. 3.

while the Vedānta considers that ignorance alone fetters the soul of man to a body, and the Yoga defines the divine Purusha (= the perfect man of Buddhism) as a being unaffected by pain (kleśa), acts, consequences of acts, and impressions derived from acts done in previous births (āśaya = saṉskāra).

Gautama's sympathy with these ideas is shown by the twelve-linked chain of causation, put forth by him as an accompaniment to his four fundamental truths (p. 43), and thus expressed (Mahā-vagga I. 1. 2):—

From Ignorance comes the combination of formations or tendencies (instincts derived from former births[1]); from such formations comes consciousness (vijñāna); from consciousness, individual being (nāma-rūpa, name and form); from individual being, the six organs of sense (including mind); from the six organs, contact (with objects of sense); from contact, sensation (vedanā); from sensation, desire (lust, thirst, taṉhā = tṛishṇā); from desire, clinging to life (upādāna); from clinging to life, continuity of becoming (bhava); from continuity of becoming, birth; from birth, decay and death; from decay and death, suffering.

It is difficult to discover a strictly logical sequence in this curious twelve-linked chain. The first link is a

---

[1] That is, Saṃkhārā = Sanskṛit Saṉskārāḥ pl. (see p. 109), 'qualities forming character.' In the Vaiśeshika system Saṉskāra is one of the twenty-four qualities, the self-reproductive quality. In the Yoga system Saṉskāra = Āśaya, 'impressions derived from actions done in previous births.' According to Childers, Saṃkāro is practically = Karma, 'act.' It may also stand for 'matter,' and for a quality, or mode of being; e.g. not only for a plant but for its greenness.

cause, the ten following are both causes and effects, while the last is an effect only. The second (saṃkhārā) is presented to us afterwards as one of the Skandhas (p. 109), and we have the whole inverted in a kind of circular chain in the form of question and answer, thus:—

What is the cause of misery and suffering? *Answer*—Old age and death. What is the cause of old age and death? *Answer*—Birth. Of birth? *Answer*—Continuity of becoming. Of continuity of becoming? *Answer*—Clinging to life. Of clinging to life? *Answer*—Desire. Of desire? *Answer*—Sensation or perception. Of sensation? *Answer*—Contact with the objects of sense. Of contact with objects? *Answer*—The organs of sense. Of the organs? *Answer*—Name and form, or individual being. Of individual being? *Answer*—Consciousness (viññāṇa = vijñāna). Of consciousness? *Answer*—Combination of formations or tendencies (or those material and mental predispositions derived from previous births which tend to form character; compare p. 109). Of such formations? *Answer*—Ignorance.

In making Ignorance (Avidyā) the first cause of the misery of life, Gautama agreed with the Vedānta (though he explained Ignorance differently, see p. 99), while in the remaining chain of causes (Nidāna) we detect his sympathy with the Sāṅkhya theory of a chain of producers and products.

His own scheme of causation (often called Paṭiććasamuppādo) occupies an important place in Buddhistic philosophy, as supplementary to, and complementary of, the four truths (p. 43). It was thought out before them (see p. 39) and is equally revered.

It is on this account that the following celebrated formula is constantly repeated like a short creed, and is found carved on numerous Buddhist monuments:—

'Conditions (or laws) of existence which proceed from a cause, the cause of these hath the Buddha explained, as also the cessation (or destruction) of these. Of such truths is the Great Śramaṇa the teacher[1].'

This was the formula repeated by Assaji to Sāriputta and Moggallāna (p. 47), when they wished to join the Buddha and asked for a summary of the spirit (artha), not the letter (vyañjana), of his doctrine (Mahā-v° I. 23. 5). Certainly the sorites-like form of statement in the scheme of causation had charms for Oriental thinkers.

Moreover the Buddha's method of clothing old truths in a new dress, or—to adopt another metaphor—his plan of putting new wine into old bottles, had in it something very attractive to all Indian minds.

Of what kind, then, was the new dress in which Gautama clothed the great central doctrine of Indian philosophy—the doctrine of metempsychosis, involving the perpetuation of the misery of life?

The Buddha, like all Indians, was by nature a meta-

---

[1] The Pāli in Mahā-v° I. 23. 5, is:—Ye dhammā hetuppabhavā tesaṃ hetuṃ Tathāgato āha tesaṃ ća yo nirodho evaṃvādī Mahāsamaṇo. The form Tathāgato is also common in Sanskrit versions. The metrical form of the sentence has become broken.

Professor Cowell informs me that the Sanskrit given in an old MS. at Cambridge is:—'Ye dharmā hetu-prabhavā hetuṃ teshāṃ Tathāgataḥ | Hy avadat teshāṃ ća yo nirodha evaṃ-vādī Mahā-Śramaṇaḥ.' Burnouf gives a slightly different version, thus:—Ye dharmā hetu-prabhavās teshāṃ hetuṃ Tathāgata uvāća teshāṃ ća etc. Sometimes both *avadat* and *uvāća* are omitted.

physician. He had at one time great sympathy with the philosophy of the Upanishads. How was it that he professed to know nothing of Spirit as distinct from bodily organism? A little consideration will make clear how he was brought to his own agnostic view.

Probably before his so-called enlightenment and attainment of true knowledge, he was as firm a believer in the real existence of one Universal Spirit as the most orthodox Brāhman. He had become imbued with Brāhmanical philosophy while sitting at the feet of his two teachers Āḷāra and Uddaka (p. 29). At that time there were no definite or formulated philosophical systems, separated from each other by sharp lines. But the Sāṅkhya, Yoga, and Vedānta systems were assuming shape, and the doctrines they embodied had been foreshadowed in the Upanishads, and were orally current.

In short, it had been repeatedly stated in the Upanishads, that nothing really existed but the one universally present impersonal Spirit, and that the whole visible world was really to be identified with that Spirit.

Then it followed as an article of faith that man's spirit, deluded into a temporary false idea of separate independent personal existence by the illusion of ignorance, was also identical with that One Spirit, and ultimately to be re-absorbed into it.

Further, it followed that man's spirit, while so deluded and so separated for a time from the One Spirit, was compelled to migrate through innumerable bodily forms, and that such migration entailed misery, from which there was no escape except by a process of disillusionment, that is, by dissipating the illusion of separate individuality, through the acquisition of perfect knowledge leading to re-union with the One Spirit, as the river blends with the ocean. And such knowledge was best gained by suppression of the passions, abandonment of all worldly connexions, and abstinence from all action. Finally, it was held, with apparent inconsistency, that the storing up of merit by good works assisted in effecting this object by raising a being not yet fit for union with the supreme Spirit, to forms of existence in which such union might be accomplished.

Now it is obvious that to believe in the ultimate merging of man's personal spirit in One impersonal Spirit, is virtually to deny the ultimate existence of any human spirit at all. Nay more—it is virtually to deny the existence of a supreme universal Spirit also.

For how can a merely abstract universal Spirit, which is unconscious of personality, be regarded as possessing any real existence worth being called true life?

To assert that such a Spirit is pure abstract Entity or (according to Vedānta phraseology) pure Existence (without anything to exist for), pure Thought or even pure Consciousness (without anything to think about, or be conscious about), pure Joy (without anything to rejoice about), is practically to reduce it to pure non-entity.

All that Gautama did, therefore, was to purge Brāhmanism of a metaphysical dogma which appeared to him to be a mere sham (Brahma-jāla I. 26).

He simply eliminated as incapable of proof the doctrine of a purely abstract, incorporeal spirit or self, whether human or divine. The assertion that any soul or self or Ego really existed (Atta-vādo) apart from the body was an error. It formed one of the constituents of Upādāna (p. 109), and was the first of the ten fetters (Sakkāya-diṭṭhi, p. 127).

And with the rejection of this dogma, as incapable of demonstration, he found himself compelled to reject also, as beyond the range of man's cognizance, the doctrine of any Supreme Being higher than the perfectly enlightened man. Like Kapila in the Sāṅkhya aphorisms (I. 92, V. 10) he felt bound to admit: 'It is not proved that there is a God.'

This, indeed, is the chief foundation on which rests the assertion that Buddhism is a mere system of atheistic negations. And there can be no doubt that from one point of view its statements are steeped in negations, or rather perhaps in evasions. Its morality has been described as more negative than positive; but this is scarcely correct, and it would be fairer to say that it delights in telling men to abstain from doing evil, rather than in urging them to active exertions for the good of others. It has many positive precepts.

But if there was no probability of a soul existing separately from a body after death, how could there be any soul-transmigration? How could there be any agreement between the teaching of the Buddha and that of the Brāhmans, in regard to this important central dogma? The real fact was that the divergence of the Buddhist doctrine from the Brāhmanical, as stated in the Upanishads, was not greater than was to be expected from the difference of belief between the two systems in regard to the existence of soul.

Plato, we know, held that souls 'found their prisons in the same natures' at death, so that an effeminate man might be re-born as a woman, a tyrannical man as a wolf, and so on. In Manu's Law-book is set forth a triple order of soul-transmigration through lower, middle, and higher planes of existence, resulting from good, middling, and bad acts, words, and thoughts. Thus—to instance only the lower—the soul of a man who spoke ill of his teacher was destined to pass into an ass or a dog (II. 201), the soul of a thief might occupy a mouse (XII. 62), the soul of one who neglected his caste-duties might pass into a demon (XII. 71, 72); and greater crimes might lead to the soul's being condemned to occupy plants, stones, and minerals. Then there was also an intermediate condition of the soul. According to one idea it went to the moon; according to another it became a hungry ghost which required food to be offered to it at the Śrāddha ceremonies.

This theory of transmigration, according to the Hindūs, explained the origin of evil. Evil must proceed from antecedent evil, and the resulting penalty must be borne by the evil-doer in succeeding existences. This was the terrible incubus which it was the great object of Indian philosophers to remove. It was equally Gautama's object, but how could he accept soul-transmigration, denying as he did the existence of any soul, as distinct from material organization? Hence he (or his disciples) put forth the following doctrine:—Every being is composed of five constituent elements called Skandhas (Pāli Khandha), which have their source in Upādāna (p. 103) and are continually combining, dissolving, and recombining, viz. 1. Form (*rūpa*), i.e. the organized body. 2. Sensation (*vedanā*) of pain or pleasure, or of neither, arising from contact of eye, ear, nose, tongue, skin, and mind with external objects. 3. Perception (*sañña = sañjñā*) of ideas through the same sixfold contact. 4. Aggregate of formations (*saṃkhāra = saṉskāra*, i.e. combination of properties or faculties or mental tendencies, fifty-two in number, forming individual character and derived from previous existences; compare the similar saṃkhārā pl. at p. 102). 5. Consciousness (*viññāṇa = vijñāna*) or thought-faculty[1]. This fifth is the most important. It is the only soul recognized by Buddhists. Theoretically it perishes with the other Skandhas, but practically is continued, since its counterpart is reproduced in a new body.

For although, when a man dies, all the five constituents of existence are dissolved, yet by the force resulting from his actions (*karma*), combined with *Upādāna*, 'clinging to existence' (one form of the fetters at p. 127), a new set of five, of which consciousness is still the dominant faculty, starts into being. The process of the new creation is so instantaneous that it is equivalent to the continuance of the same personality, pervaded by the same consciousness; though each personality is only really connected with the previous by the force of acts done and character

[1] Sometimes a human being is said to be made up of the five elements—ether, air, fire, water, earth—with a sixth called Vijñāna.

formed in each—such force operating through Upādāna. In short, to speak of transmigration of souls in Buddhism gives a wrong idea. Metempsychosis with Buddhists resolves itself into continuous metamorphosis or Palingenesis. For no true Buddhist believes in the passing of a soul from one body to another, but rather in the passing on of what may be called act-force, or of the merit and demerit resulting from a man's acts, so as to cause a continuous succession of transformations—a succession which may be compared to the rolling on of a wheel through different scenes and over every variety of ground; or to the burning on, through day and night, of a flame which suddenly dies out and then rekindles itself, so that it is not the same flame, and yet is not different. It is this act-force (Karma), combined with Upādāna, 'clinging to existence' (=abhi-niveśa in the Yoga II. 9), which is the connecting link between each man's past, present, and future bodies.

In its subtle and irresistible operation it may be compared to stored-up chemical or electric energy. It is a force which continually creates and re-creates the whole man, and perpetuates his personal identity through separate forms, whether it compels him to ascend or descend in the scale of being.

Yet to say that personality is transmitted, when there is no consciousness of any continuity of identity, amounts, after all, to denial of continuous existence.

Be it observed, too, that the scale of existence is limited in Buddhism to six classes of beings—gods, men, demons, animals, ghosts, and dwellers in hell (p. 121). Transmigration is not extended, as in the

Brāhmanical system, to plants, stocks, and stones; though a man could be born as a tree-god (p. 112).

Gautama Buddha himself was merely the last link in a long chain of corporeal forms, and he had been preceded by twenty-four Buddhas, who were to previous ages of the world what he was to the present. Every one of these Buddhas was gifted with the faculty of recollecting his previous personalities, and Gautama often gave an account of his own former existences. The stories of about five hundred and fifty of his births (Jātakas) are even now daily repeated to eager listeners in every Buddhist country, and are believed to convey important lessons, though sometimes full of puerilities.

The interchange of ideas between Brāhmanism and Buddhism is well exemplified not only by the twenty-five Buddhas, who correspond to the fourteen Manus, or representative men, in each world-period (Antara), but also by the birth-stories, many of which are mere modifications of old fables long current in India, while others have been imported from Buddhism into Sanskṛit literature. They constantly remind one of similar stories in the Pañća-tantra, Hitopadeśa, Rāmāyaṇa, and Mahā-bhārata. The noteworthy point about the repeated births of Gautama Buddha is, that there appears to have been no Darwinian rise from lower to higher forms; but a mere jumble of metamorphoses. Thus we find him born four times as Mahā-brahmā, twenty times as Indra, once as a hare, eighty-three times as an ascetic, fifty-eight as a king, twenty-four as a Brāhman, once as a gamester, eighteen times as a monkey, six as an elephant, eleven as a deer, once as a dog, four times as a serpent, six as a snipe, once as a frog, twice as a fish, forty-three times as a tree-god, twice as a pig, ten times as a lion, four as a cock, twice as a thief, once as a devil-dancer, and so on. He was never born as a woman, nor as an insect, nor as a Preta (p. 219), nor an inhabitant of hell (p. 119), and in all his births he was a Bodhi-sattva (pp. 98, 135). And in all he suffered and sacrificed himself for the good of the world.

Here is the substance of an account of Gautama's birth as a hare, given by himself (Ćariyā-Piṭaka I. 10, translated by Dr. Oldenberg):—

'In one of my lives I was a hare living in a forest. I ate grass and did no one any harm. An ape, a jackal, and an otter dwelt with me. I used to teach them their duties and tell them to abstain from evil and give alms on the four fast-days in every month. They did as I told them, and gave beans, corn, and rice. Then I said to myself:—Suppose a worthy object of charity passes by, what can I give him? I live on grass only; I cannot offer a starving man grass; I must give him myself. Thereupon the god Śakra, wishing to test my sincerity, came in a Brāhman's form and asked me for food. When I saw him I said joyfully:—"A noble gift will I give thee, O Brāhman; thou observest the precepts; thou painest no creature; thou wilt not kill me for food. But go, collect wood, place it in a heap, and kindle a fire. Then I will roast myself, and thou may'st eat me."

'He said:—"So be it," and went and gathered wood and kindled a fire.

'When the wood began to send forth flame, I leaped into the midst of the blazing fire.

'As water quenches heat, so the flame quelled all the sufferings of life. Cuticle and skin, flesh and sinews, bones, ligaments, and heart—my whole body with all its limbs—I gave to the Brāhman.'

Perhaps the best and most often recited Jātaka is the last birth but one, in which he was born as prince Vessantara (Vaiśyāntara). This is called the Mahājātaka, 'great birth.' It may be summarized thus:—

'Vessantara (afterwards Buddha) was so liberal that he gave to every one who asked. Among his possessions was a white elephant, which had the power of bringing down rain whenever it was needed. At last he gave away this also to a neighbouring country suffering from drought. This so incensed his own people that they persuaded the king his father to banish him with his wife and two children to the forest. They set out in a chariot drawn by horses. First he gave away the horses and next the chariot to Brāhmans who begged for them. Then when another Brāhman asked for the children, Vessantara gave them up too, saying: "May I for this act become a Buddha!" In short his sufferings and theirs in banishment, and his generosity to every one, led to his recall with great rejoicings. When he died he was born again in the Tushita heaven, whence he descended as a white elephant into the womb of Māyā, and was born as Gautama' (p. 23).

Another wise man of the East, who lived long before Gautama, spoke of 'the path of the just shining more and more unto the perfect day.' Of this kind of progressive advance towards higher planes of perfection, the Indian sage knew nothing. Nor to the Buddha, of course, would the Christian idea of 'original sin,' or of imputed Perfection have conveyed any meaning whatever. With Gautama, righteousness and unrighteousness, holiness and sin, were the product of a man's own acts. They were produced by no one but himself, and they were merely troublesome forces (p. 124) causing, in the one case, a man's re-birth either in one of the heavens (p. 210) or in higher earthly corporeal forms, and, in the other, his re-birth in one of the hells or in lower corporeal forms. 'Not in the heavens,' says the Dhamma-pada (127), 'not in the midst of the sea, not if thou hidest thyself in the clefts of the mountains, wilt thou find a place where thou canst escape the force resulting from thy evil actions.'

Here also is the substance of a passage in the Deva-dūta-sutta (translated by Dr. Oldenberg):—

'Do not relatives and friends welcome a man who has been long travelling, when he returns safely to his home? Even so, a righteous man, when he passes from this world to another, is welcomed by his good works, as by friends.

'Through the six states of transmigration does the power of our actions lead us. A life in the heavens awaits the good. The wardens of hell drag the wicked before the king of hell, Yama, who says to them:— "Did you not, when on earth, see the five divine messengers sent to warn you—the child, the old man, the sick, the criminal suffering punishment, and the dead corpse?"

'And the wicked man answers:—"I did see them."

'And didst thou not think within thyself:—"I also am subject to birth, old age, death. Let me be careful to do good works?"

'And the wicked man answers:—"I did not, sire; I neglected in my folly to think of these things."

'Then king Yama pronounces his doom:—"These thy evil deeds are not the work of thy mother, father, relations, friends, advisers. Thou alone hast done them all; thou alone must gather the fruit." And the warders of hell drag him to the place of torment, rivet him to red-hot iron, plunge him in glowing seas of blood, torture him on burning coals; and he dies not, till the last residue of his guilt has been expiated.'

'Heredity' in our sense has no place in Buddhism.

And this Buddhist theory of every man's destiny being dependent on his own acts is quite in keeping with Brāhmanical ideas. 'In that (new body) he is united with the knowledge gained in the former body, and then again goes on working for perfection; for even against his will he is forced on (from one body to another) by his former works' (Bhagavad-gītā VI. 43, 44). And again:—'The act committed in a former birth (pūrva-janma-kṛitaṃ karma), that is called one's destiny;' and again, 'As from a lump of clay a workman makes what he pleases, even so a man obtains whatever destiny he has wrought out for himself' (Hitopadeśa, Introduction). In Brāhmanism the influence of Karma or 'act' in determining every being's form at the time of his own re-birth is universal.

Thus also the Nyāya of Gautama (III. 132) affirms

that the new body (after death) is produced through the irresistible force of actions done in the previous body (pūrva-kṛita-phalānubandhāt tad-utpattiḥ). The cosmogony of the same philosophy (Vaiśeshika branch), taught that the concurrence of eternal atoms to form the world was the result of Adṛishṭa or the 'unseen force' derived from the acts of a previous world.

We are reminded, too, of our poet's own sentiment: 'Our deeds still travel with us from afar, And what we have been makes us what we are;' and of Don Quixote's saying, 'Every man is the son of his own works;' and of Wordsworth's, 'The child is father of the man;' and of Longfellow's, 'Lives of great men all remind us, we can make our lives sublime.'

In short, we are the outcome of ourselves. Nor can ceremonies avail aught, nor can devotion to personal gods avail aught, nor can anything whatever possess the slightest efficacy to save a man from his own acts.

It is said that Buddhism leaves the will unfettered; but surely fatalism is taught when the force of one's own deeds in previous births is held to be irresistible.

The only creator, then, recognized by true Buddhists is Act-force. 'My action is the womb that bears me,' says the Aṅguttara Nikāya. It is this Act-force that creates worlds. It is this Act-force, in conjunction with Upādāna (p. 109), that creates all beings in any of the six classes into which they are divided—gods, men, demons, animals, ghosts, and the dwellers in hell. We often talk of the force of a dead man's acts—of his being dead and yet speaking. It is this force which in Buddhism resists death; for no force can ever be lost.

And what does the modern Positivist philosopher assert? He maintains that both body and mind are resolved into their elements at death. The only immortal part of us consists in the good deeds, words, thoughts, and influences we leave behind us, to be made use of by our descendants and improved on for the elevation of humanity. And the aggregate of these, combined with the force of will, constitute, according to the Buddhist, a power strong enough to re-create not only human beings but the whole material world.

It was thus that the force of Gautama's own acts had constantly re-created him through a long chain of successive personalities, terminating in the perfect Buddha, who has no further births to undergo.

Turn we now to that division of the Buddhist system which concerns itself with the external universe, and seeks to explain its constitution, form, and the various divisions of which it consists.

And here we must be careful to note the peculiar views of Buddhism, notwithstanding the large admixture of Brāhmanical ideas.

For Buddhism has no cosmogony like the Sāṅkhya, Vedānta, and Vaiśeshika. Nor does it explain the creation of the universe, in our sense. It only concerns itself with cosmology, and it dissents from Brāhmanical cosmology in declining to admit the eternity of anything whatever, except change or revolution or a succession of revolutions. Buddhism has no Creator, no creation, no original germ of all things, no soul of the world, no personal, no impersonal, no supramundane, no antemundane principle.

It might indeed have been supposed that since Gautama denied the eternal existence of either a personal God or of Spirit, he would at least have given eternal existence to matter.

But no; the only eternal things are the Causality of Act-force and the succession of cause and effect—the eternity of 'Becoming,' not of 'Being.'

The Universe around us, with all its visible phenomena, must be recognized as an existing entity, for we see before our eyes evidence of its actual existence. But it is an entity produced out of nonentity, and destined to lapse again into nonentity when its time is fulfilled.

For out of nothingness it came, and into nothingness must it return—to re-appear again, it is true, but as a new Universe brought into being by the accumulated force of its predecessor's acts, and not evolved out of any eternally existing spiritual or material germ of any kind.

It is thus that Universe after Universe is like a succession of countless bubbles for ever forming, expanding, drifting onwards, bursting and re-forming, each bubble owing its re-formation to the force generated by its vanished predecessor. The poet Shelley might have been called a Buddhist when he wrote:

> Worlds on worlds are rolling ever
> From creation to decay;
> Like the bubbles on a river,
> Sparkling, bursting, borne away. (HELLAS.)

Or like lotuses, for ever unfolding and then decaying, each decay containing the germ of a new plant;

or like an interminable succession of wheels for ever coming into view, for ever rolling onwards, disappearing and reappearing; for ever passing from being to non-being, and again from non-being to being. It was this ceaseless rotation that led to the wheel being adopted as the favourite symbol in Buddhism (p. 122).

Christianity recognizes in a very different way this 'law of circularity' in the physical world, as the Rev. Hugh Macmillan has ably pointed out.

As to the question from whom? or whence? or how? came the original force or impetus that started the first movement, the Buddha hazarded no opinion. He held this to be an inexplicable mystery—an insoluble riddle. He confessed himself to be a thorough Agnostic. He saw nothing but countless cycles of causes and effects, and never undertook to explain the first cause which set the first wheel in motion. It was not, then, without a deep significance that Gautama placed Ignorance first in his chain of Causation (p. 102. Note, however, the explanation given at p. 99).

After all, these Buddhistic speculations amount to little else than Brāhmanism stripped of some of its transcendental mysticism. We know, for example, that the true Vedānta philosophy makes the Universe proceed out of an eternal Illusion, or Ignorance associated with the impersonal Spirit Brahmă, into which it is again absorbed.

Can it be affirmed, then, a Buddhist might say, that either this pure impersonal Spirit or Ignorance is virtually very different from pure nothingness?

What says the author of Ṛig-veda X. 120?—

In the beginning there was neither naught nor aught,
Then there was neither sky nor atmosphere above.
Then first came darkness hid in darkness, gloom in gloom;
Next all was water, all a chaos indiscreet,
In which the One lay void, shrouded in nothingness.

Then as to the vast periods called Kalpas or ages, during which (as in Brāhmanism) constant Universes are supposed to appear, disappear, and re-appear:—

Let it be supposed, say Buddhist writers, that a solid rock forming a vast cube sixteen miles high, and the same in length and breadth, were lightly rubbed once in a hundred years with a piece of the finest cloth, and by this slight friction reduced in countless ages to the size of a mango-seed; that would still give you no idea of the immense duration of a Buddhist Kalpa.

And what, in conclusion, is the existing Universe? Buddhist writers make it consist of an infinite number of Ćakkavālas (Ćakra-vālas) or vast circular planes, which for convenience may be called spheres. Each sphere has thirty-one Satta-lokas (Sattva-lokas) or dwelling-places of six classes of living beings, rising one above the other and distributed under three world-systems, built up in successive tiers through infinite space, below, upon, and above Mount Meru (or Sumeru)—the ideal central point of the whole. This gigantic mythical mountain forms the mighty base or pivot of the sphere.

First comes Hell with 136 divisions, to receive 136 varieties of offenders, all in tiers one above the other, and lying deep under the earth in the lower regions of the

Ćakra-vāla. To be re-born in Hell (Naraka) is the worst of all the six kinds of existence, reserved for the worst evil-doers, and although the punishment is not eternal, its shortest duration is for five hundred years of Hell, each day equalling fifty years of Earth. In Brāhmanism there are twenty-one hells (Manu IV. 88–90). Buddhism originally had only eight. The most terrific (Avīći) is for revilers of Buddha and his Law.

Above the subdivisions of Hell come the other sensuous worlds (Kāma-lokas), thus:—(2) the world of animals; (3) that of Pretas or ghosts; (4) that of Asuras or demons; (5) the earth, or world of men, with concentric circles of seven seas.

Having distributed all possible places of habitation for migrating beings under the three heads of Hell, four lower worlds, and twenty-six heavens (described at p. 206), Buddhism holds that there are only six forms or ways (gati) of existence through which living beings can pass, and under which every thing that has life must be classed, and of these the first two ways are good, the last four bad, thus:—1. Gods; 2. Men; 3. Asuras, or demons, inhabiting spaces under the earth; 4. Animals; 5. Pretas, or ghosts, recently inhabitants of earth, and ever consumed with hunger (see p. 219); 6. Beings undergoing torment in the hells.

As to the gods, bear in mind that Buddhism recognized most of the deities of Hindūism. See p. 206.

Such gods existed in subtle corporeal forms, and, though not omnipotent, were capable of working benefit or harm. They were subject to the universal law of dissolution, and after death were succeeded by others, so that there was not one Brahmā or one Śakra, but many successive deities so named, and many classes of deities under them. They had no power of effecting any person's salvation. On the contrary, they had to see to their own, and were inferior to the perfected man.

Moreover, to be born in the world of the gods seems not to have implied any vast accumulation of merit, for we read of a certain frog that from simply listening to the Buddha's voice, while reciting the Law, was born as a god in the Trayastrinśa heaven (Hardy, p. 392).

In short, the constant revolving of the wheel of life in one eternal circle, according to fixed and immutable laws, is perhaps after all the sum and substance of the philosophy of Buddhism (see vignette on title-page). And this eternal wheel may be regarded as having six spokes representing six forms of existence.

When any one of the six classes of beings dies, he must be born again in some one of these same six classes, for there are no other possible ways (gati) of life, and he cannot pass into plants, stones, and inorganic matter, as in the Brāhmanical system (see p. 108). If he be born again in one of the hells he is not thereby debarred from seeking salvation, and even if he be born in heaven as a god, he must at some time or other leave it and seek after a higher state still—that of the perfect man who has gained Nirvāṇa and is soon to achieve the one consummation worth living for, the one crown worth striving for—extinction of personal existence in Pari-nirvāṇa (see pp. 138–142).

LECTURE VI.

The Morality of Buddhism and its chief aim—Arhatship or Nirvāṇa.

THE first questions suggested by the subject of this lecture will probably be:—

How could a life of morality be inculcated by one who made all life proceed from ignorance, and even virtuous conduct in one sense a mistake, as leading to continuity of life, and therefore of suffering? How could the Buddha's first commandment be, 'Destroy not,' when his ideal of perfection was destruction? How could he say, 'be active,' when his theory of Karma (pp. 110, 114) made action conduce to misery?

The inconsistency is evident, but it is no less true that, notwithstanding the doctrine that all existence entails misery, and that all action, good or bad, leads to future births, Gautama taught that the life of a man in higher bodily forms, or in one of the heavens, was better than a life in lower forms, or in one of the hells, and that neither a higher form of life nor the great aim of Nirvāṇa could be attained without righteous action, meditation, and true knowledge.

Buddhism, indeed, as we have seen, could not hold forth as an incentive to good behaviour any belief in a Creator rewarding and punishing his creatures according to their works, or pardoning their sins. It could not inculcate piety; for in true Buddhism piety was impossible; yet like Manu (II. 6) it made morality (śīla) the basis of Law (Dharma); it stimulated good conduct by its doctrine of repeated births, and by pictures of its numerous heavens, and it deterred men from unrighteous acts by its terrible places of torment.

Let it then be made clear from the first that Buddhism, in inculcating morality, used no word expressive of morality, as founded on the love and fear of God, or of sin as an offence against God.

In Buddhism the words kleśa (kileso), 'pain,' and akuśala, 'demerit,' take the place of 'sin,' and its perfect saint is said to be 'free from pain' (nishkleśa) and from demerit, not from sin in our sense. By an unrighteous act it meant an act producing suffering and demerit of some kind (p. 113), and it bade every man act righteously in order to escape suffering and to accumulate merit (kuśala), and thus work out his own perfection—that is to say, his own self-extinction.

Doubtless Buddhism deserves credit for laying stress on right belief, right words, right work, instead of on ceremonial rites; and on the worship of Hindū gods; but it had its own idea of right. It urged householders to abandon the world, or else to be diligent in serving its monks for the working out of their own salvation; and while making morality, meditation, and enlightenment its indispensable factors in securing perfection, it made perfection consist in freedom from the delusion of 'I am;' and in deliverance from an individual existence inseparably bound up with misery.

Mark, too, another contradiction. It inculcated entire

self-dependence in working out this kind of perfection, and yet it set before its disciples three guides; namely, the Buddha's own example, the Law (Dharma), and the example of the whole body of monks and perfected saints (Saṅgha).

We now turn to its fuller moral system, keeping this distinct from its philosophy and metaphysics, and freely admitting that there are in Buddhist morality many things, true, honourable, just, pure, lovely, and of good report.

It is fair to point out at the outset that Buddhist morality was not a purely external matter. It divided men into the outwardly correct and internally sincere. The mere outwardly correct Buddhists might include monks as well as laymen, though a higher standard of profession was expected of monks. The internally sincere were the really earnest seekers after perfection (monks and laymen), and were divided into four classes, representing four conditions of the inner life, lower, higher, still higher, and highest, culminating in perfect Saintship, Arhatship, and Nirvāṇa (p. 132).

At the same time there was not much hope of saintship except through celibacy and monkhood; for in true Buddhism the notion of holy family-life was almost a contradiction in terms.

Of course the Buddhist moral code soon passed beyond the eightfold path propounded by Gautama in his first sermon (see p. 44), and Dr. Oldenberg has shown that in the absence of a systematically arranged code, we may still trace out amid a confusion of precepts the three leading duties of external moral conduct (śīla), of internal mental concentration (samādhi), and of acquiring true wisdom (paññā = prajñā). Compare Dr. Wenzel's 'Friendly Epistle,' 53.

The five fundamental rules of moral conduct (pañća-sīla or pañća-śīla) were promulgated early :—

1. Kill not any living thing. 2. Steal not. 3. Commit not adultery. 4. Lie not. 5. Drink not strong drink. These five, having reference chiefly to one's neighbour, were called the fivefold law *for all classes*, including laymen. They were taken from Brāhmanism, but in the vows of the Sannyāsī the fifth was not included. It was Buddhism probably that first interdicted strong drink. It prohibited too what the Brāhmans allowed—killing for sacrificial purposes.

Five others of a more trivial character for monks (often given in a different order, p. 78) were added:—

6. Eat no food, except at stated times. 7. Use no wreaths, ornaments, or perfumes. 8. Use no high or broad bed, but only a mat on the ground. 9. Abstain from dancing, singing, music, and worldly spectacles. 10. Own no gold, or silver of any kind, and accept none (Mahā-vagga I. 56). [This Buddhist Dasa-sīla may be contrasted with the Mosaic Decalogue.]

All ten were binding on monks only, and for the third was then substituted 'be absolutely chaste.'

Sometimes not only the first five but the first eight were held to be binding on laymen.

Another was added in later times:—Never think or say that your own religion is the best. Never denounce the religion of others (see p. 90).

Then, although only the first half of the eightfold

path (p. 44) was said to be necessary for lay-brethren, the whole was for monks, who also had to observe the special practices already described (p. 76).

All gambling and games of chance were prohibited (Tevijja-Sutta II). Compare Manu IX. 221–228.

Sometimes five renunciations are named:—of wife, of children, of money, of life, of craving for existence in future births.

Then sometimes three (sometimes four) corrupting influences (āsava = āsrava) are enumerated—of lust (kāma), of life, of ignorance, (of delusion.)

Most important to be got rid of are the ten fetters (saṃyojana, p. 45) binding a man to existence:—

1. Belief in the existence of a personal self or Ego (sakkāya-diṭṭhi); 2. Doubt (vićikitsā); 3. Ceremonial practices (sīlabbata = śīla-vrata); 4. Lust or sensuality (kāma); 5. Anger (paṭigha); 6. Craving for life in a material form (rūpa-rāga) either on earth or in heaven; 7. Longing for immaterial life (arūpa-rāga) in the higher heavens; 8. Pride (māna); 9. Self-exaltation (auddhatya); 10. Ignorance. Of these, 1, 3, and 4, with diṭṭhi, 'wrong belief,' are the four constituents of Upādāna, 'clinging to existence' (p. 109).

The seven jewels of the law (p. 49) are—1. the five (or four) meditations or reflections (bhāvanā); 2. the four right exertions; 3. the four steps to supernatural power; 4. the five moral forces; 5. the right use of the five senses; 6. the seven limbs of knowledge (see p. 50); 7. the eightfold path (see p. 44).

The five above-named reflections are—1. on the thirty-two impurities of the body; 2. on the duty of displaying love (Maitrī) towards all beings; 3. on compassion for all who suffer; 4. on rejoicing with all who rejoice; 5. on absolute indifference (upekshā) to joy or sorrow. These contemplations (bhāvanā) take the place of prayer. The first is also one of the four Satipaṭṭhānas (p. 49). They must not be confused with the four stages of meditation (Dhyāna, p. 209).

These (reckoning only four meditations) make up the 37 steps to Nirvāṇa, already given at pp. 49, 50.

There are also six (or ten) transcendent virtues, Pāramitās, 'leading to the further shore,' for Arhats; viz. 1. Giving (Dāna) to all who ask, even the sacrificing of limbs or life for others; this is most important; 2. Virtue or moral conduct (Śīla); 3. Patience or tolerance (Kshānti); 4. Fortitude or energy (Vīrya); 5. Suppression of desire (Nekkhamma = naishkāmya), or, according to some, profound contemplation; 6. Transcendental wisdom (Paññā = Prajñā). To which are added — 7. Truth (Satya); 8. Steadfast resolution (Adhishṭhāna); 9. Good-will or kindness (Maitra); 10. (Highest of all—) Absolute indifference or apathy (Upekshā), resulting in a kind of ecstatic quietude.

This kind of memorial tabulation in lists of 4, 5, 7, 8, 10, etc., is of course a product of later Buddhism.

I now give examples from the Dharma-pada:—

'By oneself is evil done; by oneself is one injured; by oneself is evil left undone; by oneself is one purified; no one purifies another.' (Compare Manu IV. 240.)

'Better than dominion over the earth, better than going to Heaven, or having sovereignty over the worlds, is the attainment of the first step in sanctification.'

'Not to commit evil, to accumulate merit by good deeds (kusalassa upasampadā), to purify the heart, this is the doctrine of the Enlightened' (165, 178, 183).

'As a frontier town is guarded[1] within and without, so guard thyself.' (Dh. 315.)

'He who holds back rising anger like a rolling chariot, him I call a real driver; any other merely holds the reins.' (Dh. 222. Compare Manu II. 88.)

'Let a man overcome anger by gentleness, let him overcome the evil by good; the parsimonious by liberality, the liar by truth.' (Dh. 223. Manu VI. 47, 48.)

'The fully enlightened finds no satisfaction even in heavenly pleasures; but only in suppression of desires.'

'One by one, little by little, moment by moment, a wise man frees himself from personal impurities as a refiner blows away the dross of silver.' (Dh. 187, 239.)

'There is a treasure laid up in the heart, a treasure of charity, purity, temperance, soberness. A treasure, secure, impregnable, that no thief can steal; a treasure that follows after death. (Compare Manu IV. 241.) Universal science, all the perfections, supernatural knowledge, supreme Buddhaship itself this treasure can procure.' (Childers' Nidhi-kāṇḍa.)

The following are some of the blessed states described in the Mahāmaṅgala-sutta. They prove that Gautama required married men to discharge their duties faithfully.

'The succouring of mother and father, the cherishing of child and wife, and the following of a peaceful calling, this is the greatest blessing' (maṅgalam uttamam).

[1] The body is often compared to a city with nine gates or apertures, which have to be guarded (viz. two eyes, ears, nostrils, etc.).

'The giving alms, a religious life, aid rendered to relations, blameless acts, this is the greatest blessing.'

'Reverence and humility, contentment and gratefulness, the hearing of the Law at the right time, this is the greatest blessing.'

'Patience and lowly speech, association with religious men, recitation of the Law at the right time, this is the greatest blessing.'

'Self-mortification and chastity, discernment of the noble truths, perception of Nirvāṇa, this is the greatest blessing.'

In the Aṅguttara (II. iv. 2) it is said that no adequate return can be made by children to parents 'even by menial service.' With Gautama, to honour father and mother was better than to worship the gods of heaven.

Many other examples might be given. Not only was a man forbidden to kill, he was never to injure.

Then in the Rājovāda Jātaka we have the story of the one king 'who overcomes the strong by strength, the soft by softness, the good by goodness, and the wicked by wickedness;' and of the other king 'who conquers anger by calmness, the wicked by goodness, the stingy by gifts, the liar (alika-vādinam) by truth.'

Other precepts require a man to exercise charity and respect towards all aged persons, teachers, servants, and animals. He was to set an example of self-sacrifice.

It is recorded of Gautama Buddha that on one occasion he plucked out his own eyes, and that on another he cut off his own head, and that on a third he cut his own body to pieces to redeem a dove from a hawk.

Yet we repeat that with all this apparently sublime

morality no true idea of sin, as displeasing to a Holy God, was connected with the infraction of the moral code. Nor did a Buddhist always avoid harming others from any true reverence for life. He was to cherish the life of others, but his chief motive was the fear that by not doing so he would entail the misery of continuous life on himself; and his chief motive for avoiding anger was that it was incompatible with that equanimity, which ought to characterize every wise man who aimed at the extinction of his own personality.

The ease with which charitable acts might be performed is amusingly illustrated by a story told in Huc's travels in Tibet. A certain zealous fellow-traveller (who considered that it was quite possible to be at the same time a good Buddhist and a good Christian) invited the French missionaries to co-operate with him in performing charitable acts to commemorate the termination of a fatiguing journey, especially by providing worn-out travellers, like themselves, with horses. The missionaries pleaded their own poverty, but to their surprise were told that they were only required to draw horses on paper, which were taken to the edge of a precipice, thrown up into the air, and, certain formularies being recited, were carried away by the wind and changed into real horses by the power of Buddha.

Let us by no means, however, shut our eyes to the praiseworthy feature of the Buddhist system mentioned at page 125—its recognition of the need of inner purity and sanctification—an inner Buddhism of the heart, without which even a monk was no true Buddhist. Of course the Law could be observed superficially without any real heart-belief or heart-purity.

When the inner heart-condition of a Buddhist is described, he is said to be walking on one of four paths (ćattāro Maggā), and is then called Ariyo (= Ārya), 'worthy of reverence' (distinguished from Pṛithag-jana, 'an ordinary professing Buddhist'). To avoid confounding these paths with the eightfold path (p. 44) it would be better to speak of them as four stages of inner sanctification. Dhyāna, 'meditation,' of four kinds, is the chief means of entering and passing through these stages (p. 32), which once entered can never be abandoned.

The first stage is that of the man—be he monk or layman—who is just converted, by an inner awakening, to true heart-Buddhism. This man has freed himself from the first three fetters—namely, delusion of self, doubts about the Buddha's doctrine, and dependence on external rites (p. 127). He is called Sotāpanno, 'one who has entered the stream' (Śrota-āpanna), *inevitably* carrying him onwards—though not necessarily in the same body—to the calm ocean of Nirvāṇa, and his state is called Sotāpatti. He can only be re-born as a god or man, but not in the four lower births (p. 121). Mark that the doctrine of 'perseverance' is a remarkable feature in this phase of the Buddhist system.

The second stage is that of the man who has nearly freed himself from the first five fetters, but has a sufficient number left to cause one more birth on the earth. He is called Sakad-āgāmī (Sakṛid-āg^c).

The third stage is that of the man who is quite free from the first five fetters. Such a man can only be re-born in a Brahmā heaven, from which he reaches Nirvāṇa. He is therefore called An-āgāmī, 'one who will not come back to earth.'

The fourth stage is that of the completely freed man who attains Arhatship (Arahattaṃ) in this life, and will at death experience no re-birth. There is, of course, a difference between one who has only just entered each stage of the journey and one who has reached the terminus. And this Arhatship is open to all (even to women), though only likely to be attained by true monks or true nuns. The name Arhat (Pāli Arahā, in Ceylon Rahat), 'most deserving' (root *arh*), is significant of the highest merit; for the Arhat is perfect, freed from all pain (nishkleśa), from all the ten fetters, from all attachment to existence (upādāna) whether on earth or in heaven, and from all re-creative Act-force. He has already entered Nirvāṇa, and while still living he is dead to the world. He is the Jīvan-mukta, 'emancipated living man,' of the Yoga. By the force of the fourth Dhyāna, he has gained the Abhijñās (Abhiññā), or 'transcendent faculties of knowledge,' the inner eye, inner ear, knowledge of all thoughts, and recollection of previous existences, and the extraordinary powers over matter called Iddhi (= Ṛiddhi). In short he is Asekha, 'one who has nothing to learn.'

Although, theoretically, a layman and even beings existing in other spheres, might enter the stream leading to Nirvāṇa or Arhatship (see pp. 90, 139) without becoming monks, yet it is evident that as a rule it was only likely to be entered by persons who renounced the world and led a celibate monastic life.

But of Arhats there are three grades:—

First, the simple Arhat (described above), who has attained perfection through his own efforts and the doctrine and example of a supreme Buddha, but is not himself such a Buddha, and cannot teach others how to attain Arhatship, though he associates with others.

Secondly, and second in rank, but far above the simple Arhat, the Pratyeka-Buddha or Solitary Saint, who has attained perfection for himself and by himself alone, and not as a member of any monastic Order, nor through the teaching of any supreme Buddha (except in some former birth). This solitary hermit-like Arhat—a kind of concentration of isolated or selfish sanctity—is symbolized by a rhinoceros. He does not appear on earth at the same time with a supreme Buddha, and has not the same epithets (p. 23) applied to him.

Thirdly, the supreme Buddha or Buddha *par excellence* (once a Bodhi-sattva), who, having by his own self-enlightening insight attained perfect knowledge (sambodhi), and having, by the practice of the transcendent virtues (p. 128) and through extinction of the passions and of all desire for life, become entitled to that complete extinction of bodily existence (pari-nirvāṇa), in which the perfection of all Arhatship must end, has yet delayed this consummation that he may become the Saviour of a suffering world—not in the same manner as the God-sent Saviour of Christianity, but by teaching men how to save themselves. This is the supreme Buddha, the founder of the whole monastic Order, immeasurably superior both to Pratyeka-Buddhas and to all mere Arhats.

He said of himself (Mahā-vagga I. 6, 8),—'I am the

all-subduer (sabbābhibhū); the all-wise; I have no stains; through myself I possess knowledge; I have no rival (paṭipuggalo); I am the chief Arhat—the highest teacher; I alone am the absolutely wise (Sambuddha); I am the Conqueror (Jina); all the fires of desire are quenched (sītibhūto) in me; I have Nirvāṇa (nibbuto).' See p. 42 of this volume.

This seems a marvellous assumption on the part of one who never claimed to be other than a man; yet he had taken the idea from Brāhmanism, which held that its saints could surpass all gods (Brahmā only excepted).

Such supreme Buddhas, who are perfect knowers, and also perfect teachers of the truth, are only manifested on the earth at long intervals of time.

Gautama is the fourth Buddha of the present age (Bhadra - Kalpa). He was a Kshatriya; his three mythical predecessors—Kraku-ććhanda, Kanaka-muni, and Kāśyapa—having been sons of Brāhmans. He is to be followed by the fifth Buddha, Maitreya (a name meaning 'full of love towards all beings'), but not until the doctrine of Gautama has passed out of men's memory after five thousand years (p. 181). In their previous existences Gautama and his predecessors were, (see pp. 98, 112,) Bodhi-sattvas[1], 'beings who have knowledge (derived from intellect) for their essence,' a name borne by all destined to become supreme Buddhas as well as by the first of Gautama's successors, Maitreya.

This coming Buddha is, as we shall see hereafter,

---

[1] In fact Gautama remained a Bodhi-sattva until he was thirty-four or thirty-five, when he attained perfect enlightenment and Buddhahood.

an object of universal reverence among later Buddhists of all sects as a kind of expected Messiah or Saviour. Often, indeed, he is more honoured than Gautama himself, because he is interested in the present order of things, as well as in the future, while Gautama Buddha and all his predecessors have passed away into non-being.

Twenty-four mythical Buddhas (the first being Dīpaṃkara, 'Light-causer') are held to have appeared [1] before Gautama in preceding cycles of time. Many particulars about them are given, including their birth-places, the length of their lives and their statures. Gautama himself is said to have met some of them during his transmigrations. Even the trees under which they achieved supreme wisdom are enumerated.

Sometimes the last six of the twenty-four are reckoned with Gautama Buddha as constituting seven principal Buddhas [2], who seem to have been grouped together to correspond with the Brāhmanical seven Manus of the present Kalpa. Usually, however, Gautama is held to be the last of twenty-five Buddhas.

Clearly, then, the principal lines of Buddhist moral teaching all converge to one focus—to the perfected

[1] Their names are Dīpaṃkara, Kauṇḍinya, Maṅgala, Sumanas, Raivata, Śobhita, Anavama-darśin, Padma, Nārada, Padmottara, Sumedhas, Sujāta, Priya-darśin, Artha-darśin, Dharma-darśin, Siddhārtha, Tishya, Pushya, Vipaśyin, Śikhin, Viśva-bhū, Krakućanda, Kanaka-muni (or Koṇāgamana), Kāśyapa.

[2] Beginning with Vipaśyin. These are the only Buddhas mentioned in the Dīgha-nikāya. If the coming Buddha Maitreya is reckoned, then Vipaśyin must be omitted.

Arhat or rather to a still brighter point of light in the perfect Buddha waiting for his reward—the nectar of the eternal state of complete Nirvāṇa.

And this compels us to attempt some explanation of Nirvāṇa. In the first place forty-six synonyms of it are given in the Abhidhānappadīpikā, e.g. Mokkha or Mutti, 'deliverance,' Nirodha, 'cessation,' Taṉhakkhaya (tṛishṇā-kshaya), 'destruction of lust,' Arūpa, Khema, Kevala, Apavagga, 'emancipation,' Nibbuti (= nirvṛiti), 'quietude,' Amata (Amṛita), 'deathless nectar.'

The following is from Rhys Davids' Jātaka (p. 4): 'One day the wise Sumedhā fell a-thinking, thus:—"Grievous is re-birth in a new existence, and the dissolution of the body in each successive place where we are re-born. I am subject to birth, to decay, to disease, to death. It is right, being such, that I should strive to attain the great deathless Nirvāṇa, which is tranquil, and free from birth, decay, sickness, grief and joy.

'"For as in this world there is pleasure—the opposite of pain—so where there is existence there must be its opposite, the cessation of existence; and as where there is heat there is also cold which neutralizes it, so there must be a Nirvāṇa that extinguishes (the fires of) lust and the other passions; and as in opposition to a bad and evil condition there is a good and blameless one, so where there is evil Birth there must also be Nirvāṇa, called the Birthless, because it puts an end to all re-birth.

'"Just as a man who has fallen into a heap of filth, if he beholds afar off a great pond covered with lotuses of five colours, ought to seek that pond, saying, 'By what way shall I arrive there?' but if he does not seek it, the fault is not that of the pond; even so where there is the lake of the great deathless Nirvāṇa."'

What, then, is the proper definition of Nirvāṇa (Pāli Nibbāna)? In venturing on an explanation of so controverted a term, I feel rather like a foolhardy person walking barefoot over thorny ground. Nevertheless I may fearlessly assert two things about it.

The first is, that the term Nirvāṇa was not originated by Gautama. It was an expression common to both Brāhmanism and Buddhism, and most of its synonyms such as moksha, apavarga, and nirvṛiti are still common to both. It was current in Gautama's time, and certainly occurs in the Mahā-bhārata, parts of which are of great antiquity.

In the later episode, too, of that poem called Bhagavad-gītā, V. 24, we find the following:—

'That Yogī who is internally happy, internally satisfied and internally illumined, attains extinction in the Supreme Being, and becomes that Being' (Yo 'ntaḥsukho 'ntarārāmas tathāntarjyotir eva yaḥ, | Sa Yogī Brahma-nirvāṇam[1] Brahma-bhūto 'dhigaćchati).

The second point is that it would be about as unreasonable to expect that Nirvāṇa should always be explained in one way as to restrict Brāhmanism and Buddhism—two most elastic, comprehensive, and Protean systems, which have constantly changed their front to suit changing circumstances and varying na-

[1] The expression Brahma-nirvāṇa is repeated several times afterwards. Mark, too, that one of the god Śiva's names in the Mahā-bhārata is Nirvāṇam.

tional peculiarities at different epochs and in different countries—to one hard and fast outline.

It is certainly singular that although the term Nibbāna (Sanskrit Nirvāṇa)—like some of the crucial theological terms of Christianity—has led to endless discussions, it does not occur often in the Pāli texts. The word Arahattaṃ (see p. 133) is more common.

Nirvāṇa, of course, originally means 'the state of a blown-out flame.' Hence its first meaning is properly restricted to the complete extinction of the three chief fires [1] of lust, ill-will, and delusion, and a total cessation of all evil passions and all desires [2], especially of the desire for individual existence (name and form).

Following on this is the state of release from all pain and from all ignorance, accompanied by a sense of profound rest—a state achieved by all Arhats while still living in the world [3], and notably by the Buddha at the moment when he attained Buddhahood, forty-five years before his final Pari-nirvāṇa. Nirvāṇa then is not necessarily the annihilation of all existence. It is the absence of kleśa (p. 124), as in the Yoga system, and corresponds very much to the Brāhmanical Apavarga, described in the Nyāya, and defined by a commentator, Vātsyāyana, to be Sarva-duḥkha-ćheda ('the cutting off of all pain'). In short, it is Arhatship.

---

[1] Rāga, dvesha, moha. Eleven fires are sometimes enumerated.

[2] Dr. Rhys Davids holds that the Buddha only advocated the suppression of good desires; Dr. Fausböll says 'desire in all its forms.' I agree with the latter.

[3] When I was on the confines of Tibet, this was described to me by a Tibetan scholar as the unchangeable state of conscious beatitude.

But besides Nirvāṇa we have the expression Parinirvāṇa. This is not merely the blowing out of the fires of the passions but also the entire cessation of rebirths, with extinction of all the elements or seeds of bodily existence. This took place when the Buddha died or 'passed away' after innumerable previous deaths. Practically, however, in Buddhism the death of every ordinary being amounts to this kind of Nirvāṇa; for, if there is no recollection of any former state of existence in the new being created by Karma, what is every death but utter personal extinction?

Now with regard to the Nirvāṇa of Arhatship, no one can have come in contact with the natives of India in their own country, without observing that for a genuine aristocratic Brāhman to allow others to see him give way to any passion, to exhibit any emotion or enthusiasm, is regarded as a proof of weakness.

We can easily understand, therefore, that when the Buddha exhorted his followers to strive after a wholly impassive condition, he addressed a sympathetic audience.

Long before his exhortations were heard in India, his fellow-countrymen held persons in the highest respect who claimed to have entirely suppressed their passions. The only peculiarity in Gautama's teaching was that he made this object incumbent on all true Buddhists alike, without exception. And this state of absolute imperturbability is well indicated to the eye by the usual attitude of the images which, after Gautama's death, were carved to represent him—an attitude of passionless composure, and dignified calm.

In the interesting Pāli work Milinda-praśna (Milinda-pañha), containing a conversation on the subject of Nirvāṇa between King Milinda (Menander) and the monk Nāgasena (supposed to have lived about 140 B.C.), the latter compares it to the pure water which quenches fire, and to the fathomless Ocean freed from trouble and impurities, which no river, however vast, can fill to overflowing; and to the Air, which cannot be seen or explained, though it enters our bodies and fills us with life; and to Space, which is eternal and infinite, and beyond the power of man to conceive.

I trust I shall not shock my Indian friends if I illustrate this condition by a comparison of my own drawn from the animal creation. In crossing the Indian Ocean, when unruffled by the slightest breeze, I have sometimes observed a jelly-fish floating on the surface of the transparent water, apparently lifeless. The creature is evidently neither asleep nor awake. It certainly is not thinking about anything, and its consciousness is doubtful. All that can be affirmed about it is that it seems to be drinking in the warm fluid in a state of lazy blissful repose.

No Buddhist, at least, could look at such a sight without being reminded of this idea of Nirvāṇa—the idea of, so to speak, floating in perfect repose and peace and cessation from all pain, and all work, and even all thought, on a kind of ocean of half conscious, half unconscious beatitude. It is not consciousness, neither is it unconsciousness. It is symbolized by a full-blown, perfectly formed lotus—a frequent emblem of perfection—reposing on a calm mirror-like lake.

With regard to Pari-nirvāṇa[1]—the complete termination of migrations and passing away of all the elements of bodily existence—if this is to be distinguished from the Brāhmanical idea of absorption into an impersonal spirit—whereby the Ego of personal identity is destroyed—it is a distinction without much difference.

Strictly, however, in Buddhism the dissolution of the body leaves no surviving personality or individuality, and consequently Pari-nirvāṇa is not properly described either as absorption into a void (śūnya) or as annihilation. It is simply the absolute termination of a series of conscious bodily organizations. The Buddha himself evaded dogmatic definitions, and would probably have said:—it is not life, neither is it non-life; it may be compared to infinite space (śūnya) which is not to be comprehended or explained.

We should also bear in mind that although Nirvāṇa and Pari-nirvāṇa constitute the ultimate goal to which the morality of a true Buddhist tends, they have little place either in the aims or thoughts of the ordinary adherents of Buddhism at the present day.

The apex of all the desires, the culminating point of the ambition of most of the religiously-minded Buddhists of modern times, points to a life in one of the heavens, while the great mass of the people aim only at escaping one of the hells, and elevating themselves to a higher condition of bodily existence in their next birth on this earth, and perhaps on that very part of this earth which is the scene of their present toils, joys, and sorrows.

---

[1] Or *Anupādi-sesha*, that is, Nirvāṇa without remains or remnants of the elements of existence. See Childers' Pāli Dictionary, s.v.

It only remains for me to caution those who may be impressed with the beauty of some of the precepts of the moral code and its theory of perfection, as ending in Pari-nirvāṇa, against deducing therefrom too optimistic an estimate of the Buddhist system. Buddhist morality is like a showy edifice built on the sand. It is a thoroughly fair-weather structure, incapable of standing against flood, storm, and tempest.

It may be summed up in a few words as a scheme for the establishing of a paradox—for the perfecting of one's self by accumulating merit with the ultimate view of annihilating all consciousness of self—a system which teaches the greatest respect for the life of others, with the ultimate view of extinguishing one's own.

It must, in short, be clearly understood that if any comparison be instituted between Buddhism and Christianity in regard to the self-abnegation, or self-sacrifice which each claims to inculcate, the self to be got rid of in Buddhism is not the selfishness condemned by Christianity, but rather the self of individuality—the self of individual life, and personal identity.

To be righteous in a Christian sense a man must be God-like, and to be righteous in a Buddhistic sense a man must be Buddha-like; but the righteousness of the Buddhist is not the perfection of holiness by the extinction of sin committed against God, but the perfection of merit-making, with the view of earning happiness for himself in a higher state hereafter.

For every Buddhist is like a trader who keeps a ledger, with a regular debtor and creditor account, and a daily entry of profit and loss.

He must not take, make, or hoard money. He is forbidden to store up a money-balance in a worldly bank, but he is urged to be constantly accumulating a merit-balance in the bank of Karma.

In conclusion, let the Buddha enforce his own moral teaching in his own way, by allegory and illustration drawn from real life:—When asked by a Brāhman 'why he did not plough and sow and earn his own bread?' he replied to the following effect: 'I do plough and sow and eat immortal fruit (Amata = Amṛita); my plough is wisdom (paññā); my shaft is modesty; my draught-ox, exertion; my goad, earnest meditation (sati); my mind, the rein. Faith (saddhā) in the doctrine is the seed I sow; cleaving to life is the weed I root up; truth is the destroyer of the weed; Nirvāṇa and deliverance from misery are my harvest.' (Kasi-bhāradvāja-sutta of the Sutta-nipāta.)

This may be compared with St. Luke viii. 11–15; but have we not here a contrast rather than a comparison?

Perhaps some may think that the contrast is not unfavourable to Buddhism. Nay, possibly some may complain that I have not enlarged sufficiently on the remarkable resemblance between certain moral precepts in the Buddhist code and in the Christian. I admit this resemblance—I admit that both tell us:—not to love the world; not to love money; not to show enmity towards our enemies; not to do unrighteous or impure acts—to overcome evil by good, and to do to others as we would be done by.

Nay, I admit even more:—I allow that some Buddhist precepts go beyond the corresponding

Christian injunctions. For Buddhism prohibits all killing—even of animals and noxious insects. It demands total abstinence from stimulating drinks—disallowing even moderation in their use. It excludes all who aim at perfect sanctity from the holy estate of matrimony. It bids a man, if he strives after perfection, abandon the world and lead a life of monkhood. In truth, its morality is essentially a monkhood-morality. It enjoins total abstinence, because it dares not trust human beings to be temperate. How indeed could it trust them when it promises them no help, no divine grace, no restraining power?

The glory of Christianity is that having freely given that grace and that power to man, it trusts him to make use of the gift. It seems to speak to him thus:—Thy Creator wills to trust thee and to be trusted by thee; He has endowed thee with freedom of choice, and therefore respects thy liberty of action. He imposes no rule of total abstinence in regard to natural desires; He simply bids thee keep them within bounds, so that thy moderation may be known unto all men; He places thee in the world amid trials and temptations and says to thee, 'My grace is sufficient for thee' and by its aid thou mayest overcome them all.

Yes, the grand difference between the morality of Buddhism and the morality of Christianity is not in the letter of the precepts, but in the principle and motive power brought to bear on their application.

Buddhism says:—Be righteous by yourselves, and through yourselves, and for the getting rid of all life in yourselves. Christianity says:—Be righteous through the power of God's gift of eternal life in His Son. In a word, Buddhism founds its morality on self. Christianity founds its morality on Christ.

The Buddha said to his followers:—Take nothing from me, trust to no one but to yourselves.

Christ said, and says to us still:—Take all from me; take this free gift. Put on this spotless robe. Eat this Bread of Life. Drink this Living Water.

Think you that any one who receives a priceless gift, is likely willingly to insult the Giver of it? Think you that any one who accepts a snow-white robe is likely willingly to soil it by impure acts? Think you that any one who tastes life-giving Bread is likely to relish husks? or that any one who draws deep draughts at a living Well is likely to prefer the polluted water of a stagnant pool?

Beware, then, of judging by the mere letter; or, should you insist on so judging, bear in mind that many of the precepts of Buddha are a dead letter, because the Buddha is dead; just as the Sermon on the Mount would be a dead letter, if Christ were dead.

Finally, let me say to the admirers of Buddhism:—

If you insist on placing its moral code on the same level with that of Christianity, ask yourselves one plain question—Who would be the more likely to lead a godly, righteous, and sober life, a life of moderation and temperance, a life of holiness and happiness—the man who has learnt his morality from the dead, the extinct Buddha, or the man who draws his morality and his holiness from the living, the eternal, the life-giving Christ?

LECTURE VII.

Changes in Buddhism and its disappearance from India.

In the preceding Lectures I have confined myself chiefly to the consideration of what may be called *true Buddhism* as taught by its Founder and as developed by his immediate followers and disciples during the first two or three centuries of its existence in the land of its birth, India.

To attempt an explanation of all the subsequent phases of Buddhism would, as I have before stated, require the command of unlimited time. All I can hope to accomplish in the concluding Lectures is to give a very general idea of the nature of the changes Buddhism underwent before it died out in India, and of its corruptions in some of the countries bordering on India and in North-eastern Asia.

And I may add that those who desire correct views on this subject, ought not to trust to mere inferences and theories founded on a critical perusal of the so-called Sacred Books of the Buddhists. For it is certain that without any practical experience of what Buddhism has become in modern times—I mean such an experience as can only be gained by residing or travelling in countries where Buddhism now prevails—the mere study of its ancient scriptures is likely to be misleading.

At the same time book-knowledge is indispensable, and it is essential to bring to the study of later Buddhism a scholarlike acquaintance with Sanskṛit and Pāli. Even a knowledge of Tibetan ought to be added. Nor ought the inquirer to be ignorant of the science of comparative religion, seeing that the principles of that science may throw light on many difficult questions.

For example, a student of comparative religion will be prepared to expect that all religious systems will diverge more or less from their original type in the hands of enthusiastic disciples, who are ever inclined to amplify their master's teaching and to explain it differently according to each man's peculiar temperament and mental bias, until in the end the original deposit of simple doctrine becomes overlaid with layer upon layer of adventitious matter.

Nor will he be surprised to find that the tendency of every religious movement is towards deterioration and disintegration. Nor will it appear strange to him that the chief conservative force is antagonism. As time goes on disagreements among the followers of any great leader seem to be inevitable, and always lead to sectarian divisions and subdivisions. Yet it is this opposition of religious parties that usually operates to mitigate the worst extremes of corruption, and tends to bring about re-forming movements.

Even the progress of Christianity—as history shows too well—furnishes illustrations of the law of deterioration, disintegration, and re-formation. At all events, it is certain that no mere study of the New Testament is likely to give a true idea of the varying condition of the Christian religion as exhibited at the present day in different parts of the world.

But here it is important to caution the student of religions against forcing a comparison between two systems of doctrine like Christianity and Buddhism, which are radically and essentially opposed to each other. The unchristianlike incrustations and divisions which have marred the original teaching of the Head of our religion exist *in spite* of Christianity. They are not the result of any development of its first principles; whereas, on the contrary, the corruptions and schisms of Buddhism are the natural and inevitable outcome of its own root-ideas and fundamental doctrines.

In proof of this let us revert for a moment to the insight we have gained into the origin of Buddhism.

It will be seen that the most remarkable feature of the Buddha's teaching, so far as it has been stated in the preceding Lectures, was that he altogether ignored the existence in human nature of any spiritual aspirations, affections, or instincts higher than or distinct from the natural aspirations, affections, and instincts of humanity; and of any force outside of human nature capable of aiding a man's own efforts in his struggle for salvation. Not that he reviled, or poured contempt on the religion prevalent among his fellow-countrymen, but that he found no place in his system for an external Ruler and Controller of the Universe, and would have stultified his own teaching had he acknowledged a Supreme Creator, guiding and upholding all things by His will, and always at hand to co-operate with His creatures and listen to their supplications.

If it were possible, in short, to condense into a categorical statement the scattered utterances of a man whose teaching was rarely dogmatic, we might affirm that it was to the effect that for any man to depend on a Being higher than himself, or to centre the noblest affections of his nature on a merciful, just, and holy God, whose presence he yearned for, whose aid he prayed for, and to whose image he longed to be assimilated—was a mere delusion, though perhaps a harmless one. He therefore set aside every supposed supernatural revelation as useless and incapable of proof. He prescribed no prayer, he enjoined no form of worship, he established no real church, and instead of a priesthood or clergy, ordained to aid men in their progress heavenwards or to console them in the trials of life, he founded an Order of Monks pledged to denounce human life as not worth living, and bound to abstain from all participation in human affairs.

It is true that he deserves commendation for having substituted moral conduct for useless superstitious rites, but his moral code had no other aim than the suppression of lusts and desires (p. 139, note 2), and his peculiar stoical philosophy had no other object than the removal of the ignorance which obstructed the path to true knowledge—the knowledge that all life is fraught with pain and misery, and not worth perpetuating.

It is admitted, too, that its moral precepts were of a high order; but it promised man no divine aid in observing them, it supplied him with no motive power except the selfish hope of benefiting himself in future states of corporeal existence, and it provided no remedy in case his attempts to obey its injunctions ended in failure. How, indeed, could it do any of these things when its only idea of sin was not the infraction of God's law, but the commission of an act fraught with evil consequences to the doer?

Furthermore, it was guilty of the inconsistency of bidding a man cherish a fellow-feeling for others and diligently engage in all good works, while it made his true salvation depend on his giving up all love for wife and children, and setting before himself, as his final goal, a condition of absolute indifference and inactivity.

What, therefore, I am at present concerned to point out is that, if the essential doctrines of primitive Buddhism were of the character thus summarized, a rebound from one extreme to another became inevitable, and that such a reaction was due to the very nature of the original teaching of its Founder. In point of fact it was not a development that took place, but a recoil—like the recoil of a spring held down for a time by a powerful hand and then released. And this resulted from the simple working of the eternal instincts of humanity, which insisted on making themselves felt notwithstanding the unnatural restraint to which the Buddha had subjected them; so that every doctrine he taught developed by a kind of irony of fate into a complete contradiction of itself.

Let us take a few examples:—

Buddhism, we know, started with the doctrine that all idea of marriage, or of happy home-life, was to be abandoned by wise men—by all who aimed at becoming true Buddhists; in direct contradistinction, we may note, to the primary Christian truth that it is not good for created man to be alone, and that therefore his Creator created a help meet for him—a truth confirmed in a remarkable manner by the Founder of the Christian Church when He gave the first sign of His divine commission at a marriage ceremony.

What, then, followed on the Buddha's original unnatural teaching in regard to marriage?

Of course an immediate result was that, although according to the Buddha's ordinance any one who aimed at perfect sanctity was bound to lead a celibate life, the rule against marriage was admitted to be inapplicable to the majority of human beings living in the world. The mass of the people, in short, were necessarily offenders against the primary law of Buddhism. Though called lay-Buddhists, they were not 'wise men' in the Buddhist sense of the term (pp. 86, 88). There is even evidence that among certain monkish communities in Northern countries the law against marriage was soon relaxed. It is well known that at the present day Lāmaseries in Sikkim and Tibet swarm with the children of monks, though called their nephews and nieces[1]. And far worse than this, Buddhism ultimately allied itself with Tāntrism or the worship of the female principle (śakti), and under its sanction encouraged the grossest violations of decency and the worst forms of profligacy.

It was the same in regard to the unnatural vow of

[1] This was remarked by Hooker when travelling in Sikkim. Sir Richard Temple in his Journals (II. 216) asserts that he often found married monks in Sikkim, and they make no secret of it. They are free to resign the monastic character when they choose.

poverty. Monasteries and Lâmaseries now possess immense revenues, and monks are often wealthy men.

Then again, what resulted from the Buddha's ignoring the existence of a God, and telling his disciples to abstain from depending on any Being higher than what man himself could become? Of course this was opposed to every man's innermost sense of his own needs and of his own nature. For man is so constituted that, unless his faculties become perverted or distorted, he cannot be happy without loving and trusting a Being higher than himself. Nor can man in his secret heart regard either himself or any one of his fellow-men as a being worthy of his highest adoration. Nor can he set his affections on a blank or an abstraction. And so, in spite of the Buddha's teaching, his followers would act on their own convictions. They would believe in beings higher than themselves; if not in a personal Creator knowable and lovable by themselves who takes the initiative in loving His creatures and is the proper object of their loftiest affections. It was on this account that they ultimately converted the Buddha himself into the very God he denied, calling him 'The chief god of all the gods' (Devātideva).

Again, what was the effect of the Buddha's leading men to believe that all supernatural revelation was unneeded—that all enlightenment came from within, and that every man was competent to think out true knowledge for himself by the exercise of his own reasoning powers, in the way that the Buddha himself had done?

Of course the result was that the generality of men who shrank from the effort of thinking out truth for themselves, and were wholly destitute of any faculty for doing so, insisted on believing in a revelation from an external power, and ended in attributing infallibility to the Buddha's own teaching, and worshipping the Law of Buddhism—as a visible embodiment of their deceased teacher—with all the ardour of enthusiastic bibliolatrists.

Furthermore, what followed on the Buddha's denying that any prayer, however earnest, could have any power to modify the operation of natural laws?

Of course men longed for some form of supplication to a higher power, and so the Buddha's disciples not only composed prayer-formularies, but invested the mere letters and syllables of such forms with an efficacy which no other body of religionists has ever thought of attributing to prayer of any kind (p. 371).

They not only repeated mystical sentences, which were called prayers, though really mere charms, believing that an occult virtue was inherent in the words, but invented a method of manufacturing such sentences (Dhāraṇī) like marketable commodities.

They fabricated prayers, in fact, by machinery, inscribing them on wheels or on rolls inserted in cylinders, which in the present day are made to revolve by hand or by the force of water and wind, and will possibly, with the spread of science, be impelled by steam-power, so that each revolution may count for an infinite number of repetitions, and be set down to the credit of the owner or manager of the mechanism.

Yet again, what was the inevitable consequence of the Buddha's rejection of the doctrine that any benefit could accrue to human beings from religious services conducted by regularly ordained priests, and of his instituting in their stead an Order of Monks, who were little better than a community of drones, contributing nothing to the wealth of the world, doing nothing of any utility to any one, and taught to regard inaction as the path of true wisdom?

Naturally, men craved for spiritual helpers, guides, and intercessors, and so by degrees these very monks conducted elaborate religious services, and a complicated hierarchy was organized in Tibet, even more intricate and far-reaching in its ramifications than that of the modern Romish Church.

And once more, what resulted from the Buddha's objection to provide visible images and material objects of worship, with a view to stimulate devotion or aid meditation?

Of course concrete and objective Buddhism of some kind became a necessity. It became essential to make concessions to the weakness and infirmity of human nature, which required external aids, and declined to be devoted to an ideal void, or to meditate on a pure abstraction. Even the Founder of Buddhism himself seems to have felt, as we shall see, that his hold on the memory of his followers would depend on their venerating certain objects and symbols after his death. Unhappily for the purity of Buddhism, but quite in conformity with the inveterate tendencies of humanity, the Buddha's disciples pushed veneration of external objects to an extreme. They were not contented with mere reverence shown to the relics of the Buddha's burnt body and the shrines containing them. They worshipped the tree under which he attained Buddhahood, the seat on which he sat, the prints of his feet, his shadow supposed to be impressed on rocks, the utensils he used, the books containing the Law, the wheel which symbolized both the propagation and the character of his doctrine, and finally bowed down before carved representations of his body and images of all kinds (p. 467).

In Buddhist countries idols are far more numerous than among any other idolatrous people in the world.

Lastly, what resulted from the Buddha's teaching that the ultimate end to which men's efforts ought to be directed was Nirvāṇa—that is, the total extinction of all individual existence and personal identity?

Of course men instinctively recoiled from utter self-annihilation, and so the Buddha's followers ended in changing the true idea of Nirvāṇa and converting it from a condition of non-existence into a state of hazy beatitude in celestial regions, while they encouraged all men—whether monks or laymen—to make a sense of dreamy bliss in heaven, and not total extinction of life, the end of all their efforts.

But it was not only this natural and inevitable recoil to the opposite extreme that ultimately brought about an entire change in primitive Buddhism. Another cause must also be taken into account.

We have already explained the nature of the tie which bound Buddhism to Brāhmanism, from the first day on which Gautama sat as a disciple at the feet of the Brāhman philosophers Udraka and Āḷāra (p. 29).

Now, although this tie was soon loosened, and although the Buddha struck out a line of his own, and a separation took place, yet the two systems stood on so much common ground that they were always ready to draw together again.

At all events, it is probable that one system never expelled the other, and that the constant attrition and contact which took place between Brāhmanism and Buddhism, led to a considerable splitting up of the original fabric of Buddhism, involving, of course, many divisions and subdivisions of Buddhistic thought, some of which were closely allied to the later developments of Brāhmanical philosophy.

In the Sarva-darśana-saṅgraha four principal sects of Buddhism are enumerated, which must have taken root early on Indian soil.

These four were the Vaibhāshika, Sautrāntika, Mādhyamika, and Yogāćāra. Of these the first two with their subdivisions[1] were realistic, and were established —though not perhaps thoroughly formulated and systematized—in very early times, long before the council of Kanishka; while the two later schools are described as idealistic, the Mādhyamika being a Buddhistic form of the Vedānta philosophy, and the Yogāćāra agreeing generally with the Yoga system.

Indeed there is good evidence that Buddhism developed in India a greater number of schools and phases

---

[1] The Vaibhāshika was divided into Sarvāstivāda (assertion of the real existence of all things), Mahāsaṅghika, Sammatīya (said to have been founded by Upāli), and Sthavira; the Sautrāntika had also its own subdivisions.

of thought than Brāhmanism itself. Some authorities enumerate eighteen divisions (corresponding perhaps to the eighteen original disciples, pp. 47–73) which existed in king Kanishka's time—that is, in the first century of our era, while others specify thirty-two; and in the fourth century we find the Chinese traveller Fā-hien (p. 160) making allusion to as many as ninety-six (Dr. Legge's translation, p. 62).

We cannot wonder then that the author of the Sarva-darśana-saṅgraha expressed himself in rather strong language to the following effect:—

'Though the venerated Buddha be the only one teacher, his disciples are manifold; just as when the sun has set, the thief and other evil doers, the theological student and others understand that it is time to set about their occupations, according to their several inclinations.'

Yet, after all, it was chiefly in the North, and in consequence of the council held by Kanishka, India's greatest Buddhist king after Aśoka[1] (see p. 69), that the original features of Buddhism underwent the greatest change and became overlaid with coating after coating of extraneous matter. It was there, in Northern regions, in the valley of the Indus, that the Protean system called Mahā-yāna arose, and grew, by the operation of the usual laws of accretion, conglomeration,

[1] Another great king was the celebrated Harsha-vardhana or Śilāditya of Kanauj, who flourished about A.D. 610–650, and who is said to have founded an era formerly much used in Northern India. He ruled from the Indus to the Ganges, and his doings are described by Hiouen Thsang. (Beal's Records, I. 210–221.)

disintegration, and reintegration, into a congeries of heterogeneous doctrines, including the worship of Bodhi-sattvas, deified saints, and personal gods.

Naturally the adherents of this wider method spoke disparagingly of the simpler system prevalent in the South, whose sacred books were the Tri-piṭaka of Ceylon written in the ancient vernacular (Pāli). That system they designated Hīna-yāna, 'the Lesser method,' not denying however that their own enlarged system grew out of and included the simpler one.

There arose, too, a third method, or 'vehicle' of salvation, called 'the Middle method' (Madhyama-yāna). This, however, is not so well known, and, being a compromise between the other two, never gained many adherents, though it is still recognised in Tibet—the Tibetans often speaking of Tri-yāna, or 'the three vehicles.'

At all events, it is only necessary for practical purposes to recognize the distinction of the Great and Little Vehicle—the Mahā-yāna[1] and the Hīna-yāna. And it may be stated generally that the inhabitants of Nepāl, Tibet, China, Manchuria, Mongolia, and Japan have always shown a preference for the Mahā-yāna, or 'Great Vehicle,' while the people of Ceylon, Burma, and Siam have always preferred the 'Little Vehicle.'

At the same time, it is important to note that while the Buddhists of Northern countries are supposed to be disciples of the Mahā-yāna or Great Way of

---

[1] The Mahā-yāna is said to be connected with the Mādhyamika and Yogāćāra Schools, and the Hīna-yāna with the Vaibhāshika and Sautrāntika.

Salvation, the Buddhism of each Northern country differs greatly from that of the other, and that the countries nearest to India have still further complicated the Mahā-yāna system by adopting mystical doctrines, and introducing magic and other practices supposed to aid in the acquisition of supernatural powers.

It must also be borne in mind that, although the Mahā-yāna or Great Method originated on the Indus, and the Hīna-yāna or Little Method, on the Ganges, the two streams of teaching were not always confined to these two areas, even on Indian soil.

In point of fact they were often intermixed, and the changes thus brought about in Buddhism will become more evident by referring to the narratives of three well-known Buddhist travellers from China.

Buddhism was introduced into China between 58 and 75 of our era[1], but it was not till much later that Chinese pilgrims visited India—the holy land of Buddhism.

The first traveller of whom we have any record was a certain Chinese Buddhist monk named Fā-hien, who set out on a pilgrimage to India about the year 399 of our era, with the definite object of searching for and carrying back to China complete copies of the Vinaya or Rules of discipline for the Order. He wrote a very simple and straightforward account of his travels[2]—which lasted for fourteen years—and of his visits to all the spots in India held most sacred by Buddhists. He

[1] Professor Legge's Travels of Fā-hien, p. 28.

[2] Translated from the Chinese by the Rev. S. Beal and more recently by Mr. Herbert Giles and Professor Legge.

was followed by a Chinese traveller of less mark, named Sung Yun, who started about 518 A.D., and seems to have ended his journey at Peshawar, or at least not to have penetrated much further South. Peshawar, we know, was a great Buddhist centre, and there was a fine Stūpa there, containing the alms-bowl of Buddha. Then after another interval a much more celebrated Chinese pilgrim named Hiouen Thsang[1] started for India (A. D. 629–644). The narrative of his travels for about fifteen years is perhaps the best known and most commonly quoted of the three. In Chang Yueh's preface[2] to these travels Hiouen Thsang is described as 'a Doctor of the three Piṭakas, and is said to have translated 657 works from the original Sanskṛit. In all the districts through which he journeyed he learnt the dialects and investigated the deep secrets of religion.'

All three travellers give information in regard to the prevalence of Buddhism in India up to the seventh century of our era, and the narratives of two—Fā-hien and Hiouen Thsang—are invaluable for the light they throw on the changes which Buddhism underwent in the interval of their travels. Here and there the pilgrims exaggerate, especially when they venture on numerical statistics or write from hearsay; but on the whole their accounts may be accepted, and we learn that Hiouen Thsang found some monasteries in ruins which were flourishing in Fā-hien's time, and that the Mahā-

[1] According to Dr. Legge's orthography this name should be written Hsüen Chwang.

[2] See Beal's 'Records of the Western World,' which gives a translation of these travels in two volumes.

yāna had supplanted the earlier form of Buddhism, or rather co-existed with it in many parts of the South as well as of the North, and was to be found even in Ceylon[1].

And this brings us face to face with the greatest change of all—the total dying out of Buddhism in the place of its origin. How is it to be accounted for that no adherents of either the greater or lesser Buddhist systems—of either the Mahā-yāna or Hīna-yāna—are to be found in India at the present moment?

The problem is difficult of solution, and I can only offer a few suggestions for its elucidation.

In the first place, I think it may be confidently asserted that the disappearance of Buddhism from India was a very gradual process, and unattended by any serious or violent religious revolution.

We have already alluded to the tolerant, liberal, and eclectic spirit which has characterized Buddhism ever since the period of its first promulgation at Benares.

Such toleration of the doctrines and ideas of co-existing systems had its advantages, especially in the early stages of the Buddhistic movement. It certainly had a prophylactic effect in warding off violent attacks, and helped to promote the diffusion of Buddhism throughout the numerous countries to which it ultimately spread. In India itself, as we have already seen, Buddhism was never aggressive or combative. Its motto

---

[1] Hiouen Thsang describes the Sthavira form of the Mahā-yāna as existing as far south as Ceylon. He found many monks studying both the Great and Little Vehicles in Central India. Beal's Records, ii. 247, 254, 257.

everywhere was persuasion and conciliation. Composure, tranquillity, and absence of acrimony were stamped on all its features. The very foundation on which it was reared—the very establishment of a celibate monastic Order, by means of which true knowledge was to be propagated—had in it something altogether agreeable to the spirit and usages of Brāhmanism.

We have seen, too, that the Buddha took care to show his respect for Brāhmanical traditions, even while promulgating a philosophical theory and preaching doctrines opposed to all sacerdotalism, priestly privileges, supernatural revelation, and Vedic ceremonial.

It does not, of course, follow that the great teacher, to whom the majority of Asiatic races have for centuries looked as their chosen example, had not the courage of his opinions, and was not competent to fill the rôle of a religious reformer.

The real fact was that he was too wise to enter upon any open crusade against inveterate customs and ideas. The peculiar calm of an Indian atmosphere, though occasionally disturbed by political storms sweeping from distant regions, has rarely been stirred by violent religious antagonisms. The various currents of Hindū religious life have flowed peacefully side by side, and reformers have generally done their work quietly. As for Gautama, there can be little doubt that his whole career was stamped with the impress of his early surroundings, and that he imbibed his tolerant ideas from the Brāhmanism in which he had been trained.

It has been usual to blame the Brāhmans for their arrogant exclusiveness, but their arrogance has been rather shown in magnifying their own caste-privileges and carrying them to an extravagant pitch, than in preventing any discussion of their own dogmas, or in resenting any dissent from them.

The very essence of Brāhmanism was tolerance. Every form of opinion was admissible under a system which made every person and every object in existence manifestations of the one Being, Brahmă.

The only delicate ground, on which it was dangerous for any reformer to tread, was caste. The only unpardonable sin was infringement of caste-rules. Nor was any one tempted to adopt the rôle of a violent agitator, when all were free to express any opinion they liked without hindrance, provided they took care to abstain from any act of interference with caste-privileges.

It does not appear, in short, that the preachers of either Buddhism, or Vaishṇavism, or Śaivism, or Śāktism, or of any form of these sectarian systems, ever incurred the special animosity of the Brāhmans or of each other, or ever indulged in very violent denunciations of each other's religious doctrines.

In real truth, these systems of doctrine were all evolved out of Brāhmanism. They were, therefore, not only tolerated by Brāhmanism, but accepted as the inevitable outcome of its own pantheistic creed.

No doubt each received at first a strong stamp of individuality from its founder, marking it off from other systems, but with the lapse of years the deeper shades of difference grew fainter. Then it became a question which should become merged in the other. In such a competition between rival systems Buddhism had less chance of holding its own than either Vaishṇavism or Śaivism; for its root-ideas—as we have seen—were not rooted in the eternal instincts of human nature.

Buddhism, in fact, could never have maintained itself in India till the twelfth or thirteenth century of our era, had it not gradually, and to a great extent through interaction with Vaishṇavism and Śaivism, dropped its unnatural pessimistic theory of life and its unpopular atheistic character, and accommodated itself to those systems.

But Buddhism in parting with its ultra-pessimism and its atheistic and agnostic ideas, lost its chief elements of individuality and its chief independent stand-point.

Vaishṇavism, on the other hand, was quite alive to its own interests, and had an eye to the spread of its own doctrines. It took care to adopt all the popular features of Buddhism. It vied with Buddhism in inculcating universal love, toleration, liberality, benevolence, and abstinence from injury. It preached equality, fraternity, and even in some cases the abolition of caste distinctions. It taught a succession of incarnations or rather descents (Avatāra[1]) of divine beings upon earth (as Buddhism taught a succession of Buddhas), and it even adopted the Buddha himself as one of the incarnations of Vishṇu.

This, indeed, is the best explanation of what has happened at Purī in Orissa, where a temple once

[1] As I have shown in 'Brāhmanism and Hindūism,' the term incarnation is not strictly expressive of the Hindū idea of Avatāra, which means 'a descent' upon earth of a god, or of a portion of his essence, in various forms.

dedicated to Gautama Buddha, and supposed to contain a relic of his burnt body, was afterwards dedicated to the Jagannāth form of Kṛishṇa and supposed to enshrine one of his bones, and where low-caste and high-caste both eat together the food cooked in the house of that popular god.

The same may be said of the interaction which took place between Buddhism and Śaivism; for Śaivism, of course, was quite as bent on the propagation of its own creed as other systems were. It vied with Buddhism in encouraging abstract meditation, and although it had less sympathy than Vaishṇavism had with that system, it approached in some respects so closely to its rival, that when Buddhism disappeared from India, images of Gautama were converted into representations of Śiva seated in profound contemplation.

Ultimately, the interaction between the three systems proceeded to such a point that each was influenced and modified by the other; each learnt something, or adopted some practice from the other.

It was thus, too, that Śāktism, i.e. the worship of energy or force (Śakti), identified with Śiva's consort, was imported into Buddhism; its doctrine of the self-evolution of all things from Prakṛiti having much that harmonized with the Buddhist theory of the origin of the Universe. Thus, too, even Tāntrism in its worst forms became intermixed with Buddhistic practice.

Enough, then, has been said to justify the assertion that Buddhism was not forcibly expelled from India by the Brāhmans. It simply in the end—possibly as late as the thirteenth century of our era—became blended with the systems which surrounded it, though the process of blending was gradual.

It would certainly be easy to prove from the records of the three Chinese travellers, that Buddhism and Brāhmanism existed together in Northern and Central India as quite distinct systems till at least the seventh century of our era, if not always quite amicably, yet without any violent internecine conflict. Bitter controversies between the two rival creeds are without doubt clearly alluded to, and Fā-hien in one passage states that 'the Brāhmans with their contrary doctrine became full of hatred and envy in their hearts[1].' Yet, on the other hand, we find that at a Council held by the great Buddhist king Śilāditya (Harsha-vardhana), whose meritorious acts are fully described by Hiouen Thsang (ch. v), and who had his capital at Kanauj, in the year 634 of our era[2], controversial points relating to both Buddhism and Brāhmanism were discussed in a tolerant spirit, though it is said that in discussing questions between the Northern and Southern Buddhists, the 'Little Vehicle' was condemned.

Again, the Buddhist drama called Nāgānanda, 'joy of the snake world[3],' throws great light on the amicable

[1] Professor Legge's translation, p. 56.

[2] There are four great Buddhist kings of India who may be called historical, the dates of whose reigns may be fixed with fair certainty:— 1. Ćandra-gupta, who was at any rate a sympathiser with Buddhism, B.C. 315–291. 2. Aśoka, a decided Buddhist, B.C. 259–222. 3. Kanishka (see p. 69). 4. Śilāditya, above. Some consider Kanishka to have founded the Śaka era, dating from A.D. 78.

[3] Translated in 1872 by Mr. Palmer Boyd, and published with an interesting introduction by Professor Cowell.

relations existing between the various sectarians and religionists in the days of king Śilāditya. It is the only Sanskṛit play in which the Nāndī or opening prayer invokes the power of Buddha, thus :—

'"On whom dost thou meditate, putting on a pretence of religious abstraction, yet opening thine eyes? See, saviour that thou art, thou dost not pity us sick with the shafts of Love. Falsely art thou compassionate. Who is more cruel than thou?" May Buddha, the conqueror, who was thus jealously addressed by the Apsarasas (daughters) of Māra (p. 34), protect you!'

Professor E. B. Cowell has shown in his valuable Preface that both this play and the sister Hindū play called Ratnāvali were probably put forth or at least patronised by Harsha-vardhana (Śilāditya), and that both were probably acted at the same period, the king being as much a Hindū as a Buddhist. Hiouen Thsang praises Harsha-vardhana for his support of Buddhism, but in his description of the two Convocations held by that king, states that both Buddhists and Brāhmans were equally honoured by him, and intimates that half his subjects held one doctrine and half the other. In the second Convocation which took place at Prayāga (now Allahābād) eighteen kings were present and 500,000 monks and laymen. On the first day the statue of Buddha was installed; on the second day that of the Sun, and on the third that of Śiva. Alms were distributed to Brāhmans and Buddhists alike, and even to the Nirgranthas or Jaina naked heretics.

Again the well-known play called Mālatī-Mādhava (by Bhava-bhūti, who lived at Kanauj in the beginning of the eighth century) has an opening prayer addressed to Śiva, and yet a female Buddhist ascetic and her attendant constitute two of the principal dramatis personæ, proving that an intermixture of the two creeds prevailed everywhere.

It was also during the reign of Śilāditya that the immense monastery at Nālanda near Rāja-gṛiha formed a seat of learning, which might suggest a comparison with the learned monkish communities and even with the universities of mediæval Europe [1]. In that monastery might be seen several thousand novices and monks of the eighteen Buddhist schools—all of them supported by royal grants, and thus enabled both to perform their religious duties, and to prosecute the study of philosophy, law, and science in literary ease. It is probable that if disputes and disagreements upon burning questions occurred, they rarely led to serious conflicts, and were not general throughout India, but confined to particular localities; and I think it may be safely affirmed that if Buddhism was ever anywhere persecuted, it never anywhere persecuted in return.

I myself was much struck in a visit I paid to Elorā in the Nizām's territory by the evidence I there saw of the friendly tolerance which must have prevailed between Brāhmans, Buddhists, and Jains. Brāhmanical, Buddhist, and Jaina caves are there seen side by side, and their inmates no doubt lived on terms of fairly friendly tolerance, much as the members

---

[1] See Beal's Records, ii. 167–172; a long account of this monastery visited by Hiouen Thsang is there given.

of the Anglican, Roman Catholic, and Wesleyan communions live in Europe at the present day.

Even at Benares, the stronghold of Brāhmanism, I witnessed similar proofs of amicable mutual intercourse, and at Nāsik—the Benares of Western India—the proximity of the Buddhist caves and ruined monasteries which I visited made it abundantly clear that Brāhmans and Buddhists agreed to differ and to avoid serious quarrels.

It must nevertheless be admitted, that in the extreme South of India, and perhaps eventually at Benares and a few other strongholds of Brāhmanism, the difference between the systems became so accentuated as to lead to grievous conflicts. Whether blood was shed it is impossible to prove; but it is alleged, with some degree of probability, that violent crusades against Buddhism were instituted by Kumārila and Śaṅkara—two well-known Southern Brāhmans noted for their bigotry—in the seventh and eighth centuries of our era. It does not appear, however, that they were very successful either in the conversion or extermination of Buddhists.

It may, I think, be confidently affirmed that what ultimately happened in most parts of India was, that Vaishṇavas and Śaivas crept up softly to their rival and drew the vitality out of its body by close and friendly embraces, and that instead of the Buddhists being expelled from India, Buddhism gradually and quietly lost itself in Vaishṇavism and Śaivism. In fact, by the beginning of the thirteenth century very little Buddhism remained on Indian soil. In a philosophical drama, called 'the Rise of the Moon of Knowledge' (Prabodha-ćandrodaya), written probably about the twelfth century, the approaching triumph of Brāhmanism over Buddhism is clearly indicated; for the Buddhist and other heretical sects are represented as belonging to the losing side.

Yet, after all, it is scarcely correct to say that Buddhism ever wholly died away in India. Its name indeed perished there, but its spirit survived, and its sacred places remain to this day. Its ruined temples, monasteries, monuments, and idols are scattered everywhere, while some of these have been perpetuated and adopted by those later phases of Hindūism which its own toleration helped to bring into existence.

At all events it may be safely affirmed that the passing away of the Buddhistic system in India was on the whole like the peaceful passing away of a moribund man surrounded by his relatives, and was at least unattended with any agonizing pangs[1].

---

[1] No doubt there are places in the South of India where there is evidence of some violent persecution. I may instance among the places I visited Tanjore and Madurā. When I concluded the reading of a paper on this subject at the meeting of the Royal Asiatic Society on February 15, 1886, the then President, Colonel Yule, justly remarked that the members of two religious communions who hold very similar doctrines, often on that account hate and oppose each other all the more; but my point was that the ultra-tolerance which was of the very essence of both Brāhmanism and Buddhism must have prevented actual persecution, except under special circumstances. Brāhmanism was much more likely to have adopted Buddhism as part of its system, than to have persecuted and expelled it. In point of fact, the Brāhmans, as is well known, are ready to regard any great teacher as one of Vishṇu's incarnations, and in this way are even willing to pay homage to the Head of Christianity.

LECTURE VIII.

Rise of Theistic and Polytheistic Buddhism.

In the preceding Lecture we have endeavoured to show generally how Buddhism was evolved out of Brāhmanism, how it flourished side by side with Brāhmanism, and how after a chequered career and protracted senility in the land of its birth—lasting for at least fifteen centuries[1]—it ultimately merged its individuality in Vaishṇavism and Śaivism, or, in other words, disappeared and became lost in a composite system called Hindūism.

We have now to trace more closely the gradual sliding of a simple agnostic and atheistic creed, into a variety of theistic and polytheistic conceptions.

We have already seen how the expansion of the Hīna-yāna into the Mahā-yāna became an inevitable result of the Buddha's own teaching—in other words, how a re-bound from atheism to theism was as unavoidable as the return swing of a heavy pendulum. We need only repeat here that it could not have been otherwise, when a teacher, who never claimed to be more than a man, attempted to indoctrinate his human followers with

---

[1] Buddhism began to lose ground in India about the fourth or fifth century after Christ, but it maintained a chequered career for several succeeding centuries even after Hiouen Thsang's time. See p. 161.

principles opposed to the inextinguishable instincts and eternal intuitions of humanity.

In fact the teachers of the Mahā-yāna school were not slow to perceive that, if Buddhism was to gain any hold over the masses, it was essential that it should adapt itself to their human needs. It became imperatively necessary, as a simple preservative measure, to convert a cold philosophical creed, based on an ultra-pessimistic theory of existence, into some sort of belief in the value of human life as worth living. And if life was not to be an invariable current of misery it followed that there must also be some sort of faith in a superintending God controlling that life, and interesting Himself in Man's welfare.

Unfortunately, having once advanced beyond definite limits, the more progressive teachers found it impossible to draw the line at any given point.

No doubt the theistic movement began by simple saint-worship—that is, by veneration for the extinct Buddha as for a perfect saint. This was accompanied by homage offered to his relics and to various memorials of his person.

Then mere veneration and homage led to actual worship, and the Buddha, who from first to last made his own perfect humanity an essential principle of his teaching, became elevated to a pinnacle far above humanity and converted into a veritable god.

Next, it is easy to see that a further development of the theistic movement became inevitable.

For indeed it was only natural that in process of time some of the more eminent of the Buddha's followers should become almost equally revered with himself. It was not, however, till some time after their death that they received any homage resembling that accorded to their Master.

It was then that, instead of being thought of as extinct, according to the orthodox Buddhist doctrine, they were continually elevated in the imagination of their admirers to heavenly regions of beatitude.

Of course this constant increase of saint-worship tended to land men by degrees in a mass of theistic and polytheistic conceptions.

And polytheism could not prevail in Eastern countries without its usual reverse side—polydemonism; and polydemonism could not prevail without its usual adjuncts of mysticism and magic. And all of these again entailed idolatry, relic-worship, fetish-worship, and various other gross superstitions.

Such was the natural termination of the process of degeneration. Let us now trace it more in detail.

And in the first place it must not be forgotten that Gautama himself seems to have foreseen this result.

He seems to have been quite aware of the ineradicable tendency inherent in the nature of human beings, impelling them to elevate their saints and heroes to the position of gods. He therefore took pains to make his beloved disciple and cousin Ānanda understand that the truth embodied in the Dharma or Law which he had taught, was all that ought to take his place and represent him when he was gone.

Accordingly we learn from ancient inscriptions that for many years afterwards the only allowable object of veneration among primitive Buddhists was the Law—that is, the precepts, rules, and ordinances propounded by Gautama himself—many of which may have been committed to writing in early times, though oral transmission was at first the usual rule, as it was among Brāhmans.

In time, however, the interconnexion between Brāhmanism and Buddhism, and the tendency to group sacred objects in triads [1], which showed itself very early in Hindū religious thought and mythology, seems to have led to the idea of a corresponding triple arrangement of venerated objects among Buddhists. Hence three precious things—sometimes called the three jewels (*tri-ratna*), or the 'three Holies [2]'—came first to be held in honour and then actually worshipped; a kind of personality being accorded to all three, very similar to that supposed to belong to the three chief gods of the Hindū Pantheon.

This triad of personalities consisted of (1) the Buddha himself, that is to say, Gautama Buddha, or the Buddha of the present age of the world; (2) his Dharma or Law, that is, the word and doctrine of the Buddha personified, or so to speak incarnated and manifested in written books after his Pari-nirvāṇa; and (3) his Saṅgha or Order of monks, also in a manner

[1] First, the Vedic triad of gods, Agni, 'Fire,' Indra, 'wielder of the thunderbolt,' and Sūrya, 'the Sun,' followed by the Tri-mūrti or Brahmā, Śiva, Vishṇu. Then the three Guṇas or constituents of the material Universe, Sattva, Rajas, and Tamas, and lastly the triple name of Brahmă, Saé-ćid-ānanda.

[2] Sarat Chandra Dās, in his interesting Tibetan journal, describes them as the 'three Holies.'

personified—that is, embodied in a kind of ideal impersonification or collective unity of his true disciples.

This last word, Saṅgha, which means in Sanskṛit, 'a collection' or 'assemblage,' is sometimes, as we have already seen (p. 85), very unsuitably rendered by the expression 'Buddhist Church.' It simply denotes 'the collective body of Buddhist monks;' that is to say, the entire monastic fraternity, comprising in its widest sense the whole assemblage of monks, Arhats, Pratyeka-Buddhas, Bodhi-sattvas, perfected Buddhas and not yet perfected saints of all classes, whether on the earth or in any other division of the Universe; but not including—be it carefully borne in mind—the still vaster community of living persons constituting the whole body of the Buddhist laity.

These three, then,—the Buddha, his Law, and his Fraternity of Monks,—passed into the first three divine personifications of early theistic Buddhism, commonly known as the first Buddhist Triad.

Hence we find that the Khuddaka-pāṭha or 'lesser readings[1]' of the fifteen divisions of the Khuddaka-nikāya (p. 63) begins thus:—

'I put my trust in the Buddha, in the Law, in the Fraternity of Monks' (repeated three times).

'Ye beings (Bhūtāni) here assembled of earth and air, let us bow, let us bow before the Buddha, revered by gods and men. May there be prosperity!

'Ye beings of earth and air, let us bow before the Law.

[1] Edited by Childers. See Journal R. A. S., N. S. iv. 318, and Kern's Buddhismus, ii. 156.

'Ye beings of earth and air, let us bow before the Fraternity of Monks.'

When Fā-hien was on his return home and in great peril at sea, he committed his life to the protection of the Saṅgha, saying:—'I have travelled far in search of the Law, let me, by your dread and supernatural power, return from my wanderings and reach my resting-place.'

And again, on ending his travels, he gratefully acknowledged that he had been guarded in his perils by the dread power of the 'three honoured ones' or 'three precious ones' or 'three Holies'—thus acknowledging the personality of the Law as well as of the Buddha himself and of the Saṅgha or collective body of Monks (Legge's Fā-hien, pp. 112–116).

But it must be borne in mind that this did not necessarily imply any worship of idols. It is certain that for a long time even Buddha himself was not represented visibly. This is proved by the sculptures on the Bharhut Stūpa. Even in the present day the simple expression of trust in the three revered ones constitutes the only formula of worship current in Ceylon. It is true that images of the Buddha are now common in that country, and while travelling there I saw numbers of persons offering homage and flowers at the idol-shrines. But no prayer, in the Christian sense, is addressed to the Buddha or to his visible representations, although in Ceylon, as in Northern countries, wishes are expressed and prayer-formularies repeated before the images, and the fulfilment of the wishes is attributed to the efficacy of the repetitions. (See pp. 371–386.)

Nor, when I was at the Buddhist monastery near Darjīling, did I see any image of the personified Law or of the Monkhood, though every book examined by me in the temple-library began with the words :—Namo Buddhāya, 'reverence to the Buddha;' namo Dharmāya, 'reverence to the Law;' namo Saṅghāya, 'reverence to the Order.' The only visible symbol of the three so-called 'Holies' was a long staff with three prongs, like the Indian Tri-śūla.

It seems clear, however, that while, in process of time, images of Gautama Buddha were multiplied everywhere—and, as we shall see, in various attitudes and shapes—images of the personified Law and Saṅgha also became common among Northern Buddhists. Those images of the Law which I have examined, and of which there are numerous examples in Sikkim, have four arms and hands. Two hands are joined in worship, while another holds a book (or sometimes a lotus) and another a rosary[1].

Sometimes the representation of a book alone is held to be a sufficient symbol of the Law.

The Saṅgha, on the other hand, is generally symbolized by the image of a man with two arms and hands, one of which rests on the right knee and the other holds a lotus. (See drawing at p. 485.)

And it may be observed here that of the three images of the Buddha, the Law, and the Order, some-

[1] According to Capt. R. C. Temple, Dharma, 'the law,' is personified in Sikkim as a white woman with four arms, two raised in prayer, the third holding a garland (or rosary), the fourth a lotus.

times one occupies the central position and sometimes the other. This circumstance has led scholars to speak of what it is the fashion to term a Buddhist trinity; but in real fact neither Buddhism nor Brāhmanism has any trinity in the true meaning of the term, for although Buddhists claim a kind of tri-unity for their triad, and say that the first contains the second, and that the third proceeds from the first two and contains them, yet the first is clearly never regarded as either the Father or Creator of the world, in the Christian sense.

It appears, in fact, that the earliest Buddhist worship was exactly what might have been expected to follow on the death of a religious Reformer and author of a new system. It was merely the natural expression of deep reverence for the founder of Buddhism, his doctrine, and the collective body of his disciples.

So simple a form of worship, however, did not long satisfy the devotional aspirations of the Buddha's followers, even in the sacred land of pure Buddhism.

The mere offering of homage, either to a system of Law, or to a community of living monks or to departed human saints—even though their memory was kept alive by visible representations, and stimulated by meditation and repetition of prayer-formularies—had in it nothing calculated to support or comfort men in seasons of sickness, bereavement, or calamity. This kind of simple Buddhism might have satisfied the needs of men in times of peace and prosperity. Under other conditions it broke down. It could offer no shelter and give no help amid the storms and tempests of life. Hence the development of the later phases of the Mahā-yāna system, the chief feature of which was a marked change in the meaning attached to the term 'Bodhi-sattva.'

This change will be better understood if we go back to what has already been mentioned (at p. 98). We have before explained that, according to the original theory of Buddhism, a Bodhi-sattva is one who has knowledge (derived from self-enlightening intellect) for his essence; that is, he is a being who through all his bodily existences is destined in some final existence to become a Buddha, or self-enlightened man. Until his final birth, however, a Bodhi-sattva is a being in whom true knowledge is rather latent and undeveloped than perfected. Gautama had been a Bodhi-sattva of this character (see p. 134), the merit of whose actions (Karma) in each of his countless previous existences (see p. 109) had been transmitted to succeeding corporeal forms, till in the state immediately preceding his last birth on earth he existed as a Bodhi-sattva in the Tushita heaven (see pp. 113, 207). There he continued until the time came for him to be born on earth as the Buddha of the present age, when he entered the right side of his mother in the form of a white elephant (p. 23)[1].

[1] One legend says:—'Thus, O monks, Buddha was born, and the right side of his mother was not pierced, was not wounded. It remained as before.' Foucaux, p. 97. Hiouen Thsang relates that there is a Vihāra at Kapila-vastu indicating the spot 'where the Bodhi-sattva descended *spiritually* into the womb of his mother,' and that there is a representation of this scene drawn in the Vihāra. I have myself seen many representations of it in Buddhist sculptures.

And it may be repeated here that the white elephant, as something rare and beautiful of its kind, was simply symbolical of the perfect Arhatship which he was destined to achieve in the ensuing birth.

Born, then, at last as the child Gautama, son of Śuddhodana, and purified by a long observance of the six transcendent virtues (p. 128), he ultimately attained to perfect knowledge and Arhatship under the Bodhi-tree, and in so attaining passed from the condition of a Bodhi-sattva to that of the highest of all Arhats—a supreme Buddha. Then, after about forty-five years of diligent discharge of his self-imposed task as a teacher of the right way of salvation, he ultimately passed away in Pari-nirvāṇa, or absolute non-existence.

It is important, however, to remember, that at the moment of his attaining Buddhahood he had transferred the Bodhi-sattvaship to Maitreya, 'the loving and compassionate one,' who became the Buddha-elect, dwelling and presiding as his predecessor had done in the heaven of contented beings (Tushita; see p. 207). There he watches over and promotes the interests of the Buddhist faith, while awaiting the time when he is to appear on earth as Maitreya, or the fifth Buddha of the present age. His advent will not take place till the lapse of five thousand years after the Nirvāṇa of Gautama, when the world will have become so corrupt that the Buddhist Law will be no more obeyed, nor even remembered.

No wonder then that this Maitreya—whose very name implies love and tenderness towards mankind, and who was destined to become, like Gautama, a

Saviour of the world by teaching its inhabitants how to save themselves—became a favourite object of personal worship after Gautama Buddha's death. Even when the worship of other Bodhi-sattvas was introduced, Maitreya retained the distinction of being the only Bodhi-sattva worshipped by all Buddhist countries, whether in the South or in the North. Not that Gautama's memory was neglected. He was, of course, held to be superior to Maitreya, who was still a mere Bodhi-sattva or Buddha-designate. But the feeling towards Gautama Buddha, after his Nirvāṇa and death, became different, and the object of bringing flowers and offerings to his shrines was simply to honour the memory of a departed, not an existing saint. It was a mere mechanical act, fraught with beneficial consequences, but not supplying any real religious need. On the other hand actual prayers were addressed to Maitreya, as to a living merciful being, whose favour it was all-important to secure, and whose heaven was believed to be a region of perfect love and contentment, to which all his worshippers were admitted.

In Hiouen Thsang's Travels a heavenly Ṛishi is represented as saying:—'No words can describe the personal beauty of Maitreya. He declares a law not different from ours. His exquisite voice is soft and pure. Those who hear it can never tire; those who listen are never satiated[1].'

In fact, the aspirations of few pious Buddhists in early times ever led them to soar higher than the

[1] Beal's Records, i. 228.

happiness of living with Maitreya and listening to his voice in his own Tushita heaven.

It is true that afterwards when the worship of the Dhyāni-Buddha Amitābha came into vogue in Northern countries this Buddha's heaven, called Sukhāvatī, fabled to be somewhere in the Western sky, seems to have taken the place of the heaven of Maitreya. But this belongs to a later phase of Buddhism, to be explained when we speak of the Dhyāni-Buddhas (p. 203).

It was for Maitreya's Tushita heaven that Hiouen Thsang, and other devout men of his day, prayed on their death-beds, and the one Chinese inscription found at Buddha-Gayā is full of expressions indicative of the same longing[1].

If then, we are able to enter into the feelings of Buddhists everywhere in depending on the living, loving, and energizing Maitreya, rather than on the extinct Buddha who existed only in their memories, we shall find it less difficult to understand how it came to pass that the idea of, so to speak, canonizing every great saint or popular head of a monastic community, and elevating him at death to the position of a Bodhisattva like Maitreya, living in permanent regions of bliss, and able to help his votaries to the same position, came into vogue.

It may make the course of development of Theistic Buddhism clearer if we here revert to the early constitution of the Buddhist monastic brotherhood, and endeavour to show how the homage paid to eminent

---

[1] Beal's Records, i. 134, note.

and saint-like men led, first to the multiplication of Bodhi-sattvas, and then to polytheism and every form of polytheistic superstition.

A full explanation of the early monastic system is given in the learned work of Koeppen[1]. It is clear that as long as Gautama was alive he was the sole Head of the brotherhood of monks. After his death the Headship (as in the Christian brotherhood after the death of Christ) was not assigned to any one leader. The Buddha himself forbade this. The term Saṅgha at that time merely denoted a republican fraternity of monks, bound by no irrevocable vows and subject to no hierarchical Superior, but all intent on following the example, and propagating the doctrines of their departed leader. Soon, however, the formation of separate centres of union and teaching became inevitable, and the term Saṅgha was then applied to each separate society, and sometimes even to a separate Conclave of each society, as well as to the whole body. It seems at least certain that each monastic association had the right to admit monks, to hear confession, and to excommunicate. Naturally, too, in course of time it became necessary for each society to have some sort of governing body and choose a kind of president, and this presiding officer was originally the senior monk, and accordingly had the simple title of Sthavira (Thera), 'Elder.' This

---

[1] This work, 'Die Religion des Buddha,' by Carl Friederich Koeppen, has been long out of print, and has unfortunately never been translated into English. The German is not often difficult, and I have endeavoured to give a correct idea of Koeppen's statements in the instances in which I have made use of them. It is now somewhat out of date.

title appears to have been introduced immediately after Gautama's death.

It is believed that ever since the time of the great Aśoka, Sthaviras or Elders who became actual superintendents of monasteries, exercised administrative powers, like those of Abbots; each over his own monastic community. This was the first kind of Headship recognized. It was simply a superiority of age.

As to any still higher form of authority corresponding to that of Pope, Archbishop, or Bishop, and extending over several monasteries, this did not belong to early Buddhism or to its earliest developments. Lists of uninterrupted series of pretended Buddhist Hierarchs exist, but are mere fanciful fabrications. Nevertheless, it is certainly a historical fact that along with the superiority of mere age, seniority, and experience, there rapidly grew up *pari passu* a superiority of knowledge, learning, and sanctity, which were generally, though not invariably, combined in the person of the presiding Elder.

Any one, in fact, who was distinguished for the practice of the highest degree of meditation, for complete acquaintance with the Law, for special purity of conduct, and perfect fulfilment of the precepts, was naturally elevated above the class of ordinary Bhikshus. Such a monk was from the earliest times dignified by the title Arhat, 'very reverend,' i.e. more worthy of honour than the generality. Arhat, in short, was from the first a name for the higher grade of saint-like Bhikshu. Such a man, too, before long, was raised to a still higher level in the estimation of his fellow-monks.

He was believed to have delivered himself from all the consequences of acts, whether bad or good—from all the fetters (see p. 127) of life, and therefore from all re-birth. He was even elevated to a still loftier pinnacle. He was believed by his superstitious admirers to possess unlimited dominion over nature, space, time, and matter; to be all-seeing, all-powerful, and capable of working every kind of miracle. Then, of course, at death he passed away in Pari-nirvāṇa and was, so to speak, canonized. Be it noted, however, that such canonization was never accorded to an Arhat till after his departure from the world.

Probably the immediate disciples of Gautama Buddha—that is, his so-called 'great pupils' (see p. 47), were all considered perfect Arhats. And these perfect Arhats were probably the only saints of the earliest period of Buddhism. Yet there was one who surpassed them all by an immeasurable interval, and that one was Gautama Buddha himself. It was the distinguishing mark of a supreme Buddha that he was infinitely greater than all other Arhats, because he had not only gained perfect knowledge himself, but had become the Saviour of the whole world by imparting to men the knowledge of how they were to save themselves.

It seems, therefore, only natural that the followers of Buddha, and probably the Buddha himself, before his decease, should have thought it desirable to establish a more systematic gradation of saintship by filling up the immense gap between ordinary Arhats and the supreme Buddha. It was this that led to the idea of Pratyeka-Buddhas, that is, self-dependent solitary

Buddhas[1] (see p. 134), as well as to the notion of a still higher being called a Bodhi-sattva, who, as the Buddha-designate and future successor of Gautama, occupied a still more exalted intermediate position than a Pratyeka-Buddha.

Of course it became difficult to fix on any living man, or any recently deceased saint worthy of the highest stage of Bodhi, to which a being about to become a perfect Buddha was supposed to attain.

The first to be so elevated (though apparently not by Gautama himself) was, as frequently mentioned before, the mythical individual Maitreya. He was, we repeat, for a long time the only Bodhi-sattva recognized by all Buddhists alike, whether adherents of the Hīna-yāna or Mahā-yāna. But he was not a historical personage, like Gautama or his immediate disciples. He was a mere mythological personification of that spirit of love—of that kindly and friendly disposition towards all living beings by force of which Buddhism hoped one day to conquer the world, and win it over to itself.

And in conformity with his mythical character, and probably to prevent the rivalry of pretenders among future ambitious heads of monasteries, he was not to appear for five thousand years, till the teaching of Gautama had lost its power.

Indeed, it was only to be expected that this rank should at first have been accorded to one person alone

---

[1] It is obvious to remark that in the same way those who are intellectually self-dependent and self-raised among ourselves generally rise to a higher level of popular esteem than those taught by other men.

—just as in worldly affairs there could be only one Heir-apparent to the throne.

Such was the more simple doctrine of early Buddhism in regard to the relative position of the members of the Buddhist community.

How then did the teachers of the Mahā-yāna proceed to amplify this doctrine?

They taught that there were two methods of salvation or, so to speak, two ways or two vehicles—the Great and the Little (Mahā-yāna and Hīna-yāna)—and indeed two Bodhis or forms of true knowledge which these vehicles had to convey[1]. The 'Great Method' was for the generality, the 'Little' was far more exclusive in its teaching. The 'Little Method' was the early doctrine and had many Arhats but only one Bodhi-sattva. The 'Great Method,' on the other hand, was the later and broader, which had many Bodhi-sattvas as well as many Arhats. He who satisfied the usual requirements of Saintship received the rank of an Arhat in both systems. But in the 'Great' system every one who aimed at unusual sanctity on the one hand, and knowledge (Bodhi) on the other, might walk on the broad road leading to Bodhi-sattvaship, and receive the title Bodhi-sattva.

We have seen (p. 136) that the Hīna-yāna, or 'Little system,' taught that there were only twenty-four Buddhas who had preceded Gautama. Three of these (viz. Kraku-ććhanda, Kanaka-muni, and Kāśyapa), with Gautama as a fourth, had appeared in the present age, and only one Bodhi-sattva (Maitreya) was to come.

[1] There was also a 'middle way,' see p. 159.

But according to the 'Great System,' it was a mistake to limit the acquisition of the highest Saintship in this manner. It maintained that there would be numberless supreme Buddhas (and, in addition to them, self-taught, solitary Buddhas, called Pratyeka-Buddhas), as well as numberless Bodhi-sattvas, even in the present age of the world. In other words, it propounded the doctrine that the practice of the six (or ten) transcendent virtues (p. 128), and especially the acquisition of transcendent wisdom (prajñā pāramitā), might qualify many saints for the attainment of Bodhi-sattvaship and Buddhaship. According to one theory, there were to be at least a thousand Bodhi-sattvas, followed by a thousand Buddhas, while, according to others, Buddhas and Bodhi-sattvas were to be reckoned by myriads.

But this theory of numberless Bodhi-sattvas involved an entirely new view of their nature and of the meaning of the term.

In fact, the Bodhi-sattvas of the more developed Mahā-yāna school were not Bodhi-sattvas at all, according to the strict sense of the term. It is true they resembled the genuine Bodhi-sattva in having gone through a long series of existences leading them at last to perfect saintship and to a heaven of their own, but they were under no obligation to give up their Bodhi-sattvaship, quit their celestial abodes, or descend ultimately as human Buddhas upon earth.

Furthermore, they never appeared to aim at Pari-nirvāṇa like their earthly counterparts. Their most obvious *raison d'être* seems to have been to supply the need of personal objects of worship, and though in Tibet they were believed to have their own secondary corporeal emanations—sometimes called their 'incarnations,' but more properly described as descents (avatāra) of portions of their essence in a constant succession of human saints, —they never really left their own permanent stations in the heavenly regions. Indeed, it is probable that the chief cause of their popularity, as personal objects of adoration, was that they were able to help their worshippers to attain to the same permanent and unchangeable regions of bliss.

It was thus that the 'Great Vehicle' took up an attitude which raised it not only above the simple effort to suppress the passions and desires, but also above the hopeless Nihilism of early Buddhism; for it soon became the fashion for the most devoted and pious of Buddhist monks to aspire to the title and actual blessedness of Bodhi-sattvaship rather than to the doubtful blessedness of utter personal annihilation involved in Buddhahood. At any rate the numerous Bodhi-sattvas of the 'Great Method' appear to have remained quite contented with their condition, so long as it involved perpetual residence in the heavens, and quite willing to put off all desire for Buddhahood and Pari-nirvāṇa.

Without doubt, this more amplified system was the result of a reaction of Brāhmanism on Buddhism. It was at first a mere plan for creating a close Hierarchy like that of the Brāhman caste—that is to say, a privileged class of men possessed of higher knowledge and sanctity and superior to the majority of Bhikshus of the common stamp. Then it soon developed into a scheme for satisfying the craving of the masses for divinities of some kind to whom they might appeal for help in time of need.

In all probability the first to receive the title of Bodhi-sattva, next to Maitreya, were the most celebrated Arhats before mentioned, who were immediate disciples of Gautama, not however till death had separated them from their human frames, when, as a matter of course, they received a kind of worship like that accorded to all leaders of men, just as the earliest saints, heroes, and teachers of Brāhmanism did.

To specify all the Arhats who were elevated to the rank of Bodhi-sattva and became objects of veneration in later times would be a difficult and unprofitable task.

We may also dismiss, as unworthy of note, statements such as that in the Lalita-vistara, in which it is declared that 32,000 Bodhi-sattvas joined the Buddha's assembly in the Jetavana garden. But we may notice the quasi-deification of a few historical personages mentioned by the two Chinese travellers, whose account of the state of Buddhism in India from the fourth to the seventh centuries has been so often quoted.

First of all came the immediate followers and so-called 'great pupils' (see p. 47) of Gautama, namely, his two chief disciples, Ṡāri-puttra and Moggallāna (Maudgalyāyana = Modgala-puttra)[1], both of whom are believed to have died before him. Then came the three great leaders at the first Council: 1. Kāṡyapa (pp. 46, 55); 2. Gautama's cousin and beloved pupil Ānanda; 3. Upāli (note, p. 56).

[1] See pp. 47, 104. Koeppen compares them to St. Peter and St. Paul.

Next to these perhaps the most celebrated teacher elevated to Bodhi-sattvaship was Nāgārjuna [1]—noticed before as the alleged founder of the Mahā-yāna system and its introducer into Tibet. According to one account he was the son of a Brāhman of Vidarbha, and taught Buddhism in the south of India. He had a celebrated disciple named Deva (or Ārya-deva) [2]. Nāgārjuna was at any rate a great teacher and developer of the Mahā-yāna. A legend relates that he was skilled in magic, and was able thereby to prolong his own and a Southern Indian king's life indefinitely. This caused great grief to the mother of the Heir-apparent, who instigated her son to ask Nāgārjuna for his own head. Nāgārjuna complied with the request, and cut his own head off with a blade of Kuśa grass, nothing else having the power to injure him. He is said by Hiouen Thsang to have lived in Southern Kośala about 400 years after the death of Gautama, and is worshipped under different epithets in Tibet, China, Mongolia, and even Ceylon. Probably he lived in the first or second century—Beal places him between A. D. 166 and 200. Wassiljew considers him a wholly mythical personage. The additions he made to Buddhist doctrines were undoubtedly great. When he died Stūpas were erected to his memory, and in some places he was even worshipped as Buddha.

---

[1] The Rev. S. Beal (Ind. Antiquary for Dec., 1886) shows that Nāgārjuna and Nāgasena are two different persons. Sir A. Cunningham is of the same opinion. It may be noted that Padma-sambhava is credited with introducing the more corrupt form of Buddhism along with magic into Tibet at a later date, probably in the eighth century.

[2] For the account of Nāgārjuna's disciple Deva, mentioned by Hiouen Thsang, see Beal's Records, ii. 97.

Among other deified, or partially deified Bodhisattvas, whose images and Stūpas (p. 161) the Chinese pilgrims found scattered in various parts of India, may be mentioned, those of the mythical Buddhas who preceded Gautama, especially Kāśyapa[1]. Then we have Rāhula (son of Gautama), the patron of all novices, and founder of the realistic school called Vaibhāshika[2]; Dharma-pāla, Vasu-mitra (or Vasu-bandhu), Aśva-ghosha, Guṇamati, Sthiramati, and others. In this practice of deifying their saints, Buddhists merely followed the example of the adherents of Hindūism. And we may add that this tendency is constantly repeating itself in the religious history of all nations.

There is even a tendency to press the saints of other countries into the service. This is exemplified in the history of Barlaam and Josaphat, written by St. John of Damascus in the eighth century. The story of Josaphat is almost that of Buddha (Josaphat being possibly for Bodhisat). The zealous Roman Catholics of those days thought that they could not exclude so noble a monk from the list of their saints, and so registered him as St. Josaphat. Sir Henry Yule (Marco Polo, II, 308) states that a church in Palermo is dedicated to this saint.

And here mention may be made of a modern deified Hindū teacher or sage, named Gorakh-nāth, who is said to have gone from India into Nepāl, and is worshipped

---

[1] Of course not to be confounded with Gautama's disciple of the same name, who is generally called Mahā-Kāśyapa.

[2] According to Eitel he is still revered as the patron-saint of all novices, and is to be re-born as the eldest son of every future Buddha; see Legge's Fā-hien, p. 46.

there as well as at Gorakh-pur and throughout the Panjāb. Very little is known about him, and he belongs more to Hindūism than to Buddhism. Some say that he was a cotemporary of Kabīr (1488–1512), and, according to a Janamsākhī, he once had an interview with Nānak, the founder of the Sikh sect. Such legendary accounts as are current are wrapped in much mystery. One legend describes him as born from a lotus.

Others describe him as the third or fourth in a series of Śaiva teachers, and the founder of the Kānphāṭā sect of Yogīs. The remarkable thing about him is that he succeeded in achieving an extraordinary degree of popularity among Northern Hindūs and among some adherents of Buddhism in Nepāl. His tomb is in the Panjāb, and he is to this day adored as a kind of god by immense numbers of the inhabitants of North Western India under the hills.

But the canonization of such historical teachers in India and their elevation to semi-divine rank did not satisfy the craving of the uneducated masses, either among Buddhists or Hindūs, for personal deities, possessed of powers over human affairs far greater than any departed human beings, however eminent. In Buddhism the supposed existence of the more god-like Bodhi-sattva Maitreya—venerated by both the Mahā-yāna and the Hīna-yāna schools—was not sufficient to satisfy this craving.

Hence the 'Great Vehicle' soon began to teach the existence of numerous mythological Bodhi-sattvas, other than Maitreya, to whom no historical character belonged, but whose functions were more divine.

LECTURE IX.

Theistic and Polytheistic Buddhism.

In the preceding Lecture I have endeavoured to sketch the rise of theistic and polytheistic Buddhism.

We have now to turn our attention to its development, especially in regard to the worship of mythical Bodhi-sattvas, and of the Hindū gods and other mythological beings.

Some of the Bodhi-sattvas of the Mahā-yāna or Great System were merely quasi-deifications of eminent saints and teachers. Others were impersonations of certain qualities or forces; and just as in early Buddhism we have the simple triad of the Buddha, his Law, and his Order, so in Northern Buddhism the worship of mythical Bodhi-sattvas—other than Maitreya—was originally confined to a triad, namely (1) Mañju-śrī, 'he of beautiful glory;' (2) Avalokiteśvara, 'the looking-down lord,' often called Padma-pāṇi, 'the lotus-handed;' (3) Vajra-pāṇi or Vajra-dhara, 'the thunderbolt-handed.'

These three mythical Bodhi-sattvas were not known to early Buddhists, nor to the Buddhists of Ceylon. They are not even found in the oldest books of the Northern School (such as the Lalita-vistara), though they occur conspicuously in the Saddharma-puṇḍarīka.

All we can say with certainty is, that when Fā-hien visited Mathurā on the Jumnā 400 years after Christ, their cult certainly existed there at that time.

We shall not be far wrong if we assert that it was adopted in about the third century of our era.

As already indicated (see p. 175), the idea of the first Buddhist triad—the Buddha, the Law, and the Monastic Order—accepted by the adherents of both Vehicles—was probably derived from the earliest Brāhmanical triad. (See also Brāhmanism and Hindūism, pp. 9, 44, 74.)

In the same way the second Buddhist triad introduced by the advanced teachers of the 'Great Vehicle,' viz. Mañju-śrī, Avalokiteśvara (=Padma-pāṇi), and Vajra-pāṇi, corresponded to the later Hindū triad (tri-mūrti) of deities, Brahmā, Vishṇu, and Śiva.

I have explained in 'Brāhmanism and Hindūism' (pp. 54, 73) how the gods Vishṇu and Śiva gradually usurped the position of the god Brahmā, whom they dispossessed of his co-equality with themselves, and how the whole mythology of the Hindūs, which was originally complicated by a large admixture of pre-Āryan and Vedic elements, ultimately became more simplified by arranging itself under the two heads of Vaishṇavism and Śaivism, all other mythological personages being regarded as forms of either Vishṇu or Śiva.

In contradistinction to this, we find that each member of the two Buddhist triads holds its own, and we are led on to a system which bewilders us by ever increasing complications—a system which preserves the individuality of its own triads and deified saints, and yet recognizes almost all the gods, demigods, demons, and supernatural beings of Hindūism.

I propose now to offer some account of the development of the Buddhist Pantheon, beginning with the mythical conceptions peculiar to Buddhism, and passing on to those held in common with Hindūism.

And first as to the second Buddhist triad abovenamed, it may be noted, as a proof of the very gradual growth of Buddhistic mythology, that in the earlier developments of Buddhism the three Bodhi-sattvas constituting that triad have very restricted functions.

When I visited the Buddhist caves at Elorā, I noticed that in the ancient sculptures there, Padmapāṇi and Vajra-pāṇi (but not Mañju-śrī) are represented as attendants of the human Buddha.

Of course it is easy to understand that the duty of guarding the Buddha ultimately expanded into that of watching over and protecting the whole Buddhist world, though it is difficult to determine which of the three mythical Bodhi-sattvas became first celebrated for the effective discharge of this duty, or to which of the three chronological precedence ought to be assigned.

Without taking the order already given, we may begin with Padma-pāṇi as the most popular, and may note that he has a name, Avalokiteśvara, composed of the two Sanskṛit words avalokita, 'looking down[1],' and Īśvara, 'lord,' the latter being the Brāhmanical name for the Supreme God—a name wholly unrecognized by early Buddhism, but assigned by the Hindūs to the three personal gods, Brahmā, Vishṇu, and Śiva, especially to the latter.

---

[1] The use of the passive participle in an active sense is not uncommon in Sanskṛit, but is generally confined to verbs involving some idea of motion.

In the duty of watching over and protecting the whole Buddhist world, Avalokiteśvara (= Padma-pāṇi), that is, 'the lord who looks down with pity on all men,' certainly takes the lead, and his name was in keeping with the reputation for answering prayer which he soon achieved.

In the Lāmism of Tibet, he is, as we shall see hereafter, a kind of divine Pope, existing eternally in the heavens as Vicar of one of the Buddhas of the present age, but delegating his functions to a succession of earthly Popes in whom he is perpetually incarnated and re-incarnated, while at the same time preserving his own personality in his own heaven.

Indeed, the popularity of his worship is one of the chief characteristics of the Mahā-yāna system, and is not confined to Tibet, though he is believed to be the special patron of that country. It is he who during the continuance of the present age of the world presides over the whole cycle of soul-migration. In a word, the temporal welfare of all living beings, and of all who have to wander through the worlds of the gods, men, demons, ghosts, animals, and livers in hell, is especially assigned to him.

People, therefore, pray to him more frequently than to any other Bodhi-sattva, and not only for release from the misery of future re-births, but in all cases of present bodily danger and domestic affliction. Hence he has numerous other names or epithets, such as 'God of mercy,' 'Ocean of pity' (Karuṇārṇava), 'Deliverer from fear' (Abhayaṃ-da), 'Lord of the world' (Lokeśvara), 'World-protector' (Loka-pāla), 'Protector of the

Āryas' (Ārya-pāla); and the Chinese traveller Fā-hien says of himself, that he prayed in his heart for the aid of Avalokiteśvara when in great peril during a storm at sea.

That his worship was very prevalent among Buddhists of the Mahā-yāna School all over India, as well as in Tibet, from the fourth to the seventh century, is attested also by Hiouen Thsang. Both travellers tell us that they frequently met with his images, which were often placed on the tops of mountains. Possibly this fact may account for the name he acquired of the 'Looking-down lord.' Or, on the other hand, it is possible that his name may have led to the selection of high situations for his temples and images.

And it may be observed here that although Avalokiteśvara bears a close resemblance in character to Vishṇu, yet his images often conform to the Brahmā type, and sometimes to that of Śiva [1]. He has generally several faces—sometimes even eleven or twelve—and usually four or eight arms. These faces are placed one above the other in the form of a pyramid, in three tiers, and probably indicate that he looks down on all three worlds, namely, the worlds of desire, of true form, and of no form (pp. 213, 214), from all points of the horizon.

Note, however, that two of his hands are generally folded, as if adoring the Buddha, while his two other hands hold such emblems as the lotus and wheel (especially the lotus). This distinguishes the images

[1] See Beal's Records, i. 114, note 107.

of the mere Bodhi-sattva Avalokiteśvara from those of the god Vishṇu, who, although he has four arms, is never represented in an attitude of adoration. Note, too, that the many-headed images of Avalokiteśvara probably belong to the later phase of the Mahā-yāna, when he was regarded as an emanation or spiritual son of the Dhyāni-Buddha Amitābha, whose head forms the eleventh above his own ten. There are descriptions of earlier idols, which make it probable that Avalokiteśvara was originally represented in ordinary human shape.

When his worship was introduced into China the name he received was Kwan-she-yin or Kwan-yin (in Japan Kwan-non)—a name denoting (according to Professor Legge) 'one who looks down on the sounds of the world, and listens to the voices of men.'

We know that each of the chief Hindū gods had his female counterpart or Śakti, who is often more worshipped than the male. Similarly the female counterpart of the male Avalokiteśvara is the form of the god chiefly worshipped in China and Japan[1]. In those countries he is only known in the feminine character of 'goddess of mercy,' and in this form is represented with two arms, but oftener with four or more, and even with a thousand eyes.

The connexion of Avalokiteśvara with Śiva, as well as with Vishṇu, is proved by the fact that in some characteristics Kwan-yin corresponds to the Durgā

[1] Professor Legge tells us that an intelligent Chinese once asked him whether 'the worship of Mary in Europe was not similar?'

form of Śiva's wife, and in others to the form called Pārvatī, who, as dwelling on mountains, may be supposed to look down with compassion on the world.

As to Vajra-pāṇi (or Vajra-dhara), 'the thunderbolt-handed,' this Bodhi-sattva corresponds in some respects to Indra. He is the fiercest and most awe-inspiring of all the Bodhi-sattvas, and was, in time, converted into a kind of Buddhistic form of Śiva, resembling that god in his character of controller of the demon-host and destroyer of evil spirits. Hiouen Thsang describes how eight Vajra-pāṇis surrounded the Buddha as an escort, when he journeyed to visit his father Śuddhodana. Vajra-pāṇi is of course a popular object of veneration in all Northern Buddhist countries, where a dread of malignant spirits is so prevalent that the waving to and fro of an implement symbolizing a thunderbolt (Vajra, or in Tibetan Dorje) is practised as a method of keeping them at bay and averting their malice.

Nevertheless, Vajra-pāṇi is not so popular as the third Bodhi-sattva, Mañju-śrī, 'he of glorious beauty,' also called Mañju-ghosha, 'having a beautiful voice,' and Vāgīśvara, 'lord of speech.' This Bodhi-sattva, as 'wisdom personified,' and as 'lord of harmony,' may be regarded as a counterpart of the Brāhmanical Brahmā or Viśva-Karman, the supposed creator of the universe. Brahmā, however, in his character of chief god, needed no Buddhistic substitute, having been incorporated by name into Buddhism. Mañju-śrī, as 'lord of speech,' seems also to be a counterpart of Brahmā's consort Sarasvatī.

According to some, a learned and eloquent Brāhman teacher, named Mañju-śrī, introduced Buddhism from

India into Nepāl about 250 years after the Nirvāṇa of Buddha, and the mythical Mañju-śrī may have been a development of the historical personage. His worship is mentioned by both Fā-hien and Hiouen Thsang[1], and seems to have been very popular.

A personification of Prajñā pāramitā, 'transcendent wisdom,' is also named. And indeed it seems natural that so soon as the Buddhists began to personify qualities and invest them with divine attributes, learning should have been among the first selected for deification, as it was by the Hindūs in early times.

Mark, however, that the popular Mañju-śrī has no place assigned to him in the Dhyāni-Buddha theory.

This mystical theory was a later development. It may be explained thus:—The term Dhyāna (Jhāna) is a general expression for the four gradations of mystic meditation which have ethereal spaces or worlds corresponding to them (p. 209), and a Dhyāni-Buddha is a Buddha who is supposed to exist as a kind of spiritual essence in these higher regions of abstract thought.

That is to say, every Buddha who appears on earth in a temporary human body—with the object of teaching men how to gain Nirvāṇa—exists also in an ideal counterpart, or ethereal representation of himself, in the formless worlds of meditation (p. 213). These ideal Buddhas are as numerous as the Buddhas, but as there are only five chief human Buddhas in the present age—Kraku-ććhanda, Kanaka-muni, Kāśyapa, Gautama, and

[1] Translation, p. 46. Beal, i. 180, ii. 220. According to Schlagintweit, a historical teacher named Mañju-śrī taught in the eighth or ninth century A. D.

the future Buddha Maitreya—so there are only five corresponding Dhyāni-Buddhas:—Vairoćana, Akshobhya, Ratna-sambhava, Amitābha, and Amogha-siddha (sometimes represented in images as possessing a third eye). But this is not all. Each of these produces by a process of evolution a kind of emanation from himself called a Dhyāni-Bodhi-sattva, to act as the practical head and guardian of the Buddhist community between the interval of the death of each human Buddha and the advent of his successor. Hence there are five Bodhi-sattvas—Samanta-bhadra, Vajra-pāṇi, Ratna-pāṇi, Padma-pāṇi (= Avalokiteśvara), and Viśva-pāṇi—corresponding to the five Dhyāni-Buddhas and to the five earthly Buddhas respectively. In Nepāl five corresponding female Śaktis or Tārā-devīs are named (see p. 216).

It is remarkable that the Chinese pilgrims from the fifth to the seventh centuries, while often mentioning the Bodhi-sattvas, make no allusion to any of the Dhyāni-Buddhas—whence we may gather that Amitābha, though adopted into Indian Buddhism, was not actually worshipped in India at least as a personal god.

In point of fact, it was only the Buddhism of the North which was not satisfied with the original triad of the Buddha, the Law, and the Monkhood. It, therefore, invented in addition five triads, each consisting of a Dhyāni-Buddha, a Dhyāni-Bodhi-sattva, and an earthly Buddha, though of these triads only one was of importance, namely, that consisting of Amitābha, Avalokiteśvara, and the human Buddha, Gautama. But the Lalita-vistara does not mention this theory.

It should be observed, too, that an important addition to the Mahā-yāna doctrine was made in certain Northern countries about the tenth century of our era.

A particular sect of Buddhists in Nepāl, calling themselves Aiśvarikas, propounded a theory of a Supreme Being (Īśvara), to whom they gave the name of a 'primordial Buddha' (Ādi-Buddha), and who was declared to be the source and originator of all things, and the original Evolver of the Dhyāni-Buddhas, or Buddhas of contemplation, while they again were supposed to evolve their corresponding Dhyāni-Bodhi-sattvas.

It is clear, of course, that this addition was a mere adaptation of Buddhism to Brāhmanism, and that the Ādi-Buddha was invented to serve as a counterpart of the One Universal Spirit Brahmă—the one eternally existing spiritual Essence, from which all existing things are mere emanations.

Sometimes, however, this Ādi-Buddha is said to have produced all things through union with Prajñā (mentioned before, p. 202), in which case he is rather to be identified with the personal Creator Brahmā.

Observe, moreover, that even in early times one of the Dhyāni-Buddhas—the one called Amitābha, 'diffusing infinite light,'—lost his purely abstract character, and was worshipped by Northern Buddhists as a personal God. He is in the present day held by them to be an eternal Being, the ideal of all that is beautiful and good, who receives his worshippers into a heaven called Sukhāvatī, 'paradise of pleasures' (see p. 183).

But it must also be noted that neither Ādi-Buddha nor Amitābha, when regarded as personal gods, were held to be Creators of the World in the Christian sense.

They were merely Supreme rulers outside and above it; for Northern Buddhists agree with Southern in thinking that the world exists of itself, and that its only Creator is the force of its own acts.

We pass on now to consider how far and with what modifications the mythology of Brāhmanism and Hindūism was incorporated into Buddhism.

I have already pointed out that although the Buddha changed the character of much of the existing mythology, he never prohibited his lay-followers from continuing their old forms of worship, or bowing down before the deities honoured by their fathers and grandfathers.

Apart indeed from the shrewd policy of not assuming an attitude of hostility to popular creeds and usages, the tolerant tendency and universality of the Buddha's teaching obliged him, in common consistency, to recognize, and as far as possible appropriate, the various religious elements existing around him, and to subordinate them to his own purposes.

In fact, according to the theory of true Buddhism, as has been well pointed out by other writers, there was only one system of doctrine and only one Law—that Law (Dharma) which Gautama Buddha came to renovate for the benefit of the world in the present age.

Hence all the apparently conflicting creeds, dogmas, forms, ceremonies, and usages of all nations, tribes, and races, were in reality mere outcomes, or dim recollections, or corruptions, of that one and the same universal Dharma which countless Buddhas had preached to mankind, in countless ages before the time of Gautama, and would continue to preach in ages to come.

Hindūism, therefore, like all other creeds, was contained in the Dharma of Buddhism, and the great object of Gautama's advent was not to uproot the old religion, but to purify it from error and restore it.

It was on this account that he regarded the Hindū gods as occupying a place in his own system, though not without some modification of the nature of their supposed position, offices, and functions.

And here it will be necessary to give an account of the later Buddhist theory of twenty-six successive tiers of heavens, one rising above the other (p. 213).

In the centre of the world-system stands, as we have seen, the vast mass of the mythical mountain Meru. On the upper portion of this stupendous axis of the universe and above the eight chief hells and the worlds of animals, ghosts, demons, and men, is situated the lowest heaven of the gods, where abide the four Mahā-rājas, 'great champions,' or guardians of the earth and the heavens against the demons, who are ever engaged in assailing them from their world below. These four are represented in full armour, with drawn swords; one quarter of the heavens being assigned to the guardianship of each; viz. the East to Dhṛita-rāshṭra, king of the Gandharvas; the South to Virūḍhaka, king of the Kumbhāṇḍas; the West to Virūpāksha, king of the Nāgas; the North to Kuvera (Vaiśravaṇa), king of the Yakshas. The inhabitants of this heaven are called Ćatur-mahārāja-kāyikas, or simply Mahārājika-devāḥ. Above this lowest heaven, and on the highest summit of the world's axis, Meru, is enthroned the god Śakra (Indra), known in the Veda as god of the atmosphere. He is a lord of a heaven of his own, and no god is more popular among Buddhists or oftener named in their legends; yet he is inferior to Mahābrahmā and to Māra (p. 208). Buddha himself was Indra in some of his births (p. 111). To this heaven he ascended to preach the Law to his mother (see pp. 414–418).

Hence we may infer that in the early days of Buddhism, Indra, who was perhaps the chief god of the Ṛig-veda, was still the favourite god of the people.

His heaven forms the second tier, reckoning from the lowest upwards (see p. 213), and is called Trayastrinśa (Tāvatinsa), that of the thirty-three divinities—as recognized in the Vedic hymns—consisting of the three groups of eleven Rudras, eight Vasus, and twelve Ādityas, together with personifications of Heaven and Earth.

The remaining heavens of the gods, which rise in succession above the lowest and above Indra's and therefore in the sky above Mount Meru, are the third, fourth, fifth, and sixth. These are not illuminated by the sun and moon, since the gods who live in them give out a sufficient light from their own persons. The first of them, or third of the heavens, is inhabited by beings called Yāmas. They were known to the Brāhmans and probably presided over the periods of the day. They are called 'strifeless,' because they have not to take part in the war constantly being waged by the gods of the two lower heavens against the demons (Asuras), who are unable to advance into the regions above Meru.

The fourth heaven is that of the Tushitas or 'perfectly contented beings.' It is a peculiarly sacred region, as it is the home of all the Bodhi-sattvas destined to become Buddhas. Gautama Buddha once dwelt there (p. 113), and Maitreya now presides in it.

The fifth heaven is inhabited by the Nirmāṇa-rati-devāḥ, that is, 'beings who constantly enjoy pleasures provided by themselves.'

The sixth heaven, and the highest of the Deva-lokas, is the abode of the Para-nirmita-vaśa-varti-devāḥ, 'beings who constantly enjoy pleasures provided for them by others.' These beings are also called Māras, and are 'lords of sensuous desires.' When the theory of races of gods was invented, it led to the figment of millions of Māras ruled over by a chief Māra, who tempts men to indulge their passions (pp. 28, 33, 41), and is always on the watch to enter the citadel of the body by the gates of eye, ear, etc. (see note, p. 129). One of Māra's names is Kāma, 'desire.' He is superior to all the gods of the worlds of sense, even to Śakra or Indra. In every Ćakravāla or Universe of worlds there is a Māra. He is sometimes called the Buddhist Satan, but this is misleading. He is rather a superior god, whose power consists in exciting sensual or carnal desires.

So far, then, the heavens are all worlds of sense,—like the earth and the lower regions,—and are spheres inhabited by beings who have sexual feelings and live active lives. But at this point in the ascent upwards all sensuality ceases, and we are introduced to beings who enjoy a higher condition of existence in which there is no distinction of sex, and all sensuous desires and objects have lost their hold over the frame—a condition supposed to be induced by the exercise of mystical abstract meditation (Dhyāna, Pāli Jhāna).

The importance of Dhyāna or intense abstract meditation in the Buddhist system has been pointed out before (p. 32). It is the chief religious exercise in which a true follower of Buddha can engage, and although it is divided into four stages, the man who exercises himself perfectly in any one of the four, becomes so sublimated and refined that he cannot be re-born in any of the sensuous heavens, or in any region lower than the Brahmā worlds.

The first stage of Dhyāna consists in fixing (Dhāraṇā) the mind and at the same time exercising the thinking faculties on some object, in such a way that a state of ecstatic joy and serenity is attained.

The second consists in concentrating the mind or soul so intensely on itself that the thinking faculties cease to act and only ecstatic joy and serenity remain.

In the third, nothing remains but perfect serenity.

The fourth is a trance-like condition of utter indifference and torpor, in which there is neither any exercise of thought, nor any conscious joy or serenity, but the whole being is released from the fetters of sense and soars to a transcendental condition, characterized by latent energy and a power of working miracles (p. 133).

These four stages of abstract meditation must not be confused with the four earnest reflections and the five contemplations (pp. 49, 127), which are not so abstract and require more earthly objects on which to be exercised.

The fourth and last Dhyāna is also called Samādhi, and properly means such a perfect concentration of the soul's faculties, that the soul becomes merged in itself. It is often used to denote an ecstatic condition, scarcely to be distinguished from trance or hypnotism or catalepsy. Those devotees in India who practise it are buried, not burnt, and their tombs are called Samādhs.

To return now to Buddhist Cosmology, the theory of later Buddhism is that he who has practised the first Dhyāna will rise at death to one of the three tiers of heavens connected with that first Dhyāna, i.e. to the first and lowest of the four groups of worlds of true form (rūpa), *in which all sexual distinctions are obliterated*.

This first or lowest group consists of the worlds of the Brahmās, a high order of gods divided into three classes with three tiers of abodes.

The first class of Brahmā gods, inhabiting the first or lowest of the tiers of the Brahmā abodes, consists of the Brahma-parisajjā devāḥ, or beings who constitute the retinue of the god Mahā-brahmā—the chief of all the Buddhist gods.

The second class of Brahmā gods, inhabiting the second tier, consists of the Brahma-purohitā devāḥ, 'beings who are the ministers of Mahā-brahmā.'

The third class of Brahmā gods, inhabiting the highest of the three tiers, consists of the Mahā-brahmās, 'great Brahmās,' of whom Mahā-brahmā is the chief.

The inhabitants of these three worlds are sometimes called the Brahma-kāyikā devāḥ, 'gods having a Brahmā form.'

It is important, however, to note that Brahmā or Mahā-brahmā, sometimes called Brahmā Sahām-pati, 'lord of those who have to suffer[1],' is the king of *all* the higher heavens (p. 214), ruling there, as Māra and Indra do in the lower worlds and heavens of sense and desire. Out of deference to Brāhmanism he has been adopted as the chief god of the Buddhist Pantheon, and yet he is far inferior to the Buddha.

Furthermore, it is to be observed that every Ćakra-vāla or 'system of worlds' (see p. 120) has its own Mahā-brahmā ruling over its own higher heavens, and that as there are countless Ćakra-vālas, so there are countless Mahā-brahmās. Nor is any of these chief gods eternal. Each has to pass into some other form of existence at the end of vast periods of time, and is then succeeded by another. Gautama Buddha himself was born four times as Mahā-brahmā (see p. 111).

The second group of worlds of true form has also three tiers of heavens like the first, and is assigned as an abode to those who have risen to the second degree of contemplation.

The characteristic of these three heavens is that they are regions of true light—not of the sun's light, but of mental enlightenment, and each of the three is inhabited by beings who have raised themselves to different heights of knowledge and intelligence.

In the first are the Parīttābhā (Parīttābhā) devāḥ, 'beings of circumscribed or limited enlightenment;' in

[1] Even the Brahmās, after immense periods of life in the Brahmā heavens, have to go through other births in one of the six ways of migration. Saham-pati may therefore mean 'the lord of sufferers,' 'all life involving suffering,' and this excludes the idea of his 'being lord over the Buddha who has not to be born again.'

the second are the Apramāṇābhā (Appamāṇābhā) devāḥ, 'beings of infinite light;' in the third are the Ābhāsvarā (Ābhassarā) devāḥ, 'beings of the clearest light.'

The third group of worlds of true form has again three tiers of heavens, which are assigned to those who have raised themselves to the third stage of contemplation.

The peculiarity of these three seems to be that they are regions of the greatest purity, and that each of the three is the abode of beings distinguished by higher and higher degrees of purity. In the first are the Parītta-śubhā (Parītta-subhā) devāḥ, 'gods or beings of limited purity;' in the second are the Apramāṇa-śubhā (Appamāna-subhā) devāḥ, 'beings of unlimited purity;' in the third are the Śubha-kṛitsnā (Subha-kiṇṇā) devāḥ, 'beings of absolute purity.'

The fourth group of worlds of true form has seven tiers of heavens, occupied by those beings who have risen to the fourth or highest grade of abstract meditation (Dhyāna), which is really a state of meditating on nothing and of complete indifference to all concrete objects. These beings are the emancipated Arhats who have delivered themselves from the cycle (Saṃsāra) of constant re-birth (p. 134).

In the first tier are the Vṛihat-phalā (Vehapphalā) devāḥ, 'beings enjoying great reward;' in the second are the Asañjñi-sattvā (Asañña-sattā) devāḥ, 'beings lost in total unconsciousness;' in the third are the Avṛihā (Avihā) devāḥ, 'beings who make no efforts;' in the fourth are the Atapā (Atappā) devāḥ, 'beings who never endure any pain;' in the fifth are the Sudarśā (Sudassā) devāḥ, 'beings who see clearly;' in the sixth are the Sudarśino (Sudassī) devāḥ, 'beings of beautiful appearance;' in the seventh are the Akanishṭhā (Akaniṭṭhā) devāḥ, 'highest of all beings.' In this last must be included all Arhats and Pratyeka-Buddhas.

High above the worlds of true form and above the abode of pure contemplative beings, rise the four heavens of formless entities—beings who have no material frames, even of the subtlest kind, but are mere abstractions, such as the Dhyāni-Buddhas (pp. 202, 203).

In the first of these formless heavens (Arūpa-loka) are the Ākāśānantyāyatanā devāḥ, 'beings who are capable of conceiving the idea of infinite space;' in the second are the Vijñānānantyāyatanā devāḥ, 'beings who are capable of conceiving the idea of infinite intelligence;' in the third are the Ākiñćanyāyatanā devāḥ, 'beings who can conceive the idea of absolute nonentity,' or, in other words, that nothing whatever exists anywhere; in the fourth and highest of all are the Naivasañjñānāsañjñāyatanā devāḥ (Nevasaññānāsaññāya°-), 'beings who abide in neither consciousness nor unconsciousness.' This is the most sublime of all conditions, but these heavens belong to mystical Buddhism.

Subjoined is a synopsis of all the heavens and their inhabitants explained above (see Koeppen i. 260).

A.

Heavens of beings liable to sensuous desires.

(1) Heaven of the four Mahā-rājas.
(2) Heaven of the Trayastriṉśas.
(3) Heaven of the Yāmas.
(4) Heaven of the Tushitas.
(5) Heaven of the Nirmāṇa-rati-devāḥ.
(6) Heaven of the Para-nirmita-vaśa-vartins.

B.

Heavens of beings possessing true forms.

First Dhyāna.

(7) Heaven of the Brahma-parisajjā devāḥ.
(8) Heaven of the Brahma-purohitā devāḥ.
(9) Heaven of the Mahā-brahmā devāḥ.

Second Dhyāna.

(10) Heaven of the Parīttābhā devāḥ.
(11) Heaven of the Apramāṇābhā devāḥ.
(12) Heaven of the Âbhāsvarā devāḥ.

Third Dhyāna.

(13) Heaven of the Parītta-śubhā devāḥ.
(14) Heaven of the Apramāṇa-śubhā devāḥ.
(15) Heaven of the Śubha-kṛitsnā devāḥ.

Fourth Dhyāna.

(16) Heaven of the Vṛihat-phalā devāḥ.
(17) Heaven of the Asañjñi-sattvā devāḥ.
(18) Heaven of the Avṛihā devāḥ.
(19) Heaven of the Atapā devāḥ.
(20) Heaven of the Sudarśā devāḥ.
(21) Heaven of the Sudarśino devāḥ.
(22) Heaven of the Akanishṭhā devāḥ.

C.

Heavens of formless entities.

(23) Heaven of the Ākāśānantyāyatanā devāḥ.
(24) Heaven of the Vijñānānantyāyatanā devāḥ.
(25) Heaven of the Ākiñćanyāyatanā devāḥ.
(26) Heaven of the Naiva-sañjñānāsañjñāyatanā devāḥ.

This elaborate description of higher and higher conditions of future existence may be contrasted with the reticence of the Bible and its simple allusion to a new heaven and a new earth, wherein dwelleth righteousness.

The description, however, belongs to later Buddhism. It enables us to understand the true position of the Buddhist gods. They merely constitute one of the six classes of beings, and, as they have to go through other forms of life, are inferior to Arhats and Buddhas.

Mahā-brahmā is often named, whereas Vishṇu, the popular god of the Hindūs, is neglected. In point of fact he was, as we have seen, represented by Padmapāṇi (Avalokiteśvara, p. 198), who seems to have taken his place in later Buddhism.

At all events the more modern form of Vishṇu called Kṛishṇa, who is generally worshipped by the lower orders of Hindūs as the most popular god of mediæval Hindūism, has not been adopted by the inhabitants of Buddhist countries.

When I was at Kandy in Ceylon I found one solitary shrine (Devālī) dedicated, not to Kṛishṇa, but to Mahā-Vishṇu. It was near the well-known Tooth-temple and appeared almost deserted. The shrine was at the end of a bare room, and contained a small silver-gilt image of Mahā-Vishṇu (as Vishṇu is called when worshipped by Buddhists, just as the chief of the Brahmā gods is called Mahā-Brahmā) about half a foot high. In the hands of the image was a thin metal bar with a kind of locket or amulet suspended from it, while round its neck was a long rosary and in front of the body a large plate for offerings. The folding doors of the sanctuary had representations of the sun and moon.

Turning to the god Śiva, we may note that he was adopted by later Buddhism in his character of Yogī, or Mahā-yogī (see 'Brāhmanism and Hindūism,' p. 83).

Then, as the Buddhism of the North very soon became corrupted with Śaivism and its accompaniments, Śāktism, Tāntrism, and Magic, so in Northern countries various forms of Śiva—such as Mahā-Kāla, Bhairava, Bhīma—and of his wife (Pārvatī, Durgā, etc.), are honoured, and their images are found in temples. Sometimes bloody sacrifices are offered to them.

Among the female deities forms of Tārā are chiefly worshipped, and regarded as Śaktis of the Buddhas.

It is even held by the disciples of the more advanced Mahā-yāna—especially in Nepāl—that there are five Śaktis or female Energies (corresponding to the five human Buddhas) whose names are given in corresponding order thus:—Vajra-dhātrī, Loćanā, Māmakī, Pāṇḍarā, and Tārā or Tārā-devī (the latter being the Tārā *par excellence*)[1].

But the goddess Tārā was also worshipped by Buddhists in India proper; for we find that Hiouen Thsaṅg alludes to having seen images of Tārā Bodhi-sattva[2] in the country of Magadha.

I may mention, too, that at Buddha-Gayā, not far from the Vāgīśvarī temple, which contains the circular so-called Vajrāsana or thunderbolt-seat of Gautama (see p. 395), I noticed a small shrine with an image of Tārā-devī, which, from the crown of fresh flowers encircling its head, appeared to have been recently worshipped by some Buddhist pilgrims, who had arrived on the day of my visit in 1876.

[1] See Wright's Nepāl, p. 43.
[2] Beal's Records, ii. 103, 174.

The god Indra, usually called Śakra (Sakka), is, as we have seen, the most popular god of the early Buddhist Pantheon (pp. 51, 207). He is a friendly deity and never exerts evil influences over men, like Māra. On the contrary, if any good man is in need of his services he descends from his own heaven to render assistance; and the fact of his aid being required is made known to the god by his throne becoming hot.

The Dharma-pada (107, 392) mentions Agni, god of fire, and again (48), Antaka, god of death, sometimes identified with Māra or with Yama, 'ruler in Hell.' A form of Yama called Yamāntaka is also recognized.

In Ceylon I observed several shrines to Kanda-Kumāra, a form of Skanda (son of Śiva), who is said to have received the gift of healing from Buddha.

There also I observed shrines of Saman (sometimes spelt Samanta, sometimes Sumana), the tutelary deity of Adam's Peak, which is thence called Samanta-kūṭo and Sumana-kūṭo.

Then there were shrines dedicated to a demoniacal goddess called Paṭṭinī (regarded sometimes as protecting from small-pox), and to certain good and evil genii, called Nāths (Nāthas?) in Burma.

No doubt the worship of devils and demons existed in Ceylon long before the introduction of either Brāhmanism or Buddhism. At Colombo in 1877 I witnessed a so-called devil-dance, performed late at night before the then Governor, Sir William Gregory.

First, three men dressed in coarse, loose, jet-black dresses, engaged in a wild dance together. They had shaggy hair, blackened faces daubed with white paint, and a set of six or eight long projecting false teeth, which protruded far below the lower lip, sometimes one, sometimes two at a time. Their legs were completely covered with small bells, which rattled like chains when they moved. In their hands they held three flaring torches, branching from one handle. At intervals they increased the glare and smoke from these torches by sprinkling resin upon them.

Their dance was of the wildest description, in a circle, sometimes moving in and out, and crossing each other, and all the while beating the ground violently with their jingling legs, which kept time to the noisy music of tom-toms, flageolets, horns, etc., played by attendant musicians. These three men were supposed to represent the various forms of typhus fever. At intervals during their dance they assumed frightful black masks with hideous open mouths.

Then with them were two other dancing demons dressed in red, not so hideous in appearance, who also danced holding torches. These represented another form of devil. They danced in the interval of the two performances of the black devils. There were also three men dressed in reddish garments, who formed part of the group and moved about quietly among the others. They were described to me as devil-charmers or exorcisers.

Every disease—every calamity has its presiding demon, and all such demons are the servants of Buddha.

In regard to the other supernatural beings and figments of Hindū mythology adopted, with a few unimportant modifications, by Buddhists, the first that call for mention are the Pretas (see p. 121).

The Pretas are beings of the nature of ghosts and goblins who have recently inhabited the earth, and are often of gigantic size and terrific appearance, with dried-up limbs, hairy countenances, enormous bellies, ever consumed with hunger and thirst, and yet never able to eat and drink by reason of their contracted throats. Some are represented as trying to swallow sparks of fire; others try to eat up dead bodies, or their own flesh. Possibly this form of re-birth was invented to deter the laity from withholding food from the monks. The Pretas inhabit a region above the hells. Some, however, assign them habitations above the surface of the earth or in desert places on the earth itself.

The Asuras or Daityas are evil demons who, like the Titans of Greek mythology, are always at war with the gods. They dwell under the foundations of Mount Meru, as far underneath the surface of the earth as their great enemy Indra is above it. In short, if he may be supposed to live at the zenith, they live at the nadir, and their battle-field is on the slopes of Meru.

Closely connected with them are the Rākshasas, who are also enemies of the gods and are represented as monsters of frightful form and man-eating propensities. They haunt cremation-grounds and cemeteries and way-lay human beings in solitary places to devour them.

Then there is a class of very malignant demons called Piśāćas (described in 'Brāhmanism and Hindūism,' p. 242), who are the authors of all evils.

On the other hand, the Yakshas and Yakshiṇīs are a class of good genii ruled over by Kuvera, 'god of wealth,' who is often referred to in Buddhist writings under his patronymic Vaiśravaṇa (Pāli Vessavaṇo)[1]. These beings are commonly represented in sculptures in human form and held to be harmless, though some Buddhist legends describe them as cruel. Stories are told about some of them being converted to Buddhism.

Then come the Nāgas, who are constantly alluded to. They properly belong to a class of serpent-demons, having human faces with serpent-like lower extremities, who live in one of the lower regions below the earth called Pātāla, or under the waters. They are introduced into Buddhist sculptures as worshippers of the Buddha and friends of all Buddhists, but usually represented as ordinary men. The Nāga Mućalinda (also Mućilinda), who sheltered Buddha, was a real serpent (see p. 39). Nāga-kanyās or female Nāgas (serpents from the waist downwards) are also not uncommon[2]. In Kashmīr Nāgas are connected with fountains and the sources of rivers.

Then there are the Mahoragas, 'great dragons,' who also belong to the Nāga class of demons.

We ought also to notice the Kumbhāṇḍas, a class of demons who attend on Virūḍhaka (p. 206); the Garuḍas,

---

[1] The images of this deity represent him as coarse and ill-favoured in form (his name in fact signifying 'deformed'). He has sometimes three legs. As guardian of the northern quarter he is sculptured on the corner pillar of the northern gate of the Bharhut Stūpa. He had a metropolis of his own, according to Hindū mythology (as we know from the Megha-dūta), called Alakā, on the Himālayas.

[2] A very interesting specimen of ancient sculpture representing a Nāga-kanyā may be seen in the museum of the Indian Institute, Oxford. It belongs to a collection of Buddhist antiquities lent by Mr. R. Sewell, of the Madras Civil Service.

a bird-like race ruled over by the mythical Garuḍa, king of birds and enemy of the Nāgas and serpents; the Apsarases, or nymphs produced at the churning of the ocean. These last are sometimes described in Hindū mythology as the Hūrīs of Indra's heaven, who are assigned to heroes killed in battle. In Buddhist sculptures they are represented as beautiful females, who are properly the wives of Indra's celestial musicians called Gandharvas.

Finally, mention should be made of the Kinnaras and Kinnarīs—beings who ought properly to be represented with human bodies and equine heads, and are, like the Gandharvas, heavenly musicians. It is even recorded in one legend that the Buddha himself in a former life was a Kinnarī.

All this proves the close connexion of Buddhism with the Hindūism which, like Buddhism, grew out of Brāhmanism. In short, the one mythology is so interpenetrated with the other, that Buddhism in making proselytes throughout Eastern Asia could not avoid propagating Hindū mythological doctrines along with its own.

The consequence was that Hindūism, though often regarded as an unproselyting and wholly national religion, really exercised a vast influence outside its own boundaries and among alien races.

It is, at any rate, a remarkable fact that no mythological system has ever spread over so large an area of the earth's surface as that which, originating in India, was accepted to a great extent by all Buddhist communities. And this Indo-Buddhistic system of mythology, with its, to us, absurd idolatry, rests on an extremely subtle form of pantheism, which is not to be brushed aside as too contemptible for investigation.

It is usual to denounce all such systems as simple Heathenism; but 'Heathenism' means the religion of 'the nations'—the religion evolved by the men of all countries out of their own imaginations and by their own natural faculties, without the aid of any true supernatural revelation.

And assuredly this religion of human nature is still a strong citadel entrenched behind the formidable forces of pride, passion, prejudice, and ignorance. Yet the walls of the fortress have numerous weak places, which the wise missionary, armed with the still more powerful forces at his command, will endeavour to discover and quietly undermine. By patient and quiet working he must win the day.

With man, speed and rapidity of action are supposed to be the chief evidences of progress and the chief factors in success. The Evangelist, on the other hand, is a worker for God and a fellow-worker with God, and ought not to be discouraged by the tardy advance of the Truth which he advocates. He may have his moments of despondency, but he has only to look around and observe that God works everywhere throughout His own Universe by slow and almost imperceptible processes. The ripe fruit falls from the tree in a second, but its maturity is not effected without a whole year of gradual preparation.

LECTURE X.

Mystical Buddhism in its connexion with the Yoga philosophy.

THE first idea implied by Buddhism is intellectual enlightenment. But Buddhism has its own theory of enlightenment—its own idea of true knowledge, which it calls Bodhi, not Veda. By true knowledge it means knowledge acquired by man through his own intellectual faculties and through his own inner consciousness, instincts, and intuitions, unaided by any external or supernatural revelation of any kind.

But it is important to observe that Buddhism, in the carrying out of its own theory of entire self-dependence in the search after truth, was compelled to be somewhat inconsistent with itself. It enjoined self-conquest, self-restraint, self-concentration, and separation from the world for the attainment of true knowledge and for the accomplishment of its own *summum bonum*—the bliss of Nirvāṇa—the bliss of deliverance from the fires of passion and the flames of concupiscence. Yet it encouraged association and combination for mutual help. It established a universal brotherhood of celibate monks, open to persons of all castes and ranks, to rich and poor, learned and unlearned alike —a community of men which might, in theory, be co-extensive with the whole world—all bound together by the common aim of self-conquest, all animated by the wish to aid each other in the battle with carnal desires, all penetrated by a desire to follow the example of the Buddha, and be guided by the doctrine or law which he promulgated.

Cœnobitic monasticism in fact, as we have already pointed out, became an essential part of true Buddhism and a necessary instrument for its propagation.

In all this the Buddha showed himself to be eminently practical in his methods and profoundly wise in his generation. Evidently, too, he was wise in abstaining at first from all mystical teaching. Originally Buddhism set its face against all solitary asceticism and all secret efforts to attain sublime heights of knowledge. It had no occult, no esoteric system of doctrine which it withheld from ordinary men.

Nor did true Buddhism at first concern itself with any form of philosophical or metaphysical teaching, which it did not consider helpful for the attainment of the only kind of true knowledge worth striving for—the knowledge of the origin of suffering and its remedy—the knowledge that suffering and pain arise from indulging lusts, and that life is inseparable from suffering, and is an evil to be got rid of by suppressing self and extinguishing desires.

In the Mahā-parinibbāna-sutta (Rhys Davids, II. 32) is recorded one of the Buddha's remarks shortly before his decease:—

'What, O Ānanda, does the Order desire of me? I have taught the law (desito dhammo) without making any distinction between esoteric and exoteric doctrine (anantaram abahiram karitvā). In the matter of the law, the Tathāgata (i.e. the Buddha) has never had the closed fist of a teacher (āćariya-muṭṭhi)—of a teacher who withholds some doctrines and communicates others.' In short, he was opposed to mysticism.

Nevertheless, admitting, as we must, that early Buddhism had no mysteries reserved for a privileged circle, we must not shut our eyes to the fact that the great importance attached to abstract meditation in the Buddhist system could not fail in the end to encourage the growth of mystical ideas.

Furthermore, it is undeniable that such ideas were, in some countries, carried to the most extravagant extremes. Efforts to induce a trance-like or hypnotic condition, by abstracting the thoughts from all bodily influences, by recitation of mystical sentences, and by superstitious devices for the acquisition of supernatural faculties, were placed above good works and all the duties of the moral code.

We might point, too, to the strange doctrine which arose in Nepāl and Tibet—the doctrine of the Dhyāni-Buddhas (or 'Buddhas of Meditation')—certain abstract Essences existing in the formless worlds of thought, who were held to be ethereal and eternal representatives of the transitory earthly Buddhas. These have been adverted to in a previous Lecture (see p. 202).

Our present concern is rather with the growth and development of mystical Buddhism in India itself, through its connexion with the system of philosophy called Yoga and Yogāćāra.

The close relationship of Buddhism to that system is well known; but the various practices included under the name Yoga did not owe their origin to Buddhism. They were prevalent in India before Gautama Buddha's time; and one of the most generally accepted facts in his biography is that, after abandoning his home and worldly associations, he resorted to certain Brāhman ascetics, who were practising Yoga.

What then was the object which these ascetics had in view?

The word Yoga literally means 'union' (as derived from the Sanskṛit root 'yuj,' to join; compare the English word 'yoke'), and the proper aim of every man who practised Yoga was the mystic union (or rather re-union) of his own spirit with the one eternal Soul or Spirit of the Universe. A true Yogī, says the Bhagavad-gītā (VI. 13, 25), should be indifferent to all earthly things. To him a clod, a stone, and gold should be all alike.

Doubtless this was the Buddha's first aim when he addressed himself to Yoga in the fifth century B.C., and even to this hour, earnest men in India resort to this system with the same object.

In the Indian Magazine for July, 1887 (as well as in my 'Brāhmanism and Hindūism,' p. 529), is a short biography of a quite recent religious reformer named Svāmī Dayānanda-Sarasvatī, whose acquaintance I made at Bombay in 1876 and 1877, and who only died in 1883. The story of his life reads almost like a repetition of the life of Buddha, though his teaching aimed at restoring the supposed monotheistic doctrine of the Veda.

It is recorded that his father, desiring to initiate him into the mysteries of Śaivism, took him to a shrine dedicated to the god Śiva; but the sight of some mice stealing the consecrated offerings, and of some rats playing on the heads of the idol, led him to disbelieve in Śiva-worship as a means of union with the Supreme Being. Longing, however, for such union and for emancipation from the burden of repeated births, he resolved to renounce marriage and abandon the world. Accordingly, at the age of twenty-two, he clandestinely quitted his home, the darkness of evening covering his flight. Taking a secret path, he travelled thirty miles during the night. Next day he was pursued by his father, who tried to force him to return, but in vain. After travelling farther and farther from his native province, he took a vow to devote himself to the investigation of truth. Then he wandered for many years all over India, trying to gain knowledge from sages and philosophers, but without any satisfactory result, till finally he settled at Ahmedābād. There, having mastered the higher Yoga system, he became the leader of a new sect called the Ārya-Samāj.

And here we may observe that the expression 'higher Yoga' implies that a lower form of that system had been introduced. In point of fact, the Yoga system grew, and became twofold—that is, it came in the end to have two objects.

The earlier was the higher Yoga. It aimed only at union with the Spirit of the Universe. The more developed system aimed at something more. It sought to acquire miraculous powers by bringing the body under control of the will, and by completely abstracting the soul from body and mind, and isolating it in its own essence. This condition is called Kaivalya.

In the fifth century B.C., when Gautama Buddha began his career, the later and lower form of Yoga seems to have been little known. Practically, in those days, earnest and devout men craved only for union with the Supreme Being, and absorption into his Essence. Many methods of effecting such union and absorption were contrived. And these may be classed under two chief heads—bodily mortification (tapas) and abstract meditation (dhyāna).

By either one of these two chief means, the devotee was supposed to be able to get rid of all bodily fetters—to be able to bring his bodily organs into such subjection to the spiritual that he became unconscious of possessing any body at all. It was in this way that his spirit became fit for blending with the Universal Spirit, of which it was originally a part.

We learn from the Lalita-vistara that various forms of bodily torture, self-maceration, and austerity were common in Gautama's time.

Some devotees, we read, seated themselves in one spot and kept perpetual silence, with their legs bent under them. Some ate only once a day or once on alternate days, or at intervals of four, six, or fourteen days. Some slept in wet clothes or on ashes, gravel, stones, boards, thorny grass, or spikes, or with the face downwards. Some went naked, making no distinction between fit or unfit places. Some smeared themselves with ashes, cinders, dust, or clay. Some inhaled smoke and fire. Some gazed at the sun, or sat surrounded by five fires, or rested on one foot, or kept one arm perpetually uplifted, or moved about on their knees instead of on their feet, or baked themselves on hot stones, or submerged themselves in water, or suspended themselves in air.

Then, again, a method of fasting called very painful (atikṛiććhra), described by Manu (XI. 213), was often practised. It consisted in eating only a single mouthful every day for nine days, and then abstaining from all food for the three following days.

Another method, called the lunar fast (VI. 20, XI. 216), consisted in beginning with fifteen mouthfuls at full moon, and reducing the quantity by one mouthful till new moon, and then increasing it again in the same way till full moon.

Passages without number might be quoted from ancient literature to prove that similar practices were resorted to throughout India, with the object of bringing the body into subjection to the spirit. And these practices have continued up to the present day.

A Muhammadan traveller, whose narrative is quoted by Mr. Mill (British India, i. 355), once saw a man standing motionless with his face towards the sun.

The same traveller, having occasion to revisit the same spot sixteen years afterwards, found the very same man in the very same attitude. He had gazed on the sun's disk till all sense of external vision was extinguished.

A Yogī was seen not very long ago (Mill's India,

i. 353) seated between four fires on a quadrangular stage. He stood on one leg gazing at the sun, while these fires were lighted at the four corners. Then placing himself upright on his head, with his feet elevated in the air, he remained for three hours in that position. He then seated himself cross-legged, and continued bearing the raging heat of the sun above his head and the fires which surrounded him, till the end of the day, occasionally adding combustibles with his own hands to increase the flames.

I, myself, in the course of my travels, encountered Yogīs who had kept their arms uplifted for years, or had wandered about from one place of pilgrimage to another under a perpetual vow of silence, or had no place to lie upon but a bed of spikes.

As to fasting, the idea that attenuation of the body by abstinence from food facilitates union of the human soul with the divine, or at any rate promotes a keener insight into spiritual things, is doubtless as common in Europe as in Asia; but the most austere observer of Lent in European countries would be hopelessly outdone by devotees whose extraordinary powers of abstinence may be witnessed in every part of India.

If we now turn to the second method of attaining mystic union with the Divine Essence, namely, by profound abstract thought, we may observe that it, too, was everywhere prevalent in Buddha's time.

Indeed, one of the names given by Indian philosophers to the One Universal Spirit is Ćit, 'Thought.' By that name, of course, is meant pure abstract thought, or the faculty of thought separated from every concrete object. Hence, in its highest state the eternal infinite Spirit, by its very nature, thinks of nothing. It is the simple thought-faculty, wholly unconnected with any object about which it thinks. In point of fact, the moment it begins to exercise this faculty, it necessarily abandons for a time its condition of absolute oneness, abstraction, and isolation, to associate itself with something inferior, which is not itself.

It follows, therefore, that intense concentration of the mind on the One Universal Spirit amounts to fixing the thought on a mere abstract Essence, which reciprocates no thought in return, and is not conscious of being thought about by its worshipper.

In harmony with this theory, we find that the definition of Yoga, in the second aphorism of the Yoga-sūtra, is, 'the suppression (nirodha) of the functions or modifications (vṛitti) of the thinking principle (ćitta).' So that, in reality, the union of the human mind with the infinite Principle of thought amounts to such complete mental absorption, that thought itself becomes lost in pure thought.

In the Śakuntalā (VII. 175) there is a description of an ascetic engaged in this form of Yoga, whose condition of fixed meditation and immovable impassiveness had lasted so long that ants had thrown up a mound as high as his waist, and birds had built their nests in the long clotted tresses of his tangled hair.

Not many years ago, I, myself, saw at Allahābād near the fort a devotee who had maintained a sitting, contemplative posture, with his feet folded under his body, in one place for twenty years. During the Mutiny cannon thundered over his head, and bullets hissed around him, but nothing apparently disturbed his attitude of profound meditation. Even Muhammadans practise the same. The Russian correspondent of the *Times* states (Sept. 18, 1888) that he saw in a mosque at Samarkand men who voluntarily remained mute and motionless for forty days. On a curtain being pulled aside he beheld a motionless figure seated in profound meditation like a squatting mummy. The guide said that a cannon fired off in front of his face would have left him equally unmoved.

It is clear, then, that, supposing Gautama to have made up his mind to devote himself to a religious life, his adoption of a course of profound meditation was a most usual proceeding.

A large number of the images of Buddha represent him sitting on a raised seat or throne (called the Bodhi-maṇḍa), with his legs folded under his body, and his eyes half-closed, in a condition of abstraction (samādhi) —sometimes called Yoga-nidrā; that is, a trance-like state, resembling profound sleep. (Compare frontispiece.)

He is said to have seated himself in this way under four trees in succession (see p. 39 of these Lectures), namely, under the Bodhi-tree or sacred fig-tree, under the Banyan-tree, under the Mućalinda-tree (protected by the serpent), and under the Rājāyatana-tree.

And those four successive seats probably symbolized the four recognized stages of meditation[1] (dhyāna)

---

[1] I give this as my own theory. I am no believer in the learned M. Senart's sun theory, or in its applicability to this point.

rising one above the other, till thought itself was converted into non-thought (see p. 209).

We know, too, that the Buddha went through still higher progressive stages of meditation at the moment of his death or final decease (Pari-nirvāṇa), thus described in the Mahā-parinibbāna-sutta (Davids, VI. 11):

'Then the Venerable One entered into the first stage of meditation (pathamajjhānam); and rising out of the first stage, he passed into the second; and rising out of the second, he passed into the third; and rising out of the third, he passed into the fourth; and rising out of the fourth stage, he attained the conception of the infinity of space (ākāśānañćāyatanam, see p. 214); and rising out of the conception of the infinity of space, he attained the conception of the infinity of intelligence (viññāṇañćāyatanam); and rising out of the idea of the infinity of intelligence, he attained the conception of absolute nonentity (ākiñćaññāyatanam); and rising out of the idea of nonentity, he entered the region where there is neither consciousness nor unconsciousness; and rising out of that region, he entered the state in which all sensation and perception of ideas had wholly ceased.' (See p. 213 of these Lectures.)

Clearly, even four progressive stages of abstraction did not satisfy the requirements of later Buddhism in regard to the intense sublimation of the thinking faculty needed for the complete effacement of all sense of individuality. Higher and higher altitudes had to be reached, insomuch that the fourth stage of abstract meditation is sometimes divided and subdivided into what are called eight Vimokhas and eight Samāpattis

—all of them forms and stages of ecstatic meditation[1].

A general name, however, for all the higher trance-like states is *Samādhi*, and by the practice of Samādhi the six transcendent faculties (Abhiññā) might ultimately be obtained, viz. the inner ear, or power of hearing words and sounds, however distant (clair-audience, as it might be called); the inner eye, or power of seeing all that happens in every part of the world (clair-voyance); knowledge of the thoughts of others; recollection of former existences; the knowledge of the mode of destroying the corrupting influences of passion; and, finally, the supernatural powers called Iddhi, to be subsequently explained.

But to return to the Buddha's first course of meditation at the time when he first attained Buddhahood. This happened during one particular night, which was followed by the birthday of Buddhism.

And what was the first grand outcome of that first profound mental abstraction? One legend relates that in the first watch of the night all his previous existences flashed across his mind; in the second he understood all present states of being; in the third he traced out the chain of causes and effects, and at the dawn of day he knew all things.

According to another legend, there was an actual outburst of the divine light before hidden within him.

We read in the Lalita-vistara (chap. i) that at the supreme moment of his intellectual illumination brilliant flames of light issued from the crown of his head,

[1] These are described in Childers's Pāli Dictionary, s.v.

through the interstices of his cropped hair. These rays are sometimes represented in his images, emerging from his skull in a form resembling the five fingers of an extended hand (see the frontispiece).

Mark, however, that Gautama's meditation never led him to the highest result of the true Yoga of Indian philosophy—union with the Supreme Spirit. On the contrary, his self-enlightenment led to entire disbelief in the separate existence of any eternal, infinite Spirit at all—any Spirit, in fact, with which a spirit existing in his own body could blend, or into which it could be absorbed.

If the Buddha was not a materialist, in the sense of believing in the eternal existence of material atoms, neither could he in any sense be called a 'spiritualist,' or believer in the eternal existence of abstract spirit.

With him Creation did not proceed from an Omnipotent Spirit or Mind evolving phenomena out of itself by the exercise of will, nor from an eternal self-existing, self-evolving germ of any kind. As to the existence in the Universe of any spiritual substance which was not matter and was imperceptible by the senses, it could not be proved.

Nor did he believe in the eternal existence of an invisible Self or Ego, called Soul, distinct from a material body. The only eternity of true Buddhism was an eternity of 'becoming,' not of 'being'—an eternity of existences, all succeeding each other, and all lapsing into nothingness. If there were any personal gods they were all inferior to the perfect man, and all liable to change and dissolution.

In brief, the Buddha's enlightenment consisted, first, in the discovery of the origin and remedy of suffering, and, next, in the knowledge of the existence of an eternal Force—a force generated by what in Sanskṛit is called Karman, 'Act.' The accumulated force of the acts of one Universe produced another.

Every man, therefore, was created by the force of his own acts in former bodies, combined with a force generated by intense attachment to existence (upādāna). Who or what started the first act, the Buddha never pretended to be able to explain. He confessed himself in regard to this point a downright Agnostic. The Buddha himself had been created by his own acts, and had been created and re-created through countless bodily forms; but he had no spirit or soul existing separately between the intervals of each creation. By his protracted meditation he attained to no higher knowledge than this, and although he himself rose to loftier heights of knowledge than any other man of his day, he never aspired to other faculties than were within the reach of any human being capable of rising to the same sublime abstraction of mind.

He was even careful to lay down a precept that the acquisition of transcendent human faculties was restricted to the perfected saints called Arhats; and so important did he consider it to guard such faculties from being claimed by mere impostors, that one of the four prohibitions communicated to all monks on first admission to his monastic Order was that they were not to pretend to such powers (see p. 81).

Nor is there any proof that even Arhats in Gautama's

time were allowed to claim *superhuman* faculties and the power of working physical miracles.

By degrees, no doubt, powers of this kind were ascribed to them as well as to the Buddha. Even in the Vinaya, one of the oldest portions of the Tri-piṭaka, we find it stated (Mahā-vagga I. 20, 24) that Gautama Buddha gained adherents by performing three thousand five hundred supernatural wonders (Pāli, pāṭihāriya; see p. 46). These were thought to be evidences of his mission as a great teacher and saviour of mankind; but the part of the narrative recording these, although very ancient, is probably a legendary addition.

It is interesting, however, to trace in portions of the early literature, the development of the doctrine that Buddhahood meant first transcendent knowledge, and then supernatural faculties and the power of working miracles.

In the Ākaṅkheyya-sutta (said to have been composed in the fourth century B.C.) occurs a remarkable passage, translated by Prof. Rhys Davids (S. B. E., p. 214):—

'If a monk should desire through the destruction of the corrupting influences (āsavas), by himself, and even in this very world, to know and realise and attain to Arhatship, to emancipation of heart, and emancipation of mind, let him devote himself to that quietude of heart which springs from within, let him not drive back the ecstasy of contemplation, let him look through things, let him be much alone.

'If a monk should desire to hear with clear and heavenly ear, surpassing that of men, sounds both human and celestial, whether far or near; if he should desire to comprehend by his own heart the hearts of other beings and of other men; if he should desire to call to mind his various temporary states in the past, such as one, two, three, four, five, ten, twenty, a hundred, a thousand, a hundred thousand births, or his births in many an age and æon of destruction and renovation, let him devote himself to that quietude which springs from within.'

Then, in the Mahā-parinibbāna-sutta (I. 33, Rhys Davids) occurs the following:—

'At that time the blessed One—as instantaneously as a strong man would stretch forth his arm, or draw it back again when he had stretched it forth—vanished from this side of the river, and stood on the further bank with the company of the brethren.'

And, again, the following:—

'I call to mind, Ānanda, how when I used to enter into an assembly of many hundred nobles, before I had seated myself there, or talked to them, or started a conversation with them, I used to become in colour like unto their colour, and in voice like unto their voice. Then, with religious discourse, I used to instruct, incite, and quicken them, and fill them with gladness. But they knew me not when I spoke, and would say, "Who may this be who thus speaks? a man or a god?" Then, having instructed, incited, quickened, and gladdened them with religious discourse, I would vanish away. But they knew me not even when I vanished away; and would say, "Who may this be who has thus vanished away? a man, or a god?"'—(Mahā-parinibbāna-sutta III. 22, Rhys Davids.)

Such passages in the early literature afford an interesting exemplification of the growth of supernatural and mystical ideas, which led to the ultimate association of the Buddhistic system with Śaivism, demonology, magic, and various so-called spiritual phenomena.

I now proceed to show that the development of these ideas in Buddhism resulted from its connexion with the later Yoga, which developed similar ideas.

In the aphorisms of this later Yoga, composed by Patañjali, eight chief requisites are enumerated (II. 29); namely, 1. abstaining from five evil acts (yama); 2. performing five positive duties (niyama); 3. settling the limbs in certain postures (āsana); 4. regulating and suppressing the breath (prāṇāyāma); 5. withdrawing the senses from their objects (pratyāhāra); 6. fixing the thinking faculty (dhāraṇā); 7. internal self-contemplation (dhyāna); 8. trance-like self-concentration (samādhi).

These eight are indispensable requisites for the gaining of Patañjali's *summum bonum*—the complete abstraction or isolation (kaivalya) of the soul or spirit in its own essence—and for the acquirement of supernatural faculties.

Taking now these eight requisites of Yoga in order, we may observe, with regard to the first, that the five evil acts to be avoided correspond to the five commandments in Buddhism, viz. 'kill not,' 'steal not,' 'commit no impurity,' 'lie not.' The fifth alone—'abstain from all worldly enjoyments'—is different, the Buddhist fifth prohibition being 'drink no strong drink' (p. 126).

With regard to the second requisite, the five positive duties are—self-purification, both external and internal (both called śauća); the practice of contentment (saṃtosha); bodily mortification (tapas); muttering of prayers, or repetition of mystical syllables (svādhyāya, or japa), and contemplation of the Supreme Being.

The various processes of bodily mortification already described (see p. 228) were repudiated by Buddhism.

As to the muttering of prayers, the repetition of mystic syllables such as Om (a symbol for the Triad of gods), or of any favourite deity's name, is held among Hindūs to be highly efficacious [1]. In a similar manner among Tibetan Buddhists the six-syllabled sentence: 'Om maṇi padme Hūm'—'Om! the jewel in the lotus! Hūm!'—is used as a charm against the sixfold course of transmigration (see pp. 121, 371–373).

Mystical syllables are very common. Sir A. Cunningham gives the following as current in Ladāk:—Bhyo, Rakmo-bhyo! Rakmo-bhyo-bhyo! Ru-lu, Ru-lu, Hūm Bhyo Hūm! (Ladāk, 386.)

Other mystical syllables (such as Sam, Yam, Ram, Lam, etc.) are supposed to contain some occult virtue.

The third requisite—posture—would appear to us a somewhat trivial aid to the union of the human spirit with the divine; but with Hindūs it is an important auxiliary, fraught with great benefit to the Yogī.

The alleged reason is that certain sitting postures (āsana) and cramping of the lower limbs are peculiarly efficacious in producing bodily quietude and preventing restlessness. Some of the postures have curious names, for example:—Padmāsana, 'the lotus posture;' vīrā-

---

[1] See my 'Brāhmanism and Hindūism,' p. 105.

sana, 'the heroic posture;' siṉhāsana, 'the lion posture' (see note, p. 336); kūrmāsana, 'tortoise posture;' kukkuṭāsana, 'cock posture;' dhanur-āsana, 'bow posture;' mayūrāsana, 'peacock posture.' In the first the legs are folded under the body and the right foot is placed on the left thigh, and the left on the right thigh.

In short, the idea is that compression of the lower limbs, in such a way as to prevent the possibility of the slightest movement, is most important as a preparation for complete abstraction of soul.

Then, as another aid, particular mystical twistings (called mudrā) of the upper limbs—of the arms, hands, and fingers—are enjoined.

Even in Muhammadan countries certain movements of the limbs are practised by devotees with the view of uniting the human spirit with the Divine. Those who have seen the whirling and 'howling' dervishes at Cairo can testify that fainting fits result from their violent exertions, inspirations, expirations, and utterances of the name of God, and such fits are believed to be ecstatic states of union with the Deity.

The fourth requisite—regulation and suppression of the breath—is perhaps the one of all the eight which is most difficult for Europeans to understand or appreciate; yet with Hindūs it is all-important. It is sometimes called Haṭha-vidyā. Nor are the ideas connected with it wholly unknown in Europe.

According to Swedenborg[1], thought commences and corresponds with respiration:—

[1] Quoted in Colonel Olcott's 'Yoga Philosophy,' p. 282.

'When a man thinks quickly his breath vibrates with rapid alternations; when the tempest of anger shakes his mind his breath is tumultuous; when his soul is deep and tranquil, so is his respiration.' And he adds: 'It is strange that this correspondence between the states of the brain or mind and the lungs has not been admitted in science.'

The Hindū belief certainly is that deep inspirations of breath assist in concentrating and abstracting the thoughts and preventing external impressions. But, more than this, five sorts of air are supposed to permeate the human body and play an important part in its vitality. They are called Prāṇa, Vyāna, Apāna, Samāna, Udāna. In the Ćhāndogya Upanishad (V. 19, etc.) they are described as if they were divine beings to be adored and to be honoured by offerings of food. The Haṭha-dīpikā says: 'As long as the air remains in the body, so long life remains. Death is the exit of the breath. Hence the air should be retained in the body.'

In regulating the breath, the air must first be drawn up through one nostril (the other being closed with the finger), retained in the lungs, and then expelled through the other nostril. This exercise must be practised alternately with the right and left nostril. Next, the breath must be drawn forcibly up through both nostrils, and the air imprisoned for as long a time as possible in the lungs. Thence it must be forced by an effort of will towards the internal organs of the body, or made to mount to the centre of the brain.

The Hindūs, however, do not identify the breath

with the soul. They believe that a crevice or suture called the Brahma-randhram at the top of the skull serves as an outlet for the escape of the soul at death. A Hindū Yogī's skull is sometimes split at death by striking it with a sacred shell. The idea is to facilitate the exit of the soul. It is said that in Tibet the hair is torn out of the top of the head, with the same object.

In the case of a wicked man the soul is supposed to escape through one of the lower openings of the body.

The imprisonment of the breath in the body by taking in more air than is necessary for respiration, is the most important of the breath exercises. It is said that Hindū ascetics, by constant practice, are able by this means to sustain life under water, or to be buried alive for long periods of time. Many alleged feats of suspended animation are of course mere and sheer trickery. It seems, however, open to question, whether it may not be possible for human beings of particular constitutions to practise a kind of hibernation like that of animals, or acquire some power of suspending temporarily the organic functions. A certain Colonel Townsend is said to have succeeded in doing so.

A well-known instance of suspended animation occurred in the Panjāb in 1837. A Hindū Yogī was there, by his own request, buried alive in a vault for forty days in the presence of Runjit Singh and Sir Claude Wade; his eyes, ears, and every orifice of his body having been first stopped with plugs of wax. Dr. McGregor, the then residency surgeon, also watched the case. Every precaution was taken to prevent deception. English officials saw the man buried, as well as exhumed, and a perpetual guard over the vault was kept night and day by order of Runjit Singh himself. At the end of forty days the disinterment took place. The body was dried up like a stick, and the tongue, which had been turned back into the throat, had become like a piece of horn. Those who exhumed him followed his previously-given directions for the restoration of animation, and the Yogī told them he had only been conscious of a kind of ecstatic bliss in the society of other Yogīs and saints, and was quite ready to be buried over again.

What amount of fraud there may be in these feats it is difficult to say. They may possibly be accounted for by the fact that Indian Yogīs have studied the habits of hibernating animals; but in some cases the secret introduction of food has been detected.

I may add that it is commonly believed throughout India that a man whose body is sublimated by intense abstract meditation never dies, in the sense of undergoing corruption and dissolution. When his supposed death occurs he is held to be in a state of trance, which may last for centuries, and his body is, therefore, not burnt, but buried—generally in a sitting posture—and his tomb is called a Samādh.

With regard to the fifth requisite—the act of withdrawing the senses from their object, as, for example, the eye from visible forms—this is well compared to the act of a tortoise withdrawing its limbs under its shell.

The sixth requisite—fixing the principle of thought—comprises the act of directing the thinking faculty (ćitta) towards various parts of the body, for example, towards the heart, or towards the crown of the head, or concentrating the will-force on the region between the two eyebrows, or even fixing the eyes intently on the tip of the nose. (Compare Bhagavad-gītā VI. 13.)

The seventh and eighth requisites—viz. internal self-contemplation and intense self-concentration—are held (when conjoined with the sixth) to be most important as leading to the acquisition of certain supernatural powers, of which the following are most commonly enumerated:—(1) Animan, 'the faculty of reducing the body to the size of an atom;' (2) Mahiman, or Gariman, 'increasing the size or weight at will;' (3) Laghiman, 'making the body light at will;' (4) Prāpti, 'reaching or touching any object or spot, however apparently distant;' (5) Prākāmya, 'unlimited exercise of will;' (6) Īśitva, 'gaining absolute power over one's self and others;' (7) Vaśitā, 'bringing the elements into subjection;' (8) Kāmāvasāyitā, 'the power of suppressing all desires.'

A Yogī who has acquired these powers can rise aloft to the skies, fly through space, pass through the key-hole of a door, pierce the mysteries of planets and stars, cause storms and earthquakes, understand the language of animals, ascertain what occurs in any part of the world, or of the universe, recollect the events of his own previous lives, prolong his present life, see into the past and future, discern the thoughts of others, assume any form he likes, disappear, reappear, and even enter into another man's body and make it his own.

Such were some of the extravagant ideas which grew with the growth of the Yoga system, and were incorporated into the later developments of Buddhism.

We learn from Mr. Sarat Chandra Dās that in the monastery of Galdan in Tibet there is at this moment a college specially devoted to the teaching of Esoteric and Mystical Buddhism; while magic and sorcery are taught in the monasteries founded by Padma-sambhava (see pp. 272, 274, 441).

Of course it was only natural that, with the association of Buddhism with the later Yoga and Śaivism, the Buddha himself should have become a centre for the growth of supernatural and mystical ideas.

Hence the Buddha is fabled by his followers to have ascended to the Trayastriṇśa heaven of Indra, walked on water, stepped from one mountain to another, and left impressions of his feet on the solid rock. Although in the Dhamma-pada it is twice declared (254, 255), 'There is no path through the air.'

Perhaps the climax was reached when the later doctrine made every Buddha possess a threefold existence or three bodies, much in the same way as in Hindūism three bodies are assigned to every being.

The first of the Buddha's bodies is the Dharma-kāya, 'body of the Law,' supposed to be a kind of ethereal essence of a highly sublimated nature and co-extensive with space. This essence was believed to be eternal, and after the Buddha's death, was represented by the Law or Doctrine (Dharma) he taught. The idea seems to have been invented as an analogue to Brahman, or the Universal spiritual Essence of Brāhmanism[1].

The second body is the Sambhoga-kāya, 'body of conscious bliss,' which is of a less ethereal and more material nature than the last. Its Brāhmanical analogue appears to be the intermediate body (belonging to departed spirits) called Bhoga-deha, which is of an ethereal character, though composed of sufficiently gross (sthūla) material particles to be capable of experiencing happiness or misery.

For observe that it is an essential part of the Hindū doctrine of transmigration or metempsychosis, that a soul *without a body* is incapable of feeling either happiness in heaven or pain in hell.

The third body is the Nirmāṇa-kāya, 'body of visible shapes and transformations,' that is to say, those various concrete material forms in which every Buddha who exists as an invisible and eternal essence, is manifested on the earth or elsewhere for the propagation of the true doctrine.

The Brāhmanical analogue of this third body appears to be the earthly gross body, called Sthūla-śarīra.

It is evident that the extravagances of mystical Buddhism have their counterparts in Brāhmanism.

There is a Brāhmanical legend which relates how the great Brāhman sage Śaṅkarāćārya entranced his gross body, and then, having forced out his soul along with his subtle body, entered the dead body of a recently deceased king, which he occupied for several weeks.

---

[1] See my 'Brāhmanism and Hindūism,' p. 35.

The Yoga of the Brāhmans, in fact, held that adepts, skilled in occult science, might throw their gross bodies into a state of unconsciousness, and by a determined effort of will project or force out the ethereal body through the pores of the skin, and make this phantasmal form visible in distant places [1].

And now it is declared to be a fact that a community of Buddhist 'Brothers' called Mahātmas, are living at this moment in the deserts of Tibet, who, having emancipated their interior selves from physical bondage by profound abstract meditation, have acquired 'astral' bodies (distinct from their gross bodies), with which they are able to rise in the air, or move through space, by the mere exercise of will.

Sir Edwin Arnold on the other hand, in his 'India Revisited' (p. 273), states that he asked Śrī Weligama of Ceylon whether there existed anywhere Mahātmas, who elevated in this way above humanity, possessed larger powers and more profound insight than any other living philosophers? Weligama answered, 'No! such do not exist; you would seek them vainly in this island, or in Tibet, or in Siam, or in China. It is true, O my friend, that if we had better interpretations of the Lord Buddha's teaching, we might reach to heights and depths of power and goodness now quite impossible, but we have fallen from the old wisdom, and none of us to-day are so advanced.'

I believe that the Psychical Research Society once sent

---

[1] Colonel Olcott and Mr. Sinnett mention this faculty as a peculiar characteristic of Asiatic occultism.

delegates to India who inquired into this subject, and exposed the absurdity of some of the alleged phenomena.

Curiously in agreement with these extravagant notions are the beliefs of various uncivilized races. Dr. Tylor, in his 'Primitive Culture' (i. 440), relates how the North American Indians and others believe that their souls quit their bodies during sleep, and go about hunting, dancing, visiting, etc. It is stated by Mr. Finn, late H. M. Consul for North Persia, that he never could induce his Persian servants to awaken him in the morning. They gave as their reason that the soul during sleep wanders away from the body, and that a sleeper will die if awakened before the soul has time to rejoin the body. The Indian tribes in Central Brazil have the same belief, so says Dr. Karl von den Steinen (recently quoted in the *Times* newspaper).

Furthermore it is clear that the possibility of acquiring supernatural faculties is not an idea confined to one country.

Old legends relate how Simon Magus made statues walk; how he flew in the air; how he lept into the fire, made bread of stones, changed his shape, assumed two faces, made the vessels in a house move of themselves (Colonel Yule's Marco Polo, i. 306).

We are told that the phenomena of European spiritualism are to be kept distinct from those of Asiatic occultism. Modern spiritualism, it is said, requires the intervention of 'mediums,' who neither control nor understand the manifestations of which they are the passive instruments; whereas the phenomena of occultism are the 'achievements of a conscious living operator,' produced on himself by an effort of his own will. According to Mr. Sinnett, the important point 'which occultism brings out is, that the soul of man, while something enormously subtler and more ethereal and more lasting than the body, is itself a material body. The ether that transmits light is held to be material by any one who holds it to exist at all; but there is a gulf of difference between it and the thinnest of gases.' In another place he advances an opinion that the spirit is distinct from the soul. It is the soul of the soul.

And again: 'The body is the prison of the soul for ordinary mortals. We can see merely what comes before its windows; we can take cognisance only of what is brought within its bars. But the adept has found the key of his prison, and can emerge from it at pleasure. It is no longer a prison for him—merely a dwelling. He can project his soul out of his body to any place he pleases with the rapidity of thought[1].'

It is perhaps worth noting that many believers in Asiatic occultism hold that a hitherto unsuspected force exists in nature called Odic force (is this to be connected with Psychic force?), and that it is by this that the levitation of entranced persons is effected.

Others, like the Yogīs, maintain that any one may lighten his body by swallowing large draughts of air, and by an effort of will forcing this air to diffuse itself through every part of the frame. It is alleged that this phenomenon has been actually witnessed.

The connexion, however, of similar phenomena with

[1] 'The Occult World,' by A. P. Sinnett, Vice-President of the Theosophical Society, pp. 12, 15, 20.

feats of conjuring is undeniable. In the Asiatic Monthly Journal (March, 1829), an account is given of a Brāhman who poised himself *apparently* in the air, about four feet from the ground, for forty minutes, in the presence of the Governor of Madras. Another juggler sat on three sticks put together to form a tripod. These were removed, one by one, and the man remained sitting in the air [1].

Long ago Friar Ricold related that 'a man from India was said to fly. The truth was that he did walk close to the surface of the ground without touching it, and would seem to sit down without any substance to support him' (Colonel Yule's Marco Polo, i. 307).

On the other hand, it is contended, that 'since we have attained, in the last half-century, the theory of evolution, the antiquity of man, the far greater antiquity of the world itself, the correlation of physical forces, the conservation of energy, spectrum analysis, photography, the locomotive engine, electric telegraph, spectroscope, electric light, and the telephone (to which we may now add the phonograph), who shall dare to fix a limit to the capacity of man [2]?' Few will deny altogether the truth of such a contention, however much they may dissent from Colonel Olcott's theosophical views.

There may be, of course, latent faculties in humanity which are at present quite unsuspected, and yet are capable of development in the future.

---

[1] At a meeting of the Victoria Institute, where I repeated the substance of the present Lecture, Mr. W. S. Seton-Karr, who was for some time Foreign Secretary at Calcutta, stated that he also had witnessed the performance of this feat in India.

[2] Colonel Olcott's 'Lectures on Theosophy and Archaic Religions,' p. 109.

According to Sir James Paget, in his recent address on 'Scientific Study,' many things, now held to be inconceivable and past man's imagination, are profoundly and assuredly true, and it will be in the power of Science to prove them to be so [1].

Most persons will assent to these propositions, and at the same time agree with me when I express my conviction that mystical Buddhism and Asiatic occultism are no more likely than modern European spiritualism, to bear the searching light of true scientific investigation.

Nevertheless the subject of mystical Buddhism ought not to be brushed aside as unworthy of consideration. It furnishes, in my opinion, a highly interesting topic of inquiry, especially in its bearing on the 'neo-Buddhism,' and 'Theosophy' of the present day. At all events it is clear from what we have advanced in the present Lecture, that the practices connected with spiritualism, mesmerism, animal magnetism, telepathy, clairvoyance, thought-reading [2], etc., have their counterparts in the Yoga system prevalent in India more than 2,000 years ago, and in the practices of mystical Buddhism prevalent in Tibet and the adjacent countries for many centuries.

'The thing that hath been, it is that which shall be; and that which is done is that which shall be done: and there is no new thing under the sun.'

---

[1] Report in the *Times* newspaper.

[2] See Mr. Walter Besant's recent interesting story, 'Herr Paulus.'

LECTURE XI.

Hierarchical Buddhism, especially as developed in Tibet and Mongolia.

Early Buddhism was, as we have seen, opposed to all ecclesiastical organization. It had no hierarchy in the proper sense of that term—no church, no priests, no true form of prayer, no religious rites, no ceremonial observances. It was simply a Brotherhood consisting of men who had renounced all family ties, all worldly desires—even all desire for life—and were pledged to devote themselves to meditation, recitation of the Law, self-restraint, and the accumulation of merit, not for the sake of saving others, but for their own deliverance.

It was on this account that when the Buddha died he abstained from appointing a successor, and gave no directions to his followers as to any particular form of government. All that he said was, 'Hold fast to the Law; look not to any one but yourselves as a refuge.' In short, the Society (Saṅgha) he left behind was a simple brotherhood of monks which claimed some kind of corporate authority for the enforcement of discipline, but had no Head except the Law. Nor did Buddhism for a long time think of contravening the last injunctions of its Founder. Nor has it ever attempted to establish a universal hierarchy under one Head and under one central authority, and although the great

Kāśyapa as president of the first Council (p. 55) is sometimes held to have been the first successor of Buddha, and Ānanda the second (p. 56), these men never claimed any supremacy like that of Popes. In point of fact Buddhism simply organized itself in separate monastic institutions according to local ideas and necessities. And indeed the exigencies of healthy growth, and even the simple instinct of self-preservation compelled the scattered members of the Buddhist Brotherhood to attempt some such organization very soon after the death of their Founder. In ancient times communication was carried on with difficulty, and the Buddhist Brotherhood could only hold together by combining for mutual support in various centres, and adopting some sort of monastic government.

It was thus that every collection of monks naturally tended to crystallize into a distinct organized society with certain definite rules.

Naturally, the earliest constitution of each was moulded according to the family pattern. The living Head of every monastery was a kind of spiritual father, while its inmates were his children, and these, again, resolved themselves into two classes: the first consisting of the more youthful members of the society; the second, of those whose more mature experience entitled them to greater respect and reverence. Then, again, some kind of pre-eminence was assigned to individuals who were remarkable for greater knowledge, or sanctity of character.

It is easy to understand, therefore, how it happened that the Saṅgha or collective community of monks was compelled in the end to establish several gradations of rank and position among its members.

The following were soon recognized :—1. The Śrāmaṇera or 'novice' (who began by being a Ćhela or 'pupil' under education); 2. The Śramaṇa (also called Bhikshu) or full monk; 3. The Sthavira or 'elder,' who was merely superior to others in virtue of his age; 4. The Mahā-sthavira or 'great elder' (sometimes called Sthaviraḥ Sthavirāṇām); 5. The Upādhyāya and Āćārya. These last were teachers of different kinds, who received honour in virtue of their knowledge; the two positions of elder and teacher being frequently united in the President of particular monasteries.

No doubt gradations of this kind existed in very early times in India, Ceylon, and Burma. But in India the whole Buddhistic Order of monks passed away.

In Ceylon and Burma, on the contrary, Buddhism has held its own. It may even now be found in a purer form in those countries and in Siam than in any other region of Eastern Asia, although it must be borne in mind that, when it was introduced there, it was grafted on serpent-worship, Nāga-worship [1], demon-worship, and Nath-worship [2], with all of which, as well as with the worship of numerous Hindū gods, it continues to be adulterated in the present day.

The Sinhalese (Koeppen, i. 207, 386) give a list of the first five successive enforcers of discipline (viz.

---

[1] Nāga-worship is not always identical with serpent-worship. See p. 220.

[2] The Naths are certain demons or spirits of the air more worshipped in Burma than in Ceylon. See p. 259.

Upāli; Dāsaka, Sonaka, Siggava, and Moggali-putta), and another list of ten successive Sthaviras or elders, beginning with Sāri-putta. These lists are untrustworthy, especially as omitting the great Kāśyapa.

And I may here state that the condition of Buddhism in Ceylon is a subject which I have had an opportunity of investigating personally. I visited Ceylon in 1877, and had many interesting conversations with intelligent monks, heads of monasteries, and a few really learned men, including a leading monk named Sumaṅgala, who described himself to me as 'High Priest of Adam's Peak [1].'

I found, too, that a lofty idea prevails in Ceylon in regard to the status of the monkhood. Theoretically, a true monk is regarded as a kind of inferior Buddha, and revered accordingly. There are boy-pupils, novices, and full monks, as in Burma (see p. 259). The admission-ceremonies resemble those before described (p. 77.) Admission confers no priestly powers. Those monks who are Anglicized by contact with our civilization call themselves 'priests,' but they are not real priests, and have no sacerdotal functions except teaching, intoning the Law, and preaching. They live as celibates and cœnobites in Pān-sālās ('houses made of leaves,' p. 430), or monastic buildings of the simplest structure.

The number of such monks is said to be about 8,000, and their chief duties are supposed to be to meditate a great deal, to perform Baṇa, that is, to recite the

[1] His proper title is Śrīpāda Sumaṅgala Unnānse. The title Unnānse is used by all the superior monks of Ceylon for 'venerable' (Sanskṛit *vandya*).

Tri-piṭaka with its commentary the Aṭṭha-kathā in a sing-song voice, to repeat constantly the three-refuge formula (p. 78)[1], to teach and to preach, to fast and to make confession to each other on at least four days in every month, at the four changes of the moon called Uposatha (or commonly Poya) days (see p. 84); these days being generally in modern times made to coincide with the Christian Sunday.

True Buddhism does not require monks to perform public religious services in temples. Nor is it the daily practice of monks to set the people an example of worshipping and presenting offerings there. So far as I was able to observe, the duty of visiting temples belongs rather to the laity. The monks receive offerings, rather than present them. As to their dress, it resembles that represented in the Buddha's images, and ought to consist of three pieces of cloth stained yellow or of a dull yellowish colour. The principal garment is in one piece, but torn and sewn together again, the object being to reduce its value and assimilate it to a dress made of rags. The end of the dress is brought over the left shoulder, and generally so as to leave the right shoulder bare. In some cases both shoulders are covered, or the right partially so.

A good deal of care seems to be taken in Ceylon to instruct the youthful members of the Order in Pāli;

---

[1] Sumaṅgala informed me that this was the only prayer used in Ceylon. It is no real prayer, but only an expression of reverence. Often, however, wishes for good luck are expressed like prayers. They are called Maṅgala or Jaya-maṅgala. For example: 'May I for this particular act of merit obtain some particular piece of good fortune!'

that is, in the language of their sacred books (p. 60), and to make them conversant with the sacred texts.

I visited two principal colleges for monks at Kandy, which enjoy a reputation rather like that of Oxford and Cambridge in our own country. One is called Mālwatte, and the other Āsgirīya. In the former I noticed a large central hall, in which the ceremony of admission to the monkhood takes place.

At Colombo there has been recently a revival of learning, and a modern Oriental College (called Vidyodaya), for the cultivation of Sanskṛit, Pāli, and Sinhalese, has been established under the superintendence of the learned Sumaṅgala, 'the High Priest of Adam's Peak,' mentioned before.

Each monastery in Ceylon has a presiding Head, and generally a temple and library attached, with considerable property in land, but there is clearly no organized hierarchy in the proper sense of the term, and no supreme authority like that of an Archbishop; though it is said that the Heads of the two Kandy Colleges exercise a kind of control over the after-career of the monks they have trained. I found that a certain amount of intelligence and learning exists among the monks both at Colombo and Kandy, but it must be evident to every impartial observer that the habit of living in houses apart from the laity, of repeating the Law by rote, and of engaging in a kind of meditation which generally amounts to thinking about nothing in particular, must tend, in the majority of instances, to contract the mind, induce laziness, and give a vacant and listless expression to the countenance. It may be safely affirmed that the chief religious aim of the Buddhists of Ceylon is to acquire merit with a view to 'better' themselves in future states of existence, and that their highest aspiration is to attain to the heaven of Indra (Śakra, p. 207). They have no real desire for Nirvāṇa (p. 141), and still less for Pari-nirvāṇa (p. 142).

Passing on to Burma we may remark that although in Burma, as in Ceylon, a pure form of Buddhism has prevailed ever since its introduction by Buddha-ghosha (p. 65), and is still existent, yet we find that the purer system is mixed up, as in Ceylon, with the worship of Nāgas, demons, spirit-gods called Naths (commonly spelt Nats, p. 217), and with a kind of Shamanism derived from the surrounding hill-tribes.

In regard to the gradations of the monkhood a more complete organization exists in Burma than in Ceylon.

To begin with the boy-pupils:—In Burma nearly all boys become inmates of monastic houses (called Kyoung) with the one object of learning to read and write. They are simply school-boys and nothing more. Indeed, until our advent, the monasteries monopolized the education of the country, and to a great extent do so still. The real gradations are as follow:—

1. The Sheṅ or Shiṅ, that is Śrāmaṇeras or novices. These are properly youths of at least fifteen years of age (but see p. 307); their hair is cut off and yellow garments are put on for a time.

It should be noted that every male throughout Burma is required to enter a monastery and become a novice for a portion of his life, if only for a single Vassa. This is because the Buddha taught that every true Buddhist ought to conform to his example and become a monk, although he wisely abstained from imposing any irrevocable vows. The whole process is often merely formal, and sometimes only lasts for seven days.

2. The Pyit-seṅ or Pyit-siṅ (sometimes pronounced Patzin) or full monks, who have the title Pungī or Phungī (sometimes spelt Phungee or Phongie), 'full of great glory,' when they have been at least ten years members of the order. They correspond to the Śramaṇas, and are by Europeans called Talapoins (from their carrying fans of palm leaves). Their dress usually consists of three pieces of yellow cotton cloth.

3. The Hsayā (always a Phungī) or Head of a separate monastery, who corresponds to the Abbot of European countries.

4. The Gaiṇ-ok or provincial Head, who has a kind of episcopal jurisdiction over all the monasteries of a district.

5. The Thāthanā-paing (Thāthanā = Sanskṛit Śāsanā) or supreme rulers, who correspond to Archbishops. They superintend all religious affairs. According to Mr. Scott, there are now eight of them.

Occasionally instances occur of hermit-monks who lead solitary lives, and sit motionless in meditation for years.

In Siam the gradations of monkhood are nearly similar to those in Burma, and we learn from Mr. Alabaster that the monastic vow is not binding for life, but can be cancelled at any time. This rule leads to every Siamese man spending at least three months of his life in a monastery.

We have now to pass from Ceylon, Burma, and Siam to Tibet (properly called Bod or Bot or Bhot, Sanskṛit Bhoṭa). And here we leave the simpler forms of Buddhism and are brought face to face with that highly developed system which, though nominally resulting from an expansion of the Hīna-yāna, 'Little Method,' into the Mahā-yāna, 'Great Method' (p. 158), was really the product of a still further expansion of the 'Great Method' and its combination with other creeds.

In truth, Tibetan Buddhism is so different from every other Buddhistic system that it ought to be treated of separately in a separate volume, as Koeppen has done. In his elaborate and excellent work on this subject he has remarked that for the development of a hierarchy no circumstance is more favourable than isolation, and that this advantage was offered in the highest degree by Tibet. Up to the moment of its conversion to Buddhism a profound darkness had rested on it. The inhabitants were ignorant and uncultivated, and their indigenous religion, sometimes called Bon, consisted chiefly of magic based on a kind of Shamanism.

To describe exactly what Shamanism is would be no easy task. The word is said to be of Tungusic origin [1], and to be used as a name for the earliest religion of Mongolia, Siberia, and other Northern countries.

Perhaps we shall not be far wrong in asserting that the two principal constitutents of Shamanism are the worship of nature and the dread of spirits.

---

[1] Some connect the wizard-priest Shaman with the Buddhist Śramaṇa.

The inhabitants of Tibet and Mongolia and indeed of other Northern countries believed that spirits, good and bad, influenced the whole course of nature. They held that such spirits were able either to cause or to avert diseases and disasters, to control the destinies of men, and even to decide the fate of the lower animals. Hence it is easy to understand that the chief function of the Shamans, or wizard-priests, was to exorcise evil demons, or to propitiate them by sacrifices and various magical practices. In this way they pretended to prevent storms, pestilences, and other calamities. They were supposed, too, to understand omens and to predict the future by watching the flights of birds, by examining the shoulder-blades of sheep, and by similar devices. Shamanism, in fact, with its Tibetan offshoot, Bon, had much in common with the lowest types of Śaivism, Śāktism, and Tāntrism, with which the Buddhism of Northern India, Nepāl, and the countries bordering on Tibet, had already become adulterated.

When, therefore, this mixed form of Buddhism advanced from those countries into Tibet, its approach was not resisted as an intrusion. On the contrary, Tibetan Shamanism, although it had possession of the field, was quite ready to meet the new religion halfway. The result was an alliance, or rather perhaps an amalgamation; and this led to the establishment of a complex religious system which I have ventured to call Lāmism[1].

---

[1] Lāma (written in Tibetan bLama) is the Tibetan name for a superior teacher (Sanskṛit Guru), and from this word the hierarchical system of Tibet is usually called Lāmaism. It seems, however, as

Lāmism, then, is a form of Buddhism which, although based on the Hīna-yāna and Mahā-yāna of India, is combined with Shamanism, Śiva-worship, and magic, and has a marked individuality and a peculiar hierarchical organization of its own. This organization has been compared to that of the Roman Catholic Church. Doubtless in its great receptivity Buddhism may have borrowed from Christianity, but Lāmism possesses certain unique features which distinguish it from every other system in the world.

Unfortunately few Europeans have, as yet, penetrated into Tibet, and its sacred literature has been little studied. It follows therefore that the various gradations of the Tibetan hierarchy are not easily described, and only a general idea of them can be given.

We ought first to note the boy-pupil called Genyen, sometimes spoken of as Bandi or Bante (= Bandya [1], a term more properly applicable to monks). Boy-pupils are inmates of every Tibetan monastery; but under exceptional circumstances a pupil may live with his parents. He may be received after seven years of age, and until fifteen, as in Burma (p. 259). He is placed under a full monk, who teaches him and makes him promise to keep the five chief commandments (p. 126). Though sometimes called a novice he is merely under

---

legitimate to form a word Lāmism from Lāma, as Buddhism from Buddha. At any rate my adjective Lāmistic is less awkward than Lāmaistic. As to ā in Lāma, see Rules for pronunciation at p. xxxi.

[1] This is the Sanskṛit *vandya*, 'to be saluted.' I cannot help thinking that Bante and Bandya may be the origin of the term Bonze, applied to monks or priests in China, though I believe Professor Legge connects Bonze with Munshī.

education, and not necessarily a candidate for the monkhood. The real degrees of the Lāmistic hierarchy, as explained by Koeppen and others, are as follow :—

1. First and lowest in rank comes the novice or junior monk, called Gethsul (Getzul), who has been admitted after fifteen years of age to the first stage of monkhood by a Khanpo Lāma or his representative. His hair is cut off and he wears the monkish garments, and has 112 rules to observe. He waits on the full monk, and assists in all functions except blessing and consecrating. He has been compared to the deacon of the European ecclesiastical system, but the comparison is misleading, as shown at p. 76.

2. Secondly and higher in rank we have the full monk, called Gelong (or Gelon̄). He corresponds to the Bhikshu, who has received complete consecration, and is often called by courtesy a Lāma (see note, p. 262), though he has no real right to that title. He is not properly a priest, yet it is certain that in Tibet he often discharges sacerdotal functions. The ceremony of admission to the full monkhood can only be performed after the twentieth year, and binds the recipient to 253 rules of discipline[1].

3. Thirdly we have the *superior Gelong* or Khanpo (strictly mKhan po), who has a real right to the further title Lāma, and from his higher knowledge and sanctity sometimes becomes a kind of head-teacher (Sanskṛit Upādhyāya or Āćārya). As the chief monk in a monas-

---

[1] According to Dr. Schlagintweit the number of rules is 250, and they are detailed in the first or Dulva portion of the Kanjur.

tery he may be compared to the European Abbot; but in respect of consecration he is only a Gelong. Nor are any of the higher grades of monks—so far as the forms of consecration are concerned—higher than Gelongs and Khanpos.

At this point, however, we have to note the special peculiarity of the Lāmistic system, namely, that some of the higher Khanpo Lāmas are supposed to be living re-incarnations or re-embodiments of certain canonized saints and Bodhi-sattvas who differ in rank. These are called Avatāra Lāmas (see p. 190), and of such there are three degrees, which we may denote by the letters A. B. C. as follow :—

A. The lowest degree of Avatāra Lāma. He may be called an ordinary Khubilghan (from a Mongolian word—written by Huc, Hubilghan). He represents the continuous re-embodiment of an ordinary canonized saint (p. 188), or founder of some great monastery. He is higher by one degree than the Khanpo Abbot, as presiding over a more important monastery.

B. A higher grade of Avatāra Lāma called Khutuktu. He exercises a kind of episcopal jurisdiction over a still more important monastery than that presided over by the ordinary incarnated Lāma. He represents the incarnation of a higher Bodhi-sattva or deified saint, but he sometimes claims to be an incarnated Buddha.

C. The highest Avatāra Lāma commonly called a Supreme or Grand Lāma. He is not an incarnation of a mere ordinary Bodhi-sattva (p. 188), but a continuous re-embodiment of either a supreme Buddha or of his Bodhi-sattva. The two notable examples of this highest degree are the Dalai and Panchen Lāmas, who claim an authority, like that of a Pope or Archbishop, over extensive regions outside their own monasteries. They will be more fully described in the sequel (see p. 284).

It may be stated generally, therefore, that the Lāmistic hierarchy consists of three lower and three higher grades. We have, besides, to reckon certain other distinctions of rank, such as those of the Rabjampa, 'doctor of theology or philosophy,' the Ćhorje (strictly Ćhos-rje), 'lord of the faith.' These are sometimes associated with the Khanpo or Abbot, though slightly inferior in rank to that dignitary. It is said that the Ćhorje often acts as a kind of coadjutor Abbot. Practically they rank below the incarnated or Avatāra Lāmas. Moreover, in every monastery there are numerous other subordinate officials; for example, schoolmasters, teachers who explain the Law and guide the studies of the brotherhood, precentors or choir-masters, secretaries, collectors of revenue, treasurers, stewards, overseers, physicians, painters, sculptors, manufacturers of relics, of amulets, of rosaries, of images, and in some monasteries—especially those of the Red sect—astrologers, fortune-tellers, magicians (Ćhos-kyong or Ćhos-kyoṅ), and exorcists. The Lāma is not only the priest; he is the educator, schoolmaster, physician, astrologer, architect, sculptor, painter; he is 'the head, the heart, the oracle of the laity.'

There is also a whole class of mendicant Lāmas, who have vowed to live a vagabond life for a certain number of years. They are better known than some others, for they often find their way into British territory.

When I was staying at Dārjīling, I encountered two specimens of the vagabond class who came from some distant part of Tibet. They called themselves Lāmas, though, of course, they had no real right to that title. They were clothed in ragged garments made up of thirty-two patches of different cloths, and wore thick buskins to protect them from the snows. Then they carried a kind of knapsack or wallet of goat-skin behind their backs, and in their hands a sort of sacred drum or tabour called Ḍamaru (see p. 384).

According to M. Huc, these vagabond Lāmas travel for the sake of travelling. They wander through China, Manchuria, Southern Mongolia, Kuku Nūr, Tibet, Northern India, and even Turkestān.

There is scarcely a river which they have not crossed; a mountain which they have not ascended; a Grand Lāma before whom they have not prostrated themselves; a people among whom they have not lived, and of whom they do not know the manners and language.

It should be noted that when an incarnated Lāma is the spiritual Head of a monastery there is generally a temporal Head to manage its affairs.

Then we must not forget that Tibetan Buddhism has also its organized female hierarchy, on the highest steps of which are female Khutuktus and incarnated Abbesses, as well as lower gradations of nuns and novices, living together in their own convents.

The rules of discipline for the whole Lāmistic hierarchy fill at least thirteen out of the 108 volumes of the Tibetan Canon (see p. 272). They do not differ materially from those of other Buddhist countries. The 253 rules of the Pratimoksha-sūtra (see p. 62) are said to contain commands and prohibitions relating to five sides of the monastic life—conduct, dress, food, habitation, and occupation.

It must be borne in mind that early Lāmism, like true Buddhism, had properly no secular priesthood and encouraged no intercourse with the outer world, except for the reception of alms and food from the laity. All grades of the hierarchy were supposed to live together as one celibate fraternity in monastic seclusion, apart from mundane associations. Their only duties were to meditate, recite the Law, and obey certain strict rules of discipline. This strictness of discipline, however, was not long borne with equal patience by the whole fraternity. It soon became irksome to a large section, and the same state of things which arose in early Buddhism and generally arises in all religious communities, occurred in Lāmism. The fraternity of Lāmas became split up into two chief parties or sects—the strict and the lax. We shall see in the end that these two sects were distinguished from each other by the colour of their garments, and especially of their caps, the former adopting yellow and calling themselves Gelug pa or Galdan pa, the latter adopting red (Shamār). Of course the lax or Red-cap sect soon infringed the rule in regard to celibacy, and allowed the marriage of monks under certain conditions, though such marriages seem at first to have been exceptional.

It is said, indeed, that in Nepāl, under modern Gorkha rule, the celibate occupies a lower position than the married monk, to whom the services in the temples are committed. It is said, too, that the Lāmas of Sikkim and other northern countries constantly have children living with them, though they do not admit them to be their own (p. 152). Yet, for all that, celibacy is the rule, and nominally, at any rate, the great majority of Lāmistic monks in Eastern Asia are unmarried cœnobites, who live together in monasteries.

Certainly in no other country in the world are monasteries so numerous or on so vast a scale as in Tibet and Mongolia (see p. 426).

And, indeed, in all probability it was the difficulty of enforcing discipline and order in these immense establishments, without some method of securing obedience to a presiding Head acceptable to all the inmates, that led to that strange re-incarnation or 'Avatāra' theory which is one chief distinguishing feature of Lāmism.

The process by which this remarkable theory was developed is so interesting and so important in relation to the subject of the present Lecture that it deserves careful investigation, and to clear the ground we must here make a brief digression and advert to some circumstances in the early history of Tibet and Mongolia, as given in Koeppen's laborious work.

We learn from him that Nya Khri Tsanpo, who lived in the Yarlung valley, was the first king of Tibet. After several successors came Srong Tsan Gampo. This king was born in 617, and, according to a legend, exhibited at his birth certain marks of perfection like those of Amitābha or Avalokiteśvara (p. 198). He is worshipped as a great Conqueror and Reformer.

In the year 632, or about the time when Muhammad died in Arabia, he began the work of civilizing his subjects. To this end he directed his minister Thumi (or Thonmi) Sambhoṭa to proceed to India, and make himself acquainted with Buddhist writings. This great man was the first to design the Tibetan alphabet on the model of the Indian letters then in use (called Lañćha), but rejecting certain consonants and certain vowels as unsuitable for the representation of Tibetan sounds, and adding six new letters. Hence he was the first to introduce the art of writing along with Buddhism into Tibet.

It may be noted here that Buddhism, to its great credit, has generally given some sort of literary education to the barbarous nations to which it has imparted its own doctrines. It has also made the vernacular of the people its medium of instruction, though it has not always translated its sacred literature or ritualistic formularies into that vernacular.

The first Tibetan author was Thumi Sambhoṭa himself, who is said to have composed a grammar and other books during his sojourn in India. An important work translated by him into the vernacular was the Maṇi Kambum—a Tantra work, alleged to have been revealed by Amitābha and his son Avalokiteśvara. This book describes the introduction of Buddhism into Tibet as well as the origin of the well-known six-syllabled prayer-formula of Tibet—Om maṇi padme Hūm (see pp. 371–374). It contains 100,000 precepts.

The teaching of Thumi Sambhoṭa seems to have been of an orthodox character. He may perhaps be regarded as the founder of the strict school of Tibetan Buddhism (already mentioned), which was afterwards called Kadampa, and finally developed into the Yellow-robed sect, as distinguished from the Red. After Thumi Sambhoṭa the propagation of Buddhism in Tibet was chiefly carried on by the two princesses, wives of King Srong Tsan Gampo, called Dolkar and Doljang. They were worshipped under the name Dolma, as forms of the wife of Śiva or of the goddess Tārā; one being called the white mother, and the other, the dark; representing the mild and fierce forms of Śiva's consort[1].

The first two Lāma monasteries in Tibet (called Lā brang and Ra mo che, founded about A.D. 650; Edgar, p. 38) were erected at Lhāssa[2] by them or in their honour, and each monastery contained a renowned wonder-working image, which each princess had brought with her (see pp. 440, 441, 492).

After King Srong Tsan Gampo, Buddhism declined in Tibet. One of his successors, named Khri Srong De Tsan, who was born in 728 A.D. and reigned from 740 to 786, tried to restore it. For this purpose, he sent for religious teachers in great numbers from India. These seem to have brought with them a very corrupt

---

[1] One was a Nepālese princess (called Bribsun) and the other a Chinese princess (called Wenching). According to Koeppen, they were worshipped under the general name Dāra Eke—Dāra standing for the Sanskṛit Tārā and Eke meaning Mother.

[2] Some write Lhāsa (strictly Lhasa). I prefer Lhāssa as best representing the pronunciation. It means 'the city of the gods' (lha or lhā).

form of Buddhism, which aimed chiefly at counteracting the evil influences of demons by magical spells.

First came Śānta Rakshita, with twelve companions from Bengal.

Then the celebrated Padma-sambhava was sent for out of the land of Udyāna (= Dardistān)—west of the Indus, north of Peshawar—where the people were addicted to Śaivism and witchcraft. It was under him that the great monastery at Samye (strictly Samyas) was built (see p. 448). He was celebrated for his skill in magic, sorcery, and alchemy, and became the real founder of the Red sect, after instructing several young Tibetans in his own lore. At the same time he was remarkable for his knowledge of Indian languages, and was active in promoting a taste for literature in Tibet. It redounds much to his credit that he was the first to further the translation of the whole Buddhist Canon (almost entirely from Sanskṛit books) into Tibetan.

But the sacred books had by that time greatly increased, so that the Tibetan Canon commonly called Kanjur (or more strictly Kangyur and Ka-gyur, pp. 70, 267) consisted of at least 108 volumes.

Then we have the Tanjur (Tangyur) consisting of 225 folio volumes of translations, commentaries, and treatises, corresponding to the Aṭṭha-kathā of Ceylon (p. 65), and embracing works on all subjects (often mere translations from the Sanskṛit), such as grammar, logic, rhetoric, poetry, medicine, astrology, alchemy, magic, and the use of spells.

A sect called Urgyanpa (or Urgyenpa), another called

Brugpa (or Dugpa or Dukpa), another called Sakyapa—all belonging to the Red-clothed (in Tibetan, Shamār) Lāmas who are numerous in Nepāl, Bhutān, Sikkim, Ladāk, and in portions of Southern Tibet—follow the rules of Padma-sambhava.

After Khri Srong De Tsan came a number of kings who caused Buddhism to decline; but in the second half of the eleventh century it began to recover, and learned men were sent for from Kashmīr and India, one of whom was Atīsha (strictly Atīśa), who might be called the re-founder of Lāmism.

He had an eminent Tibetan pupil named Brom Ton (Brom-sTon or Brom Bakshi [1]). All violent opposition to Buddhism then ceased. Monastery after monastery was founded in the eleventh and twelfth centuries.

Three of the most important were (1) Raseng (or Radeng, strictly Ra sGreng), north-east of Lhāssa, founded by Brom Ton in 1058; (2) Sakya (see p. 448), situated in the district of Tsang, south-west of Shigatse, and founded by Koncho Yalpo, whose son was the first Grand Lāma of this monastery; (3) Brikhung (also written Brikuṅ or Briguṅ or Brigung), four days' journey north of Lhāssa, founded by Koncho Yalpo's son.

Atīsha belonged to a school which did not favour Śaivism and sorcery in the way that Padma-sambhava had done, and his pupil, Brom Ton of the Raseng monastery, was the founder of the sect called Kadampa [2],

[1] Bakshi is probably a corruption of Bhikshu. Koeppen says it is Mongolian for Ton. Mr. Edgar (Report, p. 39) pronounces Brom Ton Domton.

[2] Dr. Schlagintweit (p. 73) identifies this with the sect which wear *red* dresses, but this must surely be an error for *yellow*.

which enforced great strictness of monastic life—a sect which, as we have already mentioned, had its earliest origin in the teaching of Thumi Sambhoṭa, and whose tenets were adopted by the celebrated reformer Tsong Khapa (p. 277), the real founder of the Yellow sect.

On the other hand, the monks of the Sakya monastery belonged to the more lax school, and were therefore followers of Padma-sambhava. No doubt these two chief monasteries of Raseng and Sakya maintained at first their own separate independence, the presiding Lāma of each claiming equal authority with the other. Then in process of time, a rivalry sprang up between them. Moreover the Brikhung monastery strove with the Sakya, each trying to acquire predominance. Ultimately they appealed to the Chinese authorities, who decided that the highest position belonged to the monastery of Sakya and to the Red sect.

And here we have to turn for a short time to Mongolia. That country received its Buddhism, or rather Lāmism, from Tibet. It is well known that the great Mongol conqueror, Jenghiz Khān, conquered Tibet about A.D. 1206[1]. Before that period the Mongolians had come in contact with various religious cults; for example, with Zoroastrianism, Buddhism, and Islām.

They had even had some experience of Christianity; for Nestorian Missions existed in Central Asia in the fifth and sixth centuries of our era, and penetrated to China in the seventh century. All these religions strove

---

[1] Through the Mongols Tibet gradually came under the power of China from 1255 to 1720. The dynasty in China is now Manchu.

to convert the Mongolians, who soon became an important nation through the conquests of Jenghiz Khān. That conqueror, however, had a very simple religion of his own. He believed in one God in heaven, and one king on earth; that is, he believed that God had given him the dominion of the whole world, and he set himself to conquer the world. Yet he tolerated all religions. 'As the hand,' he said, 'has many fingers, so there are many ways to show men how they may reach heaven.'

Khubilai (1259–1294), the greatest of all the descendants of Jenghiz and Sovereign of a vast empire, was the first to elevate his people above a mere life of rapine and plunder; and it struck him that the best method of civilizing them would be by adopting and promoting Buddhism, which the greater number of the races subject to him already professed.

Between the indigenous Shamanism of Northern countries and the doctrines of Confucius, or of Islām, or of Christianity, there were no points of contact; whereas Shamanism, as we have seen, had much common ground with Northern Buddhism, which had become mixed up with Śaivism and magic.

It was this that led Khubilai to adopt the Lāmistic or Tibetan form of Buddhism. He also thought it wise to conciliate the spiritual potentates of Tibet, who had for many centuries taken all real power out of the hands of their temporal chiefs.

And among Lāmistic prelates, the Head of the Monastery of Sakya and of the Red school in Southern Tibet had, as we have seen, acquired a kind of sovereignty. Many monks of this Red sect married, according to the practice of the Brāhmans, and remained householders till a son and heir was born to them. At that time they had a presiding monk, called Sakya Paṇḍita, and the Emperor Khubilai appointed Mati-dhvaja, the Paṇḍita's nephew, to succeed him as Head of the monastery, conferring on him a certain amount of temporal power and making him a kind of tributary ruler of Tibet. He was known as the Phaspa (strictly Phags pa), 'excellent Lāma,' and in return for the supremacy granted to him, was required to consecrate or crown the emperors of Mongolia.

Koeppen observes that Khubilai was thus the creator of the first Lāmistic Pope; just as Pepin and Charlemagne were of the first Christian Pope.

The Mongolians also owe their written character and literature to Buddhism. It was Phaspa Lāma who invented the Mongolian alphabet. Taking the Tibetan alphabet as his model, he invented a square character with a thousand syllables. He then undertook a new revision of the Buddhist sacred writings, causing the Tibetan sacred texts (Kanjur) to be compared with the Chinese. It is said that this lasted from the year 1285 to 1306.

Twenty-nine learned men, versed in the Tibetan, Ugrian, Chinese, and Sanskṛit languages, were occupied on the task of collation, and a few years later, the first Mongolian translation of the sacred texts was begun by the Sakya Lāma Ćhoskyi Odser.

Khubilai, no doubt, was a great promoter of Buddhism, and founded many monasteries in Mongolia, and a celebrated one at Peking.

After the elevation of the Phaspa Lāma to quasi-temporal as well as spiritual sovereignty very little is known about the state of Buddhism in Tibet, except that the successive Heads of the Sakya monastery maintained their position under Khubilai's successors, and of course perpetuated and extended the doctrines of the Red school of Buddhism. Probably they resided at Lhāssa, and possibly at the Mongolo-Chinese Court.

In 1368, the last Mongol emperor was expelled by the founder of the Ming dynasty, after Jenghiz's family had occupied the throne of China for about a century.

The emperors of this dynasty did their best to bring Tibet under the Chinese Government, and to conciliate the Tibetan Lāmas by gifts, titles, and other favours. But they thought it politic to prevent the predominance of any one monastery. Hence they made three other Heads of monasteries equal in rank to the Sakya Lāma, and encouraged antagonism between them. This facilitated the great Reform which Lāmism underwent in the time of the Emperor Jong lo—a reform brought about by the celebrated Tsong Khapa, sometimes called the Luther of Lāmistic Buddhism.

Tsong Khapa, whose name is as much celebrated in Mongolia and Tibet and among the Kalmuk Tartars as that of the founder of Buddhism, is said to have been born in the year 1355 or 1357 of our era, in the land of Amdo, where the celebrated monastery of Kunbum or Kumbum—situated North of Tibet on the borders of China—now stands. All sorts of legends, but none worth repeating, are related about him. We may note, however, a probable tradition that a learned Lāma, 'with a long nose and bright eyes,' who had settled in the land of Amdo, and may possibly have been a Roman Catholic priest, became his teacher.

In process of time, Tsong Khapa set out on a journey from Amdo to Tibet, his object being to acquire a knowledge of the doctrine from original sources. He is said to have studied the Law of Buddha at Sakya, Brikhung, and Lhāssa. It was in this way that he became impressed with the necessity of purifying and reforming the discipline of Tibetan Buddhism, which the Red sect had corrupted by allowing the marriage of monks and by laxity in other matters. Innumerable pupils gathered round him, all of whom adopted, as their distinguishing mark, the orthodox yellow garments of primitive Buddhism, and especially the yellow cap (p. 268); while the followers of Padma-sambhava and the more corrupt school wore red garments and a red cap.

Tsong Khapa soon acquired vast influence, and in the year 1409 was able to build on a hill about thirty miles from Lhāssa, the afterwards celebrated monastery called Galdan (or Gahdan) of the Yellow school. Of this Tsong Khapa was the first Abbot. His followers, however, rapidly became too numerous to be comprehended within so limited an area. Hence there arose in the immediate neighbourhood of Lhāssa, two other great monasteries, Brepung (also written Dapung, etc., see p. 442), founded by Jam-yang Ćhos-rje, and Sera 'the Golden,' founded by Byam Ćhen Ćhos-rje.

These three monasteries once held 30,000 monks of the Yellow sect, but now have only 16,500.

Tsong Khapa wrote many works, which enjoy a

quasi-canonical authority among the adherents of the reformed sect. Many of them exist in Mongolian translations, but they have not yet been fully examined.

Undeniably, Tsong Khapa's chief merit was that he caused his followers to revert to the purer monastic discipline, especially to the rule of celibacy. He also purified the forms of worship, and greatly restricted without altogether prohibiting the use of magical rites. Tsong Khapa, too, is said to have re-established the original practice of retirement for religious meditation at certain seasons, although as there was no rainy season in Tibet, another period had to be chosen.

Travellers in Tibet have often described the many points of resemblance between the Roman Catholic and Lāmistic systems, such as the Popedom, the celibacy of the priesthood, the worship of saints, confession, fasting, processions, holy water, bells, rosaries, mitres, croziers, etc. These resemblances and coincidences will be more fully noted in a subsequent Lecture (see pp. 338, 339).

It is possible that Tsong Khapa may have imbibed some of his notions from his instructor at Amdo already named (p. 277), who was either a Roman Catholic missionary, or was familiar with the constitution of the Romish hierarchy. On the other hand, it is certain that celibacy, confession, and fasting existed in Buddhism before the teaching of Christ, and long before that of Tsong Khapa.

In fact, Tsong Khapa's reformation had been to a certain extent anticipated, as we have seen, by the school of Kadampa, founded in the eleventh century, by Atīsha's disciple, Brom Ton (p. 273).

Very little more is known about Tsong Khapa. He died in the year 1419, or, as his disciples believe, ascended to heaven, and that ascension is still celebrated during the festival of Lamps by all orthodox Buddhists of the Lāmistic Church (see pp. 345, 346).

When some time after his death, he was canonized, he was regarded by some as an incarnation of Amitābha, or by others of Mañju-śrī, or by others of Vajra-pāṇi (see p. 195), or even of the Mahā-kāla form of Śiva, and his image is generally found in the temples of the Yellow sect, and often between the two images of the Dalai Lāma and the Panchen Lāma, on the right and left respectively.

His followers of the Yellow school called themselves Gelugpa (or Gelukpa), 'adherents of virtue' (or, Galdanpa from their monastery); their principal characteristic being that they adhered to the purer discipline.

The chief point of interest in connexion with Tsong Khapa is the bearing of his reformation on the development of the Avatāra theory already mentioned (see pp. 190, 265).

It is said that Tsong Khapa himself, like Gautama Buddha, had two chief pupils, and that he appointed these two to succeed him with equal authority as Heads of the orthodox sect. He is also credited with having been the first to promulgate the doctrine that no election of successors to his two pupils would at any time be needed, as each of them on dying would be constantly re-born in a supernatural manner.

There is, however, no historical foundation for such a statement. Indeed, according to the opinion of some, the two Grand Lāmas were merely the lineal successors of the two eminent Lāmas, Atīsha and his pupil Brom Ton (see p. 273).

After all, it seems most likely that the whole Avatāra theory was an invention of some shrewd Head Lāma, who, perceiving that the strict enforcement of celibacy would prevent any hereditary succession, like that possible in monasteries of the Red school, and foreseeing that it would be necessary to prevent the suicidal divisions to which the intrigues of an election to the Headship of monasteries—especially of Grand Lāma monasteries—would be likely to give rise, bethought himself of a compromise between hereditary succession and election. After more than one trial, the system was found to work so well that it was eventually adopted with little modification by all Northern Buddhists, and even by those of the Red sect.

The date of its invention is as uncertain as the name of the inventor. All that can be said is, that it cannot be traced back to an earlier period than the fifteenth century.

And here we must again guard against the confusion of thought likely to arise from the usual practice of translating Avatāra by 'incarnation.'

We have seen that the doctrine of transmigration (gati) through various embodiments, as applicable to all beings, is a fundamental dogma both of Brāhmanism and of Buddhism, though in Buddhism transmigration properly means a mere continuous transformation and reconstruction of the elements (Skandhas) of being (p. 109).

The idea is very dimly, if at all, adumbrated in the Mantra portion of the Veda.

It is more clearly traceable in one of the Brāhmaṇas, and distinctly enunciated in the Ćhāndogya Upanishad (V. x. 7) thus :—'He whose conduct has been good, quickly attains to some good embodiment as a Brāhman, Kshatriya, or Vaiśya. He whose conduct has been bad, assumes an inferior embodiment, as a dog, a hog, or a Ćaṇḍāla.' In Manu the theory is fully developed.

Now it is true that in Buddhism this kind of transmigration may be described as a continuous series of incarnations, although genuine Buddhism denies the separate existence of a soul between each incarnation (see p. 110).

But the doctrine of repeated incarnations of one individual in six forms of life is quite distinct from the Tibetan Avatāra theory. This theory not only recognizes the separate existence of an immaterial essence or soul, but also teaches that the Head Lāma of certain monasteries is the living, visible embodiment, for the time being, of the continuous descent (avatāra) on earth of a portion of the essence of the canonized Founder of a monastery or of a celestial Bodhi-sattva or Buddha, who will perpetually continue to descend from heaven and re-appear in human forms for the welfare of the world (see p. 109)[1].

A similar idea, we know, prevails in India, where the doctrine of the descent (avatāra) of portions of the essence of Vishṇu and other gods is common. There is, however, a noteworthy distinction in the Hindū

---

[1] It is remarkable that the expression ὁ καταβάς is said of Christ in the New Testament.

doctrine, because the descents of Vishṇu are not continuous and uninterrupted (see 'Brāhmanism and Hindūism,' pp. 47, 107–116); and although every great Hindū teacher is supposed to be the embodiment of a portion of the essence of a deity, each such embodiment is isolated and single.

And here note that one theory is that the continuous descents of Bodhi-sattvas and Buddhas into human forms were effected by means of their third changeable body (Nirmāṇa-kāya, p. 247), which belonged to Bodhi-sattvas as well as to Buddhas; or, according to another theory, through rays of light proceeding from the essences of the Bodhi-sattvas, just as the Bodhi-sattvas themselves were held by some to have been generated by rays of light proceeding from the Dhyāni-Buddhas.

Or again, the Dhyāni-Buddhas might incarnate themselves not only intermediately through their Dhyāni-Bodhi-sattvas, but by the transmission of rays of light directly from their own essences into a continuous succession of human beings of pre-eminent sanctity.

Hence it is clear that the Avatāra Lāma is no example of the working of either Hindū metempsychosis or of Buddhist metamorphosis. And indeed, re-birth, through transmigration and transformation, according to the ordinary Hindū and Buddhist theories, is regarded as a kind of natural act, whereas continuous incarnation through the descent of a portion of a celestial essence into human bodies is a supernatural act.

Of course, as we have stated, there were lower and higher Avatāras, corresponding to the difference in rank of Saints and Bodhi-sattvas (see pp. 190, 265).

Examples of the highest Avatāras are the two quasi-Popes, or spiritual Kings, who are supreme Lāmas of the Yellow sect—the one residing at Lhāssa, and the other at Tashi Lunpo (Krashi Lunpo), about 100 miles distant, in a south-westerly direction, not far from the town of Shigatse (or Shigatze, capital of the province of Tsang), and not very far from our Indian frontier.

The Grand Lāma at Lhāssa is the Dalai Lāma, that is, 'the Ocean-Lāma, or one whose power and learning are as great as the ocean;' a half Mongolian half Tibetan title—Dalai (or Tale) meaning in Mongolian 'Ocean,' and Lāma meaning in Tibetan 'a superior Teacher' (see note, p. 262). He has also the Tibetan title of rGyamthso Rinpoche (Rin-po-ćе), 'Ocean-Jewel' (the Tibetan equivalent for Dalai being rGyamthso).

The other Grand Lāma who resides in the monastery of Tashi Lunpo, is known in Europe under the names of the Tashi Lāma (sometimes written Teshu Lāma) or Panchen Lāma (called in Mongolian Bogdo Lāma). He has the Tibetan title of Panchen Rinpoche (Pañ-ćen Rin-po-ćе), 'the great Paṇḍit Jewel' (Pan being equivalent to Paṇḍita, and chen meaning great).

Hence Tashi Lunpo is the second metropolis of Lāmism (see p. 443). It is said to have been built by Gedun grub pa, the chief pupil of the Reformer Tsong Khapa, in 1445 (see p. 291).

Neither of these Grand Lāmas are Popes in the European sense, for neither are elected by a conclave of chief Lāmas.

The belief is that when they quit their bodies at death, they re-appear after nine months, or occasionally after the second or third year, in children whose bodies they have occupied from conception.

The Dalai Lāmas are held to be continuous re-incarnations of the Dhyāni-Bodhisattva Avalokiteśvara (p. 197), while the Panchen Lāmas are continuous re-incarnations of his father the Dhyāni-Buddha Amitābha (p. 203).

Hence, as the father is superior to the son, and the master to the pupil, the Panchen Lāma at Tashi Lunpo might reasonably have ranked above the Dalai Lāma at Lhāssa. But, as Avalokiteśvara is the special patron of the Lāmistic Church in Tibet, his incarnation at Lhāssa is practically a more important personage than the incarnated Dhyāni-Buddha at Tashi Lunpo. Some hold that the Panchen Lāma is only a re-incarnation of Tsong Khapa, who was identified with Mañju-śrī.

It is said that the Dalai Lāma exercises secular authority over about four millions of people, including monks; although in the present day political power has to a great extent been taken from him by the Chinese Government, which has two permanent Commissioners or Residents (called Ampas) at Lhāssa, and sometimes sends a special Envoy (Kin-Tche) [1].

The real fact is, that since mere children, who are too young to have received any education, are elevated to the Grand Lāmaship, and most of them either die

[1] According to the *Times* Correspondent Lhāssa stands in no closer relation to China than the least dependent of Indian States to the British Empire; history, however, proves that China can, when her interests demand it, assume a very different position. The military power of China is not great, but that of the Lāma Government is nearly *nil*. The expulsion of the missionaries Huc and Gabet proves this.

naturally or are made to die before they have gained any knowledge, the re-incarnated Lāmas are generally unfit to govern, and in monasteries which have an Avatāra Grand Lāma, an elected chief Lāma acts as regent or administrator of affairs, while the incarnated Buddha is supposed to lose himself in sublime heights of meditation and receive divine homage [1]. This elected Regent also governs during the intervals of the incarnations, and at Lhāssa he is the real Head and most powerful Tibetan official. He is called Nomun-khan or Nomin-khan (or No min han).

The manner in which the Avatāra doctrine is carried into practice has varied at different times.

It is alleged that formerly the departing Lāma, before he transferred himself to another body, was in the habit of revealing where and in what family he would be re-incarnated. Or occasionally it happened that children of two or three years of age called out suddenly, as if impelled by some spiritual influence, 'I am a living Buddha, I am the chief Lāma of such and such a monastery.'

Or more commonly the sacred books were consulted; or the official soothsayers gave their opinion.

But the usual rule was that at the death of the Dalai Lāma the interpretation of the traditions and oracles about his re-birth and the duty of discovering the family in which he was to appear were committed to the Panchen Lāma. When the Panchen Lāma him-

---

[1] It is said by some that even his excreta are held sacred. They are dried, ground to powder, and either swallowed or made use of as charms. Others deny this.

self died, the Dalai Grand Lāma did the same service for him.

It was only natural that the holy land of Tibet, and especially the holy city of Lhāssa, should have been most fruitful in re-incarnations, and should even have supplied foreign countries with them.

When Messrs. Huc and Gabet were travelling in Mongolia they were about to pass a certain Lāmistic convent without stopping, when a Lāma came out and invited them to enter, that they might have an opportunity of paying adoration to the saint enthroned within. 'Our saint,' he said, 'is not a mere man. In our small convent we have the happiness to possess a living Buddha! Two years ago he deigned to descend from the holy mountains of Tibet, and he is now seven years old.' These living Buddhas, according to M. Huc, are very numerous. Sometimes a clever Lāma builds a small temple and attracts a few disciples. Then by degrees his reputation increases. Other Lāmas build their cells near the temple, and bring it into fashion, and proclaim him to be a living Buddha.

It is said, indeed, that some spiritual Heads of the Hierarchy in Lhāssa have contrived to instal their illegitimate children in the Headship of distant Lāmaseries, so that occasionally the supposed living Buddha is really the son of some Tibetan Grand Lāma.

In the present day the Emperor of China exercises so great an influence in the nomination of both the Dalai and Panchen Lāmas, that the co-operation of the Lāmistic priesthood has become little more than a form. Still the form is gone through, and the following description (chiefly resting on the authority of Koeppen and Huc) may give some idea of the whole process.

When the Dalai Lāma dies, or rather when his soul—which consists of a portion of the essence of Avalokiteśvara—has cast off one body with the object of entering another, the names of all the male children born at the time of his death in Tibet have to be sent in to the great monastery of Lā brang at Lhāssa, and those parents who have reason to suspect that their children are re-incarnations, are obliged to notify the fact.

A true decision cannot be arrived at until three children have been found, or rather (as is practically the case) until three candidates have been set up for election who are accepted by the Chinese Government or its representatives.

The first stage in the process of election is to write the names of these three children on lots, and place them in a golden urn. Then the Khutuktus assemble together in solemn conclave. For six days they remain in retirement. During all that period they are supposed to fast and to be engaged in repeating prayers. On the seventh day, the leading Khutuktu draws a lot, and the infant or child whose name comes out is proclaimed Dalai Lāma. The Panchen Lāma and the representatives of China must be present at the time[1].

---

[1] In the *Times* newspaper for June 15, 1888, is the following: '*How the Grand Lāma of Tibet is appointed.*—A recent number of the *Peking Gazette* contains a memorial to the Emperor from the Chinese Resident at Lhāssa, stating that a certain Tibetan official called the Nominhan (see p. 286 of this volume) had reported to him that he had found three young boys of remarkable intelligence and acute-

In a similar manner, the Panchen Lāmas, Khutuktus, and ordinary Avatāra Lāmas are elected.

The Mongolian mode of election is thus described by M. Huc. (The quotation is not literal, and is abridged.)

The election and enthronization of the living Buddhas is extremely curious. When a Grand Lāma is 'gone away,' that is to say, is dead, the event is by no means made a matter of mourning in the convent. There are no tears or regrets, for every one knows that the living Buddha will soon re-appear. The apparent death is only the commencement of a new existence, a new link added to a boundless and uninterrupted chain of successive lives—a simple palingenesia. While the saint is in the chrysalis state, his disciples are in the greatest anxiety, and the grand point is to discover the place where their master has returned to life. If a rainbow appears, they consider it as a sign sent to them from their Grand Lāma, to assist them in their researches.

Every one then goes to prayers, and especially the convent which has been widowed of its Buddha is incessant in its fastings and orisons, and a troop of chosen Lāmas set out to consult the Churchun or diviner of hidden things. They relate to him the time, place, and circumstances under which the rainbow has appeared: and he then, after reciting some prayers, opens his books of divination, and at length pronounces his oracle; while the Tartars who have come to consult him, listen on their knees with the most profound devotion.

'Your Grand Lāma,' they say, 'has returned to life in Tibet—at

---

ness, into one of whom beyond a doubt the spirit of the late Lāma of Tashi Lunpo (one of the two supreme pontiffs) had passed. Thereupon the Chinese Resident sent a report to Peking, asking that the ceremony of selecting one of these three children might be permitted. By the time the authority arrived, the Nominhan with the children had reached Lhāssa, and a lucky day was chosen for the ceremony. The golden vase in which the lots are cast was brought and placed before the image of the Emperor. Prayers were chanted before the assembled Lāmas, and the children were conducted into the presence of the Resident and Tibetan authorities in order that their intelligence and difference from other persons might be tested.'

such a place—in such a family;' and when the poor Mongols have heard the oracle, they return full of joy to their convent, to announce the happy news. Sometimes the living Buddha announces himself, at an age when other infants cannot articulate a word; but whether his place of abode be found by means of the rainbow, or by this spontaneous revelation, it is always at a considerable distance, and in a country difficult of access. A grand procession is then made, headed by the king, or the greatest man in the country, to fetch the young living Buddha. The Mongols often go through incredible fatigue and hardships, traverse frightful deserts, and sometimes, after being plundered by robbers, stripped of everything, and compelled to return, set out again with undiminished courage. When the living Buddha is found, however, he is not saluted Grand Lāma without a previous examination. Doubtless, the simple Mongols are in this matter often the dupes of those who have an interest in making a Grand Lāma of the baby. The title of the living Buddha having been confirmed, he is conducted in triumph to the monastery of which he is to become Grand Lāma; and as he passes along, the Tartars come in great troops and prostrate themselves before him, and bring him offerings. As soon as he arrives at the convent, he is placed on the altar, and every Tartar, from the highest to the lowest in the land, bows down before this child. There is no Tartar kingdom which does not possess one of these living Buddhas; but there is always another Grand Lāma, chosen among the members of the royal family, with whom the real government of the convent rests. The famous maxim 'Le roi règne et ne gouverne pas' has been of old application among the Tartars. [See note p. 306 of these Lectures.]

It should be noted that the Lāmistic community like to keep up the fiction of these re-incarnations; and therefore they pretend to ascertain the genuineness of every re-birth by clear signs. Hencė before a re-born saint is installed, his identity is established by his passing a kind of examination before a solemn assembly, thousands of witnesses being present.

Some of the books, clothes, and sacred or secular utensils which the dead Lāma was in the habit of using, are brought and mixed with others. The child is then asked to pick out the true ones, or he has to answer questions as to the events in his previous state of existence. If the replies are satisfactory, he is installed as the re-born Lāma amid great rejoicings.

Koeppen asserts that no positive information as to the relationship between the Dalai and Panchen Lāmas is forthcoming. Some maintain that both hierarchical systems developed simultaneously. Some say that the Panchen Lāma of Tashi Lunpo was the first Grand Avatāra Lāma, while others hold that the elevation of the Panchen Lāmas took place later, and only resulted from the increase in importance of the Tashi Lunpo monastery in which they reside (p. 284).

The Dalai Lāmas may be enumerated as follow :—

The first is said to have been Gedun grub pa (otherwise pronounced Gedun dubpa). Probably he was the nephew and chief pupil of the Reformer Tsong Khapa. t was he who founded the monastery of Tashi Lunpo in 1445, and he is by some therefore called the first Lāma of that monastery. His birth is supposed to have occurred in 1391 or 1419, and his death in 1473 or 1476. Then he was born again after ten months as Gedun GyamThso (or Gedun Yamtso), the second Grand Lāma, who is held by some to have been the real founder of the Avatāra system of perpetual succession by re-incarnations. He filled the Dalai Lāma Chair from 1474 or 1476 to 1540 or 1542.

The third embodiment took place in 1543, and bore the name Sod nam GyamThso (or Sod nam Yamtso), 'sea of virtue.' He was the first who really took the half Mongolian title of Dalai Lāma. Moreover, he laboured hard to spread Buddhism among the Mongolians, and founded the first Great Lāma's Chair in Mongolia.

In his fourth re-birth, the Dalai Lāma took the name of Yon Jan Yam Thso, 'ocean of merit,' and lived up to his 14th year (until 1602) in Mongolia, when he moved to Lhāssa.

The fifth Dalai Lāma was the great Navang Lobsang (strictly Ngag dBang bLo bSang), 'wise speaker or eloquent sage,' who is the most celebrated of all. According to some he was the first real Dalai Lāma, those who preceded him being merely supreme Lāmas of the Yellow school. His career lasted from 1617 to 1682. He was a kind of Lāmistic Innocent. But his long minority led to political disturbances. In the end, Navang Lobsang overcame all difficulties, and as a sign that the power of a king of Tibet had been made over to him, built on one summit of the triple hill Potala, where once the royal castle had stood, that palatial monastery—that wonderful Lāmistic Vatican—in which he still resides in his continual re-incarnations (see p. 330).

Indeed the successors of Tsong Khapa had good reason to be satisfied with their position at that time. They had overshadowed the Red sect, or reduced it to comparative unimportance. They had won over Mongolia, which greatly aided them in their struggle for dominion. Monastery after monastery arose there. The sacred books had been translated into the Mongolian language, and thousands of Mongolians came every year with rich presents to worship the re-born Lāmas at Lhāssa, or sent their sons there for education.

When Navang Lobsang died, his death was concealed by the Regent, and great intriguing followed. In the interregnum two Dalai Lāmas were successively set up and deposed. These are not reckoned in the list of legitimate Dalai Lāmas.

Then a child was chosen, who had all the signs of being called to the Lāmaship. This was Lobsang Kalsang Yamthso; he is reckoned the sixth Dalai Lāma. He died in 1758, after gaining some repute as a writer.

The seventh Dalai Lāma was Lobsang Jampal (or Champal) Yamthso, who is believed to have died in either 1805 or 1808.

The next was Lungtog YamThso, who died a mere infant in 1815 or 1816. He had three child-successors, who were all killed as minors by the acting Regent. The last child was made away with in 1837.

If these three children are reckoned, Ge Mure YamThso must be regarded as the eleventh Dalai Lāma. He died in 1855. The twelfth was born in 1856, and seems to have lived till 1874.

The discovery of the present Dalai Lāma is thus related by Sarat Chandra Dās.

After the death of an incarnate Lāma, his soul is said ordinarily to remain in the spiritual world for a space (called Bardo) of at least forty-nine days. In 1875, one year after the demise of the late Dalai Lāma, Thinle Gya-tsho, the Regency and the College of Cardinals at Lhāssa consulted the celebrated oracle of Nachung Chhoskyong about the re-appearance of the Dalai. The oracle declared that the Grand Lāma could only be discovered by a monk of the purest morals. Accordingly the Shar-tse Khanpo of the Galdan monastery, who was well known for his virtuous character and his profound knowledge of the sacred books, proceeded to Chhoikhor Gya, where he sat in profound meditation for full seven days. On the night of the last day he saw a vision, in which a voice from heaven directed him to go and see a miraculous sight in the Ya-tsho lake of Chhoikhor Gya. Awaking from his sleep, the Khanpo went to the lake, where in the crystal-like water he saw the incarnate Grand Lāma sitting in the lap of his mother and caressed by his father. The house with its furniture was also visible. All on a sudden this mirage-like appearance disappeared, and he heard the neighing of a horse. So much of his dream being fulfilled, he proceeded on the horse to the province of Kong-po, and, on the way, he happened to call at the house of a rich and respectable family of the district of Tag-po. Here he recognized the house, the family, and the child he had seen in the lake, and at once declared that the real end of his journey was obtained. On his report the Government officials and the College of Cardinals, headed by the Regent, visited Tag-po and escorted the infant with its parents in great pomp to the palace of Rigyal near Lhāssa. The princely child was only one year old when he was discovered. He is now ten, and bears the name of Nag-wang Lo-ssang Thub-dan Gya-tsho, 'the lord of speech, and powerful ocean of wisdom.' (This extract is abbreviated.)

A similar list of the Panchen Lāmas who have reigned at Tashi Lunpo has not been given. When Mr. Sarat Chandra Dās was there in August, 1882, the then Panchen Lāma died from grief (so it was said) because he had not been allowed to consecrate the young Dalai Lāma, according to previous custom.

The next important Lāma in great Tibet (after the Dalai and Panchen Lāmas) is the Head Lāma or Khanpo of the monastery of Galdan (Gahdan)—the oldest monastery of the Yellow sect, founded in the year 1409 by the reformer Tsong Khapa (see p. 278), who was the first Abbot. It once had 8,000 inhabitants. The body of Tsong Khapa is said to be there visible, preserved from corruption and miraculously poised in the air.

Prints of his hands and feet and his bed are also shown to pilgrims (see p. 441).

But the Grand Lāma of the Yellow school who comes next in rank to the Dalai and Panchen Lāmas is the Head of the monastery of Kurun (also written Kuren) or Urga, in the land of the Khalkhas in Mongolia. His perpetual re-incarnation began in the sixteenth century. He is generally called by the Mongolians Maidari or Gegen Khutuktu, but his proper title is Je Tsun Dampa (or Tampa) Tāranātha. A Tāranātha Lāma (born in 1575) completed a work on Buddhism in the Tibetan language in 1608 (Markham's Tibet, xlviii).

There is also a celebrated Avatāra Lāma at Kuku khotun in Tartary who is a perpetual re-incarnation of Mañju-śrī Khutuktu.

Indeed Mongolia is a kind of paradise in which the monks of Lāmism enjoy perennial bliss, for the Mongolians are simpler and more full of faith than the Tibetans.

Another Grand Lāma is the Dharma-rāja of Bhutān (p. 297), and another Great Lāma is at Peking in China (see p. 299).

As to Ladāk (the capital of which is Le or Leh), this is the most western part of Tibet that has adopted Lāmism. Aśoka's mission penetrated to Ladāk, so that the whole land in king Kanishka's time (that is, in the first century) was Buddhistic. Moreover, the Buddhist religion (both Red sect and Yellow) has maintained itself there until now, while in the neighbouring countries of Kashmīr, Kafirstān, the Panjāb, etc., it has been displaced by Brāhmanism, Islām, and Śāktism, etc. We have little knowledge of the ancient history of Ladāk. It has a large and ancient monastery at Lāma Yurru, near the Indus—in which is an enormous image of the cloven-headed Avalokiteśvara—another at Hemis, and another at Hanle. (See Cunningham's 'Ladāk,' Mrs. Bridges' 'Travels,' and p. 433 of this volume.)

In Tangut, all round the blue lake (Kuku Nūr), Lāmistic Buddhism has been the established religion since the end of the ninth century. It seems to have taken a great start upwards in the succeeding four centuries, for it was in the province of Amdo, as before mentioned (p. 277), that the great Reformer commenced his career. In the North-eastern corner close to China is the Lāmasery of Kunbum (Kumbum), where Tsong Khapa was born. When his reputation increased, Lāmas from all parts made pilgrimages there. Sarat Chandra Dās states that it is inhabited by 9,000 Lāmas of the Yellow sect. Koeppen says that it has a University with four Faculties, and an important printing-press, and that at the head of it is an incarnated living Buddha. The Lāmas from Amdo are said by Koeppen to be more highly-gifted, intelligent, learned, and religious than the monks of other monasteries. They are intrusted in Lhāssa with the most important offices, and are employed in the education of the infant representatives of Buddha. Amdo is still almost a terra incognita.

Passing on to Nepāl—this country probably adopted Buddhism before the beginning of the Christian era. It is said that Aśoka's missionaries found their way there; but there is no proof that Buddhism really flourished in Nepāl till the seventh century, and even then it never existed except in conjunction with Brāhmanism. It is probable that Buddhist monasteries and Brāhmanical temples always adjoined each other. Indeed since the immigration of the Hindūs into Nepāl, and especially since the invasion of the Gorkhas, there have always been two nationalities, two languages, two literatures, two religions in contact with each other.

In recent times Brāhmanism has gained the predominance as the State-religion, and Buddhism has degenerated, though it is everywhere tolerated.

It is a question whether the spiritual supremacy of the Tibetan Grand Lāma has ever been acknowledged in Nepāl proper. But, according to some, the Dalai Lāma formerly had a legate or representative in the largest and oldest Buddhistic temple of Khatmaṇḍu—the temple of Svayambhu-nāth, who is here at once Ādi-Buddha and Śiva. The Dalai Lāma also claimed the ownership of this temple, which, he maintained, had been dependent on him from the earliest times. But it is certain that, even if the Tibetan Legate ever possessed the authority arrogated by him, he was compelled by the Gorkhas to abandon his claims. Nevertheless the Tibetan tribes now in Nepāl still adhere to Buddhism. The same may be said of the Newars, who are the original possessors of the great valley of Nepāl. They profess a kind of Buddhism, though they reject the Lāmas, and have priests of their own, whom they call Bandya (see note p. 263).

With regard to Bhutān (capital town Punakha) it is said to have become Buddhist about 350 years ago. Its spiritual ruler and incarnated saint is called Dharmarāja (or Lāma Rinpoche). He belongs to the Red-cap school, and calls himself Chief of all the monks of the Dugpa sect. His subordination to the Dalai Lāma is little more than nominal. The temporal Governor is called Depa-rāja (Deb-rāja).

The following titles engraved on the Dharma-rāja's seal of office will give some idea of his pretensions :—

'I am the Chief of the realm. Defender of the Faith. Equal to Sarasvatī in learning. Chief of all the Buddhas. Head-expounder of the Śāstras. Caster out of devils. Most learned in the holy Laws. An Avatār of God. Absolver of sins. Head of the best of all religions.' (See Dr. Wright's Nepāl.)

It is said that there are about 10,000 monks, and about 50,000 Buddhist lay families in Bhutān. Many of the monks do not live in monasteries, but hold offices under the Government.

Next, as to Sikkim—of which Dārjīling, now the Sanitarium of the Bengal Government, once formed a part. This is a small boundary country between Bhutān and Nepāl. It seems to have adopted Buddhism about the same time as Bhutān, or perhaps a century earlier. The Lāmas there belong to the Dugpa Red sect (p. 268). The aborigines, called Lepchas, though they venerate the Lāmas, are really only half Buddhists; and their priests, called Bijna (Bhikshu ?) beggars, are half devil-exorcists. The oldest temple is that of Pemyangchi (see p. 432). Next come the important monasteries of Tassiding, Changachelling, Raklang, and Tamlung (one residence of the Rāja, the other being at Chumbi in Tibetan territory). There is also one near Dārjīling.

We ought finally to advert briefly to China and Japan. It is noteworthy that next in rank to the Mongolian Grand Lāma comes the Head Lāma of the great monastery of Peking, who represents Lāmism in that country. Koeppen informs us that in China, for at least six centuries, there have been two classes of Buddhist monks side by side, viz. first, the Ho-shang (p. 92) or Chinese monks, who had become naturalized in the year 65 after Christ; and, secondly, the Lāmas. These two schools are not distinguished so much by difference of doctrine and discipline, as by the position they hold in the empire. The Ho-shang are little more than separate fraternities of monks, tolerated by the State. They have no hierarchical organization, and no bishops, but each monastery stands independently, and has no superior except its own Abbot.

On the other hand, the Lāmas constitute in China a public organized society, acknowledged to a great extent and supported by the State, and possessing certain spiritual and temporal rights over particular districts. It is said, however, that the Lāmistic hierarchy in China is subordinated to the Government Committee for foreign affairs.

It is further stated that three great monasteries situated in or near Peking are exclusively reserved for the Tibetan and Mongolian Lāmas, and that of the three Lāmas who preside over these the chief is the before-mentioned representative of Lāmism at the Government Court (p. 295).

In China proper, within the eighteen Provinces, the number of the Lāma monasteries is said to be small, and these are generally to be found in the Provinces nearest to Tibet and Mongolia.

As to Japan, it does not appear that the Lāmistic form of Buddhism has penetrated into that country. In all probability Buddhist writings were introduced there from Corea about A.D. 552[1], but it is certain that Buddhism did not gain much ascendency in Japan till the ninth century, and even then was not able to displace either Shintoism or Confucianism and the worship of deceased ancestors. In fact, Buddhism commended itself to the Japanese, as it did to the people of every country to which it spread by its receptivity; and just as in Tibet, it adapted itself to the Shamanism which previously existed there, so in Japan it adopted Shintoism, and turned some of the Shinto deities into Bodhisattvas. Then followed the inevitable splitting up of Japanese Buddhism, as of all other religious systems, through disagreements and divisions; and in the thirteenth century various sects were developed. As to these, we need only note that while some sects adopt the early Atheistic and Agnostic form of Buddhism with its doctrine of Nirvāṇa, the principal sect called Shin is decidedly Theistic.

Sir Edward Reed, in his work on Japan (i. 84), informs us that he met a learned priest named Akamatz in company with the Archbishop of the Western sect. This priest's account of the Shin sect coincides with the information which I myself received from a learned Japanese priest at Oxford.

---

[1] Article on Japan in the last edition of the Encyclopædia Britannica.

It appears that the members of this sect believe in Amitābha Buddha as a Being of infinite light and goodness, their chief prayer-formula being Namo Amida (for Amita) Butsu, 'Reverence to the Infinite Buddha,' that is to Amitābha[1]. They place faith in the love and mercy of Amita Buddha, or rather in his readiness to receive them into his paradise called Sukhāvatī (see pp. 183, 204). At the same time they are required to lead moral lives, and salvation is practically only obtainable through their own works. The monks are allowed to marry and to eat flesh and fish.

Their doctrines have many points of contact with Christianity. The late Mr. Kasawara of Japan, who belonged to this sect and was highly esteemed by all who knew him in England, said to a Christian friend that 'it gave him great pleasure to meet in the Gospels many coincidences with the aspirations of his own Buddhist faith, and that he greatly admired the idea of the Christ as the concrete expression of the Inscrutable Essence in its twofold form of infinite Light and infinite Love.'

Another well known sect called Nichiren was founded by a celebrated student and teacher named Nichiren. The Nichirens have been called the Methodists or Revivalists of Japan. They are very strict, and esteem the book of the Law as the highest object of veneration. Their prayer is to the following effect:—'Glory be to the salvation-bringing book of the Law!'

---

[1] According to one of my Japanese informants Butsu should be Bhutsu, and the formula should be translated, 'Reverence to the Infinite Being.'

Doubtless Japan once had a peculiar hierarchical organization of its own, which crumbled away not long ago, and need not now be described. Even in the present day each sect may have its leader or Head, who exercises a kind of episcopal superintendence like that of a Bishop or Archbishop.

We have already mentioned (p. 200) that a female form of Avalokiteśvara is worshipped in Japan and China as the goddess of mercy. Her name in China is Kwan-yin, and in Japan Kwan-non; and she is represented as possessing any number of eyes and arms up to a thousand, and sometimes three faces.

In concluding this Lecture we may note that Russia is the only European country to which Lāmistic Buddhism has hitherto penetrated. There are adherents of the Dalai Lāma among the Burat (Buryad) tribes on the Baikal Lake, and among the Kalmuks on the Volga. Koeppen informs us that the chief temple and monastery of the former is on a lake thirty versts to the North-west of Selenginsk, and that the presiding monk is called the Khanpo Paṇḍita and claims to be an Avatāra Lāma. The Chief Lāma of the latter is said to be appointed by the Russian Government.

Hierarchical Buddhism naturally leads us on to the subject of ceremonial Buddhism, which must be reserved for the next Lecture.

LECTURE XII.

Ceremonial and Ritualistic Buddhism.

Having in the last Lecture described the manner in which hierarchical systems were established in various Buddhist countries, we are naturally led on to consider in the present Lecture the development of what may be called 'Ceremonial and Ritualistic Buddhism'; for no hierarchy can maintain its hold over the masses anywhere without the aid of outward manifestations, rites, ceremonies, and appeals to the senses.

Early Buddhism was, as we have already shown, vehemently opposed, not only to all sacerdotalism, but to all merely external ritualistic and ceremonial observances. It swept away the whole Vedic ritual—the whole sacrificial system of the Brāhmans; it rejected all penitential austerities and painful bodily mortifications; it denounced every form of superstition, idolatry, and priestcraft; it maintained that to lead a life of purity and high morality was better than all the forms and ceremonies of religion.

But the very vehemence of its opposition tended to bring about a reaction. Indeed, the history of all religious movements proves that the teaching of extreme doctrines of any kind is almost invariably followed by a Nemesis, though the teacher of them may himself not live to see it.

At the outset a reformer of the ultra type is sure to gain adherents by his enthusiasm and earnestness, as well as by his ardour in condemning abuses, but a time is almost certain to come when his followers will themselves lapse into the identical practices which it was his great object to denounce.

At all events, it is well known that in the present day the Buddha's followers have invented a mass of complicated forms and ceremonies wholly out of keeping and incompatible with the purer and simpler system which he himself sought to establish.

In point of fact the Buddha in promulgating his creed did not take into account the impossibility of eradicating certain deep-seated cravings inherent in human nature, which every religion aiming at general acceptance must reckon with and satisfy:—for example, the craving for the visible, for the audible, and for the tangible; the craving for some concrete impersonation of infinite goodness and power; the craving for freedom from personal responsibility and for its transference to a priesthood; the craving for deliverance from the pains and penalties of sin; the craving for an infallible guide in all matters of faith and doctrine.

Later Buddhism, on the other hand, set itself to satisfy these longings—these ineradicable yearnings of the human heart. It felt that it could not establish itself on a firm foundation without hierarchical organizations, and it could not maintain these without external forms, ceremonies, and ritual observances. It therefore turned the simple monastic brotherhood into a caste of priests, and it attracted and gratified the senses of unthinking multitudes by a great variety of religious rites, usages, and symbols, many of which are quite unique, while nearly all are accompanied with superstitious practices implying an amount of ignorance and credulity on the part of the people, quite unparalleled.

This corrupt phase of Buddhism is especially dominant in Tibet, Mongolia, and Northern countries. In real truth it might be affirmed of every Buddhist in Tibet that religious superstition colours all his thoughts, words, and deeds. It is interwoven with the tissue of his daily life, and is part and parcel of his worldly occupations. It is equally part and parcel of the national life, and enters into every Government transaction. Furthermore, it is fostered by art and science, and ministered to by painting and sculpture. Nay, it is stamped on Nature itself. It is impressed on rocks, stones, and trees. It finds its way to the summit of snow-clad mountains, to the recesses of inaccessible ravines, and to the extremities of remote deserts.

To crown all, it might be affirmed that in Tibet religious superstition goes on by machinery, quite independently of the human will. It is kept in continual activity, night and day, by the flapping of flags, and by the revolution of innumerable wheels and cylinders, which are acted on by the forces of wind and water.

It may easily, therefore, be imagined that to give an exhaustive account of all the ceremonies and superstitious practices of Tibetan, or, as it may be called, Lāmistic Buddhism, would require the command of unlimited time. They have been treated of by Koeppen in his second volume, and by Schlagintweit in his 'Buddhism in Tibet,' and have been illustrated by descriptions in Huc's travels[1], in Markham's account of the travels of Bogle, Turner, and Manning, and in the recent narrative of Mr. Sarat Chandra Dās' Journey. All I can attempt is to give a concise account of some of the chief Lāmistic observances, taking the books just named as my authorities, and adding whatever information I have been able to collect myself from other sources, while travelling in Buddhist countries.

We must, however, guard against the notion that ceremonial observances are confined to Tibet and Northern regions. They are now more or less prevalent in Burma and Ceylon, which have adopted much of the Mahā-yāna system, and to these countries we must give our first attention. Even the ceremonies now observed at the reception of novices and monks in Burma and Ceylon are less simple than the early admission-forms already described (pp. 77, 78, 256).

Of course every novice has to cut off his hair. He does this to prove that he is ready to give up the most beautiful and highly-prized of all his personal ornaments for the sake of a religious life.

But other forms have to be gone through in the present day, and I now give an account of the admission-ceremony of a novice—as performed in Burma—based

[1] My quotations from the travels of Huc and Gabet have been made from excellent translations by Mrs. Percy Sinnet and W. Hazlitt, but I have been compelled to abbreviate the extracts.

on the description in the third chapter of Shway Yoe's interesting volume called 'the Burman[1].'

It is well understood that, according to the strict letter of the law (p. 77 of the present Lectures), a boy ought not to be admitted to the novitiate until he is fifteen, but in modern times, the admission often takes place at twelve or even eleven years of age, the belief being that until a boy is so admitted he cannot claim to be more than an animal.

The first point to be noted is that his admission involves the dropping of his secular name, and the receiving of another title to mark that it is then possible for him to escape the suffering of life. As he is sure to have been a scholar or pupil in a monastery (Kyoung) before applying to be admitted as a novice, he has learnt beforehand all the forms of worship and much that will be required of him during his monastic life; for instance, that he is to address senior monks in a particular manner and to wait upon them respectfully; that he is to walk through the streets keeping his eyes fixed on the ground, without gazing about, even if he have to pass a pageant or attractive spectacle of any kind; that he is to wear his garments in the prescribed fashion; that he is to eat with moderation and dignity.

On the day appointed for the induction-ceremony, the young neophyte dresses in his gayest clothes, and mounted on a pony, passes at a foot's pace through the town or village. A band of music goes before him, and all his friends dressed in their best garments,

[1] Published by Messrs. Macmillan & Co. Shway Yoe is an assumed name. The author's real name is Scott.

follow in a crowd, the young men dancing and singing, the girls smiling and laughing. Thus he proceeds in procession to the houses of his relations, to bid them farewell. Of course the introductory observance is intended as a kind of dramatic imitation of Gautama Buddha's celebrated abandonment of his own family and worldly associates, called the Mahābhinishkramaṇa, 'the great going forth from home' (see p. 28 of this volume). When the round of visits is finished, the would-be novice turns back with all his companions to his parents' house. There he finds a large number of persons assembled, and among them the Head of the monastery, with several of his brother monks. These are seated on a raised dais in front of which are the offerings intended for presentation to them, consisting of fruit, cooked food, yellow cloth, etc.

The monks ('Talapoins') seated in a row, carefully hold up their large fan-like screens to shut out the female portion of the assemblage from their view. Portions of the Vinaya (p. 62 of this volume) are then recited, after which the would-be novice is made to throw off all his fine clothes and bind a piece of white cloth round his loins. Then his hair is cut off close, and his head is carefully shaved and washed. Next he is taken to a bath, and after immersion in pure water, is brought once more, partially clothed, before the assembled monks. Prostrating himself three times before them, he raises his hands in reverence, and, using the regular Pāli form of words, asks to be admitted to the holy brotherhood. Upon that the Head of the monastery presents him with the yellow monastic garments. These are duly put on, and the mendicant's bowl is hung round his neck. The ceremony concludes by the formal announcement of his having become a member of the monastery.

The present admission-ceremony in Ceylon appears to be of a simpler character. In fact it differs little from the ancient form. Those boys who are destined for the novitiate usually begin their connexion with the monastery to which they intend to belong by first becoming pupils in the monastery-school. The devotion of the monkhood to the education of mere boys was perhaps one of the best results of the progress and development of Buddhism. In monasteries, all boys may learn to read and write[1]. There also they gain some experience of monastic duties and requirements, so that when the time comes for any pupil to enter the novitiate, his preparedness is taken for granted. He merely makes known his intention to a superior or senior monk. Then having shaved his head, and undergone the ceremony of bathing, the applicant, who has furnished himself with the proper yellow robes, presents them to the superior monk, and requests to be allowed to receive them again that he may become a novice. Next, on his reciting the three-refuge formulary, and the ten prohibitions, he is permitted to take back the monkish garments and to put them on. He is then formally admitted, and his admission announced to the other members of the monastery

[1] I was told when in Ceylon, that many monasteries in the Kandyan provinces had misappropriated their endowments and dropped the schools, which they were bound to keep up.

(Hardy's Eastern Monachism, p. 23). It may be noted that the monkish garments do not include a head-covering as in Northern countries.

As to the ceremony of admission to the full monkhood, it differs so little from the ancient rite (described at p. 79), that no further description need here be given.

With regard to the religious services performed in the monastic institutions of modern times, they are, of course, a great advance on the simple formularies used in early days, before the establishment and organization of large monasteries.

The earlier and purer Buddhism, as we have seen, had only one religious formula, and that was a simple expression of veneration for the three jewels—the Buddha, his Law, and his Order of Monks (p. 78).

Any form of worship was altogether out of place, if not a mere mockery, when there was no supreme Being to worship; when the Buddha himself, who never claimed to be more than a perfected man, had passed away into non-existence, and when all that he left behind was the great ideal of his own memory, to be venerated and imitated.

When, however, monastic establishments were organized and the doctrine became developed, a great development of worship took place.

To illustrate this I submit a description of daily life in a Burmese monastery, based on the information given by Shway Yoe (p. 307), and often using his words.

It appears that every monastic community in Burma is roused a little before daylight by the sound of a big bell, beaten with a wooden mallet. Each monk has then to rise, rinse out his mouth, wash his hands and face, arrange his dress (the same in which he has slept all night) and recite a few formularies, among which is one to the following effect:—'How great a favour has the Lord Buddha bestowed upon me in manifesting to me his law, through the observance of which I may escape the purgatorial penalties of hell and secure salvation!' All the members of the fraternity then station themselves before the image of the Buddha, with the Abbot at their head, and the rest of the brotherhood, full monks, novices and scholars, according to their order. This done, they proceed to intone the morning service. At its conclusion each stands before the Head of the monastery, and pledges himself to observe during the day all the rules and precepts incumbent upon him. They then separate—the pupils and novices to sweep the floor of the monastery, bring drinking water, filter it, etc., the more advanced novices and full monks to tend the sacred trees; the elders to meditate in solitude on the miseries of life, such meditation being beyond all other actions meritorious. Some gather flowers and offer them before the relic-shrine (Dāgaba).

Then comes a repast, preceded by a grace to the effect that the food is eaten to satisfy bodily wants, not to please the appetite; that garments are used to cover nakedness, not for vanity; that health is desired to give strength for the performance of religious worship and meditation. After the meal, all devote themselves to study or to teaching. Then arranging themselves in file, they set out with the Abbot at their head to receive their food (not beg). Silently they move on through the streets, fixing their eyes steadily on the ground six feet before them, meditating on the vanity and mutability of all things, and only halting when a layman emerges from some door to pour his contribution of rice or fruit or vegetables into their alms-bowls. The gift received, not a word or a syllable of thanks is uttered; for is it not the receivers who confer the favour and not the givers? In this way they circle back to the monastery.

On their return from their perambulation a portion of the food is offered to the Buddha, and then all proceed to eat the remainder, consisting perhaps of cooked rice, boiled peas, fish, cocoa-nut cakes, cucumbers, or even curried flesh and fowl, usually wrapped separately in plantain-leaves. Next the bowls are washed, and a few hymns are chanted before the Buddha's image. During the succeeding hour the boy-scholars are allowed to play about, while the monks pass their time in conversation, and the Abbot receives people who come to pay their respects. All visitors prostrate themselves before him three times, once for the Buddha, once for the Law, and once for the Monkhood. The Abbot in return says: 'May the supporter' (so he calls all laymen; compare p. 89), 'as a reward for merit, be freed from the three calamities (of war, pestilence, and famine)!' At about half-past eleven the last regular meal of the day is eaten. Monks are forbidden to eat after noon. When the mid-day meal is over, all return to work. Some undertake the teaching of the boy-scholars. Others read the texts of the Tri-piṭaka with their commentaries, or superintend the writers who are copying manuscripts. Some of the older members of the monastery talk with the idlers, who are to be found lounging about the precincts, and some sink into deep meditation, which probably ends in deep sleep.

Yet this profound meditation is believed to be all important, for is it not the path to Arhatship, to Nirvāṇa, and to the acquisition of supernatural faculties (see p. 245)? Other monks tell the beads of their rosaries and repeat the prescribed formularies, such as: 'All is changeful, all is sorrowful, all is unreal,' followed by invocations to the three holies (see p. 175). Between three and four o'clock the lessons are finished, and the scholars perform any domestic duties required in the monastery. This is the chief return for the teaching they receive. Then most of the pupils go to their own homes for dinner. As to the youthful novices or junior monks, these are all obliged to fast like the full monks. Many of them go out with some of the senior monks for a solemn walk. Then at sunset the far-reaching notes of the bell summon the walkers back to the monastery. All must be within the walls before the sun goes down. The day's duties now draw to a close. The boy-pupils are made to repeat all they have learned during the day, and some of the Pāli rituals are chanted 'with spasmodic energy.' At half-past eight or nine there are further recitations before the image of the Buddha. All assemble, as in the morning, and together intone the hymns. When the last sound of the chant has died away, one of the novices stands up and proclaims the hour, day of the week, day of the month, and number of the year. Then all bow before the Buddha's image, and thrice before the Head of the monastery, and retire to rest (see Shway Yoe's 'Burman').

It is noteworthy that severe asceticism and painful austerities—as practised among the Hindūs from the earliest times up to the present day (described at pp. 228–230 of this volume)—form no part of the duties of Buddhist monks; for Buddhism has never sanctioned bodily torture, as Brāhmanism has done.

We now pass on to a description of the observances usual during the period of Vassa (see pp. 82–84).

Mr. Dickson has given us some valuable notes on the method of keeping this season in Ceylon, and I venture to found a short narrative on the information he has communicated[1].

It seems that the villagers of Ceylon esteem it a privilege and a work of great merit to send for one or two monk-priests from a monastery and to minister to their wants, as well as listen to their preaching and recitations during Vassa.

The season begins on the fifteenth day of the eighth month; that is, on the day of full moon in the month Ashāḍha (June, July). Sometimes two or three villages join in inviting a monk-priest to live with them for the whole three months. They prepare a chamber for his sleeping accommodation, a room for his meals, a temporary chapel for the reception of the Buddha's image, of the relic-casket and of the sacred books, and a place in which he can recite the law and explain it.

---

[1] Notes illustrative of Buddhism as the daily religion of the Buddhists of Ceylon, by J. F. Dickson, M.A. Oxon.

On the first day of Vassa the villagers put on their holiday dresses, and set off with music, dancers, singers, and flags for the monastery, where the priest, whom they desire to invite, resides. Thence they conduct him in procession to their homes. His first act, after his arrival, is to set up the image and arrange the relic-casket and books. An altar is placed in front of the image, and on this the people proceed to make their offerings of flowers and perfumes. Next every villager contributes something for the priest's food, such as tea, sugar, honeycomb, orange-juice, and the like. The priest, in return, pronounces a benediction, and says:—'By virtue of this first offering made for the sake of the Buddha, who is like unto the sun of gods and men, and by virtue of this second offering made to the monkhood, which is like a field of merit, may you henceforth be delivered from the evils of birth in the place of torment, in the world of beasts, in the world of ghosts, and in the world of demons, and inherit the bliss of those who ascend and descend through the worlds of gods till you are born again in the world of men (see p. 21)!'

Then the monk-priest proceeds to the preaching-chamber, in the middle of which is a chair with a cushion. He takes his seat, and, holding a screen before his face to prevent his attention being distracted, commences his recitations. The people sit on the floor—the men on one side, the women and children on the other. First he repeats the three-refuge formula (p. 78) and the five prohibitions (p. 126), the people repeating after him. Next he recites some favourite passage from the discourses of Buddha, the one generally selected being the Nidhi-kāṇḍa Sutta (see p. 129). If any listener interposes a remark, or hints that he does not understand, the priest explains the meaning. The people then make obeisance and depart.

The monk-priest next repeats to himself the appointed Pirit for the first day of Vassa—namely, the Maṅgala-sutta, Ratna-sutta, and Karaṇīya-metta-sutta (see p. 318), after which he retires to rest for a few hours. Rising before daybreak, he meditates on the virtues of Buddha, on goodwill towards all living beings, on the impurities of the body, and on death, walking up and down in his own chamber, or in any place suitable for perambulation. Next he goes to the temporary chapel, and prostrating himself before the shrine, says, 'I worship continually all the relic-shrines, the sacred Bodhi-tree, and the images of Buddha. I reverence the three jewels' (see p. 175). He then arranges his offering of flowers, and places these with a small portion of his morning meal on the altar. His meal being concluded, he teaches the children of the villagers, or he prepares for the mid-day and evening preaching (baṇa).

These preachings are generally well attended, especially on the four Poya days (p. 257). On the new-moon and full-moon days, the priest must go to the nearest monastery and join in the Pātimokkha (see p. 84); and on the full-moon day, which terminates the three months of Vassa, he must go there again as before, but on that occasion, addressing the assembled monks, he must say:—'Venerable Sirs, I have duly finished the Vassa; if you have any doubt about it, speak, and tell me in what I have erred.' If no one speaks he is held to have fulfilled his duties faultlessly. Then returning and taking with him a second priest, the two together perform the Rātri-baṇa or mid-night service, which concludes the ceremonies of Vassa. Two pulpits, made of four upright posts, supporting small platforms, are erected, and the people from the neighbouring villages, dressed in their holiday attire, attend in large numbers. These nocturnal recitations are commonly continued for about five hours.

Some account should next be given of the ceremony called Pirit, which is performed in Ceylon and Burma during Vassa, and also at other times. The name Pirit is corrupted from the Pāli *paritta,* which again is supposed to be connected with Sanskṛit paritrā or paritrāṇa, 'protection[1].' We must premise that this ceremony had its origin in the fear of evil spirits and demons everywhere prevalent in the East (see p. 218); but it must be borne in mind that Buddhism recognizes no order of beings, called demons, created by God, and eternally separate in nature from men.

Demons are beings who are regarded as created by men, rather than by God; for they may have been men in their last state of existence and may become men again (see p. 122). They are, however, represented as cherishing spiteful and malevolent feelings against the superior race to which they once belonged; and all kinds of safeguards and counteracting influences

[1] This is the derivation given by Childers; one might otherwise have been inclined to suspect some connexion with Preta, a ghost (pp. 121, 219 of this volume).

are thought to be needed to protect human beings from their malignity.

This is quite in keeping with the Hindū theory, which holds that when a man addicted to any particular vice dies, his evil nature never dies, but assumes another personality and lives after him as a demon. And this applies equally to women, so that the resulting demons may be of either sex, and the female is held to be more spiteful than the male.

The most effective of all safeguards against the machinations of such malignant beings, is believed to be the recitation or intoning of the Buddha's Law, and especially of the Sutta (Sūtra) division of it already described (p. 62). And of this division there are choice portions—twenty-nine in number [1]—supposed to possess greater prophylactic potency than other portions. Collectively, they constitute what is called the Pirit, and of these, three are most commonly recited:—the Maṅgala-sutta, the Ratna-sutta, and the Karaṇīya-metta-sutta. Part of the first of these has been already given (at p. 129 of this volume).

Part of the second or 'Jewel' Sutta (translated by Childers) runs thus:—

'All spirits here assembled,—those of earth and those of air,—let all such be joyful; let them listen attentively to my words.

'Therefore hear me, O ye spirits; be friendly to the race of men; for day and night they bring you their offerings, therefore keep diligent watch over them.

---

[1] The texts and commentaries of some of these were collected by M. Grimblot, and translated with notes by M. Leon Feer, in the Journal Asiatique. The Tibetan Pirit is said to consist of only thirteen Suttas.

'Whatsoever treasure exists here or in other worlds, whatsoever glorious jewels in the heavens, there is none like Buddha.

'Buddha is this glorious jewel. May this truth bring prosperity! There is nought like this doctrine. The Law is this glorious jewel. May this truth bring prosperity!

'The disciples of Buddha, worthy to receive gifts, the priesthood is this glorious jewel. May this truth bring prosperity!

'Their old karma is destroyed, no new karma is produced. Their hearts no longer cleaving to future life, their seed of existence destroyed, their desires quenched, the righteous are extinguished like this lamp. The priesthood is this glorious jewel. May this truth bring prosperity! Ye spirits here assembled—those of earth and those of air—let us bow before Buddha—let us bow before the Law—let us bow before the Monkhood.'

Part of the third or Karaṇīya-metta-sutta runs as follows:—

This is what should be done by him who is wise in seeking his own good. Contented and cheerful, not oppressed with the cares of this world, not burdened with riches, tranquil, discreet, not arrogant, not greedy for gifts, let him not do any mean action for which others who are wise might reprove him. Let all creatures be happy and prosperous; let them be of joyful mind. Let no man in any place deceive another, nor let him be harsh towards any one; let him not, out of anger or resentment, wish ill to his neighbour. As a mother, so long as she lives, watches over her child, her only child, so among all beings let boundless goodwill prevail. Let goodwill without measure, impartial, unmixed with enmity, prevail throughout the world, above, below, around.

The Rev. D. J. Gogerley witnessed the performance of a great Pirit ceremony in Ceylon (Hardy's Monachism, p. 240). Taking his account and that of Mr. Diçkson, I have compiled the following brief description of the Mahā-baṇa Pirit, 'great Pirit recitation':—

So soon as the sun has set crowds of people arrive at the Recitation-Hall, bringing oil-lamps made out of cocoanut-shells. The Hall is decorated, and a canopy, shaped like a pagoda, is erected over the pulpits, which are placed on a raised platform. When darkness supervenes a blaze of light illuminates the Hall. A relic of the Buddha is deposited on the platform, and a sacred thread is fastened round the Hall, one extremity of it being brought close to the relic and to the Reciters. On the morning of the next day, the recitations begin. One of the Reciters repeats the three-refuge formula, and the five commandments (see pp. 78, 126). Then incense is burnt round the platform, and the musicians outside the Hall strike up a lively air. Next, the formula of 'the twelve successive causes of existence' (see p. 102) is intoned, and a hymn of victory chanted.

The recitation of the Pirit continues uninterruptedly, day and night, for seven days. Twenty-four priests are employed, two of whom are constantly seated on the platform and engaged in reciting. Moreover three times in each day—at sunrise, mid-day, and sunset—they all assemble together and chant in chorus. Of course, when the recitation of the Suttas constituting the Pirit is concluded, it is recommenced, and in this way all the Suttas are recited again and again. On the morning of the seventh day a messenger is sent to a neighbouring temple to invite the attendance of the gods. Then by a stretch of the imagination certain of the gods and spirits are believed to answer the summons, and on their supposed arrival, the protective Suttas are chanted more energetically than ever till the morning of the eighth day, when a benediction concludes the ceremony, and offerings of robes are to the priest-reciters.

We now pass on to Tibet and Mongolia.

The ceremonies of admission to the monkhood in those countries do not deviate sufficiently from the practices just described to require special notice.

With regard, however, to the dress of Lāmistic monks after their admission to the Order, the ancient rule, as we have seen, obliged them to wear only three garments of a dirty yellowish colour, made out of rags, or picked up in cemeteries or on dust heaps. But the necessities of a colder climate have compelled the Lāmas to increase their official vestments, and the higher Lāmas sometimes wear bright silken robes enriched with ornament. The law is sufficiently obeyed by putting a patch or two at one corner.

A full equipment is supposed to consist of an under vestment, a sort of tunic worn over it, a mantle, a kind of scarf worn over the left shoulder, a loose robe brought round over the same shoulder, and a cap[1]. The right shoulder is rarely bare, as it generally is in Southern Buddhist countries.

The colour of these six articles of clothing, especially of the cap, is yellow or red, according to the sect to which a monk belongs.

The cap is an important mark of sectarian difference, and is of various forms, and when it has five points, has been compared to a bishop's mitre, but the five points really denote the five Dhyāni-Buddhas and their Bodhi-sattvas.

---

[1] A cold climate necessitates the addition of trousers, and boots and occasionally shoes are worn.

Part of every full monk's equipment in Tibet is a peculiar instrument, made of bronze or other metal, and called a Dorje (Sanskṛit Vajra, 'a thunderbolt'), the employment of which for religious objects is peculiar to Northern Buddhism. It is shaped like the imaginary thunderbolt of the gods Indra and Śiva—that is, it consists of a short bar, about four inches long, the two extremities of which swell out in globular form, or like small oval cages formed of hoops of metal. The original Dorje is supposed to have fallen direct from Indra's heaven, and to have been preserved in a monastery near Lhāssa, called Sera (pp. 278, 442). According to another legend, the original instrument belonged to Gautama Buddha himself, and on his passing away into non-existence, transported itself through the air from India into Tibet. The consecrated imitations of it are innumerable. Their primary use is for exorcising and driving away evil spirits, especially in the performance of ceremonies and repetition of prayers—the instrument being then held between the fingers and thumb and waved backwards and forwards, or from side to side.

The efficacy of the Dorje in securing good fortune and warding off evil influences of all kinds is supposed to be of wide application. The idea was really borrowed from Śaivism or from the Tantra system, introduced through Nepāl by the Red sect. It is easy to understand the enormous power supposed to belong to a priesthood which claimed to be the wielders of a formidable thunderbolt, sent to them directly from heaven.

No wonder that the original Dorje preserved at the Sera monastery has become an object of actual worship. According to M. Huc, countless pilgrims prostrate themselves before it; and at the New Year's festival, on the 27th day of the first month, it is carried in procession with great pomp to Lhāssa,—to the two centres of Lāmism—Potala and Lā brang. On its way there, the mystical implement is adored by the whole population, male and female (ii. 221).

Below is an engraving of a Dorje which I brought from Dārjīling.

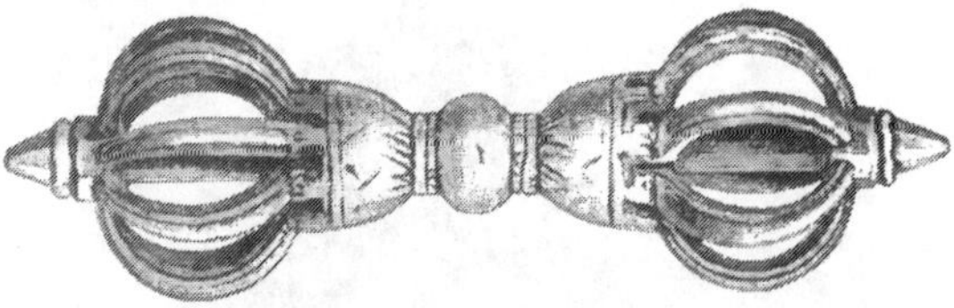

It should be mentioned that the fierce Bodhi-sattva Vajra-pāṇi (see p. 201 of this volume) is represented holding a similar Dorje in his right hand in his character of subduer of evil spirits. In some representations the evil demons are denoted by serpents.

Another important part of a full monk's equipment in Tibet is the Prayer-bell (called Drilbu) employed at the performance of daily religious ceremonies, and rung to accompany the repetition and chanting of prayers, or to fill up the intervals of worship. It often has half a Dorje as a handle, or the handle is ornamented with various mystical symbols carved on it. The object of ringing bells during worship is to call the attention of the beings who are worshipped, or to keep off evil spirits by combining noise with the waving of the Dorje in the handle.

The bell here represented was brought by me from Dārjīling.

The bells used in Burma are described at p. 526.

Other religious implements used by novices and lay-brethren, as well as by full monks, are prayer-wheels, prayer-cylinders, rosaries, amulets (see p. 358), drums (see p. 385), and the Phurbu or Phur-pa (pp. 351, 352).

As to the daily religious services and ceremonies performed by Monks in Tibet and Mongolia, these, of course, are far more ritualistic than in southern Buddhist countries. It has already been explained (at pp. 202, 225) that certain abstract essences or mystical forms of the Buddha, called Dhyāni-Buddhas, were imagined to exist, and these had their concrete energizing vice-gerents called Bodhi-sattvas—beings who received adoration as if they were actually gods. In Tibet the Bodhi-sattva Avalokiteśvara, and the canonized reformer Tsong Khapa, and other supposed saints, became prominent objects of religious worship. Then, in process of time, a complicated ceremonial was developed, which, as we shall see (p. 338), has much in common with the ritual of Roman Catholic Christianity.

The language employed in the religious services of the Lāmistic Hierarchy, whether in Tibet, Mongolia, or in the Lāma monasteries of China and Manchuria, is Tibetan. In fact, Tibetan is to the Lāmistic Church what Latin is to the Romish. It is the sole orthodox language of religion and religious ceremonial.

According to Koeppen, only one Mongolian Lāma-monastery (and that established at Peking) has the right to perform religious services in Mongolian instead of in Tibetan[1].

Dr. Edkins, however, states that there is a temple (called Fa-hai-si) near the hunting-park, in which the Manchu language is employed instead of Tibetan. (Chinese Buddhism, p. 406.)

Without doubt the acquisition of some knowledge of the Tibetan language is incumbent on every Lāma.

---

[1] This is probably permitted with a view to prevent the study of Mongolian from entirely dying out. It is certain that, although the Buddhist sacred books have long been translated into Mongolian, Chinese, and Tungusic, only the Tibetan texts are esteemed as canonical.

Nevertheless, few, except in Tibet, really understand it. They simply repeat the usual prayers and formularies mechanically[1].

[1] The indomitable persevering Hungarian traveller, Alexander Csoma de Körös, already mentioned (at p. 70), was the first European to throw light on the Tibetan language. He had been impelled to acquire it by the task he had imposed on himself of searching out the progenitors of his race. More than eighty years ago he set out on his travels, and his search ultimately brought him to Tibet. There he devoted himself to the study of the Tibetan language and its sacred literature, taking up his abode in the monastery of Pugdal, in defiance of intense cold and other hardships. But his heroic energy did not end there. In 1831 he travelled from Tibet to Calcutta, and in that city, about the year 1834, published his Grammar and Dictionary of the Tibetan language, besides his table of contents of the Kanjur and the extra-canonical treatises. At length fancying himself qualified for the accomplishment of his self-inflicted task, he started off again, and died in Sikkim in April 1842. He is buried at Dārjīling. We Englishmen, who ought to have taken the greatest share in these linguistic conquests—so important in their bearing on the interests of our Indian frontier—have hitherto, to our great discredit, almost entirely neglected them. Meanwhile, St. Petersburg and Paris have founded chairs of the Tibetan language, and nearly all that has been effected for promoting the study of Tibetan has been due to Russian and French scholars, and to German and Moravian missionaries, especially to Jäschke and Hyde.

I am glad, however, to see from the annual address delivered by the President of the Asiatic Society of Bengal, and published in the Report for February, 1888, that this reproach is now being wiped out by our fellow-subjects in India. Babu Pratāpa Chandra Ghosha is bringing out in the Bibliotheca Indica the Tibetan translation of the Buddhistic work Prajñā-pāramitā, forming the second division of the Kanjur, while Mr. Sarat Chandra Dās, C.I.E., is editing the Tibetan version of the Avadāna-Kalpalatā (a store-house of legends of Buddha's life and acts), and compiling a Tibetan-Sanskṛit-English Dictionary. Great credit is due to our Indian Government for the publication of Jäschke's Tibetan-English Dictionary.

It appears that the Lāmistic priests assemble three times a day to go through the prescribed ritual—at sunrise, at mid-day, and at sunset. We read that, before commencing the service, they enter the temple or hall of worship in procession and seat themselves on low seats in long rows. These are placed the whole length of the hall, from the entrance-door to the altar, being divided in the middle by a passage. At the further extremity, close to the altar, are two raised thrones for the Head Lāmas—a five-cushioned one on the right for the Abbot and a three-cushioned one for the Vice-Abbot.

When all have seated themselves, the choir-master or precentor gives a signal with a bell. Then the prayer-formularies are recited or chanted, certain passages out of the Law are intoned and certain litanies sung, sometimes in loud tones, accompanied by noisy music or by clapping of hands, and generally in unison, though occasionally verses are sung alternately with responses.

Then at other times a sentence of the Law is repeated by each monk in turn; or a chant is set up consisting of such words as: Praise be to the Buddha! or praise be to some Bodhi-sattva! followed by a recital of all his names, titles, and epithets; or mystical sentences and syllables are ejaculated. The result is said to be a chaos of voices and a deafening confusion of sounds.

The chief instruments used in the services are a spiral shell, a long trumpet of copper or brass (sometimes more than ten feet long), a large drum, flutes, cymbals, and horns—the last being sometimes made of the thigh-bones of human beings [1].

The ritual is imposing, and still more so when a living Buddha is present. It has been described by M. Huc, and I here give the substance of his account [2].

In front of the chief idol, and on a level with the altar, is a gilded seat for the living Buddha or Grand Lāma of the Monastery. The whole space of the temple, from one end to the other, is occupied by long low seats almost level with the ground, stretching right and left of the Grand Lāma's throne. These are covered with carpets, a vacant space being left between each row for the Lāmas to pass and repass. When the hour of prayer is come, a Lāma, whose office it is to summon the choir, places himself in front of the grand entrance of the temple and blows with all the force of his lungs into a conch-shell trumpet, the sound of which is audible for a league round. This effectually rouses the Lāmas and calls them together. Each then takes his mantle and official hat of ceremony, and repairs to the interior court. The trumpet sounds again, and when its note is heard for the third time, the great door is suddenly thrown open; the living Buddha enters, and takes his seat in front of the image on the altar. Then the Lāmas, after depositing their red boots in the vestibule, advance towards him barefoot, and adore him by three prostrations. This done, they seat themselves on the long seats according to their dignity, cross-legged and face to face. As soon as the director of the ceremonies has given the signal by tinkling a little bell, everyone murmurs the prescribed prayers, unrolling the formularies on his knees. After this recitation, there is profound silence for a minute. Then the bell is again rung, and a hymn or chant in two choruses begins. The Tibetan prayers, ordinarily arranged in verses, and written in metrical style, are well adapted to harmony; but sometimes at certain pauses indicated by the rubric, the Lāma musicians execute a strain

---

[1] As corpses are exposed to be devoured by animals in Tibet human bones are easily obtained for this purpose.

[2] As before stated (p. 306, note) I have been compelled to abbreviate the translator's version and occasionally to vary the expressions, and have therefore felt it right to omit inverted commas.

in little accord with the gravity of the psalmody. The result is a stunning noise of bells, cymbals, drums, tambourines, conch-shells, trumpets, and pipes. Each musician sounds his instrument with a sort of fury, and each strives to outdo his neighbour in the noise he can produce. (Huc's Travels, i. 88, abridged.)

One important element in some Tibetan religious services is the consecration and distribution of holy water and grain by the chief Lāmas.

Perfumes, too, are burnt, and censers containing incense are swung backwards and forwards during the ceremonies.

Then, again, some Lāmistic ceremonials include the drinking of tea poured into little cups, kept in the breast-pockets of the monks' robes, and replenished two or three times during the service.

Sir Richard Temple (Journal, ii. 208) thus describes a tea-drinking ceremonial at which he was present, at the monastery of Pemyangchi in Sikkim (see p. 298 of these Lectures).

The priests and monks, some thirty-five in all, were drawn up in full robes to receive us. Then the officials of the monastery were introduced—the steward, the rod-bearer, the deputy master, and lastly, the master. A procession was quickly formed, which we followed into the chapel, where they all took their accustomed seats, while we sat on places prepared for us. The interior of the chapel seemed an odd place for this, but we were told that it was the correct ceremonial. A chant was begun, which lasted some ten minutes, as a sort of grace, and then tea was handed round—first to us, next to the priests, and lastly to the monks. A short chant followed, and then the procession preceded us out of the chapel.

In the picture which accompanies Sir Richard's description, all the monks have head-coverings, some of which are like caps or hats of a high sugar-loaf shape, while others have several points like episcopal mitres (see p. 321).

The monks of Sikkim are generally of the Dugpa sect[1], and wear red caps (see pp. 273, 298).

When Dr. Watt was in Ladāk, he was present at a service performed by a number of monks belonging to both sects, who seemed to fraternize very amicably. All the monks of the red sect took up a position on one side of the chapel, while those of the yellow sect ranged themselves on the opposite side. The two sects entered together, as usual, in procession, and part of the ceremonial—as in that witnessed by Sir Richard Temple—consisted in drinking tea from little cups taken from the folds of their robes, and put back again, to be again taken out and replenished ; and this, too, without interrupting the continuous repetition of prayers, chants, and formularies[2].

M. Huc also describes a 'Tea-general' ceremony after morning service in a temple. Each monk drinks in silence, carefully placing his scarf before his cup, as if to prevent the sight of the apparent incongruity of drinking tea in such a sacred spot (ii. 57).

Another instance of tea-drinking as an element in Lāmistic ceremonial, occurs in Mr. Sarat Chandra Dās' highly interesting account of the ceremony of his presentation to the Dalai Lāma at the palace-monastery of Potala, in Lhāssa, on June 10, 1882. I

---

[1] According to Schlagintweit this sect (also called Brugpa, p. 272) are especially worshippers of the Dorje (see p. 322), and are therefore Tāntrikas.

[2] This I heard from his own lips.

venture to give the substance of it in an abbreviated form and not quite literally [1].

An account of other presentations both to the Dalai Lāma and Tashi Lāma will be given in a future Lecture (see pp. 439, 444, 447).

Early in the morning I was informed of the arrival of Chola Kusho, who was ready to take me to Potala for presentation to the Dalai Lāma. We sallied forth on horseback, with three bundles of incense-sticks in our hands, and a roll of scarves in our breast-pockets, chanting as we went along certain hymns, and particularly the mystic 'Om maṇi padme Hūm.' In the street we saw a calf sucking milk, and several women fetching water in our direction. My companions were delighted at these auspicious omens. Arrived at the eastern gateway of Potala, we dismounted, and walked up a long hall, on two sides of which were two rows of prayer-wheels, put there to be twirled, on going in and coming out.

A young monk now came down to conduct us, and we ascended slowly, looking only on the ground before us. The several ladders which conducted us from one story to another were steep, and placed in dark halls. I counted five, which took us as far as the ground-floor of the Red palace. Half-a-dozen ladders still remained to be scaled.

At about eight we reached the top, and there found a number of monks anxiously awaiting an interview with his Holiness. A seat was pointed out to me. A monk sat near me, and smilingly observed that it must have been on account of the sins of my former life that I was born in India, where there is no living Buddha.

From the top of the Red palace we enjoyed a grand panorama of Lhāssa and its suburbs. Shortly afterwards some Lāmas of high rank, dressed in loose yellow mantles, arrived. They entered the hall of reception one after another in solemn array. We remained outside in anxious suspense, fixing our eyes on the entrance door, and expecting to be summoned to his Holiness' presence.

At last, three Lāmas came towards us and asked us to enter in a

---

[1] The abstract has been made by me from a copy of Sarat Chandra Dās' Report kindly lent to me by Sir Edwin Arnold. But I learnt much from Mr. S. C. D. in personal conversations. In my numerous quotations I have ventured to make a few alterations in the English.

line one after another. Walking very gently, we proceeded to the middle of the audience hall—a spacious apartment supported by three rows of four wooden pillars. The walls had paintings of the exploits of Buddha, of Chanrassig[1], Tsong Khapa, and other celebrated saints, besides images of the successive incarnations of the Dalai Lāma.

As soon as we had entered the official scarf-collectors received the presentation-scarves from our hands. We seated ourselves on rugs, spread in about eight rows, my seat being in the third row, at a distance of about ten feet from the Grand Lāma's throne, and a little to his left. When all were seated, perfect silence reigned in the grand hall. The state officials walked from left to right with serene gravity, as became their exalted rank, in the presence of the Supreme Vice-Regent of Buddha on earth. At their head walked the Kuchar Khanpo, who carried in his hand the bowl of benediction, containing the sacred Thui (that is, consecrated water stained yellow with saffron) for sprinkling over the audience. The bearer of the incense-pot, suspended by three golden chains, the carrier of the royal golden tea-pot, and other domestic officials, now came up, and stood motionless as pictures, without looking on either side, but fixing their eyes and their attention, as it were, on the tips of their respective noses. Two large golden lamp-burners, resembling flower-vases, flickered on two sides of the throne. The great altar—resembling an oriental throne, and supported by lions[2] carved in wood—on which sat his Holiness, a child of eight, was covered with silk scarves of great value. It was about four feet high, six long, and four broad. A yellow mitre-hat[3] covered the Grand Lāma's head, the pendant portions veiling his ears, and a yellow mantle enveloped his person. He sat cross-legged, with the palms of his hands joined together to bless us. When it came to my turn I received his Holiness' benediction, and was able to look upon his divine face. Other Lāmas approached him with downcast looks, and resumed their respective seats, not presuming to look up. I longed to linger a few seconds, but other candidates for benediction displaced me by pushing me gently forward. I noticed that the

---

[1] This is the Tibetan name of Avalokiteśvara or Padma-pāṇi. It is often spelt Chenresi, or Chenresig, or Chenressig.

[2] The Lion is an emblem of the Buddha, and he is called Śākya-sinha, 'the Lion of the Śākya tribe' (see pp. 23, 394).

[3] See p. 321.

princely child possessed a really bright and fair complexion, with rosy cheeks. His eyes were large and penetrating. The contour of his face was remarkably Āryan, though somewhat marred by the obliquity of his eyes. The thinness of his person was probably owing to the fatigues of the court-ceremonies, religious duties, and ascetic observances, to which he had been subjected since taking the vows of monkhood. Remembering the stories about the freaks of fortune, which had lately brought him to this proud position, and had compelled his predecessors to undergo untimely transmigrations, I pitied his exalted rank: for who knows whether he will not be forced to undergo another transmigration before reaching his twentieth year?

When all were again seated after receiving the Dalai Lāma's benediction, the Sol-pon Chhenpo poured tea in his Holiness' golden cup from a golden tea-pot, while four assistant Sol-pons poured tea in the cups of the audience, consisting of the head Lāmas of Meru monastery and ourselves. Before the Grand Lāma lifted his cup to his lips, a grace was solemnly said, beginning with 'Om āh Hūm' thrice chanted, and followed by a prayer to the following effect:—'Never even for a moment losing sight of the three Holies, always offer reverence to the Tri-ratnas; let the blessings of the three be upon us.' Without even stirring the air by the movements of our limbs, we slowly lifted our cups to our lips, and drank the tea—which was delicious—taking care to make no sound with our lips. Three times was tea served, and three times we emptied our cups, after which we put them back in our breast-pockets. Then the Sol-pon placed a golden dish full of consecrated rice in front of his Holiness, which he only touched. The remainder was distributed among those present. I obtained a handful, which I carefully tied in one corner of my handkerchief. The following grace was then uttered by the assembled monks, with much gravity:—'The most precious *Buddha* is the most perfect and matchless teacher; the most unerring guide is the *Saṅgha*; the most infallible protection is in the sacred *Dharma*. We offer these offerings to these three objects of refuge. Reverence be to each of them!'

Mr. Sarat Chandra Dās also witnessed at the same time the performance of a remarkable ceremony for the translation of the soul of a chief Lāma or Khanpo to one of the heavenly mansions.

It appears that a certain well-known Khanpo had died of small-pox. He was one of the most distinguished scholars of Tibet, and held the highest position in the Court of Potala. The day on which the ceremony was performed was the twenty-seventh day of this chief Lāma's *Bardo* (p. 371); that is, of the interval of forty-nine days between his death and his translation to another world. (According to Jäschke the interval of the intermediate state only lasts for forty days.)

The Dalai Lāma, seated on his throne, chanted a hymn in a low indistinct voice. Afterwards the assembled monks in grave tones repeated what the Grand Lāma had uttered. Then a venerable personage rose from the middle of the first row of seats, and addressing the Grand Lāma as the incarnate Lord Chenressig (Avalokiteśvara), recited all the many acts of mercy performed by him, as the patron-saint of Tibet, for the benefit of its people. Next, he made offerings of certain precious things (including an imaginary presentation of the seven mythical treasures[1]) for the benefit of the soul of the late Khanpo, saying:—'I pray that you may graciously accept these presents for the good of all living beings.'

Finally, he prostrated himself three times before the Grand Lāma's throne. A solemn pause followed; after which the audience rose, and the Grand Lāma retired. Mr. Sarat Chandra Dās goes on to relate that at the end of the ceremony one of the assistant Lāmas gave him two packets of pills, and another tied a scrap of red

---

[1] See these enumerated at p. 528.

silk round his neck. The pills, he was told, were chinlab or blessings, consecrated by the Buddha and other saints; and the consecrated scrap of silk, called sungdū, 'knot of blessing,' was the Grand Lāma's usual return for presents made to him by pilgrims and devotees.

We may note here that in 1866 the Indian explorer Nain Singh saw the then Dalai Lāma. He was a handsome boy about thirteen years old, and was seated on a throne six feet high. He had the Regent on his right hand. He was said to be in his thirteenth transmigration[1].

Dr. Schlagintweit (p. 239) describes a ceremony in which consecrated water (thui) is poured from a teapot-like vessel over a metallic mirror (pp. 458, 463 of these Lectures), which is held so as to reflect the image of Gautama Buddha seated on the altar. This water falls down into a flat vessel containing a bag filled with rice, and is then suitable for ceremonial ablutions.

Another ceremony (called Nyungne? by Schlagintweit), involving long abstinence, lasts for four days.

The first and second days are passed in preparations. Those who are to take part in the ceremony rise at sunrise, bathe and prostrate themselves several times before the image of Avalokiteśvara. The head Lāma then bids them confess their faults, and meditate on the evils resulting from demerit. He next, with his attendants, recites extracts from certain books of confession. This goes on till ten o'clock, when tea is taken. After this the recitations and prayer-recitals

---

[1] See Mr. Clements Markham's Tibet, p. cxiii.

continue till two o'clock, when a meal of vegetables is eaten. Then comes a pause, but the prayers and readings are afterwards carried on till late at night, tea being handed round at intervals. Before retiring to rest, the head Lāma specifies the various duties to be performed by the devotees on the following day, and orders them, as a penance, to sleep in 'the lion-posture,' viz. to lie on the right side, to stretch out the feet and to support the head with the right hand [1].

The third day is the most important, and is passed in rigorous abstinence from all food. No one is even allowed to swallow his saliva, which must be ejected into a vessel placed before him. Not a word must be spoken. Each man prays and confesses his sins, but does so in absolute silence This continues till sunrise on the fourth day.

It was at first the rule that repetitions of the Law, confessions of sin (especially the Pātimokkha), and some of the chief religious ceremonies (including fasting) should take place, more particularly on the days of new and full moon (called Uposatha, p. 84).

Thus we read that 'on the day of full moon Ānanda purified himself, and went up to the upper story of his house to keep the sacred day' (Mahāsudassana-sutra, 1–10). This was in conformity with the ancient Brāhmanical rule that every new-moon day (Darśa) and every full-moon day (Paurṇamāsa) should be set apart for special religious observances [2].

---

[1] This was the Buddha's attitude when he died (see pp. 50, 241). He is called 'a Lion.' (See note 2, p. 332.)

[2] See my 'Brāhmanism and Hindūism,' p. 367.

In later times the intermediate quarter-moon days were also held sacred, and so the number of Uposatha days (see p. 84) was increased to four in every month, or once a week. Very strict Buddhists in Tibet eat nothing on these days between sunrise and sunset except farinaceous food with tea (p. 346).

The laity are invited to join in keeping the Uposatha days, but take no real part in the detail of the services. The same rule applies to all religious ceremonies. Laymen may be present at any rite, but without co-operating in carrying out the ritual. Still, laymen have their own part to perform. They look on—listen, tell their rosaries, and repeat short prayers—such as the 'three-refuge' and 'jewel-lotus' formula (pp. 78, 370)—and make declarations to avoid the five great sins (p. 126). Or they walk up to the image-altar and place offerings on it, or bow before it and receive the Lāma's benediction. Theoretically, the laity only exist to honour and support the monkhood, and to be blessed by them in return. At all events a layman's religion is usually restricted to a very limited range of duty.

One common way of showing piety is by walking round temples, monasteries, Stūpas, and sacred walls (see pp. 380, 505), from east to west, keeping the right shoulder towards them, and even occasionally measuring the ground with the extended body.

This last task is by no means a light or easy one. According to M. Huc (i. 202), a whole day scarcely suffices to perform the circumambulation when the monastic buildings and temples occupy an extensive area. People begin at daybreak, and the feat must be accomplished all at one time, without any break, or even a few moments' pause for taking nourishment. Moreover, the measuring-process must be perfect; 'the body must be extended to its whole length, and the forehead must touch the earth while the arms are stretched out in front and the hands joined.' At each prostration a circle must be drawn on the ground with two rams' horns held in the hands. 'It is a sorrowful spectacle, and the unfortunate people often have their faces and clothes covered with dust and mud. The utmost severity of the weather does not present any obstacle to their courageous devotion. They continue their prostrations through rain, snow, and cold. Sometimes they go through the additional penance of carrying an enormous weight of books on their backs. You meet with men, women, and even children sinking under these excessive burdens. When they have finished their circumambulation, they are considered to have acquired the same merit as if they had recited all the prayers contained in the books they have carried.' In point of fact they are generally far too ignorant to be able to read the books, and the carrying of them on their backs is taken as an adequate equivalent.

The acquisition of merit by circumambulation is not an exclusively Hindū or Buddhist idea. The Holy House at Loretto near Ancona—believed to have been transported there from Bethlehem by angels—is circumambulated by pilgrims on their knees, but keeping the sacred object to the left. Indeed, we may fitly conclude the present Lecture by a comparison between the ritual of Tibetan Buddhism and that of Roman Catholicism—

a comparison, too, drawn by the Roman Catholic Missionaries themselves:

'The cross, the mitre, the dalmatica, the cope, which Grand Lāmas wear on their journeys, or when they are performing some ceremony out of the temple; the service with double choirs, the psalmody, the exorcisms, the censer for incense, suspended from five chains, and opened or closed at pleasure; the benedictions pronounced by the Lāmas by extending the right hand over the heads of the faithful; the chaplet, ecclesiastical celibacy, spiritual retirement, the worship of the saints, the fasts, the processions, the litanies, the holy water, all these are analogies between the Buddhists and ourselves' (Huc, ii. 50). To these may be added sacred images, sacred pictures, sacred symbols, relics, lamps, and illuminations [1].

This is doubtless a true comparison. But it does not follow that the opinion which the missionaries express—'that these analogies are of Christian origin'—is equally deserving of our assent. No doubt one chief feature of Buddhism, as of Hindūism [2], is its receptivity, but may it not be the case that human nature and human tendencies will be found to assert themselves independently in every part of the world, wherever surrounding circumstances are favourable to their development?

---

[1] I found, when in the South of India, that an image of Bhavānī in a Hindū temple was very like that of the Virgin Mary in an adjacent Roman Catholic Church. I was told that the same Hindū carver carved both.

[2] We know that Hindūism, in the end, adopted Buddha himself, and converted him into one of the incarnations of Vishṇu (see 'Brāhmanism and Hindūism,' p. 114).

LECTURE XIII.

Festivals, Domestic Rites, and Formularies of Prayer.

WE must now turn to the consideration of some of the chief festivals, domestic rites, and prayer-formularies of Buddhism—a subject which follows as a natural sequel to the last Lecture.

It is well known that the Hindūs have certain festivals and holy days, celebrated at the junction of the seasons which in India are properly six in number—namely, spring, summer, the rains (Varsha), autumn, winter, and the season of dew and mist (see 'Indian Wisdom,' p. 450; 'Brāhmanism and Hindūism,' p. 428).

Buddhism has adopted the old Hindū ideas on this subject, and has added others of its own, but generally only reckons three seasons—summer, the rains (Vassa = Varsha) and winter.

The festival of the New Year is, of course, universal. It is supposed to celebrate the victory of light over darkness, and, in Buddhist countries, of Buddhism over ignorance. The corresponding Hindū festival is called Makara-saṅkrānti. In India this marks the termination of the inauspicious month Pausha and the beginning of the sun's northern course (uttarāyaṇa) in the heavens. It is a season of general rejoicing.

In Burma, where a good type of Southern Buddhism is still to be found, the New Year's festival might suitably be called a 'water-festival.' It has there so little connexion with the increase of the New Year's light, that it often takes place as late as the early half of April (see Mr. Scott's 'Burman,' ii. 48). It is, however, a movable feast, the date of which is regularly fixed by the astrologers of Mandalay, 'who make intricate calculations based on the position of various constellations.' The object is to determine on what precise day the king of the Naths (see p. 217 of this volume) will descend upon the earth and inaugurate the new year. When the day arrives all are on the watch, and just at the right moment—which invariably occurs at midnight—a cannon is fired off, announcing the descent of the Nath-king upon earth. Forthwith (according to Mr. Scott) men and women sally out of their houses, carrying pots full of water consecrated by fresh leaves and twigs of a sacred tree (p. 514 of this volume), repeat a formal prayer, and pour out the water on the ground. At the same time all who have guns of any kind discharge them, so as to greet the new year with as much noise as possible.

Then, 'with the first glimmer of light,' all take jars full of fresh water and carry them off to the nearest monastery. First they present them to the monks, and then proceed to bathe the images. This work is usually done by the women of the party, 'who reverently clamber up' and empty their goblets of water over the placid features of the Buddhas and Bodhisattvas. Then begin the Saturnalia. All along the road are urchins with squirts and syringes, with which they have been furtively practising for the last few days. The skill thus acquired is exhibited by the accuracy of their aim. Cold streams of water catch the ears of the passers by. Young men and girls salute one another with the contents of jars and goblets. Shouts of merriment are heard in every quarter. Before breakfast every one is soaked, but no one thinks of changing his garments, for the weather is warm, and 'water is everywhere.' The girls are the most enthusiastic, and as they generally go in bands and carry copious reservoirs along with them, 'unprotected males' are soon routed. Then a number of 'zealous people' go down to the river, wade into the water knee-deep, splash about and drench one another till they are tired. No one escapes. For three days no one likes to be seen with dry clothes. The wetting is a compliment. A clerk comes up to his master, bows, and 'gravely pours the contents of a silver cup down the back of his neck,' saying, 'let me do homage to you with water.'

It appears from Mr. Scott's amusing narrative that, when there was a king in Burma, an important feature of the festival was the formal washing of his Majesty's head.

The New Year's rejoicings in Ceylon require no special notice.

In Tibet the New Year's festival properly begins at new moon, and may be delayed till some time in February. The festival lasts fifteen days, and, as usual, is a season of general festivity, gifts, congratulations, mummery, dancing, and acting. It is the Lāmistic carnival.

According to M. Huc (ii. 216) the rejoicings commence (as in Burma) at midnight. At Lhāssa all the inhabitants sit up, awaiting the solemn moment which is to close the old year and open the new. The usages differ so curiously from those customary in Southern Buddhist countries, that I here give an abbreviated version of the two French travellers' experiences.

Not being at all eager to watch for the moment of separation between the two Tibetan years, we went to bed at our usual hour, and were wrapped in profound slumber, when we were suddenly awakened by cries of joy issuing from all quarters of the town. Bells, cymbals, conchs, tambourines, and all the instruments of Tibetan music, were set to work together and produced the most frightful uproar imaginable. We had a good mind to get up to witness the happiness of the inhabitants of Lhāssa, but the cold was so cutting that, after reflection, we decided to remain under our woollen coverlets, and to unite ourselves in heart only with the public felicity. Unhappily for our comfort, violent knocks on our door, threatening to smash it into splinters, warned us that we must renounce our project. We therefore donned our clothes, and the door being opened, some friendly Tibetans rushed into our room, inviting us to the New Year's banquet. They all bore in their hands a small vessel made of baked earth, in which balls of honey and flour floated on boiling water. One visitor offered us a long silver needle, terminating in a hook, and invited us to fish in his basin. At first we sought to excuse ourselves, objecting that we were not in the habit of taking food during the night, but they entreated us so warmly, and put out their tongues at us with so friendly a grace, that we were obliged to comply, and resign ourselves to a participation in the New Year's festivities. Each of us, therefore, hooked a ball, which we then crushed between our teeth to ascertain its flavour. For politeness sake we had to swallow the dose, but not without making some grimaces. Nor could we get off with this first act of devotion. The New Year was inexorable. Our numerous friends at Lhāssa succeeded each other almost without interruption, and we had perforce to munch Tibetan sweetmeats till daybreak.

It is said that other peculiar customs follow, one of which the Tibetans call the Lhāssa-Moru. This takes place on the third day, and leads to the invasion of the town and its environs by innumerable bands of Lāmas. Immense numbers of Lāmas, some on foot, some on horseback, some on asses or oxen, and all carrying cooking-utensils and prayer-books, crowd into Lhāssa from all points. The town is completely overrun. Those who cannot get lodgings encamp in the streets and squares, or pitch their tents in the suburbs. The tribunals are closed, and the course of justice is suspended. The Lāmas parade the streets in disorderly bands, uttering discordant cries, pushing one another about, quarrelling, fighting, and yet, in the midst of all, chanting their prayers (Huc, ii. 218).

In Tibet there is a 'water-festival' in the seventh or eighth month (about our August and September). At this festival the Lāmas go in procession to rivers and lakes, and consecrate the waters by benediction or by throwing in offerings. Huts and tents are erected on the banks, and people bathe and drink to wash away their sins. It concludes with dancing, buffoonery, and masquerading.

The festival of Gautama Buddha's conception, or of the Buddha's *last* birth—for it must be borne in mind that, before Buddhahood, he went through innumerable previous births—is a most important anniversary in all Buddhist countries, but the right date has been the occasion of much controversy. The event is generally celebrated at the end of April, or beginning of May, or on a day corresponding to the 15th day of the Hindū month Vaiśākha, which is also sometimes given as the date of the Buddha's attainment of Buddhahood, and of his death. Everywhere throughout the modern Buddhist world the Buddha's birthday is kept by the worship of his images, followed by processions.

As to the day of his death, Sarat Chandra Dās was at Lhāssa on June 1, 1882, and wrote thus :—'To-day being the holiest day of the year—the anniversary of Buddha's Nirvāṇa—the burning of incense in every shrine, chapel, monastery, and house, darkened the atmosphere with smoke. Men hastened to the great temple to do homage to the Buddha and to obtain his blessing.'

The 'festival of lamps' is an important anniversary with all Buddhists. The Hindūs have their Dīvālī or feast of illuminations (see 'Brāhmanism and Hindūism,' p. 432) when the cold season begins. The early Buddhists marked the end of the rainy season (Vassa = Varsha), which terminated their period of retirement, by a day of rejoicing (see p. 84). In process of time they connected the celebration of Gautama's descent from heaven (p. 417) with the termination of Vassa.

In Tibet the orthodox followers of the Dalai Lāma have a festival of their own, with illuminations, on the 25th day of the 10th month (Nov.–Dec.), to celebrate the ascension of Tsong Khapa to heaven (p. 280). Sarat Chandra Dās was at Tashi Lunpo on this day in 1881, when 'hundreds of lamp-burners were tastefully placed in rows on the roof of every building.' The illuminations of the temples, tombs, and grand monastery 'presented a magnificent appearance.'

With regard to the season called Vassa, it should be noted here that since there is no rainy period of the year in Tibet which corresponds to the Indian 'Rains,' certain seasons of abstinence from food are observed either before, or at the same time with the great Festivals. These periods of fasting are distributed equally throughout the year—one in February, one in May, one in July, one in November or December.

The festivals and holy days thus briefly described, are by no means the only festivals of Buddhism. There are numerous other special and local ones. For example, in Ceylon, the Sinhalese celebrate the coming of the Buddha to their island and his victory over the Rākshasas and evil demons by a festival in March or April, when the greater number of pilgrims flock to his supposed foot-print on Adam's Peak, or to the sacred Bodhi-tree at Anurādha-pura (see p. 519). Other Southern countries have festivals connected with the worship of special foot-prints and relics of their own.

Then the Lāmas in Lhāssa keep the day of the worship of the Dorje (see p. 322) on the 27th day of the first month, while those in Sikkim celebrate as a festival the day on which the Lepchas make offerings to the spirit of the mountain Kinchinjunga.

Then, again, at the beginning of the third month an exhibition of sacred vessels and pictures takes place at Lhāssa, accompanied by processions in masks, the Lāmas appearing as good genii, and the laity as tigers, leopards, elephants, &c.

In other places, too, there are special festivals. For example, a singular festival, called 'Chase of the spirit-kings,' is kept by Northern Buddhists on the 30th of the second month, when there is a vast amount of religious dancing (with tediously slow movements), masquerading, mummery, and buffoonery, not unlike the devil-dancing which goes on in Ceylon, and closely connected with the universal belief in demons and evil spirits.

The most hideous masks are used on these occasions. In 1884 I had an opportunity of inspecting in a Buddhist monastery near Dārjīling a most singular assortment of religious masks, which for distortion of feature and horrible unsightliness, could scarcely be matched anywhere; for indeed mask-making is an art which Buddhism has brought to the greatest perfection. I also witnessed a religious dance performed by a party of masqueraders which struck me as a remarkable example of the utter debasement of Buddhism in Northern countries.

Mrs. Bridges describes a similar religious dance in Ladāk thus:—

'A group of grinning masks—lions' heads and harlequins' bodies—came down the steps, and whirling slowly round, retreated again into the gloom and came out dragon-headed. Then a band of skeletons, the skulls (masks) admirably painted, gnashing their hideous jaws and shaking their lanky limbs, rushed out into the sunshine and executed a real "Dance of Death" before us.' ('Travels,' p. 101.)

Yet all true Buddhists are prohibited from dancing and masquerading (p. 126 of this volume); just as Manu (II. 178, IV. 15, 212) prohibited Brāhmans from engaging in similar frivolities.

Then the religious dramas performed on some of

the Buddhist festive days are not the least interesting examples of the present prevalent superstitions.

I witnessed part of a dramatic performance at a Burmese Theatre in Calcutta (during the Exhibition year), when the story of the Hindū Epic, called Rāmāyaṇa, and especially that portion of it which relates to the carrying off of Sītā by demons (see 'Brāhmanism and Hindūism,' p. 42, and 'Indian Wisdom,' p. 337), was dramatically represented. The theatre was a rude wooden enclosure open to the sky, with the exception of a portion roofed over for a band of musicians, whose noisy performances appeared to constitute an important element in the proceedings. The chief musician sat on the ground in the middle of a circular frame-work—about two or three feet high—hung round with drums of different sizes, which he struck with his hands, and occasionally tuned by the application of moist clay in larger or smaller lumps. In the centre of the open area of flat dusty soil which served for the stage, a big branch of a tree was stuck upright, possibly to represent the forest in which Rāma lived with his wife. Then the hero and heroine of the drama—Rāma and Sītā—kept up a tedious colloquy, interspersed with jokes, for hours. The former—who, be it remembered, was supposed to be a god—smoked a cigar all the while, and occasionally ejected saliva with perfect indifference to all appearances and to all laws of congruity, while every now and again Sītā, in spite of a tight dress, varied the monotony of the dialogue by executing a slow dance, characterized by strange contortions, twistings, and wrigglings of the limbs. Hideous masks were at intervals assumed by the actors, and, of course, by the demons who intervened at odd moments with much ludicrous gesticulation. The action of the play went on continuously for about ten days, during which period people came and went as they liked, and the last comers entered into the progress of the plot with as much interest as if they had witnessed the whole. There is never much originality of invention in these religious plays. The Indian heroic poems and the five hundred and fifty birth-stories (see p. 63) of the Buddha furnish the basis of all.

The religious dramas of Tibet are of a somewhat different character. The following description is founded on Dr. Schlagintweit's account (p. 233), and on that of Mrs. Bridges in her interesting 'Travels' (John Murray, 1883, p. 130).

The dramatis personæ consist of three classes.—1. Tutelary deities or good genii, called Dragshed (Dragśed), who ward off the assaults of evil demons; 2. Evil demons; 3. Men. The actors of each class are distinguished by their masks. The first class—that is the Dragsheds or good genii—wear masks of enormous size and terrific aspect[1]. The second class—that is the Evil demons—wear larger masks of a dark colour, and their garments are well padded to deaden the force of the blows showered upon them. The third class—that is the Men—wear the usual dress of human beings, and masks of a natural size and colour, while under their clothes they carry heavy wooden sticks, with which at times, during the progress of the drama, they belabour the demons. The gods also get well knocked about by the demons, much to the amusement of the spectators.

The drama is preceded by the recital of hymns and prayers and by

[1] These good deities, according to Schlagintweit, are represented with formidable countenances and dark complexions, and a third eye in the forehead—probably the eye of wisdom, as in the Dhyāni-Buddhas (see p. 203 of these Lectures).

noisy music. The Dragsheds occupy the centre, the men are on their right and the demons on their left. At short intervals the men and the demons execute slow dances, each group by itself. At last, an evil spirit and a man step forth. The evil spirit then tries, in a plausible speech, to tempt the man to violate some precept of morality, while other evil spirits approach and chime in. The man at first stands firm, but gradually gives way and is about to yield, when other men come forward and entreat him not to be seduced by the artful suggestions of the demons. He is then closely pressed by the two opposite parties, but in the end takes the advice of his human counsellors. Upon this all the men break out into praise of the Dragsheds, to whose presence and assistance they ascribe the victory. The Dragsheds now proceed to punish the evil demons. The leading Dragshed, who is distinguished by an unusually large yellow mask, advances against them surrounded by about a dozen followers. Other Dragsheds next rush out from the back-ground, shoot arrows, throw stones, and even fire with muskets upon the demons, while the men belabour them with their sticks, hitherto concealed under their clothes. The demons are routed, and run in every direction pursued by the good genii. The drama concludes by all the actors (men and demons included) singing hymns in honour of the victorious tutelary genii.

Among the spectators (at the performance witnessed by Mrs. Bridges at Leh) were six deities, represented by six Lāmas seated on a bench with umbrellas over their heads. They had incense swung before them by attendant priests.

This curious dramatic performance is paralleled in India by the Hindū drama called Prabodha-ćandrodaya, 'Rise of the moon of true knowledge,' in which we have Faith, Volition, Opinion, Imagination, Contemplation, Devotion, Quietude, Friendship, &c., on one side; Error, Self-conceit, Hypocrisy, Love, Passion, Anger, Avarice, on the other. The two sets of characters are, of course, opposed to each other, the object of the play being to show how the orthodox faith of the Hindūs became victorious over the erroneous doctrine of the Buddha—the Buddhists and other heretical sects being represented as adherents of the losing side.

Then—to take a parallel nearer home—we find similar religious dramas acted in England not so very long ago (about the time of Henry VIII). For example, in the old English morality play, called 'Every-man,' some of the dramatis personæ on the one side are—God, Death, Every-man, Fellowship, Kindred, Good-deeds, Knowledge, Confession, Beauty, Strength, Discretion; while on the other are personifications of the opposite qualities. Then, again, in 'Lusty Juventus,' we have a medley of Good Counsel, Knowledge, Satan, Hypocrisy, Fellowship, Abominable Living, God's Merciful Promises.

And here with reference to the supposed contest continually going on between good and evil, and the participation of human beings in this terrible struggle, we may note that the mystical thunderbolt called Dorje (p. 322) is not the only implement of spiritual warfare employed by the Lāmas against the demons [1]. Another important weapon is the Phurbu or 'nail,' described as triangular and wedge-shaped, with the thin end very sharp-pointed, and with the head of Tamdin (a particular Dragshed = Haya-grīva, noted for his power) emerging from the broad end and surmounted by a half-thunderbolt for a handle.

According to Schlagintweit, this weapon is often made of cardboard, on which mystical sentences (Dhāraṇīs) in

[1] See the account of the female demons called Tanma at p. 457 of these Lectures.

Sanskṛit are inscribed, some against the demons of the South, some against those of the East, and some against those of the South-east. In case of illness a Lāma goes round the house turning the point of the Phurbu in all directions and uttering magical spells.

Most of the Dhāraṇīs end with the syllables Hūm phaṭ, the potency of which in scaring evil demons is irresistible. Many charms begin with Ah Tamdin.

Those Phurbus are considered most efficacious which are inscribed with mystical syllables and words composed by either the Dalai Lāma or Panchen Lāma. These are sold for large sums. It is said (Schlagintweit, 260) that such Phurbus form an important article of trade for the Mongolian pilgrims returning from Tibet.

I was fortunate enough to meet with a remarkable specimen of a magical weapon of this kind (called Phur-pa by Jäschke) made of metal, and shaped like a dagger with three edges, one for each of the three classes of demons inhabiting the three quarters. The handle is composed of a Dorje (p. 322), and is surmounted by carvings of the heads of the three most powerful Dragsheds. I here give a representation of it[1].

[1] The shape is not quite the same as that of the Phurbu, but there can be no doubt of its being a kindred weapon. I purchased my specimen at Dārjīling, and was assured that it came from Tibet, and was used by the Tibetans in the same way as the Phurbu.

It may be easily understood that among a people, steeped in superstition, a man armed with such a weapon as this—composed of the heads of three potent genii, a divine thunderbolt and a triple-edged dagger—would be regarded as a match for the whole demon-host.

In Burma the tattooing of mystical squares, triangles and cabalistic diagrams and figures on various parts of the body, seems to be regarded as a sufficient substitute for the use of magical weapons, and is held to be highly efficacious.

Obviously we may contrast the Christian armoury described by S. Paul (Ephes. vi. 11), 'the shield of faith and the sword of the Spirit.' We might also contrast the words of Christ, 'Rejoice not, that the spirits are subject unto you; but rather rejoice, because your names are written in heaven' (S. Luke x. 20).

Domestic Rites and Usages.

I now pass on to domestic rites and usages, which are as numerous and important in Buddhist countries as in India. It is said, indeed, that in Tibet and Mongolia no one is so poor as not to possess an altar in his dwelling on which he daily lays his offerings, and before which he performs devotions.

In Ceylon and Burma certain ceremonies take place soon after the birth of a child. Mr. Scott, describing those in Burma, says that a fortnight after birth a fortunate day and hour is fixed by an astrologer for the naming of the infant. A feast is prepared, and all the friends and relations of the family are invited. 'The child's head is usually washed for the first time on this day,' and some one suggests a name.

The name actually given appears to be a matter of choice, but this is not so. The consonants of the language are divided into groups, which are assigned to the days of the week, Sunday having all the vowels to itself. 'It is an invariable rule in all respectable families that the child's name must begin with one of the letters belonging to the day on which it was born, but within these limits any name may be chosen.' A common belief is that, according to the day of the week (or rather the constellation representing that day) on which a child is born, so will its character be.

In this way every person's probable characteristics may be inferred. For example, a man born on a Monday is likely to be jealous; on Tuesday, honest; on Wednesday, hot-tempered—but soon appeased—this characteristic being intensified under the influence of Rāhu [1].

Then, again, if born on a Thursday, a man will probably be mild; on Friday, talkative; on Saturday, ill-tempered and quarrelsome; on Sunday, parsimonious. Saturday is a bad day for everything. Not only has every day its special character and its fixed letters, but there is also (according to Mr. Scott) a particular animal assigned to symbolize it—for example, a guinea-pig stands for Friday; a dragon for Saturday; a tiger for Monday—and red or yellow wax candles are made in

---

[1] See 'Brāhmanism and Hindūism,' p. 345.

the forms of these animals to be offered at the Pagoda by the pious. Each worshipper offers the creature-candle representing his birth-day.

Then a careful note is made of the exact hour of birth, with the important object of drawing up the child's horoscope. This may be delayed till the fifth or sixth year, and a Brāhman astrologer may be called in for the purpose. He records the year, the month, the day and hour at which the child was born; the name given to it and the planet in the ascendant at the moment. All this is scratched neatly on a palm-leaf with a metal style. On the other side are a number of cabalistic squares and numbers from which future calculations may be made.

A person born on Monday remains under the influence of the moon for fifteen years. Then he passes under Mars for eight years. At the age of twenty-three Mercury presides over him, and so on through all the planets to the end of his life, which may be protracted to 108 years.

Rāhu, and especially Saturn, have a particularly sinister influence. A man does most of the stupid and wicked things in his life while he is in Saturn's house. Other details will be found in 'Shway Yoe.'

The horoscope is carefully kept by the parents until the child is old enough to take care of it himself, and thenceforward it is guarded as a valuable possession.

All these Buddhist customs have their counterpart in the ceremonies of Brāhmanism and Hindūism.

For example, the Hindūs have their birth-ceremonies (Jāta-karman), and their name-giving ceremony (Nāmakaraṇa[1]), and the latter is a solemn religious act fraught with momentous consequences in its bearing on a child's future. Hence Hindū boys are generally called after some god, or the name indicates that the child is the god's servant. Horoscopes, too, are as important in India as in Buddhist countries[2].

In India, too, all Brāhman boys go through the ceremony of tonsure and cutting off the hair.

Among the Buddhists of Burma a boy is sent to the monastery school at about the age of eight. Before he can become a novice he has to undergo the hair-abscission ceremony, followed by shaving every fortnight (as before described). But those who afterwards elect to lead a secular life wear long hair, to wash which is regarded as a kind of religious ceremonial, and only to be performed about once a month, partly, says Mr. Scott, because the washing of a Burman's luxuriant hair takes a long time, and partly because too frequent ablutions 'would disturb and irritate the good genius who dwells in the head and protects the man.'

It is considered unlucky to wash the head on a Monday, Friday, or Saturday; and 'parents sending their boy to a monastery must remember not to cut his hair off on a Monday, or on a Friday, or on his birth-day.'

It is noticeable that a kind of baptism is practised in Tibet and Mongolia. It is usual to sprinkle

---

[1] See my work on 'Brāhmanism and Hindūism,' pp. 357, 358, 370, etc.

[2] See the translation of a horoscope given in 'Brāhmanism and Hindūism,' p. 373.

children with consecrated water, or even to immerse them entirely on the third or tenth day after birth. This is called Khrus-sol (according to Jäschke).

The priest consecrates the water by reciting some formula, while candles and incense are burning. He then dips the child three times, blesses it, and gives it a name. After performing the ceremony, he draws up the infant's horoscope.

Then, so soon as the child can walk and talk, a second ceremony takes place, when prayers are said for its happy life, and an amulet or little bag is hung round its neck, filled with spells and charms against evil spirits and diseases.

The use of *amulets* (Sanskṛit kavaća), charms and spells in Northern Buddhist countries is universal.

At Dārjīling I noticed that among the crowds of persons who frequented the bazaar—many of whom were travellers from Tibet, Nepāl, Bhutān, and Sikkim—almost every one wore an amulet, or a string of amulets round the neck. Most of these amulets are simply ornamental boxes or receptacles for supposed relics of saints, or for little images, or pictures, or for prayer-formularies, worn, like breast-plates or phylacteries. They are composed of wood, bone, and not infrequently of beautifully-worked filigree silver, embossed and ornamented with turquoise. The shape is sometimes square, sometimes circular or curved, and brought round to a point[1]. I purchased several specimens, but the vendor of any amulet in actual use in-

[1] According to Schlagintweit, those amulets which are curved round to a point are intended to represent the leaf of the sacred fig-tree.

variably removed the contents before consenting to part with it. Here is a specimen of one of exceptionally beautiful design which was given to me by Mr. Sarat Chandra Dās. It was taken from the neck of a woman in the bazaar, but not purchased without much difficulty.

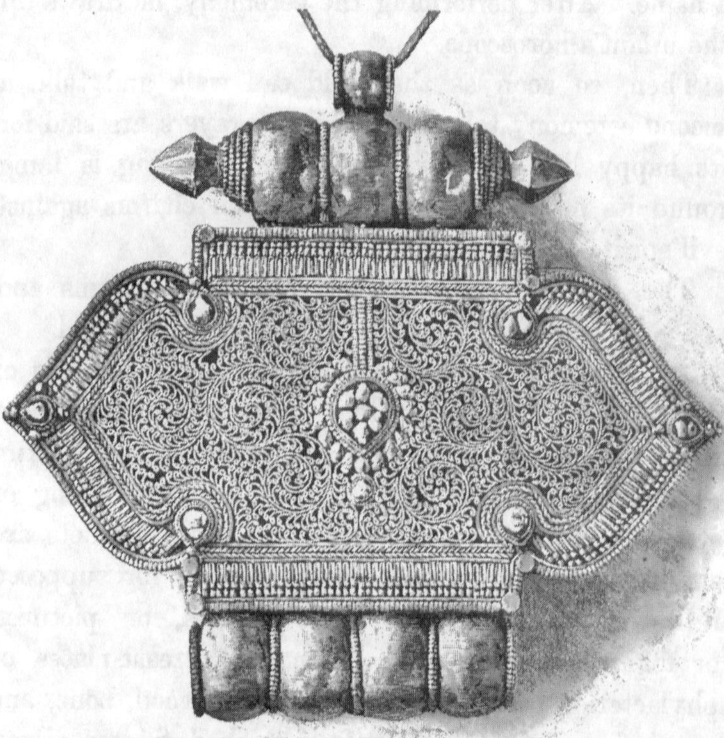

We pass on next to the Buddhist *marriage-ceremony*. This in Ceylon, Burma, Tibet, Mongolia, and indeed in all Buddhist countries, is properly a purely civil contract witnessed only by parents and guardians. We have already pointed out, that true Buddhism considers celibacy to be the only sure means of attaining real sanctity of character. Consistently with this idea, it has not prescribed any religious ceremony to be performed by monks or priests, as a condition of the validity of marriage[1].

Hence among Buddhists the ceremony of marriage is very simple, and has no religious character, or at any rate no complicated religious observances connected with it, as among the Hindūs[2]. In fact the celibate monks of true Buddhism would be much scandalized if they were asked to take part in the celebration of a wedding, or even to ratify it by their presence.

The principal ceremony consists in a feast given by the bridegroom or his parents, to which all the relations, friends, and neighbours are invited. Nevertheless, in most Buddhist countries in the present day the monks manage to have some remunerative work to do in connexion with weddings; for their business is to fix the most auspicious days for the performance of the ceremony, in return for which they receive offerings of various kinds. We know that in India astrology is a chief factor in all marriage-arrangements. Similarly in most Buddhist countries no wedding can take place till the astrologer, who is usually a monk-priest, has been

[1] In this it did good service, at least for a time; for the cost of marriage-ceremonies among the Hindūs often cripples the resources of a family for years. The marriage of the poorest persons sometimes entails expenses in gifts to the Brāhmans, etc., to the amount of 300 rupees.

[2] Mr. Scott points out in his 'Burman' that this is especially the case in Burma.

consulted as to lucky and unlucky combinations, and the benign or baleful aspects of planets and stars. For example, in Burma, Saturdays and Thursdays are pronounced unlucky days, and it would be the height of imprudence to marry in certain months of the year. Then, again, a woman born on a Friday would be guilty of utter folly if she married a man born on a Monday, seeing that one or other would soon die[1]; and so on through a long list of auspicious and inauspicious potentialities.

It should, however, be set down to the credit of Buddhism that wives and daughters are not imprisoned in Zanānas, as among Hindūs and Muhammadans. I was present at an evening-party given by a rich native of Ceylon, when the ladies of the family were introduced to the European guests, and conversed freely with the rest of the company. Nor is the marriage of mere boys and girls insisted on in Buddhist countries as in India. The bridegroom is seldom of a less age than eighteen or nineteen.

Then, again, not only births and marriages, but illnesses and death are in the present day a source of revenue to the Buddhist monkhood.

First, as to *sickness*.

In Ceylon, when any one is dangerously ill, the monk-priest is summoned from the neighbouring Vihāra, after first sending offerings of flowers, oil, and food. Then a temporary preaching-place is erected near the house, and all the relatives and friends, and if possible

---

[1] Scott's 'Burman,' p. 125.

the sick man himself, listen to the reading of the Law (Baṇa) for about six hours. The part especially read and intoned is the Ratna-valiya section of the Pirit (see p. 317). After the Baṇa a number of offerings are given to the reciting priest, including a piece of calico, one end of which is held by the priest, and the other by the sick man. Then the priest pronounces a benediction, and says words to the following effect:—'By reverence do the wise secure health, by almsgiving do they lay up treasures for themselves[1].'

When the sick man is likely to die the priest repeats the Three-refuge formula (p. 78), the five commandments (p. 126), and the Sati-paṭṭhāna Sutta (p. 49).

In Burma, if an epidemic happens to break out in any village, the people begin by painting the supposed figure of an evil spirit on a common earthenware water-pot, and then solemnly smashing it to pieces at sunset with a heavy stick[2]. Then as soon as it gets dark all the villagers shout, yell, shriek, and make every kind of deafening din, with the hope of frightening away the evil spirit who has caused the disease. This process is continued for three nights, and if no good result follows the monk-priests are called in from the monastery. They recite the ten precepts, chant the Law up and down the road, and intone a particular sermon of the Buddha, by the preaching of which he once drove

[1] My authority for this is Mr. J. F. Dickson's pamphlet called 'Notes and illustrations of Buddhism,' etc.

[2] Scott's 'Burman,' i. 282.

away a pestilence. These means are, of course, not effective unless abundant alms and gifts are bestowed upon the monastery.

According to Koeppen and Huc the art of medicine in Northern Buddhist countries is practised exclusively by the Lāmas. The theory is that there are 140 different maladies, and that most of these are caused by devils. The monk-priests are the sole doctors, and a sick person can only be cured by them. One process is simple. It begins by the Lāma doctor writing the name of a remedy upon a morsel of paper, moistening it with saliva, and rolling it into a pill. The patient takes the paper pellet with as much faith as if he were swallowing the veritable drug. Many Mongols believe that 'it is precisely the same, whether you swallow a drug or its written appellation.' Then, 'if the patient be poor, the devil is a little one, and may be dislodged by a few prayers; but, if he be rich, the case is different; fine clothes, handsome boots, or even a good horse must be presented, or he will not consent to turn out.'

A very effective medicine may be composed of the bones of some pious Lāma ground into a powder. This may be given alone or in combination with other substances.

It appears to be essential that the prayers recited on these occasions should be accompanied by terrific noises. M. Huc relates a story of an old woman—the aunt of a certain chief—who was one day attacked by intermittent fever. The Lāma, of course, announced that a devil had possession of her body; and so in the evening he and eight other Lāmas began operations for its expulsion. First they made a little figure or manikin of dried herbs, which they called the devil of intermittent fevers. This they stuck upright in the tent of the sick woman. Then at eleven o'clock at night the Lāmas ranged themselves at the back of the tent, armed with bells, tambourines, conch-shells, and other noisy instruments. Nine members of the family closed the circle in front, crouching on the ground, while the old woman remained seated on her heels in front of the manikin. Next, 'at a given signal, the orchestra performed an overture capable of scaring away the most imperturbable and obstinate devil, while all the secular assistants beat time with their hands to the hubbub of the instruments and the howling of the prayers. When this demoniacal music was over, the chief Lāma began his exorcisms, scattering millet seeds around as he proceeded; sometimes speaking low, sometimes in stentorian tones. Then, appearing to throw himself into a passion, he addressed animated appeals, with violent gesticulation, to the manikin.' Finally, after further incantations, he gave a signal; the Lāmas thundered out a noisy chorus, the instruments added to the din, and the members of the family rushing out in file, made the circuit of the tent, striking it frantically with stakes, and uttering terrific cries. Finally, the chief Lāma and his assistants, after joining in the yells, set fire to the manikin. This ended the ceremony; the demon being compelled to beat a retreat.

Mr. Sarat Chandra Dās has given an account of a somewhat similar ceremony in Tibet performed by some Lāmas to cure him of a sickness. An image representing the patient, and supposed to resemble him, was constructed, and a suit of his clothes placed in front of it, together with portions of his usual food and drink. Two Lāmas then muttered mystic sentences, ringing a bell, waving a Dorje (see p. 323 of these Lectures), and twisting their fingers and hands into the mysterious shapes called Mudrā (p. 241). Next they broke out into alternate exhortations and threats, and at the conclusion of the ceremony the officiating priests supplicated the lord of death (Yama) to accept the image in place of the moribund man.

On another occasion, when Mr. Sarat Chandra Dās was seriously ill in Tibet, an effective method of curing his disease was proposed to him, and, with his consent, actually carried out. This mainly consisted in the ransoming of fish-life. A certain Lāma started off for a fisherman's village, and in a short time returned in a high state of satisfaction. He had saved the lives of five hundred fishes for the benefit of the sick man. The merit of this deed was credited to the patient on his repeating the following prayer :—

'By virtue of my having ransomed the lives of these animals, let health, longevity, prosperity, and happiness perpetually accrue to me.'

In the same way in Burma, in times of great heat and drought, when the ponds and tanks appear to be on the point of drying up, it is held to be a work of enormous merit to rescue fish, put them in jars, and transport them alive to the rivers. (See Scott's 'Burman,' ii. 43.)

Similarly a bird-catcher will sell live birds to pious persons, that they may gain merit by releasing them.

We pass on, in the next place, to the usages and ceremonies common at death.

If a man's soul is to be separated from his body properly and peacefully, so as not to hurt the survivors, and in a manner likely to cause a happy re-birth for himself, alms must be bestowed on the monk-priests, and their presence must be invited for the repetition of prayers. In Ceylon and Burma monks go to the houses of mourners and repeat portions of the Pirit (see p. 317).

In Tibet the priest not only recites prayers but compresses the skull till it appears to crack, or else the hair is torn off and a little incision is made, to enable the dying man's soul to escape. The priest then settles what method of burial is to be followed, and the place, day and hour, all of which depend on astrological combinations, known only to him.

The method of disposing of a dead body differs in all Buddhist countries according to station, condition, rank, and wealth.

In Ceylon the bodies of monks are all burnt, and the cremation ceremonies are carried out under decorated arches or canopies, which are never removed, but left to crumble away.

In Burma the cremation of a monk distinguished for sanctity is an affair of great state and ceremonial. The body (see Mr. Scott's 'Burman,' ii. 331) is first embalmed, and next tightly wrapped in white cloth, which is varnished and afterwards covered with gold-leaf. The corpse thus gilded is placed in an unclosed inner coffin, and left exposed to view for a considerable time. When fastened down, the inner coffin is covered with gold-leaf, like the body. An outer sarcophagus is then prepared, and painted to represent scenes from the lives of the Buddha. This is placed in a building erected for the purpose, and there the body lies in state for several months, while a constant line of pilgrim-worshippers pass in and out. In process of time, when enough money for the expenses has been collected, a grand cremation takes place under a lofty canopy, which on special occasions may be fifty or sixty feet high. The calcined bones are then reverentially collected, and either buried near the temple or pounded and made up into a paste, with which an image of the Buddha is constructed for worship in the monastery.

In Tibet the bodies of the Grand Lāmas are generally embalmed and preserved in monuments or Stūpas. Other Lāmas and monks distinguished for sanctity are burnt, and their ashes are either distributed as relics, or preserved in idols or in small Dāgabas. Kings, princes, and great men are also burnt, and of course with much ceremony and repetition of prayers. Then for a long time afterwards prayers continue to be recited by the priests, the object being to propitiate Yama, god of Death, and to deliver the deceased from the possible purgatorial torments of one of the hells. It is said that this repetition of prayers is prolonged, in the case of the rich, for seven weeks, and in the case of princes, for a whole year.

Mr. J. Ware Edgar, C. S. I., in his interesting Report of his visit to Sikkim in 1873, gives a description of the remarkable funeral ceremonies performed on the occasion of the death of the Rājā of Sikkim's sister (see p. 62), which I here abbreviate :—

The Rājā's sister had died a few days after his return to Choombi. The body had been buried at Choombi, but her clothes had been sent to Toomlong, and her soul was supposed to accompany them. There a lay-figure meant to represent her, dressed in her costume as a nun, and wearing a gilt mitre and a long white veil, was placed on a kind of throne to the right of the great altar in the principal chapel. Before the figure was a table, on which were different kinds of food. On another table were various things which had belonged to her, while on a third, 108 little brass lamps were arranged in rows. Some days afterwards the lay-figure of the nun was taken to Pemyangchi. There, for three days the figure was seated before the altar, and the monks chanted the litanies for her soul, which had accompanied her clothes from Choombi. On the third day towards evening the tea-cup of the nun was freshly filled with tea, and all the monks solemnly drank tea with her. The monks chanted the litanies, and the Head Lāma went through some elaborate ceremonies. At about nine o'clock the chanting ceased, and the Lāma made a long speech to the soul of the nun, in which he told her that all that could be done to make her journey to another world easy, had been done, and that now she would have to go alone and unassisted to appear before the King and Judge of the dead.

'You will have to leave your robes, your mitre, and your veil,' said he, 'and clad in the black garment of your sins, or in the shining garment of your good deeds, you will be shown the mirror of the just King. Your gold and silver, your rank, your good name will not help you, when your good deeds are weighed against your evil deeds, in the scales of the King. If you have done ill, you will be punished; but if your sins are found to be lighter than your good works, your reward will be great indeed.'

When the Lāma had finished his address, some of the monks took down the lay-figure and undressed it, while others formed a procession and conducted the soul of the nun into the darkness outside the monastery, with a discordant noise of conch-shells, thigh-bone trumpets, Tibetan flutes, gongs, cymbals, tambourines, and drums.

In Japan small portions of the calcined remains (often not larger than peas) are preserved in globular glass shrines, and then duly honoured and worshipped.

The method of disposing of the dead bodies of the

laity and of the common people is generally much more simple. In most Buddhist countries laymen are buried, and the priests lead the processions to the grave. In Ceylon, the laity are certainly, as a rule, buried and not burnt.

In Burma rich laymen are also generally buried, and, according to Mr. Scott, the funeral is a grand affair.

The body is swathed in new white cotton cloth, leaving the face uncovered. A piece of gold or silver is placed between the teeth to serve as ferry-money over the Buddhist Styx—the terrible river of death which all deceased persons are compelled to pass. This river is clearly the counterpart of the Vaitaraṇī of the Hindūs (see 'Brāhmanism and Hindūism,' p. 297).

If the dead man's family is poor, a copper coin or even a betel nut will suffice. Next the monks are sent for, their immediate presence being necessary to keep off the evil spirits who always swarm near a corpse. After an interval the body is placed in a coffin, which is sometimes gilded and placed on a bier under a canopy. When the right day arrives for the funeral, a long procession is formed, with a number of priests in proportion to the amount of alms bestowed, and a crowd of relations, friends, and neighbours. Occasionally those who carry the bier stop and go through a sort of solemn dance, while mournful tunes are played by the musicians and funeral dirges are sung. The body is finally buried in a cemetery to the west of the town or village. A funeral must never go to the north or to the east. The ceremony concludes by alms to the priests, who in return intone the commandments and other portions of the Law in Pāli. After the funeral, great festivities go on in the family-abode for the benefit of the crowds who come to offer condolence. Then the presence of the priests is again needed, and has to be paid for by alms to the monastery, or the evil spirits, who are sure to hang about, cannot be got rid of. In some parts of Burma the cremation of rich laymen is not uncommon, and the ashes are either deposited in Dāgabas—that is, in small Stūpas or Pagodas [1]—or are pounded into paste and made into miniature Stūpas (p. 506) or into small images of the Buddha for worship at the domestic altar.

In Tibet and Mongolia the corpses of the laity, especially of the poor, are often exposed in the fields, in deserts, or on mountain tops, or rocks, or in lonely ravines, or sometimes in open places enclosed for the purpose. Occasionally they are covered with a thin layer of earth or loose stones. Usually they are devoured by vultures, dogs, and other animals.

It seems that in Lhāssa certain dogs are kept for that purpose [2]. A class of professional men exist there, whose business it is to cut up dead bodies, and throw the flesh piecemeal to dogs and vultures. Even the bones are sometimes pounded, and the dust, being mixed with flour, is given to be devoured. The strange thing is, that this kind of burial is thought desirable, and even honourable. To be eaten up by sacred dogs after death

[1] The Dāgabas of laymen have no umbrellas at the top (see p. 505). This privilege is only accorded to the monkhood (Scott's 'Burman').

[2] This is mentioned by Huc as well as by Koeppen.

is productive of great merit, and leads to re-birth in higher forms. Dogs are the mausoleums of Lhāssa.

According to M. Huc, a common funeral ceremony among the Mongols consists in carrying the corpse to the summit of a mountain, or to the bottom of a ravine. The body is walled up in a sort of kiln of a pyramidal form, with a small door at the bottom, and an opening at the top to maintain a current of air, and allow the smoke to escape. During the combustion the Lāmas recite prayers. When the corpse is consumed, the kiln is demolished. Then the bones are collected and carried to the Grand Lāma, who reduces them to a powder, and, after adding an equal quantity of wheaten flour, kneads the whole carefully, and, with his own hands, fashions a number of cakes of various sizes. These are afterwards placed in a pyramidal Stūpa, which has been built beforehand in some auspicious place.

The soil of the famous monastery of the Five Towers in the province of Shan Si, is said to be so holy that those interred there are sure to effect a good transmigration. In the deserts of Tartary, Mongols are frequently seen carrying on their shoulders the bones of their kindred, and journeying to the Five Towers—there to purchase, almost at its weight in gold, a little surface of ground whereon to erect a small Stūpa. Some of them undertake a toilsome journey of a whole year's duration, to reach this holy spot (see p. 435).

Burial in rivers, which is highly prized by the Hindūs, is not in favour among Buddhists. Only very poor people allow their dead to be thrown into rivers, though this is the only kind of Buddhist burial mentioned by Alberūnī (Sachau, ii. 169). Buddhism, from the first, repudiated the Hindū funeral ceremonies called Śrāddhas, which are still a great incubus on the people. The poorest man in India, if he be of high caste, cannot perform a Śrāddha for a relation for a less sum than forty rupees, given in fees to the priests. Buddhism did good service in delivering the people from this burden, but in Northern countries it established something similar in the Bardo ceremony (p. 334).

Formularies of Prayer.

With regard to prayer-formularies, there is in modern times a good deal of difference between Southern and Northern Buddhist countries. We have seen that the three-refuge formulary was the sole prayer of early Buddhists. Certain orthodox men whom I met in Ceylon, maintained to me that this is the only legitimate form of prayer that ought to be used even in the present day. It is certainly a form which is accepted and employed by all Buddhists of whatever nationality.

Tsong Khapa, it is said, established at Lhāssa an annual prayer-congregation called Monlam Ćhenpo (see p. 386). But the most common prayer used in Tibet is a mere formulary, the constant repetition of which is one of the most amazing instances of the tyranny of superstition to be found in any part of the world.

It consists of the six-syllabled sentence, Om maṇi padme Hūm, 'Om! the Jewel in the Lotus! Hūm!'

This prayer, or rather mystical sentence, is supposed

to have been composed by Padma-pāṇi (Avalokiteśvara), and to have reference to his own manifestation as the Patron-Saint of Tibet[1]. It is sometimes called the Maṇi or 'Jewel' prayer, and, if brevity is a valuable quality, its excellence is undeniable, since it consists of merely two Sanskṛit words, between two mystical, untranslatable auspicious ejaculations, Om and Hūm[2].

Doubtless the prayer really owes its origin to the close connexion which sprang up between Northern Buddhism and Śaivism. The worshippers of Śiva have always used (compare p. 240) similar mystical sentences and syllables called Dhāraṇīs, to which a kind of miraculous efficacy is attributed. In all probability an occult meaning underlies the 'Jewel-lotus' formula, and my own belief is that the majority of those who repeat it are ignorantly doing homage to the self-generative power supposed to inhere in the universe —a power pointed at by the popular Sāṅkhya theory of the union of Prakṛiti and Purusha, and by the universal worship of the Liṅga and Yoni throughout India[3]. No thoughtful person can have travelled much in India without being impressed with this.

---

[1] He is sometimes represented seated on a Lotus, or born from a Lotus.

[2] Om is borrowed from the Hindūs. It is their most sacred syllable, symbolical of their triad of gods, Brahmā, Vishṇu, and Śiva, denoted by the three mystical letter A, U, M (see my 'Brāhmanism,' p. 402). When imported into Buddhism it may possibly symbolize the Buddhist triad. Om is sometimes translated by Hail! Hūm, as a particle of solemn assent, is sometimes translated by Amen! I prefer to treat both Om and Hūm as untranslatable ejaculations.

[3] I had formed this opinion long before I saw the same view hinted at in one of Koeppen's notes (see my 'Brāhmanism and Hindūism,'

At all events, whatever be its origin and meaning, no other prayer used by human beings in any quarter of the globe is repeated so often. Every Tibetan believes it to be a panacea for all evil, a compendium of all knowledge, a treasury of all wisdom, a summary of all religion. But if you ask Northern Buddhists to give you the reason for this belief, very few are able to give an intelligible reply. According to the most learned doctors of philosophy who are to be found in Tibetan monasteries, it is certainly addressed to their patron deity Avalokiteśvara, and the real secret of its efficacy lies in the fact, that each one of its six syllables has a potent influence on some one of the six *Gatis* or courses of being—that is to say, on some one of the six kinds of transmigration or transformation through which every living individual has to pass (see p. 121)[1].

The oftener, therefore, this mystical formula is repeated the shorter will be an individual's course (gati) through some of these six forms of existence, every one of which involves misery or evil. Or it may be that by repeating it he will be able to escape some of the six existences altogether.

Strange indeed as it may appear to us, it is impossible to shake the faith of a Lāmistic Buddhist in the

---

p. 33). It is certainly remarkable that the name Maṇi is applied to the male organ, and the female is compared to a lotus-blossom in the Kāma-śāstras. I fully believe the formula to have a phallic meaning, because Tibetan Buddhism is undoubtedly connected with Śaivism.

[1] Some think, however, that the six syllables owe their efficacy to their symbolizing the six Pāramitās or transcendent virtues.

absolutely infallible efficacy of his six favourite mystic syllables. He repeats them, not at all as if he were praying in a Christian sense, but as if he were a farmer intent on planting the very best seed in the most productive soil, and watering it incessantly according to the most scientific principles of irrigation. A bountiful harvest is absolutely certain to reward his efforts.

It need not, therefore, surprise us if these six syllables are murmured morning, noon, and night, by every man, woman, and child, wherever the Lāmistic Hierarchy has extended. And, if not repeated by the voice, an incessant stream of repetition—an incessant scattering of the six mystic seeds—is kept going by the hand.

The words are written or printed on roll within roll of paper and inscribed in cylinders, which, when made to revolve either by educated monks or by illiterate laymen, have the same efficacy as if they were actually said or repeated. The revolutions are credited as so much prayer-merit, or, to speak more scientifically, as so much *prayer-force*, accumulated and stored up for the benefit of the person who revolves them.

The cylinder is generally made of metal, the prayer being engraved on the outside, as well as written on paper and inserted inside. It is held in the right hand and whirled round, like a child's toy, by means of a handle in a particular direction (with the sun). If made to revolve the other way, its rotations will be set down to the debtor rather than the creditor side of the owner's account. Here is a drawing of one of several hand-cylinders (commonly called prayer-wheels or prayer-mills; Tibetan, Ćhos-kor or Ćhos-kyi or Khor-lo), obtained by me at Dārjīling:—

Then, again, the words of the prayer are written or printed millions and millions of times on rolls or strips of paper, and enclosed in much larger barrel-like cylinders, which are set up in temples, chapels, monasteries, corridors, passages, houses, villages, by the road side, and in every possible corner, for the convenience of the mass of the people who are too ignorant to read, and too indolent to engage in continuous oral repetition[1].

It sometimes happens that quarrels arise from rival claims in regard to the use of such prayer-cylinders. In illustration of this an amusing story is told by the French missionaries:—

---

[1] Dr. Schlagintweit mentions (p. 121) that when Baron Schilling visited a certain convent he found the Lāmas occupied in preparing 100 million copies of Om maṇi padme Hūm to be inserted in a prayer-cylinder. He also states that the inscription relating to the foundation of the monastery of Hemis in Ladāk (see p. 433 of these Lectures) records the setting up of 300,000 prayer-cylinders along the walls and passages of the monastery.

One day when they happened to be passing a praying-machine, set up near a monastery, they saw two Lāmas engaged in a violent quarrel; and, as it appeared, all on account of their zeal for their prayers. The fact was that one Lāma had come, and, having set the barrel in motion for his own benefit, was retiring modestly and complacently to his own abode, when happening to turn his head to enjoy the spectacle of the wheel's pious revolutions, he saw the other Lāma stop it, and set it whirling again for himself. Indignant, of course, at this unwarrantable interference with his own devotions, he ran back, and in his turn put a stop to his rival's piety, and both of them continued this kind of demonstration for some time, till at last losing patience they proceeded to menaces, and then to blows, when an old Lāma came out of a neighbouring cell, and brought the difficulty to a peaceful termination by himself twirling the prayer-barrel for the benefit of both parties.

On the occasion of my visiting Dārjīling in 1884, I was desirous of judging for myself of the method of using these remarkable instruments of religion. I therefore, soon after my arrival, walked to a Buddhist temple near the town. There I found several large barrel-like cylinders set up close together in a row at the entrance, so that no one might pass in without giving them at least one twirl, or by a rapid sweep of his hand might set them all twirling at once. Inside the entrance-portico a shrivelled and exceptionally hideous old woman was seated on the ground. In her left hand she held a small portable prayer-cylinder, which she kept in perpetual revolution. In her right hand was a cord connected with a huge barrel-like cylinder, which with some exertión she made to rotate on its axis by help of a crank, while she kept muttering *Om maṇi pamme Hūm* (so she pronounced it) with amazing rapidity. In this way she completed at least sixty oral repetitions every minute, without reckoning the infinite number of rotatory repetitions accomplished simultaneously by her two hands. And all this was done with an appearance of apathy and mental vacuity in her withered face, which was so distressing and melancholy to behold, that the spectacle will never be effaced from my memory. In truth the venerable dame seemed to be sublimely unconscious that any effort of thought or concentration of either mind or heart was needed to make prayer of any value at all.

And the men of Tibet are quite as much slaves to this superstition as the women. A friend of mine when staying at Dārjīling had some conversation on serious subjects with an apparently sensible native, and observed with surprise that all the while he was engaged in talking with the Buddhist, the latter continued diligently whirling a prayer-cylinder with great velocity. My friend, being unacquainted with Tibetan customs, came away from his colloquy under the impression that Buddhists regard Christians as dangerous lunatics possessed with evil spirits, which require specially active measures in the way of exorcism. It did not occur to him that the Buddhist was merely intent on redeeming every instant of time for the purpose of storing up merit by prayer.

And the hold which this extraordinary superstition has upon the population is still more forcibly impressed on the traveller who penetrates into the regions beyond Dārjīling. He may there see immense prayer-cylinders set up like mills, and kept in incessant revolution, not by the will or hand of man, but by the blind, unconscious force of wind and water.

It is even said that great mechanical ingenuity is displayed by the monks in some parts of Tibet, their inventive powers being stimulated by a burning desire to economize time and labour in the production of prayer-merit by machinery.

An intricate arrangement of huge wheels and other wheels within wheels, like the works of a clock, is connected with rows of cylinders and made to revolve rapidly by means of heavy weights. An infinite number of prayers are repeated in this manner by a single monk, who takes a minute or two to wind up the complicated spiritual machinery, and then hastens to help his brothers in industrial occupations—the whole fraternity feeling that the ingenious contrivance of praying by clock-work enables them to promote the common weal by making the most of both worlds. The story goes that, in times of special need and emergency, additional weights are attached to the machinery, and, of course, increased cogency given to the rotatory prayers. It is to be hoped that when European inventions find their way across the Himālayas, steam-power may not be pressed into the service of these gross superstitions.

The use of prayer-wheels of various kinds is also common in Japan, as described in Sir Edward Reed's work.

But praying by machinery is not all. Beneficial results are believed to accrue through the carving of the all-powerful six syllables on every conceivable object.

The traveller, as he walks along, sees the mystic words impressed on the stones at his feet, on rocks, doors, monuments, and trees. Indeed, rich and zealous Buddhists maintain at their own expense, companies of Lāmas for the sole object of propagating the Maṇi-padme formula. These strange missionaries may occasionally be encountered, chisel and hammer in hand, traversing field, hill, dale, and desert, their only mission being to engrave the sacred six syllables on every rock in their path (Huc, ii. 194).

Absolutely incalculable is the grand total of Maṇi-padmes thus placed to the credit of the world of living beings during the short space of twenty-four hours. Yet, at the end of the New Year's festival in Tibet, the chief Lāma will sometimes pretend to proclaim the exact sum of mystic syllables supposed to have been repeated during its continuance, amounting perhaps to billions upon billions, for the consolation of all those faithful Buddhists who, oppressed by the evils of life, are seeking for some antidote.

But the 'jewel-lotus' is not the only antidote. There are other short prayer-formularies, such as Om Vajra-pāṇi-Hūm (addressed to the Bodhi-sattva Vajra-pāṇi, p. 201), and other still more mystical ejaculations (such as Om ah Hūm); and magical sentences, called Dhāranī, and profoundly significant monosyllables, such as Ram, Phaṭ, Hṛim, Hṛīm, Ṛim, Ṛīm, Hṛīs.

And here in connexion with the ubiquity of prayer-formularies, we must not omit to notice the *Praying-walls,* that is, the long stone walls or banks called (from the 'jewel-lotus' prayer inscribed upon them) *Maṇi*[1], or in the provincial dialect Man Dang (variously Man-dong, Mendong).

These remarkable stone-structures, peculiar to Lāmism, are erected by the side of high-roads, and in frequented thoroughfares, with the simple object of aiding in the accumulation of prayer-merit. Some are only a few feet long, six feet high, and from six to twelve feet broad; others have been met with nearly 1000 yards long, with pyramidal Stūpas[2] or Ćaityas (in Tibetan Ćhortens) at each end. Inserted in these walls are slabs on which the six-syllabled, and other prayer-formulas, and sometimes images of saints, are carved and dedicated as votive offerings. Passing travellers acquire merit by keeping them on their left side[3], so that they may follow the letters of the inscription without necessarily repeating the words[4].

In the same connexion we may advert to *Praying-flags* and *Praying-staffs.* And I may mention that, while staying at Dārjīling, I visited a village to which a monastery is attached, and, on approaching the spot, was surprised to see the whole neighbourhood studded with poles from which long flags were flying. On the tops

---

[1] The *Maṇi-padme* prayer is itself for shortness often called Maṇi.

[2] Stūpas and Ćaityas are explained at p. 504.

[3] So says Schlagintweit, but he adds that in some places passers by keep them to the right. Mr. Sarat Chandra Dās also mentions this.

[4] According to Sir Richard Temple (Journal, p. 198) travellers walk first on one side and then on the other.

of the poles were curious ornaments like caps, made of coloured cloth with flounces. I naturally supposed that I had arrived on a gala day, and that at least a great Lāma or other high functionary was expected, perhaps to lay the first stone of some new building connected with the monastery. On inquiry, however, I ascertained that there was nothing unusual about the appearance of the village, which was merely praying, according to custom, by means of its flag-staffs. Every time the wind, which happened to be blowing fresh, extended the long flags, a vast number of prayers were credited to the inhabitants who were themselves all absent, and probably hard at work either in the fields or at Dārjīling.

I managed to obtain facsimiles of some of the flags. On them are inscribed various versions of the inevitable Maṇi-padme formulary, together with figures of the 'flying-horse' (Lungta, strictly rLuṅ-rta, 'wind-horse')[1] and other symbols, such as those of the Norbu gem[2] and of the Phurbu—which are held to be peculiarly efficacious in warding off evil spirits or neutralizing the diseases inflicted by them. Indeed in most cases these flags are regarded by the peasantry as talismans or charms to protect the village from the malice of mischievous ghosts and demons, believed to haunt the atmosphere and swarm everywhere around.

Here are some of the mystic formularies inscribed on

[1] Schlagintweit (p. 253) says this is the horse which constitutes one of the seven treasures (see p. 528 of these Lectures). It brings good fortune to the man who keeps it flying on a flag.

[2] The gem called Norbu is another of the seven treasures.

my flags. They resemble Śaiva Mantras and Dhāraṇīs —that is, mystical words or sentences used as spells:—

Om maṇi padme Hūm Hring, Om Vajra-pāṇi Hūm, Om ā Hūm, Om Vāg-īśvarī Mūm, Sarva-siddhi-phala Hūm, Om muni muni mahā-muni, Śākya-muni svāhā, Om vajra-sattva Hūm, Hulu hulu, Rulu rulu, Hūm Phaṭ, etc. (Compare my 'Brāhmanism,' etc. p. 197).

One flag in my possession has representations of four animals at the four corners, viz. a Tiger, Lion, Eagle, and Dragon [1]—supposed to act as guards against evil spirits. It also has an inscription in Tibetan which was translated for me by Mr. Sarat Chandra Dās, thus:—

'Reverence be to the Buddhas and Bodhi-sattvas! Thus hath it been heard by me—once on a time when the adorable Śākya-Buddha was seated on a marble throne amid the gods of the Trayastrinsa heaven, Indra, the Prince of Gods, arrived there, after being completely defeated by the demons (Asuras). Seeing the Buddha, and throwing himself at his feet, he thus reverentially addressed him:—"Oh, my Lord, we the gods of the Trayastrinsa (heaven) have suffered a complete defeat at the hands of the demons; instruct us, what are we to do? how are we to triumph over our enemies?" To this the adorable one replied:—"O lord of gods, take this mystical formula called Gyatshar gyi tsemoi Punggyan, which, when repeated, will make you unconquerable. I, too, in my former existence of a Bodhi-sattva found it efficacious in securing victory."'

It is of course a work of great merit to erect prayer-flags. They form a conspicuous feature in every landscape throughout Tibet, fluttering on hills and in valleys, by the roadside, and on the river bank, on walls and on the tops of houses, in streets, squares, and gardens.

---

[1] Dr. Schlagintweit says that a Dhāraṇī to the following effect is often written on the flag: 'Tiger, Lion, Eagle, and Dragon, may they co-operate Sarva-du-du-hom! ('Tibetan Buddhism,' p. 255).

Then, again, the duty of a constant repetition of prayer-formulæ and mystical sentences has led Northern Buddhists to employ *Rosaries*, which were used both by Hindūs and Buddhists long before they came into vogue in Europe. Without these necessary aids to devotion the long rounds of repetition could not be accurately completed. In Northern Buddhist countries rosaries ought to consist of 108 beads, which in Tibet are said to represent the 108[1] volumes of the Kanjur. The same number of beads is used by the worshippers of Vishṇu, who use the rosary to aid them in repeating any one of the names of Vishṇu 800 times, the eight additional beads marking each century of repetitions.

The commonest Buddhist rosaries are made of wood, or pebbles, or berries, or bone[2]; the more costly, of turquoise, coral, amber, or silver, or even of pearls and gems. If a rosary made of the bones of some holy Lāma can be procured, it is of course prized above all others. Sometimes a Dorje is appended. Northern Buddhist worshippers hold their rosaries (like Roman Catholics) in the right hand, and move on the beads with the left, and they will do this while talking together or even quarrelling. In China and Japan Buddhist rosaries are often arranged in two rings. They sometimes consist of enormous beads with relics in the central bead.

Be it observed, however, that the prayer-formularies

[1] The number 108 seems sacred, as the sole of Buddha's foot is said to have that number of marks upon it.

[2] Common people in Buddhist countries are satisfied with 30 or 40 beads.

of Buddhists are not always a mere unintelligible string of words and syllables, muttered, iterated, and reiterated with the aid of rosaries. Their prayers sometimes contain lofty sentiments. For instance, the two vagabond mendicant monks seen by me at Dārjīling (described at p. 267) went about chanting the following :—

Reverence to all the noble Father-Lāmas ! I address this to the feet of Duang our patron saint. I, Milaraspa[1], sing it. If the soul be white (enlightened), it must be white inside and outside. I am born in consequence of the works of this world. My earthly father is a sower of the seed of sin. My mother is the soil which receives the seed of sin. The child is myself tied to the father by the cord of sin. When you think of your earthly father, think also of your Lāma (spiritual father). Your earthly father is the source of your sin. Your Lāma frees you from sin[2].

But this song, which was repeated over and over again, invariably concluded by a repetition of the inevitable six-syllabled formula. This they repeated very rapidly, pronouncing it as usual, 'Om maṇi-pamme Hūm,' and adding the mystical syllable Hṛīs. Their chanting was accompanied by an incessant agitation of their Ḍamaru or sacred drum, which I was able to purchase. It is shaped like two hemispheres, joined on their convex sides, and is encircled by sacred shells. It is sounded by means of buttons attached to two pendulous strips of leather. The sound made by these drums is out of all proportion to their size. It may be heard at a great distance, and is thought to be highly efficacious in frightening away evil spirits, who dislike loud noises

---

[1] This is a great Tibetan saint, author of a hundred thousand songs.

[2] Translated for me by Mr. Sarat Chandra Dās, who was my companion during part of my sojourn at Dārjīling.

of all kinds. Here is an exact representation of the sacred drum now in my possession :—

Again, Dr. Eitel (Lectures, iii.) mentions a manual of daily prayer used by Northern Buddhists, which shows that striking words are sometimes chanted, though they may be in Sanskṛit, and therefore unintelligible to those who repeat them. For instance, the following :—

'May all the Buddhas abide in me, instruct and enlighten me with knowledge and perfection, free me, deliver me, cleanse me, purify me ; and may the whole universe be set free (Sarva-tathāgatā māṃ samāvasantu buddhyā siddhyā bodhaya vibodhaya moćaya vimoćaya śodhaya viśodhaya samantaṃ moćaya) !'

Before, therefore, concluding this Lecture we must acknowledge, in fairness to the inhabitants of Tibet, that much of the spirit of religion may be mingled with their superstitions. The words of their prayers are not merely repeated by machinery, written on paper, and inscribed on rocks and stones. The voices of men and women, if not their thoughts, often go heartily with uttered prayers. The note of prayer is raised at all times and seasons—in the morning, mid-day, and evening, in private and in public, at home or abroad, in the midst of labour and idleness, in lying down and rising up, in moving about and keeping still, on the march and on the battle-field, on mournful occasions, and in the midst of joy and laughter. Nor is any one ashamed of praying aloud or praying together in the open streets and squares of crowded towns.

'There exists,' says the French Missionary (ii. 194), 'a very touching custom at Lhāssa. In the evening, just as the day is verging on its decline, all the Tibetans stop business and meet together, men, women, and children, according to their sex and age, in the principal parts of the town and in the public squares. As soon as groups are formed, every one kneels down, and they begin slowly and in undertones to chant prayers.

'The religious concerts produced by these numerous assemblages create throughout the town a solemn harmony, which operates forcibly on the soul. The first time we witnessed this spectacle, we could not help drawing a painful comparison between this pagan town, where all prayed together, and the cities of Europe, where people would blush to make the sign of the cross in public.'

LECTURE XIV.

Sacred Places.

It was only to be expected, that Buddhism, closely connected as it was with Brāhmanism and Hindūism, and yet in some respects opposed to those systems, should have certain sacred places and hallowed regions, some of which were identical with those of Brāhmanism and Hindūism, and some peculiarly its own.

In the Mahā-parinibbāna-sutta (V. 16–22, Rhys Davids), we have the following declaration:—

'There are four places which the believing man should visit as a pilgrim with feelings of reverence and awe. The place at which he can say, "Here the Tathāgata (one of the names of Buddha, see p. 23) was born." The place at which he can say, "Here the Tathāgata attained to perfect insight and enlightenment." The place at which he can say, "Here the Law was first preached by the Tathāgata." The place at which he can say, "Here the Tathāgata passed finally away in that utter passing away which leaves nothing whatever behind" (see p. 142, note, and p. 477).

'And they who die, while with believing heart they journey on such pilgrimages, shall be reborn, in the happy realms of heaven.'

The Chinese traveller, Fā-hien, names the same four sacred places (Chap. xxxi.), and says that the situation of the four great Stūpas (see p. 504) has been fixed, namely, (1) where the Buddha was born, (2) where he attained wisdom, (3) where he began to turn the wheel of his Law, (4) where he attained Pari-nirvāṇa (p. 142). Compare engraving of sculpture opposite p. 477.

Elsewhere Fā-hien mentions two other sacred spots—the place where the Buddha discomfited the advocates of erroneous doctrines[1], and the place where he descended after ascending to the Trayastriṃśa heaven (see p. 414 of this volume), to preach the Law to his mother (Legge's Fā-hien, 68).

These places are all situated within the area of the sacred land of Buddhism (see map opposite p. 21);—that is to say, the land which was the scene of the Buddha's itineration for forty-five years—a region about 300 miles long, by nearly 200 broad, lying in Gangetic India, within the modern provinces of Oudh and Behār (Bihār for Vihāra), or the ancient kingdoms of Kosala and Magadha, and having Śrāvastī and Buddha-Gayā for its limit towards the north and south respectively.

It will be interesting to note a few particulars in regard to these and other sacred spots scattered throughout this region, in the following order:—Kapila-vastu, Buddha-Gayā, Sārnāth near Benares, Rāja-gṛiha, Śrāvastī (often written Śrāvasti), Vaiśālī, Kauśāmbi, Nālanda, Saṅkāśya, Sāketa (Ajūdhyā), Kanyā-kubja (Kanauj), Pāṭali-putra (Patnā), Kesarīya, Kuśi-nagara. The map opposite p. 21 will make these clear.

To begin with the Buddha's birth-place (see p. 21).

Kapila-vastu.

Kapila-vastu (in Pāli, Kapila-vatthu) was long searched for by archæologists in vain, but is now identified by

---

[1] Hiouen Thsang says that this place is near Prayāga (the modern Allahābād), and that Aśoka built a Stūpa there. (Beal, i. 231.)

General Sir A. Cunningham and Mr. Carlleyle with Bhūila, a village surrounded by buried brickwork in the Bastī district under the Nepāl mountains, about twenty-five miles north-east from Faizābād, twelve north-west from Bastī, and one hundred and twenty north of Benares. Both Fā-hien (Legge, 67) and Hiouen Thsang describe the neighbouring Lumbinī (Lavaṇī) garden, where the Buddha was born from the right side of his mother (see p. 23, and engraving opposite p. 477). They also mention the Arrow-fountain where Gautama contended with others of his tribe in a shooting-match. The legend is (p. 24) that he gained the victory by shooting an arrow which passed through the target, buried itself in the ground, and caused a clear spring of water to flow forth (Legge, 65–67; Beal, ii. 23, 24). This name Śara-Kūpa, 'arrow-fountain,' has now been corrupted into Sar-Kuia (or Sar-Kuhiya), and the spot has been identified (Cunningham's 'Reports of Survey,' xii. 188).

It might have been expected that so sacred a place as Kapila-vastu—the birth-place of Buddha and the scene of his education and youthful exploits—would have been a favourite place of pilgrimage for Buddhists through all time; but we learn from the two Chinese travellers, that even in their day (from the fourth to the seventh century) the whole neighbourhood was a desert and the town in ruins (Beal, i. 50; ii. 14). The reason probably is that Hindūism gained the ascendancy over Buddhism in certain localities, and that when this happened the Brāhmans took pains to obliterate all traces of the rival creed. In later times Muhammadan invasions contributed to the same result.

Buddha-Gayā.

This was the place where the Buddha obtained perfect knowledge and enlightenment after his sexennial course of fasting and meditation (see p. 31 of this volume). It is situated six or seven miles from the town of Gayā, and about sixty miles from Patnā and Bankipur. It is of all Buddhist sacred places the most sacred, and abounds in profoundly interesting memorials of early Buddhism.

Of course it was only to be expected that memorial structures intended to mark important epochs in the life of the extinct Buddha, and calculated to foster feelings of reverence in the minds of his followers, should have been erected at this and various other holy spots of ground consecrated by the presence and acts of Gautama on great occasions. And of all such Buddhist monuments the ancient pyramidal temple at Buddha-Gayā, which I visited in 1876 and 1884, is the most striking and full of interest. Probably a monument of some kind was erected there not very long after the Buddha's death, and Hiouen Thsang (see p. 399) mentions the temple built there by Aśoka. The temple which I saw on the occasion of my first visit was probably not built till the middle of the second century, but was erected on the foundation of Aśoka's temple, the ruins of which are traceable under the present one[1]. The materials consist of bluish bricks, plastered with lime. Hiouen Thsang states that in his

---

[1] General Sir A. Cunningham puts the date at about A.D. 150.

ANCIENT BUDDHIST TEMPLE AT BUDDHA-GAYĀ, AS IT APPEARED IN 1880.

Erected about the middle of the second century over the ruins of Aśoka's temple, at the spot where Gautama attained Buddhahood.

[*To face page* 391.

time it had eleven stories and an altitude of about 165 feet. It also had niches in each story, with a golden statue of Buddha in each niche. The whole was crowned with the representation of an Amalaka fruit (Emblic myrobalan) in gilt copper (Cunningham's Report, i. 5). The Burmese probably restored the temple between 1035 and 1078 A.D. Though falling into decay in 1876, its appearance struck me as exceedingly imposing,—even more so than that of the grand pyramidal towers, built over the entrances to the great South Indian temples[1]. The annexed engraving of this ancient monument as it appeared in 1880, before its restoration, is from a photograph by Mr. Beglar, taken on the spot, and enlarged by Mr. Austen.

The original object of its erection seems to have been simply and solely to serve as a monument, and not as a Dāgaba or receptacle for relics. Very soon, however, monuments of this kind were made to enshrine images, and were used as temples and places of worship. On inquiry I found that the ancient image or images of Buddha, which once occupied the shrine in the ancient Buddha-Gayā temple, had been destroyed or carried off at different times[2], and that another stone image, believed to have been carved in the eighth century, had been recently substituted for it. It is remarkable that

---

[1] See the account given in 'Brāhmanism and Hindūism,' p. 442.

[2] Many images and sculptures were abstracted by the Burmese, but many never reached Burma, for they accidentally fell into the Ganges in the process of being transported there. The colossal image found outside the temple is now in the Calcutta Museum (see the engraving opposite to p. 466).

during the process of restoring the so-called 'diamond throne,' on which the statues were placed, a mass of fragments of coral, sapphire, cornelian, crystal, ruby, pearl, ivory, and gold, but no diamond, was found compacted or cemented together in front of it[1].

At the back of the raised terrace which surrounded the ancient temple was a Pīpal or sacred fig-tree, fabled to be the very tree under which Gautama sat during his course of profound meditation ending in Buddhahood (see p. 31). Its vitality was on the wane, for its decaying branches drooped over the parapet as if they sought, like those of a neighbouring Banyan tree, to gain new life by rooting themselves in the ground beneath. Some Buddhist pilgrims happened, at the moment of my visit, to be worshipping at the temple, deputed by the King of Burma to present offerings. I observed that they had brought packets of gold-leaf, and had gilded the stone steps that surrounded the tree. Having performed this act of homage, they sat near muttering their prayer-formularies. No doubt they believed it to be the very Bodhi-tree of Gautama's time, the stem of which had been miraculously preserved, though, had it been really so, the stem would have been about twenty-three centuries old. Considering the well-known properties of the Pīpal tree, it is possible that the worshippers were, after all, paying honour to the descendant of the original tree, the fact, no doubt, being that as each tree began to decay a new one was produced, by the dropping of seeds into the old roots and the springing up of fresh

[1] Mr. Beglar gave me specimens of the fragments, which I have still.

ANCIENT BUDDHIST TEMPLE AT BUDDHA-GAYĀ, AS RESTORED IN 1884.

[To face page 393.

scions. Probably most of the sacred trees in the neighbourhood of Buddhist temples throughout India, Ceylon, and Burma were originally raised from seeds brought from the ancient Buddha-Gayā tree.

It is a received tradition that a shoot from this tree was taken by the Missionary Mahendra, son of Aśoka, in the third century B.C. to Ceylon, and planted at Anurādha-pura, where its descendant still flourishes.

When I again visited Buddha-Gayā in 1884, I found that the old pyramidal temple had been restored according (as is conjectured) to Hiouen Thsang's description of the Vihāra of his day.

It is said that the late Burmese government, not very long ago, spent about thirty thousand rupees in building a wall round the temple and making excavations with a view to its restoration. Then our government, about 1881 or 1882, undertook the work, and I believe at least a lakh of rupees has been spent in completing it. I give a representation of the restored temple (as it appeared in 1884), from a photograph taken by Mr. Beglar, and enlarged by Mr. Austen. Its present height is 176 feet, as it has several tiers of the usual umbrella-like ornament, tapering to a point at the summit[1].

The reconstruction of the temple led of course to the removal of the sacred Bodhi-tree, but an effort was made to preserve the tree by transplanting it to a neighbouring garden. No sooner was this done than parties of pilgrims from Burma and Ceylon, in their pious desire to maintain the vitality of the venerated tree, covered the stem with gold-leaf, and, bringing

[1] The umbrella is symbolical of supremacy. See p. 523.

Eau de Cologne and other scents, poured them over the roots, at the same time manuring them with the contents of boxes of sardines steeped in oil, choice biscuits, and other delicacies. Of course, the result was the speedy destruction of the tree, root and branch. To compensate for its loss, a new Pīpal tree was planted behind the restored temple by Sir A. Cunningham in 1885. Another near the temple appeared to be in a flourishing condition in 1884, and I observed that both Hindū and Buddhist pilgrims met together there as worshippers of the same sacred object.

The idol-shrine, under the principal tower of the restored temple, consists of a small vaulted stone-chamber lighted only by the door. My first act, on arriving at Buddha-Gāya in 1884, was to descend to this interesting spot. At the further end is the principal statue of Buddha, seated, in the 'witness-attitude' (see p. 480)—on an altar-like throne having five pilasters, and supposed to represent the original Bodhi-maṇḍa. The pedestal of the statue is ornamented with diamond-shaped carvings, and sculptures of two elephants and two lions [1].

Inside the shrine, at the moment of my visit, were five Burmese pilgrims from Mandelay. They were apparently monks, as all were habited in yellow dresses. Each man bowed down before the image, with hands joined in reverence, occasionally touching the ground with his forehead, and going through a course of prayer-repetition by help of a rosary. After worshipping for some time, they deposited a quantity of offerings, of a

[1] The lion is often associated with Buddha, who is called Śākya-siṉha (see p. 23), and whose throne is therefore called a *Siṉhāsan.*

somewhat miscellaneous description, in front of the image. I noticed among other things, rice, fruit, vegetables, flowers of the Bel-tree, tin boxes filled with sardines, Huntley and Palmer's biscuits, bottles of the genuine Maria Farina's Eau de Cologne for watering the sacred-trees, and a large number of packets of gold-leaf. I left the shrine for two or three hours, and on returning found that the pilgrims had crowned their act of worship by gilding the image with the contents of these packets, reserving a supply for covering the other images in the vicinity of the temple. The cost of the whole process must have been considerable.

At the back of the great Buddha-Gayā temple, I found a stone tablet for offerings, recently brought and fixed horizontally in the ground by another pilgrim who was from Colombo in Ceylon. It bore an inscription indicating that the slab had been placed there as a votive offering by a person calling himself Guṇa-ratna Muddali Rājā of Kolamba-pur. The date carved on it (Buddha-vasse 2427) shows that the Buddhists of Ceylon are no believers in the researches of modern scholars. They still reckon from B.C. 543 for the supposed Nirvāṇa of Buddha.

At a little distance in front of the great Temple, but on the right side, are the two smaller temples called Tārā-devī and Vāgīśvarī. In the latter is a circular stone with nine circles of complicated ornaments. This is called a Vajrāsana, from the thunderbolt ornament in the second circle, but it is not the true Bodhi-maṇḍa.

I may mention here that a portion of the original Aśoka stone-railing, with an inscription, lotus-ornaments and carvings, was discovered in a fair state of preservation by Sir A. Cunningham, and is now to be seen *in situ.* The Buddha's walking place was unearthed by Mr. Beglar. The massive new brick railing which now encloses the temple has been well constructed after an ancient pattern, and ornamented with numerous carvings representing scenes in the lives of the Buddha (p. 111). The paved quadrangle sets the whole off to great advantage. Indeed, the present appearance of the square and the sacred area of ground adjoining—strewn with ruins of the Stūpas erected by Aśoka and others—and according to the legend by the gods Indra and Brahmā—is one of the most striking sights in all India, and must be seen to be appreciated.

In truth, Buddha-Gayā is a kind of Buddhist Jerusalem, abounding in associations of thrilling interest, not only to the followers of Buddha, but to all who see in that spot the central focus whence radiated a system which for centuries has permeated the religious thought of the most populous regions of Eastern Asia, and influenced the creed of a majority of the human race.

Another remarkable characteristic of this spot is that it was converted into a kind of Buddhist Necropolis, teeming with the remains of generations of the Buddha's adherents contained in relic-receptacles called Stūpas (pp. 503–506), some of which have been brought to light, while countless others still remain to be unearthed.

The fact was that immense numbers of pilgrims from all parts of India and the outlying countries once thronged in crowds to Buddha-Gayā, and nearly every pilgrim brought with him a Stūpa or relic-shrine of some kind, according to his means, and deposited it as a votive offering in this hallowed region, either with the object of acquiring religious merit for himself, or of promoting the welfare of the deceased in other states of being. Often it was inscribed with the usual Buddhist formula, Ye Dharmā, etc. (see p. 104), and sometimes bore a date and the name of the reigning king. Generally the votive Stūpa contained the relics of deceased relatives—perhaps the ashes of a father or mother, or pieces of bone, or a small fragment of a single bone placed in an earthen vessel or casket of some other material, and buried in the interior of the Stūpa.

Relics, however, were not always forthcoming, and so the votive Stūpas were frequently mere cenotaphs or models in clay or stone of actual Stūpas erected in other places. Often they were beautifully carved and ornamented with rows on rows of images of the Buddha. I obtained some beautiful specimens for the Indian Institute at Oxford, a drawing of one of which will be given (see p. 505). Layers on layers of these have been exhumed during the process of the excavations. They are of every variety of size, from three inches to several feet high, and of every variety of material, from terra cotta and clay turned on a potter's wheel to elaborately sculptured brick and stone. All the upper layers are now gone (those made of clay and pottery having naturally crumbled to pieces), but the lowest are still *in situ*, and furnish specimens of all ages from the second century to the tenth or twelfth. I noticed hundreds lying about on the ground in 1884.

A sacred tank, mentioned by Hiouen Thsang, is situated three or four hundred yards to the left of the Buddha-Gayā temple. I found, on visiting it, that this hallowed pool is quite as much venerated by Hindūs as by pilgrims from Buddhist countries.

Indeed, I was much struck by the evidence which Buddha-Gayā affords of the inter-relationship between Buddhism and Hindūism—especially that form of the latter called Vaishṇavism. For instance, on one side of the temple I noticed the tombs of the Mahants, or Heads of the neighbouring Hindū monastery, who are buried there in a sitting posture. Near these again are shrines of the five Pāṇḍava heroes (who take the place of the five Buddhas), and a shrine containing the supposed impression of the two feet of Vishṇu. The upper portion of a small Buddhist Stūpa has been sawn off and inverted[1], and Vishṇu's footsteps carved on the smooth surface. This certainly symbolizes in a remarkable manner the merging of Buddhism in Vaishṇavism, and bears out Dr. Sachau's assertion that in Alberūnī's time Vishṇu-worship was dominant in India.

Then, again, on the right of the entrance to the principal temple is a raised platform of earth, on which are images of Vishṇu, Śiva, Pārvatī, and Gaṇeśa. Here I saw a Śrāddha ceremony[2], in the act of being performed by some Hindūs—just arrived from the neighbouring town of Gayā. They were repeating their mantras,

---

[1] This will be evident to any one who examines it attentively. The socket-hole of the umbrella-ornament may be easily detected.

[2] The form of ritual observed was like that I witnessed at Gayā, and described in my 'Brāhmanism and Hindūism,' p. 310.

offering their Piṇḍas, and putting the finishing stroke to the funeral services (previously performed by them at the Vishṇu-pad temple at Gayā), under the shadow of a Pīpal tree, held as sacred by them as by Buddhists.

To give an exhaustive account of the objects crowded together at this fountain-head of Buddhism would be impossible. The following abbreviated version of the Rev. S. Beal's translation (ii. 115) of Hiouen Thsang's description, throws great light on the state of Buddhism in the seventh century:—

Going south-west from Mount Prāgbodhi, we came to the Bodhi-tree. It is surrounded by a brick wall, and is about 500 paces round. Within the wall the sacred traces touch one another in all directions. In one place there are Stūpas, in another place Vihāras. In the middle of the enclosure is the Bodhi-tree, under which is the diamond throne called Bodhi-maṇḍa. On this the Buddha sat and attained the holy path of perfect wisdom. When the earth is shaken, this spot alone is unmoved. In old days, when Buddha was alive, the Bodhi-tree—which is a Pippala or sacred fig-tree—was several hundred feet high. Although it has often been injured by cutting, it is still forty or fifty feet high. The leaves never wither either in winter or summer, but always remain shining and glistening, except on every successive Nirvāṇa-day, when the leaves fade, and then in a moment revive as before. On this day thousands and ten thousands assemble from different quarters, and bathe the roots with scented water and perfumed milk. King Aśoka, before he was converted, tried to destroy the tree by force, and after him king Saśāṅka tried again, but the roots sprang up as full of life as ever.

To the east of the Bodhi-tree, there is a Vihāra about 160 or 170 feet high, built of blue tiles covered with chunam; all the niches in the different stories holding golden figures. The four sides of the building are covered with ornamental work. The whole is surmounted by a gilded copper Amalaka fruit. To the right and left of the gate are niches; in the left is a figure of Avalokiteśvara Bodhisattva and in the right a figure of Maitreya. On the site of the present Vihāra, Aśoka at first built a small Vihāra. Afterwards a

Brāhman, who became a convert to Buddhism, reconstructed it on a larger scale.

To the north of the Bodhi-tree is the place where Buddha walked up and down, about 70 paces or so long. When he had obtained enlightenment, he remained perfectly quiet for seven days. Then rising, he walked up and down during seven days to the north of the tree. Not far to the south of the tree is a Stūpa about 100 feet high, built by King Aśoka. To the east of the tree is the place (marked by two Stūpas) where Māra tempted Gautama to become a Universal Monarch. To the north-west is a Vihāra in which is an image of Kāśyapa Buddha, noted for its miraculous qualities. Occasionally it emits a glorious light, and the old records say, that if a man, actuated by sincere faith, walks round it seven times, he obtains the power of knowing the place and condition of his previous births. Outside the south gate is a large tank, about 700 paces round, the water of which is clear and pure as a mirror. To the east of this is the lake of the Snake-king, Mućalinda. On the west bank is a small Vihāra. Formerly, when Tathāgata acquired complete enlightenment, he sat here for seven days in perfect composure, and ecstatic contemplation, while Mućalinda protected him with his folds wound seven times round his body. (Compare the frontispiece.)

By the side of the river, not far off, is the place where Buddha received the rice-milk, and where two merchants offered some wheat-flour and honey from their travelling-store (p. 40 of this volume).

Near this a Stūpa marks the spot where the four Kings presented Buddha with four golden dishes. The Lord declined such costly offerings. Then the four Kings, casting away the golden vessels, offered silver ones; and afterwards vessels of crystal, lapis-lazuli, cornelian, amber, ruby, and so on in succession; but the Lord of the World would accept none of them. Lastly, the four Kings offered stone vessels.

Near this spot the Buddha worked various wonders to convert those who were capable of conversion. For example, it was here that the Buddha overcame the fiery snake-demon (see p. 46 of this volume). In the middle of the night the Nāga vomited forth fire and smoke, and the chamber seemed to be filled with fiery flames; but the Buddha having forced the fiery dragon into his alms-bowl, came forth next day holding it in his hand, and showed it to the unbelievers.

To the south of Mućalinda's tank is a Stūpa, which indicates the spot where Kāśyapa, having embarked in a boat to save Buddha during an inundation, saw the Lord of the World walking on the water as on land.

Sārnāth near Benares.

The city of Benares (Banāras, properly Vārāṇasī) is the most sacred place of Brāhmanism[1], and is certainly the second most holy place of Buddhism. For it was from this centre that the stream of Buddhist teaching first flowed, and in the days of Aśoka and of his immediate successors, Buddhism must have vied with Brāhmanism in the number of its shrines and sacred objects collected there.

We have already seen that memorial Stūpas and temples, not intended to contain relics, were reared at various holy spots of ground, consecrated by the presence of Gautama on special occasions. The immense ruined Stūpa—once a tower-like monument—at a spot now called Sārnāth (Sāraṅga-nāth[2]), three or four miles from the modern city of Benares, is a memorial of this kind. It is all that remains of the celebrated structure erected

---

[1] See my 'Brāhmanism and Hindūism,' p. 434.

[2] That is, 'the lord of deer.' Sāraṅga is a kind of deer, and the Buddha was probably called so because he is fabled to have wandered about as a deer in this very place in one of his former births (see p. 111 of this volume). The legend is that he was born eleven times as a deer, and on this account a deer is one of the sacred symbols of Buddhism. We learn from General Sir A. Cunningham (i. 105) that the name Sārnāth properly belongs to a temple dedicated to Śiva near the Buddhist monument, and the epithet 'Lord of deer,' is equally applicable to the god Śiva, who is often represented in the act of holding up a deer in his hand.

at the spot in the Mṛiga-dāva or deer-park, once called Isi-patana (for Sanskṛit Ṛishi-patana), where Gautama first turned the wheel of the Law (Dharma-ćakra)—that is, where he preached his first sermon (p. 42). It was to this place that Buddhist pilgrims once flocked, and here vast numbers of votive relic-shrines and Stūpas were deposited, as at Buddha-Gayā.

I visited this ancient ruin, in company with the late Mr. Sherring, in 1876, and enjoyed the advantage of his guidance in inspecting it, as well as all that remains of the monastic buildings and other adjacent ruins, including the octagonal tower called Chaukandi, about half a mile distant. In his book on Benares, Mr. Sherring has followed General Sir A. Cunningham, who describes the principal monument—now of a bee-hive shape, and called Dhamek[1]—as 93 feet in diameter at the base, 292 feet in circumference, and 128 feet above the general level of the soil. The lower part—to a height of 43 feet—is built of stone, and all the upper part of bricks. There are eight projecting faces with empty niches, which once held statues.

An old man who was in charge of the ruins when we examined them, lighted a candle, and took us into the horizontal tunnel-like gallery which the General had excavated some years before, in the hope that relics or memorials of some kind might be found buried in the interior. A shaft or well had been previously sunk from the summit, and at the depth of 10½ feet a slab

[1] The name Dhamek may possibly be a corruption of Dhamma-ćakka (Dharma-ćakra).

was discovered, inscribed with the well-known Buddhist formula 'Ye dharmā,' etc. (p. 104); but the search for relics proved unsuccessful. The Stūpa, in fact, turned out to be merely memorial, like that at Buddha-Gayā.

Probably some monumental Stūpa existed here from the earliest times, and certainly from Aśoka's time. The present Stūpa was seen by Hiouen Thsang, who has described it in rather a confused manner (Beal, ii. 45). Hence it must be as old as about the ninth century. Fā-hien saw a Stūpa of some kind there in the fifth century (p. 387).

About fifty yards from the Stūpa, Sir A. Cunningham found the interesting sculpture given at p. 477.

Rāja-gṛiha.

Rāja-gṛiha (Pāli, Rāja-gaha) is the modern Rāj-gīr. The old city had the epithet Giri-vraja, 'surrounded by hills[1].' It was the first metropolis or mother-city of Buddhism, and the original capital of the powerful kingdom of Magadha, when under the rule of the Kings Bimbi-sāra (p. 48) and his son Ajāta-śatru, who were contemporaries and friends of Gautama, and converted

[1] Fā-hien says that the old city was girdled by five hills. These hills are now called Baibhār (on which are five Jain temples), Vipula, Ratna, Udaya, and Sona-giri. A long account of the place will be found in Cunningham's 'Ancient Geography of India,' pp. 462–468, and in his 'Archæological Report,' i. 20. Bimbi-sāra seems to have built the town, which was afterwards improved by Ajāta-śatru, and the site of the new portion being not quite identical, the new town was called 'new Rāja-gṛiha.' Legge's 'Fā-hien,' p. 81. There are several hot springs in this locality.

by him to Buddhism[1]. The sacred character of the place is attested by the ruins of vast numbers of Buddhist Stūpas and Vihāras which once existed here. Unhappily Brāhmans and Musalmāns have used the materials for their temples, tombs, and mosques.

It was here that Gautama first studied under the Brāhmans Āḷāra and Uddaka (p. 29), and here he first imbibed the philosophical ideas which afterwards coloured his teaching. It is not surprising, therefore, that at a later period of his career he was fond of returning to Rāja-gṛiha for retirement during Vassa; his two favourite resorts[2] being the Bambu grove (Veḷu-vana, p. 48) and the hill called Vulture-peak (Gṛidhra-kūṭa, Legge's Fā-hien, 81, 83), both in the neighbourhood of the city.

It was here, too, that several interesting incidents in the life of Buddha occurred. For example, it was here in a cavern that the Buddha often meditated. It was here that he often preached and taught; and it was here, or in the neighbourhood of the city, that the god Śakra (Indra) once appeared to Buddha, bringing a musician from heaven to entertain him, and afterwards testing his knowledge by forty-two questions. These the god traced with his finger on the rock, and the impression of them, according to Fā-hien, was to be seen

---

[1] Ajāta-śatru seems first to have sided with Buddha's enemy Devadatta.

[2] It may be mentioned here that any place or house in which the Buddha resided for a time was afterwards called Gandha-kuṭī (probably from the fragrance of the perfumed offerings always to be found in it). Hence the Bambu grove at Rāja-gṛiha, and the Jeta-vana at Śrāvastī (p. 407), were both Gandha-kuṭīs.

there in his time, and a monastery was built on the spot. With reference to this legend we may note that the answers to the forty-two questions are supposed to be contained in a celebrated Tibetan work called the 'Forty-two points on which the Buddha gave instruction[1]', the importance of which is proved by its being translated into several languages.

It was in this neighbourhood, too, that Buddha's two chief disciples—Śāriputra and Maudgalyāyana (Pāli, Moggallāna, p. 47)—had their noted meeting with Aśvajit (Pāli, Assaji), already mentioned (p. 104). Here, also, a Jaina ascetic made a pit of fire and poisoned the rice, and then invited Buddha to eat. Lastly, it was here that many of Deva-datta's plots against the Buddha's life (see p. 52) were carried on. The story of these is so interesting that I abridge it from the Sacred Books of the East (vol. xx. p. 238):—

Now at that time the Venerable One was seated preaching the Law and surrounded by a great multitude, including the king and his retinue. And Deva-datta rose from his seat, and said, 'The Venerable One is now aged, he has accomplished a long journey, and his term of life is nearly run. Let the Venerable One now dwell at ease and give up the Saṅgha to me, I will be its leader.' Then said the Buddha, 'I would not give over the Saṅgha, even to Sāriputta and Moggallāna; how much less then to so evil-living a person as you.'

Then Deva-datta thought: 'The Venerable One denies me before the king, and calls me "evil-living," and exalts Sāriputta and Moggallāna.' With these thoughts in his mind he departed, angry and displeased, and went to Ajāta-sattu and said, 'Do you, prince,

[1] A magnificent edition of this work in Tibetan, Mongol, Manchu, and Chinese came into the possession of the French Missionaries (Huc, ii. 74).

kill your father, and become Rājā; and I will kill the Venerable One and become the Buddha.' And prince Ajāta-sattu, taking a dagger, entered his royal father's chamber. And the Rājā Bimbi-sāra said, 'Why do you want to kill me, O prince? if you want the kingdom, let it be thine.' And he handed it over to Ajāta-sattu. Then Deva-datta said, 'Give orders, O king, to your men, that I may deprive the Samana Gotama of life.' And Ajāta-sattu did so. Then sixteen men were sent to kill Gotama. They went, and returned and said, 'We cannot kill him. Great is the power of the Venerable One.'

Next Deva-datta climbed up the Vulture's Peak, and hurled down a mighty rock on the Venerable One. But two mountain peaks came together and stopped that rock. [Fā-hien says that it hurt one of his toes. Legge, p. 83.] Now at that time there was at Rāja-gṛiha an elephant named Nālāgiri, fierce and a man-slayer. And Deva-datta caused the elephant to be let loose against Gotama. But the Venerable One infused a sense of love into the elephant. And the elephant extended his trunk and took up the dust from off the feet of the Venerable One and sprinkled it over his own head, and retired bowing backwards, gazing upon the Venerable One.

It may be noted here that the hell to which Deva-datta was condemned for his attempts upon the Buddha's life, is thus described by Burmese authorities:—

The impious Deva-datta, a cousin and brother-in-law of the Buddha, suffers terrible punishment in Hell. His feet are sunk ankle-deep in burning marl. His head is incased with a red hot metal cap down to the lobe of the ears. Two large red-hot bars transfix him from back to front, two horizontally from right to left, and one impales him from head to foot. (Shway Yoe's 'Burman,' i. 121.)

It should be mentioned in connexion with Rāja-gṛiha that Ajāta-śatru built a grand Stūpa there, over a portion of the Buddha's ashes, soon after his cremation.

Another fact which enhances the interest of this place is the propinquity of the celebrated Satta-paṇṇi cave (p. 55), where the Buddhist brotherhood first assembled after their leader's death.

Śrāvastī.

Śrāvastī (Pāli, Sāvatthī), sometimes spelt Śrāvasti, has been identified by General Cunningham with a place now called Sāhet-Māhet, about fifty-eight miles north of Ajūdhyā in Oudh. The town is said to derive its name from the fact that it was built by a certain King Śrāvasta. Other native authorities derive it from a Ṛishi named Sāvattha, who is said to have resided there. It was certainly the ancient capital of Kosala (Oudh), and was ruled over by King Prasena-jit (Pāli, Pasenadi), who was Gautama's contemporary. Moreover, it was the Buddha's favourite place of retreat [1] during the rainy seasons (p. 48 of this volume), about half of his Vassas having been spent there [2] in the Jeta-vana monastery built for him by the wealthy merchant Anātha-piṇḍika (Anepidu), sometimes called Su-datta.

Doubtless on this account Śrāvastī was once much resorted to by the Buddha's followers, and ultimately became an important seat of Buddhist learning.

The celebrated monastery, the ruins of which still exist, was erected in the garden (vana) of Prince Jeta, who parted with the land to Su-datta on condition that he would cover it with gold coins. This was done, till eighteen krores of coins had been spread out like a

---

[1] Here, therefore, there was a Gandha-kuṭī (see note, p. 404).

[2] Fā-hien says, 'Here lived Buddha for a longer time than at any other place,' and on that account, perhaps, was called Dharma-pattana (Beal's 'Records,' ii. 1). It was at this place that the Brahmaćārīns killed a courtesan, and accused Buddha of adultery and murder (see Legge, p. 59; Beal, ii. 8).

pavement on the ground. Both Fā-hien and Hiouen Thsang mention this incident, and the former states that the monastery was seven stories high [1]. The pavement of coins is represented in one of the sculptures belonging to the Stūpa of Bharhut (Cunningham, pp. 84–87), as well as on one of the pillars of Aśoka's railing at Buddha-Gayā.

Śrāvastī was the place where, according to Fā-hien, the first sandal-wood image of Buddha was set up in a monastery by King Prasena-jit (see p. 471) [2]. A colossal erect figure of the Buddha was found here in a temple excavated by Sir A. Cunningham, but this was of stone.

With regard to the celebrated sandal-wood image, Fā-hien (p. 57) relates a strange legend of its preservation by a miracle :—

'The kings and people of the countries around vied with one another in their offerings (to the image). Hanging up about it silken canopies, scattering flowers, burning incense, and lighting lamps. It happened that a rat, carrying in its mouth the wick of a lamp, set one of the canopies on fire, which caught the Vihāra, and the seven stories were all consumed. The kings and people were all very sad, supposing that the sandal-wood image had been burned; but lo! when a small Vihāra to the east was opened, there was seen the original image!'

Fā-hien goes on to describe another miracle :—

'To the north-west of the Vihāra there is a grove called "The getting of Eyes." Formerly there were five hundred blind men, who lived here; Buddha preached his Law to them, and they all got back their eyesight. Full of joy they stuck their staves in the earth, and

e, pp. 57, 59; Beal, ii. 5.

[2] Another statue, claiming to be the genuine sandal-wood image, was at Kauśāmbī (see p. 412).

did reverence. The staves immediately began to grow, and formed a grove' (Legge, pp. 58, 59).

Hiouen Thsang states that in his time the towns and monasteries about Śrāvastī were mostly in ruins. He, too, gives an interesting account of a miraculous incident which occurred there:—

To the north-east of the Jeta-vana garden is the place where the Buddha washed a sick Monk, who lived apart by himself in a solitary place. The Lord of the World seeing him inquired, 'What is your affliction?' He answered, 'In former days, my disposition being a careless one, I never looked on any sick man with pity, and now when I am sick, no one looks on me.' Thereupon the Buddha said to him, 'My son! I will look on you,' and touching him with his hand, he healed the sickness. Then leading him forth, he washed his body, and gave him new clothes, and said, 'From this time forward be diligent and exert yourself.' Hearing this, the penitent monk, moved by gratitude and filled with joy, followed the Buddha and became his disciple. (Founded on Beal, ii. 5, abridged.)

Vaiśālī.

Vaiśālī (in Pāli Vesālī, now Besārh) lies twenty miles north of Hāji-pur, on the left bank of the Ganges, and twenty-seven north-east of Patnā. This town (the city of the Liććhavis) is celebrated as the scene of the second Council (p. 57). Near it, at a place called Bakhra, is a celebrated ancient pillar surmounted by a lion (see Cunningham, i. 59). Vaiśālī, however, is chiefly noted as one of the places where Gautama often preached and taught, and where he stopped on his way to Kusinārā, the place of his death. His usual residence was in a Vihāra, described by Fā-hien as double-galleried, and in a garden presented to him by the courtesan Amba-pālī, whom he converted and induced to live a virtuous life.

He also resided for the fifth year of his teaching in a building called the Kūṭāgāra[1] hall.

Hiouen Thsang speaks of the town and of the objects of interest round it thus (Beal, ii. 66–75):—

Both heretics and believers are found here living together. There are several hundred monasteries (Saṅghārāmas) which are mostly dilapidated. There are also several Deva temples, occupied by sectaries of different kinds. The followers of the Nirgranthas (i.e. of the Jains) are very numerous.

To the north is a Stūpa which indicates the place where Tathāgata stopped and took leave of the Liććhavis, on his way to Kuśi-nagara to die. Wishing him to quit the world, Māra (compare p. 41) came to Buddha and said, 'You have now dwelt sufficiently long in the world. Those whom you have saved from the circling streams of transmigration are as numerous as the sand.' The Buddha replied, 'No, those who are saved are as the grains of dust on my nail; those who are not saved are like the grains of dust on the whole earth. Nevertheless, after three months I shall die.' Māra hearing this was rejoiced, and departed.

Both within and without the city of Vaiśālī and all round it, the sacred vestiges are so numerous, that it would be difficult to recount them all. To the north-west is a Stūpa at the spot where Buddha dwelt when he recited the history of his former birth (Jātaka) as a Ćakra-vartin or Universal Monarch (compare p. 423) possessed of the seven treasures. To the south-east is a great Stūpa, marking the place where the convocation of the seven hundred sages and saints was held, one hundred and ten years after the Nirvāṇa of Buddha, to compel the monks who had broken the laws of Buddha to obey them.

It appears that the Liććhavis of Vaiśālī obtained a large quantity of the relics of the Buddha's body, and built a Stūpa over them.

According to Fā-hien they also erected a Stūpa over

[1] A kūṭāgāra is properly any building with a peaked roof (kūṭa) or pinnacle.

half the relics of the burnt body of Ānanda (see p. 47 of this volume), the other being deposited near Rāja-gṛiha. His narrative runs as follows:—

When Ānanda was going from Magadha to Vaiśālī, wishing his Pari-nirvāṇa to take place there, king Ajāta-śatru heard of his intention, and set out with his retinue to follow him.

The Liććhavis, too, when they heard that Ānanda was coming to their city, went out to meet him. In this way both parties arrived together at the river, and Ānanda, thinking to himself that he ought to please both, burnt his own body in the middle of the river, and thus attained Pari-nirvāṇa in a fiery ecstasy of Samādhi. Then his body was divided into two, so that each got one half as a sacred relic (Legge, pp. 75–77).

Kauśāmbī.

Kauśāmbī (in Pāli Kosāmbī), now Kosam[1], on the river Jumnā, about thirty miles from Allahābād, was once a place hallowed by many Brāhmanical associations, and is mentioned in the Rāmāyaṇa. It was the capital of the Kauśāmba country, and is said to have been founded by Kuśāmba, tenth in descent from Purūravas. Without doubt it was one of the most ancient cities of India. It was also the city of King Udayana, whose story is alluded to by the greatest of all Sanskṛit poets, Kāli-dāsa, in his 'Cloud-Messenger[2].' Furthermore, Kau-śāmbī is the city in which the scene of the Sanskṛit drama Ratnāvalī was laid[3].

The Buddha resided there in the sixth and ninth

---

[1] Cunningham (i. 301) gives a full account of the place.

[2] The story is fully narrated in the second and third books of the Kathā-sarit-sāgara of Soma Deva. See my 'Indian Wisdom,' p. 511. King Udayana is said to have been a contemporary of the Buddha.

[3] See my 'Indian Wisdom,' p. 486.

years of his Buddhahood, and probably visited the place at other times. This was the chief cause of its reputation in connexion with Buddhism. But it also derived its sacred character from the fact that it contained the celebrated sandal-wood image[1] of the Buddha, believed to have been carved during his life-time, by a sculptor sent by Moggallāna (see last line, p. 414) at King Udayana's request, to the Trayastriṇsa heaven, when the Buddha was there preaching the Law to his mother (see p. 207).

In a village near at hand Sir A. Cunningham (i. 308) found two sculptured pillars, and the pedestal of a statue inscribed with the 'Ye dharmā' formula (see p. 104). A great monolith was also discovered there. In Fā-hien's time a Vihāra existed at the spot where the Buddha had explained the Law (Legge, p. 96). Hiouen Thsang mentions that a lofty Stūpa, 200 feet high, was erected by Aśoka near at hand.

There was also a cavern in which the Buddha had left his shadow impressed on the rock. He also speaks of ten monasteries all in ruins.

Nālanda.

Nālanda[2] was the greatest seat of Buddhist learning in India. It has been identified by Sir A. Cunningham with the village of Baragaon, about seven miles north of

---

[1] See Hiouen Thsang's account of it, p. 471. Another similar image belonged to King Prasenajit at Śrāvastī, see pp. 408, 471.

[2] The name is said to have been derived from that of a Nāga, who lived in a neighbouring tank. See the description in two Chinese Buddhist inscriptions found at Buddha-Gayā. R. A. S. Journal, vol. xiii.

Rāja-gṛiha, about thirty miles south-east of the modern Patnā, and about forty miles from Buddha-Gayā. Sir Alexander states that Baragaon possesses immense ruins and more numerous specimens of sculpture than any other place visited by him. According to Hiouen Thsang, the Buddha preached the Law there for three months. The vast extent and importance of the monastery (Saṅghārāma) or monasteries at Nālanda have been already alluded to (p. 169). Fā-hien, however, does not mention them, which seems to indicate that they were built subsequently to A.D. 425. Hiouen Thsang, who travelled in the seventh century, is said to have resided there for five years as a student. Ten thousand monks, renowned for their learning, lived and studied in six magnificent buildings. The following is an extract from the later Chinese traveller's description of it (Beal, ii. 70):—

The monks of Nālanda, to the number of several thousands, are men of the highest ability. Their conduct is pure and unblamable, although the rules of the monastery are severe. The day is not sufficient for asking and answering profound questions. From morning till night the monks engage in discussion; the old and the young mutually helping one another. Those who cannot discuss questions out of the Tripiṭaka are little esteemed, and are obliged to hide themselves for shame. Hence learned men from different cities come here in multitudes to settle their doubts; and thence the streams of their wisdom spread far and wide. For this reason some persons usurp the name of Nālanda students, and in going to and fro receive honour in consequence.

If men from other quarters desire to enter and take part in the discussions, the keeper of the gate proposes some hard questions; those who are unable to answer have to retire. One must have studied deeply both old and new books, before gaining admission. Those students who come as strangers, have to show their ability by hard discussion; those who fail compared with those who succeed are as seven or eight to ten.

Saṅkāśya.

Saṅkāśya, now called Saṅkisa, about fifty miles north-west of Kanouj, was identified by Sir A. Cunningham in 1842. It was evidently once a large town with many remarkable monuments, and ought to be reckoned among the most sacred places of Buddhism. Hiouen Thsang describes it under the name Kie-pi-tha (Kapitha).

It is said that the Buddha's mother died seven days after his birth (see p. 24 of this volume), and was thus deprived of the advantage of hearing the Law from her son's lips. To compensate her for this loss, the Buddha ascended by his own supernatural power in three steps to the Trayastriṉśa heaven of Indra (p. 207), to which his mother had been transported, and there recited the Law for three months for her benefit. His return to earth seems to have been a more difficult matter; for his descent was not effected without the help of a ladder with three parallel flights of steps, made for him by the god Indra.

Fā-hien describes this miraculous incident in the following manner (Legge, 48, abridged):—

Saṅkāśya is the place where Buddha came down after ascending to the Trayastriṉśa heaven, and there preaching his Law for three months for his mother's benefit. Buddha had ascended there by his supernatural power, without the knowledge of his disciples; but seven days before his return, Anuruddha, by his own supernatural vision, saw him in heaven, and requested Moggallāna (see p. 47 of this volume) to ascend to Indra's heaven to inquire after 'the World-honoured one.' Moggallāna did so, and returned with the information that in seven days the Buddha would return. Then the kings of eight countries with their people, not having seen Buddha for a long time, were all eagerly looking up for him to return. But the female mendicant Utpalā[1] thought in her heart, 'To-day, the kings, with their ministers and people, are all going to meet Buddha. I am but a woman; how shall I succeed in being the first to see him?' Then Buddha, by his supernatural power, changed her into the appearance of a Universal Emperor, so that she was the foremost of all to meet and to do reverence to him.

At his descent three flights of steps were created. Buddha descended on the middle flight, composed of the seven precious substances; Mahā-Brahmā, king of the Brahmā heavens (see p. 211 of this volume), came down by a flight of silver steps on the right side, and Śakra (Indra), lord of the thirty-three divinities (p. 207), descended by steps of gold on the left side, holding a canopy made of the seven precious substances. An innumerable multitude of gods followed. No sooner had the Buddha come down than all three flights disappeared in the ground, except seven steps, which continued to be visible.

Afterwards King Aśoka, being eager to ascertain where their ends rested, sent men to find out by digging. They dug down till they reached a yellow spring, but could not discover the bottom of the steps. Hence the king felt an increase of devotion, and built a Vihāra over the steps, with a standing image of Buddha sixteen cubits high. Behind the Vihāra he erected a stone pillar, about fifty cubits high, with a lion on the top of it. A dispute arose between some heretics and the Buddhist monks about the ownership of the place, and the former agreed to give up their claim if any supernatural sign occurred; upon which the lion on the column gave a great roar.

Fā-hien adds that a Stūpa was erected on the spot where Buddha descended; another where the female mendicant caught the first sight of Buddha at his descent.

The basement of King Aśoka's pillar was found by General Cunningham in 1876. On a previous occasion

---

[1] This Utpalā must be the same as Utpala-varṇā (see p. 48 of this volume).

he discovered the capital of the ancient pillar surmounted by an elephant, which may have been mistaken by Fā-hien for a lion (see Cunningham, i. 274).

Hiouen Thsang, in his account of the three ladders (Beal, i. 202), says that they were arranged side by side from north to south, so that those who descended might have their faces to the east, and that the flight by which Indra descended was of crystal (not of gold), while that used by Brahmā was of silver, and the Buddha's steps were of gold (or of the seven precious substances, of which gold was one). This indicated the superiority of Buddha over the two gods who accompanied him.

In harmony with these ideas Indra and Brahmā are sometimes represented in Buddhistic sculptures standing one on each side of the Buddha, and protecting him. They were also present at his birth (see p. 483 and engraving opposite p. 477).

Hiouen Thsang adds that some centuries before his time the ladders still existed in their original position; but, when he visited the spot, they had sunk into the earth, and disappeared. Saṅkāśya, however, was still much frequented. A magnificent image of the Buddha was preserved in a large monastery there, and 1000 priests were studying the doctrines of the Sammatīya, a school of the Hīna-yāna, in four monasteries. Furthermore, many 'myriads' of pious laymen lived in the neighbourhood.

The story of Buddha's descent from heaven by help of golden steps is commonly believed both in Ceylon and Burma to the present day. The legend, as current in Ceylon, is given by Spence Hardy (Manual, p. 311).

It appears that when Buddha was about to return to earth from the god Indra's heaven, the god reflected that, although Buddha had ascended in three steps, his descent ought to be celebrated 'with special honours.' He therefore caused a ladder of gold to extend from the Mountain Meru (see p. 206 of the present Lectures) to Saṅkāśya, 80,000 Yojanas[1] in length. The steps were alternately of gold, silver, coral, ruby, emerald and other gems. At the right side of the ladder he created another, also of gold, by which Indra, blowing the conch, descended, accompanied by his own gods; and on the left another ladder of silver, by which Brahmā and the Brahmā gods (p. 210) descended, holding umbrellas over the Buddha. The three flights of steps appeared to the people of the earth like three rainbows. When Buddha commenced his descent all the worlds were illuminated by the light from his body.

With this extravagant myth—believed in as a historical fact by most Buddhists—we may contrast the simple narrative of Jacob's dream in Genesis xxviii.

Nevertheless the legend is curious, and I was greatly pleased by discovering in the Indian Section of the South Kensington Museum, a small bronze model of the triple ladder, lately dug up at Moulmein. Mr. Purdon Clarke, C.I.E., the present Keeper, kindly had the model photographed, and presented me with a drawing of it. This I have had engraved, and here give.

---

[1] A Yojana is variously estimated at 4 or 5 or 9 English miles.

It will be observed that an image of the Buddha is represented above the ladder, as if seated in Indra's heaven, and as if engaged in the act of teaching there; while the earth is typically represented below in the shape of a square platform, with four small Buddhist temples, one at each of the four quarters of the compass (compare p. 85).

A ruder representation of the ladder occurs in the sculptures of the Bharhut Stūpa (Cunningham, p. 92).

The General found an imperfect representation of it carved in soap-stone at Saṅkisa in 1876 (Report, xi. 26).

Sāketa.

Sāketa is a name of the ancient city Ayodhyā (now Ajūdhyā) described in Valmīki's great epic the Rāmāyaṇa, and believed to have been founded by Manu, the progenitor of the human race. This renowned city, which was a great centre of Brāhmanism, was also, no doubt, at one time a considerable centre of Buddhism. At all events, the identification of certain Buddhist sites there has been made clear by Sir A. Cunningham, who considers Sāketa to be the same as the Pi-so-kia (Viśākhā) of Hiouen Thsang and the Shā-che or Shā-khe of Fā-hien. The former found twenty monasteries there, and 3000 priests studying the Little Vehicle according to the Sammatīya school; also fifty Deva temples and very many heretics.

In one of the monasteries resided the Arhat Devaśarmā, who wrote a treatise called the Vijñāna-kāya-śāstra in defence of the doctrine of the non-existence of any Ego or personal self. A Stūpa, 200 feet high, was built by Aśoka in the place where Buddha is supposed to have preached and taught during six years.

Both Fā-hien and Hiouen Thsang mention the legend that he one day threw on the ground a twig he had used to clean his teeth (danta-kāshṭha), which sprouted and grew into a miraculous tree seven cubits high, at which height it always remained. The Brāhmans became jealous of the miracle and sometimes cut the tree down, sometimes uprooted it, but it always grew again and remained at the same height. Here also is the place where the four Buddhas (p. 400) walked and sat (Legge, pp. 54, 55; Beal, i. 240).

Kanyā-kubja (Kanouj).

Kanyā-kubja[1] is the Sanskṛit name for the ancient city of Kanouj (often spelt Kanoj), once the capital of Northern India, and said to be the oldest city in India, next to Ayodhyā.

When Hiouen Thsang visited this place it was the capital of the celebrated monarch Harsha-vardhana, also called Śilāditya (see p. 167 of this volume), whose kingdom extended from Kashmīr to Assam and from the river Narbadā to Nepāl. When he carried off a tooth-relic of the Buddha from Kashmīr, his procession back to his capital was attended by a large number of tributary kings. Hiouen Thsang, in describing the piety of this great monarch, says of him, that 'he sought to plant the tree of religious merit to such an extent that he forgot to sleep and to eat.' He goes on to state as follows:—

> King Śilāditya forbade the slaughter of any living thing as food on pain of death. He built several thousand Stūpas, each about 100 feet high. Then in all the highways of the towns and villages throughout India he erected hospices, and stationed physicians there with medicines for travellers and the poor persons round about. On all spots where there were holy traces of Buddha, he built monasteries. Once in five years he held the great assembly called Moksha. Then

---

[1] Hiouen Thsang states that this name, which means a 'hump-backed virgin,' is derived from the fact that an old sage (Ṛishi), who possessed supernatural powers, cursed ninety-nine daughters of king Brahma-datta for refusing to marry him, and made them deformed (Beal, i. 209). A different legend is given in my Sanskṛit-English Dictionary.

every year he assembled the monks, and bestowed on them the four kinds of alms (food, drink, medicine, clothing). He ordered them to carry on discussions, and himself judged of their arguments. He rewarded the good and punished the wicked. He promoted the men of talent, and degraded evil men. Wherever he moved he dwelt in a travelling-palace, and provided choice meats for men of all sorts of religion. Of these the Buddhist priests would be perhaps a thousand; the Brāhmans five hundred[1]. He divided each day into three portions. During the first he occupied himself on matters of government; during the second he practised himself in religious devotion (Beal, i. 214).

Notwithstanding Hiouen Thsang's description of various Stūpas, monasteries and monuments seen by him, General Sir A. Cunningham was not able to identify any of the existing ruins in the neighbourhood of Kanouj, 'so completely has almost every trace of Hindū occupation been obliterated by the Musalmāns' (Report, i. 284).

Fā-hien mentions a Stūpa near the town, built on the spot where the Buddha preached a discourse on 'the bitterness and vanity of life,' comparing it to 'a bubble or foam on water' (Legge, 54).

Pāṭali-putra.

Pāṭali-putra (now Patnā) seems to have existed as a village at a very early period. Its ancient name was Kusuma-pura. It was enlarged and practically founded about the time of the Buddha's death by Ajāta-śatru[2],

[1] This is very instructive in regard to the numerical proportion between Brāhmans and Buddhists at this place.

[2] According to Cunningham, about B.C. 450.

who did not, however, remove there from his own capital city Rāja-gṛiha. One of his successors, the great King Aśoka, the well-known patron of Buddhism (p. 66), converted Pāṭali-putra into the metropolis of the kingdom of Magadha, and it thenceforward became an important centre of Buddhism. Sir A. Cunningham states that it continued flourishing as the capital of the great Gupta kingdom during the fourth and fifth centuries of the Christian era.

Fā-hien relates a tradition that King Aśoka's palace in the city was built by genii (spirits), who brought great rocks and constructed chambers by heaping them together. He describes a monastery belonging to the Great Vehicle, and a temple belonging to the Little Vehicle, in the neighbourhood of the city, and gives an account of a Buddhist procession of four-wheeled cars and images which took place once a year. Each car was twenty-two feet or more high, and had five stories, with niches on four sides, in which were placed images of the Buddha and the Bodhi-sattvas, along with images of the gods (dēvas). They were made to look like moving pagodas (or Dāgabas). The Hindūs, as we know, have similar car-processions to this day, when the images of Kṛishṇa are dragged through the streets of towns and villages.

Fā-hien mentions the interesting fact that the nobles of the country had founded hospitals in the city to which destitute, crippled, and diseased persons might repair, and receive advice, food, and medicines suited to their cases, gratuitously. He adds that Aśoka, wishing to build 84,000 Stūpas[1] in place of the eight originally constructed over the Buddha's ashes, built the first Stūpa and a pillar near Pāṭali-putra.

Near it he says was an impression of the Buddha's foot, over which a temple with a door towards the north had been erected (Legge, pp. 77–80; Beal, i. lv–lviii). The position of the Stūpa and column has been discovered by Sir A. Cunningham (xi. 157, 158).

Kesarīya.

Kesarīya is a large village about thirty miles distant from Vaiśālī (Besārh). It is chiefly remarkable for a mound of ruined brick-work, 62 feet in height, supporting a solid brick Stūpa (nearly 68½ feet in diameter), which is also partly in ruins. The people call it the Stūpa of the Ćakravartī (Universal Monarch) Veṇa, father of King Pṛithu. In Manu, VII. 41; IX. 66, 67, King Veṇa is described as an arrogant monarch who resisted the authority of the Brāhmans. Probably he favoured the Buddhists. At any rate the Buddhists assert that the remarkable Stūpa at this place was built to mark the spot where Gautama Buddha preached a discourse, in which he described one of his previous births as a Ćakravartī king.

Not far from the Stūpa a small mound has been excavated, and the head and shoulders of a colossal statue of Buddha brought to light (Cunningham, i. 67).

---

[1] One for each of the 84,000 elements of the body (p. 499). The real number of Stūpas was 84, but, as usual, three ciphers have been added.

Kuśi-nagara.

Kuśi-nagara (in Pāli Kusi-nārā) was the place where the Buddha died, or—to speak more correctly—passed away in Pari-nirvāṇa (see pp. 48, 49, 140). It was long searched for in vain, but has recently been identified by Sir A. Cunningham with the modern Kasia, eighty miles east of Kapila-vastu, and 120 miles N.N.E. of Benares.

Neither Fā-hien nor Hiouen Thsang say much about Kuśi-nagara, except that it was deserted and had few inhabitants; but the latter's allusion to the Buddha's passing away out of the world at this place, and his account of the subsequent assembling of the first council at Rāja-gṛiha by order of the great Kāśyapa (pp. 47, 55), is so interesting and curious that I here give an abstract of his narrative, based on Mr. Beal's translation (ii. 161):—

Once when the great Kāśyapa was seated in meditation, suddenly a bright light burst forth, and the earth shook. Then, exerting his faculty of supernatural vision, he saw the Lord Buddha passing away into Pari-nirvāṇa between two trees. Forthwith he ordered his followers to accompany him to the city of Kuśi-nagara. On the way there they met a Brāhman, who, on being asked whence he came, replied, 'From Kuśi-nagara, where I saw your master entering into Nirvāṇa. A vast multitude of heavenly beings were around him.'

Kāśyapa having heard these words said, 'The sun of wisdom has extinguished his rays. The world is now in darkness. The illustrious guide—the King of the Law—has left us; the whole world is empty and afflicted. Men and gods are left without a guide.' Accordingly, he proceeded to the two trees, and looking on Buddha, offered worship. But certain careless monks said one to another, with satisfaction, 'Tathāgata has gone to rest. This is good for us; for now, if we transgress, who is there to reprove us?' Then Kāśyapa was deeply moved, and resolved to secure obedience to the teaching of Buddha.

Addressing the assembled multitude, he said, 'We ought to collect the Law. Those who have kept it without failure, whose powers of discrimination are clear, such persons may form the assembly. Those who are only learners must depart to their homes.'

On this they went away, and only 999 men were left, including Ānanda. But the great Kāśyapa excluded Ānanda as being yet a learner. Addressing him, he said, 'You are not yet free from defect; you, too, must leave the assembly. You were a personal attendant on Buddha, you loved him much, and are, therefore, not free from the ties of affection.'

So Ānanda retired to a desert place. Wearied out, he desired to lie down. Scarcely had his head reached the pillow, when lo! he obtained the condition of an Arhat. Then he returned to the door of the assembly. But Kāśyapa said to him, 'Have you got rid of all ties? If so, prove it; exercise your spiritual power and enter without the door being opened.' Then Ānanda entered through the key-hole, and having paid reverence to the assembled monks, sat down.

This power of reducing the body to the size of an atom, so as to be able to pass through so minute an aperture as a key-hole, was one of the supernatural faculties supposed to belong to perfected saints or Arhats (compare pp. 133, 245 of these Lectures).

The consideration of Buddhist Sacred Places might lead us on to various hallowed spots in other Buddhist countries, for example, Anurādha-pura, Adam's Peak and Kelani in Ceylon; the site of the great pagoda at Rangoon, and of that near Mandalay in Burma; the site of the Buddha's foot-print (Phra Bat) in Siam; the snows of Kinchinjunga in Sikkim; the city of Lhāssa and its monasteries in Tibet; Kuren in Mongolia; but all these, and other places, have either been incidentally mentioned in previous Lectures or will be more fully noticed hereafter.

LECTURE XV.

Monasteries and Temples.

Buddhist monasteries deserve a fuller notice than the incidental allusions we have made to them in previous Lectures.

The duty of dwelling under trees, and not in houses, according to the example set by all the Buddhas (see p. 136), and especially by Gautama Buddha himself, during his long course of meditation (see p. 31), was in theory supposed to be binding on all true monks. 'The root of a tree for an abode' was one of 'the four Resources,' of which every monk was allowed to avail himself, and the enumeration of which formed part of the admission-ceremonies (see p. 80).

At the same time certain dispensations or indulgences were specially granted at those ceremonies, one of which was permission to live in covered residences, when not itinerating. The five kinds of dwellings permissible under varying circumstances are described in Ćulla-vagga (VI. 1, 2). They are Vihāras (monasteries), Aḍḍhayogas (i. e. houses of a peculiar shape), storied dwellings (prāsāda)[1], mansions (harmya), and caves (see note, p. 81 of this volume).

It is clear that any painful exposure of the body to

---

[1] It is difficult to understand exactly what these Aḍḍhayoga, Prāsāda and Harmya were. In some Buddhist countries storied houses are considered objectionable, as no one likes to submit to the indignity of having the feet of another person above his head.

the violent storms of India was incompatible with one of the principles of Buddhism, which, though it taught self-denial and self-sacrifice of a particular kind, deprecated all personal self-inflicted pain and austerity.

Yet it appears (from Mahā-vagga, III. 15) that at the time of his first residence at Rāja-gṛiha (see p. 29 of these Lectures), the Buddha had not yet instituted 'the Retreat' during the rains (Vassa). Hence the monks were in the habit of going on their travels alike during winter, summer, and the rainy season.

The people complained of this, and said that the monks in walking about during wet weather were unable to avoid crushing vegetable life and treading on minute living things. Thereupon the Buddha prescribed that the monks were to keep 'Vassa,' and refrain from peregrination during the rains.

Soon afterwards, when the Buddha had left Rāja-gṛiha and had taken up his abode during Vassa in the Jeta-vana garden at Sāvatthī (see p. 407), a wealthy and pious layman (Upāsaka) who had built a monastery (Vihāra) for the monks, sent to invite them to reside in it, saying that he wished to hear them recite the Law and to bestow gifts upon them. The Buddha permitted them to go, but required them to return in seven days. He gave the same permission when another rich and pious layman had provided other residences and conveniences for the monks, such as a storied house, a mansion, a store-room, a cave, a refectory, a bathing room, a well-house, a pavilion, a park, etc.

On the other hand, when, on a particular occasion, a monk wished to keep Vassa in a cattle-pen (Mahā-vagga, III. 12) the Buddha permitted him to do so. So, again, on another occasion he allowed a man to keep Vassa in a caravan, and on a third occasion in a covered boat or ship. But it is recorded that he prohibited Vassa from being kept in the open air, or in the hollow of trees[1] (see Mahā-vagga, III. 12, 3).

It is evident from all this, that even in the early days of Buddhism, rich laymen were in the habit of seeking to acquire religious merit by providing comfortable habitations for the monks; and although at first the use of such luxuries was only permitted in the rainy season, this restriction was soon removed, and a residence in covered dwellings became usual at all seasons of the year.

Then, as Buddhism spread, kings, princes, and rich men competed with each other for the privilege of erecting vast monasteries—sometimes called Vihāras[2], sometimes Saṅghārāmas—to which temples, libraries, and schools were generally attached, and in which dwelt wealthy communities of monks, who were allowed to hold property in land.

The founding of extensive and important institutions of this kind was, of course, an exceptional proceeding. As a general rule, collections of monastic dwellings were of a simple and unostentatious character. In various parts of India are to be seen in the present day ancient Buddhist cave-monasteries now untenanted, some of

---

[1] The objection to the hollow of trees was that spirits, ghosts, and goblins often took up their abode there.

[2] The term Vihāra was afterwards usually applied to temples, or to buildings combining temple and monastery in one.

them—such as the caves of Barābar—as old as the third century B.C.

I myself visited those at Elorā (Elurā), twelve miles from Aurangābād in the Nizām's territory, as well as others at Nāsik, Kārle, and other places. The Elorā caves are possibly as old as the third century[1], and with the adjoining Brāhmanical and Jain caves of later date, extend for one mile and a quarter along the scarp of an elevated plateau. The three groups of caves rival each other in the beauty and interest of their sculptures, and together constitute one of the wonders of India—their position side by side proving that the adherents of the three systems lived together in harmony. Among the Buddhist caves are beautiful 'Ćaityas' or halls for general worship (see p. 450), refectories for commensality, and cells without number for the habitation of the monks. All the excavations had become partially filled up; but the visit of the Prince of Wales in 1876 stimulated the Nizām's government to clear away the dust and rubbish of centuries.

Then, besides cave-monasteries, the ruins of extensive monastic establishments built of brick, stone, or other less durable materials, are scattered everywhere throughout India.

Those of the vast monastery of Nālanda near Rājagṛiha, and others at various other sacred places, have been already described (see p. 412).

Turning next to the monastic structures of modern Buddhist countries, and beginning with Ceylon, we find

[1] Some authorities place them in the sixth century of our era.

that in that island, as Spence Hardy has pointed out, and as I myself observed during my sojourn there, the residences of the monks are of very simple construction, and often extremely mean in appearance. They are called Pān-sālās (Paṇṇa-śālā = Sanskṛit Parṇa-śālā) because supposed to be made of leaves. In general, however, they are constructed of wattle filled up with mud, the roof being covered with straw, or with the platted leaves of the cocoa-nut. They are always dirty and always abound in cobwebs.

A monastery which I saw near Kandy consisted of an oblong rectangular court-yard, surrounded in the interior by a kind of roofed cloister or verandah, out of which opened the monks' cells, lighted only from the sky above the court. The interior walls of both cloister and cells were begrimed with patches of dirt and masses of cobwebs, which are never touched for fear of breaking the first Buddhist commandment, 'kill not' (p. 126).

Of course there are monasteries of a better and more imposing type, such as that attached to the Māligāwa temple of the sacred eye-tooth on the Kandy lake (see p. 454).

In Burma the ordinary residences of the monks appear to be simple in character, like those in Ceylon. In Siam, on the contrary, they are sometimes elaborate, and often have richly-covered entrances. At the same time the Siamese monks (according to Mr. Alabaster) are in the habit of itinerating a good deal, only remaining in their monasteries during the three months of rains, when residence there is imperative.

Speaking of the larger and more imposing monasteries (Kyoung) in Burma, Mr. Scott says (I give his account in an abbreviated form):—

The monasteries are built of teak, or, sometimes in Mandalay and Lower Burma, of brick. The shape is always oblong, and the inhabited portion is raised on posts and pillars, eight or ten feet above the ground. They are, like all the other houses in the country, only one story high; for if it is an indignity to a layman to have anyone's feet over his head[1], it is much more so to a member of the brotherhood. The space between the ground and the floor is always kept open, and is never used except by the monastery school-boys. A flight of steps of stone or wood leads up to the verandah, which extends along the north and south sides, and frequently all round. From the raised floor thus reached, rises the building, with tier upon tier of massive roofs (in diminishing stages), giving the appearance of many stories when there is only one. The accommodation is simple. It consists in the main of a central hall divided into two portions, one level with the verandah where the scholars are taught, and most of the duties of the monastery carried on, and the other a dais, raised about two feet above the level of the rest of the building. Seated upon this, the monks are accustomed to receive visitors, and at the back, against the wall, are arranged the images of Buddha, a large one usually standing in the centre on a kind of altar, with candles, flowers, praying flags, and other offerings placed before it. On shelves alongside are a number of smaller figures of gold, silver, alabaster, clay or wood, according to the popularity of the monastery, and the religious character of the neighbourhood. Occasionally there are dormitories for the monks, but as a rule they sleep in the central hall, where the mats which form their beds may be seen rolled up against the wall. The whole area of the extensive compound in which the monastery stands is enclosed

---

[1] This is curiously illustrated in a recent letter from a resident in Burma to the Editor of the *Times* newspaper, in which it is stated that about six months after King Theebaw had been deported, some of his things were exhibited by us in the lower rooms of the Rangoon Museum, to the great disgust of his Burmese admirers, who asked, 'how we dared place their king's things in a lower room where people could walk above them?'

by a heavy teak fence with massive posts and rails, seven or eight feet high. The laity, when they enter, take off their shoes and carry them in their hands. This rule applies to the highest in the land.

The daily life of the monks inhabiting monasteries of this kind in Burma has been already described (see pp. 311–314 of these Lectures).

If we now pass to northern Buddhist countries we shall find that, as a general rule, the dwellings of monks are insignificant tenements of poor construction, attached to or built round small chapels or shrines. Sometimes the monks live in the rooms built over such chapels.

Sir Richard Temple (Journal, ii. 207) visited a so-called monastery at Pemyangchi (in Sikkim), which consisted of a single building with two stories. In the upper some of the monks resided, and a chapel formed the lower.

The temple-monastery I myself visited in British Sikkim, near Dārjīling, is similar. The exterior appearance might be compared to that of some small Dissenting chapel in an English village. The thatched roof, which once gave it a picturesque appearance, has recently been removed, and a roof of modern construction substituted. The shrine or temple is on the ground floor, while the upper floor is the abode of the attendant priests, and seems also to serve as a store-room with cupboards for their equipments. The contents of the ground-floor temple, with its altar at the further end and shelves for the sacred books on one side, are very indistinctly seen, being only lighted up by a 'dim religious light,' when the door is kept wide open. I noticed three images on the altar.

The case is different when large numbers of monks congregate in particular places. In some districts of Ladāk, Mongolia and Tibet, monasteries (or Lāmaseries as they are sometimes called) have been erected, which for vastness, magnificence, and grandeur of situation amid splendid scenery, are unequalled in any part of the world.

According to strict rule, retired localities should be chosen. Hence large monastic establishments are often found in solitary places[1] and elevated situations; for instance, in Ladāk those at Lāma Yurru and Hemis are more than 11,000 feet above the sea, and that at Hanle is 14,000 feet. They resemble romantic castles towering upwards in the midst of rocks, crags, and snowy mountains.

Another monastery at Kīlang (Kyelang), in the British Tibetan province of Lahūl (contiguous to Ladāk), stands on the spur of a mountain, at an elevation of 12,000 feet, and is approached through grand ravines and glaciers, so that occasionally, after snow-storms, those who pass to and fro are buried in avalanches.

The outer walls of large monasteries of this kind in secluded situations are generally lofty. Often they are made of stone or brick, plastered with mud and surmounted with little pinnacles and poles, on which are prayer-flags. Within the walls are cells for the monks, the abode of the Head or Abbot, a room for holding books, a temple, an assembly-hall, a refectory, storehouses, receptacles for musical instruments, masks,

---

[1] It is for this reason that in the Tibetan language they are called Gonpa.

staves, etc.; the buildings being often arranged in rows, and always intermixed with Stūpas (see p. 504) and monuments. The walls of the vestibules and of the great hall are usually ornamented with fresco-paintings, representing subjects from the Buddhist Jātakas (p. 111). Generally there are corridors or covered cloisters lined with prayer-wheels, or open walks paved with stone, called in Sanskrit Ćankramaṇa (Pāli, Ćankamana), for the monks to perambulate up and down in meditation. These are supposed to be constructed after the pattern of the stone walking-places used by the Buddha himself (see p. 400).

In the monastery at Kīlang the roof of the great hall is supported by massive beams garnished with belts, swords, yaks' tails, huge and terrible masks, and all sorts of odds and ends. On one side is a huge praying-wheel, on each revolution of which a bell is struck. A dim subdued light pervades the entire hall, exaggerating the ghastly hideousness of the figures [1].

To take as another instance—the monastery or Lāmasery of Kunbum (or Kumbum) north of Tibet, celebrated as the birth-place of Tsong Khapa (p. 277), and situated, according to M. Huc, on a mountain intersected by a broad and deep ravine:—

On either side of the ravine, and up the slopes of the mountain, rise, in amphitheatrical curves, the white dwellings of the Lāmas, each with its little terrace and enclosing wall, while here and there above them 'tower the temples, with their gilt roofs glittering with a thousand colours.' The houses of the superior monks are distinguished by pennants, floating above small hexagonal turrets, while

[1] So described in a pamphlet on Buddhist Monasteries in Lahoul, by a Moravian Missionary.

those of the ordinary monks are simple cells. On all sides mystical sentences, in the Tibetan character, meet the eye (see p. 381), some inscribed on doors, some on walls and stones, or on linen flags fixed on poles.

Almost everywhere are conical vessels, in which incense and odoriferous wood are burning; while numbers of Lāmas circulate through the streets of the monastery in their red and yellow dresses—grave in their deportment, and, although under no obligation to silence, speaking little, and that little in a low voice.

This Lāmasery of Kunbum enjoys so great a reputation, that the worshippers of Buddha make pilgrimages to it from all parts of Mongolia, Tartary, and Tibet, and on the occasion of great festivals the confluence of strangers is immense. It is much frequented by Eastern Tibetans.

Near Kunbum is a much smaller monastery, devoted to the study of medicine. It is at the foot of a rocky mountain, on the heights of which dwell certain contemplative monks. M. Huc saw one of these hermits, who never communicated with the outer world except for food, which he drew up to his rocky cell by the help of a bag tied to a long rope (ii. 73).

Some mention should also be made of the monasteries at Kuku khotun, 'the blue city' in Tartary. That town contains no less than five great Lāmaseries and fifteen affiliated monasteries, with a grand total of 20,000 Lāmas dwelling in them. The chief monastery is that of the 'Five Towers'—not to be confounded with one of the same name in the Chinese province of Shan si.

This latter is a celebrated place for burials (see p. 370), and pilgrims may there be edified by a sight of the Buddha's shadow impressed on a rock.

Another example of a monastery in a remote situation is that of Kurun or Kuren (see p. 295), situated on the slope of a mountain in Mongolia. In this celebrated monastery of the Grand Lāma Tāranātha 30,000 Lāmas (according to M. Huc) are lodged and supported.

The plain at the foot of the mountain is constantly covered with tents of various sizes for the convenience of pilgrims. Hither throng the worshippers of Buddha from the most remote countries.

Viewed from a distance, the white cells of the Lāmas, built on the declivity in horizontal lines one above the other, resemble the steps of an enormous altar, of which the temple of the Tāranātha Lāma appears to constitute (in Roman Catholic phraseology) 'the tabernacle.' In this country Tāranātha is the saint par excellence, and there is not a Tartar Khalka who does not take a pride in calling himself his disciple.

Passing on now to Tibet, we find that in its principal provinces the number of monastic institutions connected with its two respective capitals of Lhāssa and Tashi Lunpo, is more than a thousand, with 491,242 Lāmas. This is the estimate of the latest traveller [1].

According to Huc, more than thirty large monasteries may be reckoned in the neighbourhood of Lhāssa alone.

Adverting for a moment to Lhāssa itself, we may note that this 'city of the gods'—the chief town of the province of U, situated on the Ki-ćhu river [2]—had in 1854 about 15,000 inhabitants within a circumference of two-and-a-half miles. According to a Chinese proverb, its chief inmates have always been 'priests, women, and dogs.' Koeppen affirms that Lhāssa has always been a greater nest of monk-priests than Rome has ever been.

---

[1] Mr. Sarat Chandra Dās gives the names of 1026 monasteries. Koeppen makes 3000 monasteries and 84,000 Lāmas.

[2] A small river flowing into the Tsanpo or Brahma-putra.

Doubtless its population is now increased, and includes a considerable proportion of laymen; yet, in all likelihood, at least two-thirds of the inhabitants are monks; and it cannot be too often repeated that, according to the true theory of Buddhism, the only raison d'être of the laity is to wait upon the monkhood.

Moreover, Lhāssa, next to Benares and Mecca, is, perhaps, the most frequented place of pilgrimage upon earth. Scarcely a day passes on which the streets do not overflow with crowds of pilgrims—some from every quarter of Tibet, some from Bhutān and other Himālayan regions, some from all parts of Mongolia. All meet here to worship the incarnated representative of the Bodhisattva (Avalokiteśvara) manifested in the Dalai Lāma—to receive his blessing, his consecrated pills, and his prayer-papers (see p. 331 of these Lectures). The residence of this Lāmistic Pope is at Potala.

In fact Potala on the north-west side of Lhāssa is what the Vatican is to Rome. It existed in ancient times as a palace, but was rebuilt and converted into a palace-monastery by the celebrated fifth Dalai Lāma Navang Lobsang, A.D. 1617–1682 (p. 292 of this volume), and from that time forward became the residence of all the Dalai Lāmas, who had before lived either at Sera or at Brepung (Dapung, see p. 442).

In its striking and unique position, it is even more imposing than the Vatican.

Imagine a lofty structure erected on an isolated hill[1],

---

[1] The hill is called Potala, and the palace-monastery is named after it. Koeppen says it has three peaks, but the illustration in Mark-

rising abruptly from the plain with three long summits or eminences, and watered at the base by the Ki-ćhu river, which flows into the great Tsanpo. The south-western ridge is the so-called Iron-hill, on which is a monastery where Tsong Khapa himself is said to have taught. The north-eastern bears the name of the Phagmo hill[1], while the highest is the hill of Potala, with its palace-monastery towering in four stories to the height of about 367 feet, and ending in a cupola covered with plates of pure gold.

From this vantage ground the incarnated Bodhisattva looks down on the crowds of pilgrims approaching to worship him, or kneeling at the foot of the hill. The buildings grouped in the vicinity are said to contain 10,000 rooms, for the accommodation of as many monks. Countless are the statues of Buddha, with other idols and images of saints, not to mention obelisks and pyramidal monuments, which meet the eye everywhere. All sacred objects are manufactured out of gold, silver, or copper, according to the wealth of those who have brought them as offerings. Two ascending avenues lead up from Lhāssa to Potala, which are constantly thronged with foreign pilgrims, troops of Lāmas in official vest-

ham's account of Manning's journey (p. 256) shows three long summits rather than peaks. The hill is called Buddha-la by Huc (ii. 140), but Koeppen (ii. 341) is more correct in stating that Potala is the name of a sea-port on the river Indus, called Pattala by the Greeks, and now Tatta. There is a tradition that this Potala was the original home of the Śākya tribe (see p. 21 of this volume).

[1] Koeppen translates this by the German *sau*, but says it may also mean 'Hintere Berg.'

ments, higher Lāmas and courtiers in full uniform. Yet we are told that a solemn religious silence prevails, for the thoughts of all are fixed in meditation.

I have already given an abstract of Mr. Sarat Chandra Dās' narrative of his visit to Potala, and his presentation to the Dalai Lāma on June 10, 1882 (see p. 331 of these Lectures). I now add an account of Mr. Thomas Manning's interview with the Dalai Lāma on December 17, 1811. No European, except Mr. Manning[1], has ever set eyes on a Dalai Lāma, and no other Englishman has ever seen Lhāssa (for M. Huc was misinformed; Moorcroft was never there):—

We rode to the foot of the mountain on which the palace is built, or out of which, rather, it seems to grow; but having ascended a few paces to a platform, were obliged to dismount. From here to the hall where the Grand Lāma receives visitors is a long and tedious ascent. It consists of about four hundred steps, partly stone steps in the rocky mountain, and the rest mere ladders from story to story in the palace. Besides this, from interval to interval along the mountain, wherever the ascent is easy, there are stretches interspersed, where the path continues for several paces together without steps. At length we arrived at the large platform on which is built the hall of reception. There we rested awhile, arranged the presents, and conferred with the Lāma's Chinese interpreter.

The Tí-mu-fu was in the hall with the Grand Lāma. I was not informed of this until I entered, which occasioned me some confusion. I did not know how much ceremony to go through with one, before I began with the other. I made the due obeisance, touching the ground three times with my head to the Grand Lāma, and once to the Tí-mu-fu. I presented my gifts, delivering the coin and the handsome silk scarf with my own hands into the hands of the Grand Lāma. I then took off my hat, and humbly gave him my clean-shaven head to

---

[1] Messrs. Huc and Gabet failed in their attempt to obtain an interview with the Dalai Lāma of 1846.

lay his hands upon. The ceremony of presentation being over, the Munshī and I sat down on two cushions not far from the Lāma's throne, and had tea brought to us. It was most excellent, and I meant to have emptied the cup, but it was whipped away suddenly, before I was aware of it. The Lāma's beautiful and interesting face and manner engrossed almost all my attention. He was at that time about seven years old; and had the simple and unaffected manners of a well-educated princely child. His face was, I thought, poetically and affectingly beautiful. He was of a gay and cheerful disposition; his beautiful mouth perpetually unbending into a graceful smile, which illuminated his whole countenance. Sometimes, particularly when he had looked at me, his smile approached to a gentle laugh. No doubt my grim beard and spectacles somewhat excited his risibility. He inquired whether I had not met with molestation and difficulties on the road; to which I promptly returned the proper answer. A present of dried fruit was brought and set before me, and then we withdrew. (Mr. Clements Markham's Tibet, p. 264, abridged.)

As to the monasteries grouped around this Vatican of Lāmistic Buddhism, we may make special mention of four, noting a few particulars.

To begin with the oldest monastery, that of *Lā brang*, said to mean 'abode of Lāmas[1],' which was built by King Srong Tsan Gampo (see p. 271 of this volume), and founded in the seventh century. This ancient institution is in the very centre of Lhāsta, and is regarded as the centre of the whole country. All the main roads of Tibet converge towards it. Doubtless the area of the monastery has been enlarged by occasional additions in the course of one thousand years, but not since it was partly rebuilt and restored in the seventeenth century. Its magnificent temple (Cho Khang) is the St. Peter's of Lāmism (see p. 459).

---

[1] It may also mean temple of Lhāssa and 'abode of gods,' in which case Lā would be for Lhā.

The immense number of monks inhabiting this monastery is proved by the fact that a huge cauldron is shown which holds more than 1200 gallons of tea for the Lāmas who perform the daily services.

The other three monasteries near Potala and Lā brang, according to Koeppen, are devoted to the study of magic and the art of exorcising. We may take them in the following order :—

First, at a short distance north of Lā brang, stands the monastery *Ramoćhe*, 'the great enclosure,' which was the other ancient monastery built by Srong Tsan Gampo, or by one of his wives (see p. 271). It is now a great school of exorcism, and has a celebrated temple (see pp. 462, 463), containing the celebrated image of the Buddha, and also one of Nanda, Gautama's step-brother and disciple. Those who study here may gain the degree of 'Doctor of Magic.'

Next comes the monastery of *Moru* (or Muru or Meru), close to the city. It is noted for its order and cleanliness, and for its printing-press. Like the last, it contains a school for instruction in magic.

Then, at a short distance east of Lā brang (according to Koeppen), is the monastery of *Gar Ma Khian*—the mother monastery of soothsayers, fortune-tellers, and exorcisers (Ćhos-kyong, see p. 266).

Let us next turn to the three ancient 'mother-monasteries' of the Yellow sect—Galdan, Sera, and Dapung.

Galdan (or *Gahdan*), the 'heaven of contented beings' (Sanskṛit Tushita, see pp. 207, 213)—the oldest monastery of the Yellow sect—is situated on the hill of the same name, about thirty miles[1] east of Lhāssa. As already stated (pp. 278, 294), it was founded by Tsong Khapa A.D. 1409. It is three-quarters of a mile in circumference, and has 3300 monks.

Sera, 'the golden,' founded by Tsong Khapa (p. 278), or by one of his disciples immediately after his death, lies about three miles north of Lhāssa, on a declivity of a hill, over which passes the road leading to Mongolia. It has 5500 monks, and numerous temples, towers, and houses curving round like an amphitheatre. On the hills above the town are rows of cells of contemplative monks and recluses.

Sera has three great temples several stories high, the halls of which are richly gilded. In one temple the staff of Gautama Buddha is preserved.

Dapung (variously Dapuṅ, Depung, Debung, Debang, Brepung, Brebung, Prebung), 'rice-heap,' so called from the shape of the hill, was also founded by Tsong Khapa three years before Sera, and is situated four miles west of the city of Lhāssa. It has 7700 monks. The great temple in the middle is surrounded by four small ones. One of these four belongs to the exorcisers and professors of magical arts, of whom there are nearly three hundred. In the centre of the monastery is a residence for the Dalai Lāma, when he pays his annual visit. Numbers of foreigners study here, especially Mongolians. In front of the monastery stands a Stūpa, which contains the bones of the fourth Dalai Lāma, Jon Tan Yam Thso, who was of a Mongolian family.

---

[1] Huc says 'four leagues;' Koeppen 'drei meilen,' which is incorrect.

Mr. Edgar (Report, p. 41) mentions four other monasteries of the Yellow sect around Lhāssa, *Chemiling*, *Tengiling*, *Chechuling*, and *Kenduling*[1]. The last is said to be the residence of the Regent (p. 286 of these Lectures). Sarat Chandra Dās gives a long list of monasteries, some containing 5000 monks (e.g. Rnam rgyal grvatsang, Gongdkar rDorjegdan, etc.) and some 7000.

We have next to describe the great monastery of the second Grand Lāma of Tibetan Buddhism—I mean that at *Tashi Lunpo*, also belonging to the Yellow sect.

Tashi Lunpo, near *Shigatse*, is the seat of government of the Tashi Lāma or Panchen Lāma (see p. 284 of these Lectures), and the second metropolis of Lāmistic Buddhism. Our knowledge of this celebrated place is derived from the record of the journeys of Mr. Bogle and Captain Turner, as well as from the narratives of Indian explorers.

According to some of these authorities, Tashi Lunpo is situated about 140 English miles in a nearly westerly direction from Lhāssa. It is built on a level plain enclosed on all sides by rocky hills, through which a small river (the Painam) rushes into the great Tsanpo (Brahma-putra). The monastery is said to have been built by the first Dalai Lāma, Gedun grub pa, in 1445 (see p. 291 of these Lectures), though the final seat of the Dalai Lāmas was at Lhāssa.

According to Koeppen four roads meet at Tashi

[1] These are also mentioned by Sarat Chandra Dās and by Markham (p. 130, note 3), and again, differently spelt, at p. 264, note 1.

Lunpo; one leading to Lhāssa, one to Ladāk, one to Nepāl, and one to Bhutān.

Near at hand, on the north-east side of the Tashi Lunpo monastery, on a rocky eminence protecting it from the cold winds, stands the fort of Shigatse (also written Shigatze), which, with its surrounding houses, forms the capital of the province of Tsang, just as Lhāssa constitutes that of the province of U.

Our fellow countryman, Mr. Bogle, commissioned by Warren Hastings to open communications between Bengal and Tibet, arrived at Tashi Lunpo in 1774. His description of it is to the following effect. I give it abbreviated (from Mr. Clements Markham's Tibet):—

We passed by the foot of Tashi Lunpo, which is built on the lower declivity of a steep hill. The roof of the palace is all of copper-gilt. The building is of dark-coloured brick. The houses of the town rise one above another. Four churches with gilt ornaments are mixed with them. Altogether the town presents a princely appearance. Many of the courts are spacious, flagged with stone, and have galleries running round them. The alleys, which are likewise paved, are narrow. The palace is appropriated to the Lāma and his officers, to temples, granaries, warehouses, etc. The rest of the town is entirely inhabited by priests, who are in number about four thousand.

The following is the substance of Mr. Bogle's account of his interview with the Tashi Lāma on November 8, 1774 (abbreviated from Markham's Tibet):—

In the afternoon I had my first audience of the Tashi Lāma. He is about forty years of age, of low stature, and inclining to be fat. His complexion is fairer than that of most Tibetans, and his arms are as white as those of a European; his hair, which is jet black, is cut very short; his eyes are small and black. The expression of his countenance is smiling and good-humoured. He was upon his throne, formed of wood carved and gilt, with some cushions above it, upon which he sat with his legs folded under him. He was dressed in a mitre-shaped cap of yellow broadcloth, with long bars lined with red satin, a yellow cloth jacket without sleeves, and a satin mantle of the same colour thrown over his shoulders. On one side of him stood his physician, with a bundle of perfumed sandal-wood rods burning in his hand; on the other stood his cup-bearer. I laid the Governor's presents before him, delivering the letter and the pearl necklace into his own hands, together with a white handkerchief on my own part, according to the custom of the country. He received me in the most engaging manner. I was seated on a high stool covered with a carpet. Plates of boiled mutton, boiled rice, dried fruits, sweetmeats, sugar, bundles of tea, dried sheep's carcases, etc., were set before me and my companion, Mr. Hamilton. The Lāma drank two or three dishes of tea with us, but without saying any grace, asked us once or twice to eat, and on our retiring threw white handkerchiefs over our necks. After two or three visits, he used to receive me without any ceremony, his head uncovered, and dressed only in the large red petticoat worn by all full monks, red boots, a yellow cloth vest, with his arms bare, and a piece of coarse yellow cloth thrown across his shoulders. He sat sometimes in a chair, sometimes on a bench covered with tiger-skins, and nobody but the cup-bearer present. Sometimes he would walk with me about the room, explain the pictures, or make some remarks upon the colour of my eyes, etc. For, although venerated as God's vicegerent through all the eastern countries of Asia, and endowed with a portion of omniscience and with many other divine attributes, he throws aside in conversation all the awful part of his character, accommodates himself to the weakness of mortals, endeavours to make himself loved rather than feared, and behaves with the greatest affability to everybody, particularly to strangers.

In 1783, when Tashi Lunpo was visited by Captain Turner, the monastery consisted of 400 houses, many of which were built of stone and marble, and at least two stories high. They contained about 3700 monks (now 3800). Around the houses were gilded temples, pinnacles, pyramidal monuments (Stūpas), and above all the palace of the Tashi Lāma, forming a striking spectacle.

Captain Turner had a remarkable interview with the Grand Lāma at the neighbouring monastery of Terpaling, on December 4, 1783. He found the princely child, then aged eighteen months, seated on a throne, with his father and mother standing on the left hand. Having been informed that, although unable to speak, he could understand, Captain Turner intimated to him 'that the Governor-General, on receiving news of his decease, had been overwhelmed with sorrow, and continued to lament his absence from the world until the cloud was dispelled by his re-appearance. The Governor hoped that he might long continue to illumine the world by his presence.'

The infant looked steadfastly at the British envoy, and appeared to be listening to his words with deep attention, while he repeatedly nodded his head, as if he understood every syllable. He was silent and sedate, and conducted himself with astonishing dignity. Captain Turner thought him one of the handsomest children he had ever seen. It seems that he grew up to be an able and devout ruler, gratifying the Tibetans by his presence for many years, and living to a good old age.

Tashi Lunpo was not visited by the French missionaries, but M. Huc informs us (ii. 157) that in 1846 the then Panchen Lāma was 60 years of age, and still vigorous. M. Huc was told that he was of Indian origin, and that he had declared of himself that his first incarnation had taken place in India some thousands of years before.

Mr. Sarat Chandra Dās, from whose notes of a journey in Tibet so many extracts have been already given, writes thus of his arrival at Tashi Lunpo on the 9th of December, 1881 (the extract is not given literally, and is abbreviated):—

In the afternoon we arrived at Tashi Lunpo. In front of the western entrance I noticed two Chortens (that is, 'Ćaityas or Stūpas,' see p. 504 of these Lectures), one very large, with a gilt spire, and the other small. On entering the grand monastery, I mustered all my knowledge of Buddhist ceremonies and monkish etiquette, that I might not be criticised by the passing monks as one unacquainted with the duties of the wearers of the sacred costume. I walked slowly and with gravity, but secretly observing everything around me. There were a few yaks under the charge of three or four herdsmen, waiting probably for the return of some of their number from within the monastery. Some monks, riding on mules, passed us from north to south. A few parties with heavy grain packages on their backs were entering the monastery along with us. The rays of the sun, now slanting on the gilded spires of houses and tombs in the monastery, presented a very magnificent view to the eye.

While residing in the monastery I saw people busily engaged in out-door work, such as collecting fuel and tending cattle. In fact, this was the busiest part of the year, when the Tibetans remain on the move for the purpose of buying and selling, at a time when the intensely cold winds wither up the vegetation, freeze the streams, harden the soil, and dry up the skin. The monks, like the lay-people, are remarkable for their habit of early rising. No monk within the walls of the monastery rose later than five in the morning, and the usual time for getting up was four a.m. Those who slept later, without any special cause, were subject to correction. At three in the morning the great trumpet summons all the monks to the religious service in the congregation hall. Whoever fails to attend is punished next morning. No register is kept, yet the officer who superintends the discipline can tell what monk out of two thousand has absented himself on any particular day. I was the only man who slept up to six in the morning. The monks used often to remark that, were I a regular monk of the monastery, the superintendent's birch would have stript my body of its flesh.

About six miles from Tashi Lunpo, and on the road

leading from it in a south-westerly direction towards the monastery of Sakya (see below), is the monastery of *Narthang*, whence issued one of the three copies of the Kanjur (p. 272) brought to Europe by Brian Hodgson.

We have now to notice the two most important monasteries of the Red sect.

First, *Sam ye* (Sam yas) is on the great river Tsanpo, about forty miles from Lhāssa, in a south-easterly direction. It was the first monastery founded in the eighth century by Padma-sambhava, after King Khri Srong De Tsan's restoration of Buddhism (pp. 271, 272). It is the metropolitan monastery of the Red-capped monks and Urgyanpa sect. Sam ye was visited by the Indian explorer Nain Singh in 1874, on his final journey to Lhāssa[1], and by Sarat Chandra Dās in 1882. Many of its images are of gold, and it possesses an extensive library. Padma-sambhava was a master of Indian Yoga and magic. He is fabled to have worked many miracles—such as filling empty jars with divine water—at Sam ye. He undertook to expel all evil demons from Tibet, but was opposed by the Bon priests.

The other chief monastery of the Red sect is that of *Sakya* (Saskya), situated about fifty-five miles from Tashi Lunpo, on the road leading in a south-westerly direction towards Nepāl. It has four great sanctuaries and a celebrated library, and is surrounded by a large town, with temples and houses mostly painted red (p. 273).

---

[1] For his services as an explorer and surveyor Nain Singh enjoys a Government pension, and has been awarded the gold medal of the Geographical Society. Sarat Chandra Dās has been made a C.I.E.

It should be noted that in all the large monasteries of Northern Buddhist countries, varied assortments of vestments, robes, costumes, and masks are kept for use in the religious dances, masquerades, and dramatic performances which are a characteristic of Northern Buddhism. Indeed, some of the richer monasteries possess extensive wardrobes of great value, and the monks in their masquerading dances change their costumes very frequently and with great rapidity (see pp. 347–350).

Note, too, that the libraries of such monasteries generally contain large and valuable collections of books. The 108 volumes of the northern canon called Kanjur, with the commentaries called Tanjur (see p. 272), constitute a library in themselves. In addition to these, there are vast numbers of other treatises written to elucidate the mysteries of Northern Buddhism, most of which are still a terra incognita to European scholars. It is well known that in mediæval times some Buddhist monasteries became seats of learning, which might have vied with the most learned Universitics established at that period in Europe.

Temples.

Although temples have been already adverted to as forming an important feature in all monasteries, and often an actual part of the edifice constituting the monastery; it will be worth while to devote a short space of time to their separate consideration.

In the earliest days of Buddhism neither temples nor halls nor rooms for meeting together (saṅgha-gṛiha) were much needed. The monk recited the Law in the open air or in the houses of the laity. It was only when collections of monks crystallized into regularly organized communities, and a kind of congregational recitation of the Law became a part of every day's duty, that the monks required places of assembly like churches for the performance of religious services.

Such places of meeting were often, like the cells for the monks, excavated out of rocks. And, since relic-shrines called Ćaityas (as well as Stūpas, see p. 504) were erected at the further extremity of the excavated hall, the hall itself was generally called a Ćaitya.

The two principal rock-excavated Ćaitya-halls visited by me were at Elorā (also spelt Ellora and Elurā) and at Kārle (Kārlī). I was also much interested in a smaller one at the Nāsik caves. In their interior structure they are all strikingly like ancient Christian churches.

The *Elorā* Ćaitya forms one of the series of caves already mentioned (p. 169). It is probably as old as the sixth century of our era, and is of an elongated horse-shoe shape, with a massive ribbed roof arched like that of a cathedral, supported on twenty-eight octagonal columns, over which runs a curious frieze, having on it a carved representation of a buffalo-hunt and boar-chase. There is a nave with side-aisles about 86 feet long by 43 broad. Moreover, over the entrance, supported by two square columns, is a gallery which may have served for a choir or for a band of musicians. A lofty solid Dāgaba, in shape like a massive dome resting on a cylindrical base, stands at the further end of the nave, the aisles being continued round it, so that worshippers may circumambulate the apse. The front of this immense relic-receptacle is hollowed out to receive a colossal sedent figure of the Buddha, about 17 feet high[1], with the Bodhi-tree carved in an arch above his head. Two images of attendants are in an erect attitude, one on each side, but are not so prominent as to draw off the eye from the immense central figure.

The Brāhmans have now appropriated this cave, and dedicated it to Viśva-karma, the supposed patron deity of builders and carpenters. I was told that carpenters come from all parts of the country to worship the image in its Brāhmanical character. As a token of honour, they smear it with red paint.

I noticed a remarkable sculpture carved out of the rock near this cave-temple. It represented worshippers praying to Padma-pāṇi to be delivered from fire, from sword, from captivity, from wild beasts, from snakes, and from the skeleton Death who is seen approaching.

The Ćaitya cave at *Kārle*, near Poona, which I visited in 1876, is in all its dimensions and arrangements similar to the Viśva-karma cave at Elorā, but is still larger, finer, and more imposing. It has a nave and side aisles, terminating in an apse, round which the aisle is carried. The whole is about 124 feet long by 45½ feet broad and 46 feet in height. There are fifteen pillars on each side, separating the nave from the aisles, and under the dome of the apse is the Dāgaba (or Ćaitya)—a two-storied cylindrical drum, surmounted by a Tee ornament (p. 456), on which is a wooden umbrella. There is a cavity in the Dāgaba for relics, though none are now to be found there.

---

[1] My authority for all these details is Dr. Burgess' Report.

This wonderful excavation at Kārle is one of the most magnificent monuments of ancient Buddhism, and one of the most interesting examples of early Buddhistic art to be seen anywhere in India. And, more than this, it is probably one of the most striking places of congregational worship to be seen anywhere in the world.

Of course these rock-excavated churches soon developed into temples (Vihāras) built of stone or brick, some of which were of a monumental character, like that at Buddha-Gayā, already described (see p. 390), while others were unpretending structures near villages, where the laity could repeat their prayers or make offerings. Others, again, formed the most important edifice among the group of buildings constituting a monastery.

The village temples might more suitably be called chapels. All have some features in common. At the further end of a dimly-lighted room is an altar of stone or wood. On this are placed the idols, and around them are arranged vases and cups, in which the offerings of the laity are deposited. The larger edifices have vestibules, and at the entrance are generally rude images of the four great kings (p. 206), who are supposed to be the guardians of Buddhism (p. 206), while inside there are sculptures, frescoes, and pictures illustrative of the various births and transmigrations of the Buddhas and Bodhi-sattvas. In the precincts is always to be found a Bodhi-tree (Bo-tree, p. 519), if the climate and soil will admit of its being reared. The greater number of sacred structures, however, even those of a more important kind and more entitled to be called temples, are mere square or oblong rectangular buildings, without architectural design or ornamentation.

In Ceylon I visited a temple of this kind on the shore of the Kandy lake. It consisted of a large bare room or small hall, at the further end of which was a curtain concealing a highly venerated image of the Buddha. The attendant drew aside the curtain and showed us the image, which had representations of rays of light issuing from all parts of his body, as well as five rays emerging from the crown of his head. In the enclosure or 'compound' of the temple, was a bell-shaped Dāgaba or relic-shrine of solid brick-work, covered with Chunam, and having a receptacle for lights in front of it. Close at hand was the usual sacred Pīpal-tree.

At *Kelani*, about eight miles from Colombo, is a larger and much more important temple which I also visited. Those who make pilgrimages to this temple gain great stores of merit. It contains a colossal recumbent image of the Buddha, thirty-six feet long, lying on his right side, and representing the founder of Buddhism when about to pass into Pari-nirvāṇa (see p. 50). The image is protected by a screen, in the centre of which is a figure of the King of Serpents, while at the sides are gigantic images of the temple-guardians. Around the interior are fresco paintings of various incidents in the previous lives of the Buddha. There are also images of the Hindū gods Vishṇu, Śiva, and Gaṇeśa (see p. 206). In the garden of the temple are residences for the monks, a cloister-like enclosure, a room with a good printing press, and an immense Pīpal-tree.

A still more important temple is that called the

Dalada Māligāwa or temple of the sacred eye-tooth, at Kandy in Ceylon. This is a very picturesque structure, situated on the margin of the lake close to the town. It has no surrounding walls, and is easily accessible to all comers. Steps lead up to a kind of open corridor, in which is the main entrance, and the walls of which are decorated with coloured frescoes of the eight principal hells—the supposed abode of evil-doers undergoing purgatorial torments during one of their states of existence (see p. 120)[1].

Some are represented in the act of being cut in pieces by demons, or fixed on red-hot iron spikes, or torn asunder with glowing tongs, or sawn in two with saws, or crushed between rocks, or consumed by flames entering the apertures of their bodies. The European visitor inquires with amazement how it is that a system so mild, merciful, and tolerant, should have invented the horrible tortures here exhibited. The explanation is not difficult, and his astonishment ceases when he is reminded that Buddhism, recognizing no moral Governor of the Universe, is compelled to resort to such artifices for the coercion and intimidation of evil-doers.

In the interior of the building is the shrine, in which is preserved behind iron bars, the golden Dāgaba or receptacle of one of the Buddha's eye-teeth (see p. 500). On each side are images, and when I visited the shrine, the whole chamber was redolent with the fragrance of masses of flowers—chiefly jasmine—recently deposited before them as offerings.

---

[1] Copies of these were made for me by a Sinhalese artist.

Behind the building I found an open quadrangle with cells for the monks, and a residence for the Head of the monastery. Not far from the entrance was a spacious library, where I was greeted by a number of youthful monks, dressed in simple toga-like vestments, but with their right shoulders left bare. Some were engaged in writing. I therefore asked for a specimen of their penmanship. Upon which they wrote down for me on palm leaves, in the Sinhalese character, forty-eight epithets of the Buddha, such as the following:—God of the gods, Indra of Indras, Brahmā of Brahmās, the Almighty, Omniscient, Existing in his own Law, Lord of the Law, Saviour of all, Conqueror, King of doctrine, Ocean of grace, Treasury, Jewel, Sun, Moon, Stars, Lotus, Ambrosia of the World, the Five-eyed one, the Bull, Elephant, Lion among men, stronger than the strongest, mightier than the mightiest, more merciful than the most merciful, more meritorious than the most meritorious, more beautiful than the most beautiful, etc.

The temples in Burma are commonly called 'pagodas,' a word corrupted from the Pāli Dāgaba (Sanskṛit Dhātu-garbha), 'receptacle of the (sacred) elements' or relics of the body. They are also called Dagohn. According to Mr. Scott ('Burman,' i. 184), the number of temples in Burma far exceeds those in Ceylon or Tibet or China. No village so poor as to be without its 'neatly kept shrine, with the remains of others mouldering away around it; no hill so steep as to be without its glittering gold or snow-white spire rising up to guard the place; no work of merit so richly paid as the building of a pagoda.' Some are of simple construction, others elaborate; but of all the temples the great Rangoon pagoda is the grandest and most crowded with worshippers and pilgrims.

The peculiar sacredness and popularity of this wonderful structure (said to have been founded 588 B.C.), arises from its containing relics of Gautama and his three predecessors, that is, eight hairs from Gautama's head, the staff of Kāśyapa, the robe of Kanaka-muni, and the drinking-cup of Kraku-ććhanda (see p. 135 of these Lectures). The stately pile stands upon a mound—partly natural, partly artificial—cut into two rectangular terraces one above the other, the upper being 166 feet above the ground, and each side facing one of the cardinal points of the compass. The ascent is by very dilapidated steps, some of stone, some of 'sun-dried bricks, worn almost into a slope by the bare feet of myriads of worshippers.' None but Europeans may ascend with covered feet. The stairs lead to a 'broad, open flagged space, which runs all round the pagoda, and is left free for worshippers.' From the centre of this springs, from an octagonal plinth, the 'profusely gilt *solid brick* pagoda,' which has a circumference of 1355 feet, and rises to a height of about 328, 'or nearly as high as St. Paul's cathedral.' On the summit is 'the Tee,' a gilt umbrella-shaped ornament with many tiers of rings, on each of which 'hang multitudes of gold and silver jewelled bells.' It was 'placed there at a cost of not much less than £50,000[1].' At the foot of the pagoda are four chapels, having colossal figures of Buddha

[1] In this description I have chiefly followed Mr. Scott.

at the sides, and their gilded interiors darkened by the vapour of thousands of burning tapers. 'Hundreds of Gautamas,' large and small, white and black, gilded and plain, sitting, standing, and reclining, surround the larger images. It is said that the great pagoda has been thrice covered with gold-leaf.

There is a still higher pagoda (332 feet high) at Pegu, and the most ancient of all is at Arakan.

Passing to Northern Buddhist countries, we find that the temples are generally simple, and not to be compared with the grand pagodas of Burma.

For example, at Tassiding in Sikkim, Sir Richard Temple (Journal, ii. 204) found that the two principal temples were chapel-like structures with 'overshadowing umbrella-shaped roofs, thatched with split bamboos.' The walls were of rough stone, the upper half being painted red. The interiors, which were dimly lighted, had two stories, the walls being covered with coloured frescoes illustrating the punishments in the various hells, 'some of which would be suitable for illustrations of Dante's Inferno.' The ends opposite to the entrance were filled with images. In other parts of the chapels were praying-machines, and on shelves the remnants of a library of sacred Buddhist manuscripts. Sir Richard attended a religious service in one of these chapels, which consisted of a series of chants and invocations to a female demon called Tanma, represented by a hideous lay figure dressed in robes. According to tradition, it was the malevolent action of the twelve Tanmas in bringing pestilences on the Tibetans, that led them to send for Padma-sambhava, who introduced the debased Buddhism subsequently prevalent in Tibet (Note by Capt. R. C. Temple).

According to Dr. Schlagintweit (p. 189) and Koeppen the generality of temples in Mongolia and Tibet consist of one large square or rectangular room, with an entrance-hall or vestibule, which in Mongolia looks to the south and in Tibet to the east. 'The inside surface is whitewashed or covered with a kind of plaster,' and decorated with paintings representing episodes taken from the life of the Buddhas, or with pictures of gods and goddesses of terrible aspect. Generally images of the four great kings are placed here as guardians of the sanctuary (p. 206 of this volume). Sometimes there are side chambers, which may be compared to transepts, and give the building the form of a cross. These chambers often have shelves for the sacred books, wrapped in silk. In the corners are tables for images of the deities, religious dresses, musical instruments, etc. Other articles required for the daily service are hung up on wooden pegs along the walls. Benches for the Lāmas are placed in the hall of the temple.

The altar at the further extremity rises in steps made of wood, beautifully carved and richly ornamented. Upon these are arranged images of the Buddhas and Bodhi-sattvas, and especially the chief idol representing Gautama Buddha in some of his forms and attitudes. Here also are vessels for offerings, bells, Dorjes (p. 323), and other utensils used in religious worship. Among the latter may be seen the mirror (Melong, see p. 463) used in the ceremony described at p. 335. There is also a vase with peacock's feathers, and a sacred book is never wanting.

The vessels for offerings are of brass, and like tea-cups. They are usually filled with barley, butter, and perfumes, and in summer with flowers. Near at hand is a Chorten (p. 380) containing relics, and having a niche with the image of a Buddha or Bodhi-sattva, to whom the temple may perhaps be dedicated.

Finally, in the entrance-vestibule, at both sides of the door, as well as in the interior, stand rows of large and small prayer-cylinders, which are perpetually kept revolving by the attendant Lāmas.

Of course the temples at the great centres of Tibetan Buddhism in and near Lhāssa, Tashi Lunpo, and other important places, are far more imposing. Indeed, for magnificence, few religious edifices in any part of the world can compare with them.

The great temple (called *Cho Khang*) in the monastery of *Lā brang* at Lhāssa is a kind of centre of the Lāmistic Church. It is the first and oldest temple, and, as before stated (p. 440), the St. Peter's of Lāmism[1].

The facade of this vast structure looks to the east, and in front of it is a square place, with a kind of obelisk or monolith, commemorating the victory of the Tibetans over the Chinese in the ninth century, as well as more recent treaties of peace and friendship between the two countries. The main building is three stories high. Before the entrance stands a lofty flag-pole, forty

---

[1] This description is based on Koeppen, ii. 234, and on the narrative of Sarat Chandra Dās' journey in 1881, 1882.

feet high[1], and not far off is a poplar, said to have sprung 'from the consecrated hair of Buddha.' The portico of the temple consists of a colonnade of six thick wooden columns. The walls of the portico are covered with rude paintings, representing scenes in the biography of Gautama Buddha. In the middle are folding doors adorned with bronze carvings in relief. Through these is the entrance into the front hall, over which is the first story. In the wall opposite to the entrance is a second door, on each side of which stand two colossal statues of the four great kings (see pp. 23, 51, 53, 54 of this volume).

This second door leads into the interior of the building. On entering, the visitor finds himself in a vast temple, shaped like a basilica, divided by rows of columns into three naves and two transepts. The broad central nave is lighted from above by transparent oil-cloth instead of glass. This is the only light which finds its way into the temple, as there are no side windows. On the outside of the two secondary naves is a row of small chapels, fourteen on one side and fourteen on the other. The two transepts form the back-ground of the great hall, and are separated from the naves by a silver lattice-work. Here, at the ordinary services, are the seats of the inferior monks. From the west transept a staircase leads to another pillared transept, which forms the vestibule of the

[1] Sarat Chandra Dās mentions a 'flag-pole forty feet high, on which are some inscriptions, two tufts of yak hair, and several yak and sheep-horns.' Possibly this may be the obelisk mentioned by Koeppen.

sanctuary. In the middle of the sanctuary, which is square in form, is the altar for offerings. Beyond the altar, at the west side of the sanctuary, and therefore in the furthest recess of the whole building, is a quadrangular niche. In front of this niche on the left is the throne of the Dalai Lāma, very lofty, richly adorned and furnished with five cushions, as is customary in the case of Grand Lāmas. On one side of the Dalai Lāma's throne is a similar throne for the Panchen Lāma, and then, in regular order, the thrones of the Khutuktus and other Avatāra Lāmas. The Khanpos and the whole non-Avatāra monkhood have seats in the transept.

Opposite to the throne of the Dalai Lāma, on the right of the niche, is the chair of the Regent, which is less elevated than the thrones of the Avatāra Lāmas. Behind are the seats of the four ministers, which again are less elevated than those of the non-Avatāra Lāmas. At the west end of the niche is the high altar, which rises in numerous steps. On the upper steps are small images of deified saints, in massive gold or silver. On the lower ones, as on all Buddhist altars, are lamps, incense-holders, bowls for offerings, etc. On the highest elevation, behind silver and golden lattice-work, is the celebrated image of Gautama Buddha richly gilded. This image is said to have been constructed in Magadha during the lifetime of the Buddha. Others hold it to be self-produced; and another tradition ascribes its origin to the god Viśva-karma, who, instructed by Indra, constructed it with equal parts of five metals and five precious stones. Besides this highest object of worship, the temple contains countless images and pictures of Buddhas and Bodhi-sattvas (such as Dīpaṃkara, Amitābha, Maitreya, the eleven-faced Avalokiteśvara, Mañju-śrī, etc.), besides gods and goddesses[1], and historical personages, such as Tsong Khapa, who have benefited the Lāmistic church (among them being a statue of Hiouen Thsang), as well as relics, and gold and silver vessels, which are exhibited every year at the beginning of the third month.

Mr. Sarat Chandra Dās, who, in his 'Narrative,' records his visit to the great Lhāssa temple, informs us that when he was there, five thousand oil-burners were lighted in the court of the temple, and those before the principal image were all of gold. He found some of the subordinate chapels infested by mice, which are never touched, because supposed to be metamorphosed monks. He observed some Buddhists from Nepāl chanting Sanskṛit hymns, and others engaged in circumambulation, while the muttering of Om Maṇi padme Hūm (p. 372) was incessant.

Mr. Sarat Chandra Dās also describes a visit he paid to the famous shrine of *Ramoćhe*, before adverted to (see p. 441). I give his description in an abbreviated form :—

Our equipment was as usual a bundle of incense-sticks, clarified butter, and a few scarves. Our road turned westward by the side of a long Mandong (see p. 380). I left it to my right-hand side, seeing that to have kept it on my left would have been heretical. A few hundred

[1] One of these is the terrific goddess Paldan (p. 491), worshipped by all Tibetans and Mongols, and identified with the goddess Kālī.

paces brought us to the gate of the famous temple of Ramoche, erected by the wife of King Srong Tsan Gampo, the first Chinese princess who introduced Buddhism into Tibet. It is a lofty edifice, flat-roofed, and three stories high, surrounded by a stone wall, with a high and wide porch. About thirty monks were solemnly seated to perform a religious service, on two sides of a row of pillars which supported the roof. The image brought by the Nepālese princess, lay midway between the pillars. It was grand-looking; and, though its face was gilded, its antiquity was manifest. In the northern lobby of the temple was a vast collection of ancient relics, such as shields, spears, drums, arrows, sabres, long knives, trumpets, etc. In a room to the left of the entrance, enclosed by iron lattice-work, were a few images considered especially sacred. We were also shown a brass mirror, called Melong, said to be possessed of wonderful properties.

The history of the shrine, according to the same traveller, is this:—The princess being thoroughly versed in astrology, found that there was a spot close to the new-built city of Lhāssa which was connected with the lower regions of torment. On that plot of ground she erected the shrine of Ramoche, on the chief altar of which she placed the famous statue of Buddha, brought from China. In this way she hoped to intercept the passage (*gati*) of wicked people to a life in one of the hells (see p. 121). Whoever, at the time of death, was brought to this sanctuary, could only be born again in the worlds of either men or gods.

Finally we come to the temple at the second great Metropolis of Buddhism:—

Mr. Bogle (Markham's Tibet, p. 100) describes the temple in the monastery at Tashi Lunpo as simply a long room or gallery containing thirteen gigantic figures made of copper gilt, all in a sedent attitude, with their legs folded under them. He found them all draped, with jewelled crowns and necklaces of coral, pearls, and other stones. The thrones on which they sat were also of copper gilt, and adorned with turquoises and cornelians. Behind them were a variety of conch-shells, set in silver, ostrich-eggs, cocoa-nuts, and other articles. At each end of the gallery was a large collection of books deposited in pigeon-holes. Mr. Bogle was present when the Tashi Lāma himself entered the temple, and, as he passed along, sprinkled rice upon the images. This was a kind of consecration-ceremony.

As an instance of the tolerant character of Buddhism and its readiness to accommodate itself to the indigenous creeds of the countries into which it was introduced, we may note, in conclusion, that in Japan may be seen Buddhist and Shinto temples side by side or even occasionally combined in one building. Buddhism in fact adopted Shintoism in Japan just as it adopted Shamanism in Tibet. It took the deities and demi-gods of Shintoism and turned them into Bodhi-sattvas[1].

The subject of Monasteries and Temples naturally leads us to that of images and image-worship; but this and the whole subject of 'Sacred Objects' must be reserved for the next two Lectures.

[1] My authority for this is Bishop Edward Bickersteth, the present Bishop in Japan.

LECTURE XVI.

Images and Idols.

On several occasions during my travels through all parts of India, I asked intelligent Paṇḍits how they could reconcile the gross idolatry and fetish-worship which meet the eye at almost every step throughout the length and breadth of their land, with the doctrine repeatedly declared to be the only true creed of Brāhmanism—the doctrine that nothing really exists but the one eternal, omnipresent Spirit of the Universe (named Brahman or Brahmă)[1].

The answer I generally received to this inquiry was, that spiritual worship was at first the only form of religion dominant in India, till the Buddhists set the example of worshipping material objects and images (pratimā-pūjā).

Of course it is impossible to say what amount of truth there may be in this accusation. It seems probable that material impersonations of the forces of nature existed before the Buddha's time. Yet there is no evidence of the prevalence of actual idolatry at the time when the Ṛig-veda was composed. Nor is there any very clear allusion to it in Manu. Nor have any images of Hindū gods been found which are

---

[1] See my 'Brāhmanism and Hindūism' (published by Mr. Murray of Albemarle Street), pp. 2–20.

so ancient as some Buddhist images. At the same time nothing is said about image-worship in the Buddhist Piṭakas. The statement that the Buddha himself sanctioned idolatry is wholly legendary (see p. 177). Nor is there any proof that carved images of his person were common in India till several centuries after his death.

The Bharhut sculptures of about the second century B.C.—though representing many scenes connected with the Buddha (see pp. 408, 523)—exhibit no representations of the Buddha himself. Nor are there any on the Sānchī gateway of still later date.

The only objects of reverence in the Bharhut sculptures, according to Sir A. Cunningham, are Bodhi-trees, Wheels, the Tri-ratna symbol, Stūpas, and foot-prints (see pp. 521–522 of these Lectures). The bas-reliefs on the railing at the Buddha-Gayā Temple, which is of a little earlier date, agree in making the Tree, Wheel, Tri-ratna, and Stūpa the great objects of reverence. On the other hand, in the edicts of king Aśoka veneration for the Bodhi-tree alone is enjoined. Among the historical scenes represented in the Bharhut sculptures, are the processions of the kings Ajāta-śatru and Prasena-jit on their visits to the Buddha; 'the former on his elephant, the latter in his chariot, exactly as they are described in the Buddhist chronicles.' There are also bas-reliefs which seem to represent Rāma, during his exile, besides images of other gods, Yakshas and Nāgas, but no figure of Buddha himself is to be seen anywhere.

Yet it is undeniable that in the early centuries of our era, images of Gautama Buddha and other Buddhas and

REMAINS OF A COLOSSAL STATUE OF BUDDHA, PROBABLY ONCE IN THE ARGUMENTATIVE OR TEACHING ATTITUDE (see p. 481).

Found in the ruins close to the south side of the Buddha-Gayā temple, the date (S. 64 = A.D. 142) being inscribed on the pedestal.

[*To face page 467.*

Bodhi-sattvas had become common among the Buddhists in every part of India.

One of the oldest statues of the Buddha that has yet been brought to light is the colossal image (now in the Calcutta Museum) dug up in the ruins outside the ancient temple at Buddha-Gayā (p. 390), the date inscribed on which corresponds to about A.D. 142. The engraving (opposite) is from a photograph of this statue, belonging to Sir A. Cunningham [1]. The thick lips are certainly remarkable. The attitude was probably the 'argumentative' or 'teaching' (described at p. 481). Another colossal statue of about the same date was found by Sir A. Cunningham at Śrāvastī (see p. 408).

It was indeed by a strange irony of fate that the man who denied any god or any being higher than himself, and told his followers to look to themselves alone for salvation, should have been not only deified and worshipped, but represented by more images than any other being ever idolized in any part of the world. In fact images, statues, statuettes, carvings in bas-relief, paintings, and representations of him in all attitudes are absolutely innumerable. In caves, monasteries, and temples, on Dāgabas, votive Stūpas, monuments and rocks, they are multiplied infinitely and in endless variety, and not only are isolated images manufactured out of all kinds of materials, but rows on rows are sculptured in relief, and the greater the number the

---

[1] Another ancient statue but not so old, though of a highly interesting type, was procured by me (for the Indian Institute at Oxford) from Buddha-Gayā on the occasion of my last visit in 1884, through the kind assistance of Mr. Beglar. It is in the erect attitude.

greater religious merit accrues to the sculptor, and—if they are dedicated at sacred places—to the dedicator also.

And not only images of the Buddha, but representations of every object that could possibly be connected with him, became multiplied to an indefinite extent.

The gradual growth of what may be called objective Buddhism, and the steps which led to every kind of extravagance in the idolatrous use of images, may be described in the following manner :—

It was only natural that the disciples of an ideally perfect man, who had taught them that in passing away at death he would become absolutely extinct, should have devised some method of perpetuating his memory and stimulating a desire to conform to his example. Their first method was to preserve the relics of his burnt body, and to honour every object associated with his earthly career. Then, in process of time, they began to worship not only his relics but the receptacles under which they were buried, and around these they placed sculptures commemorative of his life and teaching. Thence they passed on to the carving or moulding of small statuettes of his person in wood, stone, metal, terra-cotta, or clay, and on these they often inscribed the well-known Buddhistic formulæ mentioned before (see p. 104). Eventually, too, painting was pressed into the service, and frescoes on walls became common. Indeed in some temples paintings take the place of images, as objects of adoration.

It seems likely that the use of images and paintings was at first confined to the brotherhood, and it is alleged that they were only honoured and not worshipped. But the more the circle of uncultured and unthinking Buddhists became enlarged, the more did visible representations of the founder of Buddhism become needed, and the more they became multiplied.

Nor was this all. The reaction from the original simplicity of Buddhism led to a complete repudiation of its anti-theistic doctrines. It adopted polytheistic superstitions even more rapidly and thoroughly than Brāhmanism did. People were not satisfied with representations of the founder of Buddhism. They craved for other visible and tangible objects of adoration—for the images of other Buddhas and Bodhisattvas—of gods many and lords many—insomuch that a Buddhist Pantheon was gradually created which became peopled with a more motley crowd of occupants than that of Brāhmanism and Hindūism.

Furthermore, it was only natural that the manufacture of the whole array of divinities and semi-divinities, of saints and sages, should have been committed to the monks. They alone possessed this privilege. They alone, too, had the power of consecrating each image by the repetition of mystical texts and formularies. And when images and idols were thus consecrated, they were believed to be animated with the spirit, and to possess all the attributes of the beings they represented.

In fact, the development of every phase of idolatrous superstition reached a point of extravagance unparalleled in any other religious system of the world. The monks of Buddhism vied with each other in the 'pious fraud' with which they constructed their idols. They so manipulated them that they appeared to give out light or to flash supernatural glances from their crystal eyes. Or they made them deliver oracular utterances, or they furnished them with movable limbs, so that a head would unexpectedly nod, or a hand be raised to bless the worshipper. Then they clothed them with costly vestments, and adorned them with ornaments and jewels, and treated them in every way as if they were living energizing personalities.

It ought, however, to be noted here, that in some temples images of the Buddhas and Bodhi-sattvas were said to exist which were not manufactured or consecrated by monks. They were believed to have been self-produced, or to have been created supernaturally out of nothing, or to have emerged in a miraculous manner out of vacuity. The child-like faith of uncultured and imaginative races in the virtue supposed to be inherent in such images was perhaps not surprising. The power of working all kinds of miracles was gradually ascribed to them; sicknesses were said to be healed by them, rain to be produced, and the course of nature itself to be subject to their direction and control.

The two Chinese pilgrims Fā-hien and Hiouen Thsang are never tired of describing the wonders supposed to have been wrought by the statues and idols they saw during their travels, especially by the marvellous sandal-wood statue mentioned before (see p. 408).

The following tradition in regard to this image, narrated by Fā-hien (Legge, 56, 57), is especially interesting as showing that the general belief among all classes of Buddhists in his time was, that Gautama Buddha himself was the first to sanction the making of visible representations of himself:—

When Buddha went up to the Trayastriṇśa heaven and preached the law for the benefit of his mother for ninety days, Prasenajit longing to see him, caused an image to be carved in Gośīrsha sandal-wood, and put in the place where he usually sat. When Buddha, on his return, entered the Vihāra, this image immediately left its place, and came forth to meet him. Buddha then said to it: 'Return to your seat. After I have attained Pari-nirvāṇa you shall serve as a pattern to the four classes (paths, see p. 132) of my disciples.' Thereupon the image returned to its seat. This was the very first of all the images of Buddha, and that which men subsequently copied.

In Hiouen Thsang's narrative, which is of much later date (see p. 413), we find the following account of this celebrated sandal-wood image (Beal, ii. 322):—

At the town of Pimā (Pi-mo) there is a figure of Buddha in a standing position made of sandal-wood. The figure is about twenty feet high. It works many miracles, and reflects constantly a bright light. Those who have any disease, according to the part affected, cover the corresponding place on the statue with gold-leaf, and forthwith they are healed. People who address prayers to it, with a sincere heart, mostly obtain their wishes. This is what the natives say: 'This image in old days, when Buddha was alive, was made by Udayana, King of Kauśāmbī (see p. 412 of these Lectures). When Buddha left the world, it mounted of its own accord into the air, and came to the north of this kingdom to the town of Ho-lo-lo-kia (Urgha?).'

With regard to the form and character of the countless images now scattered everywhere, they vary according to country and period (see p. 485). It should be observed, however, that Buddhism, when it began to encourage idolatry, did not make it hideous by giving monstrous shapes to its idols. In this respect early Buddhism contrasted very favourably with Hindūism. Nor did the Buddhists of India, as of other countries, adopt the practice of endowing their idols with extra heads and arms to symbolize power, or of inventing grotesque combinations of the human figure with the shapes of elephants, birds, serpents, and other animals. They seemed rather to have tried in the first instance to neutralize the tendency to extravagant symbolism common among all Eastern peoples, by delineating their great teacher as an ideal man, simply and naturally formed, according to the Buddhist ideal of perfection with symmetrical limbs, and a dignified, calm, passionless, and majestic bearing. What can be a greater contrast than the four-armed elephant-headed village-god of India,—Gaṇeśa, son of Śiva[1]—and the purely human figure of the Buddha as shown in his statues!

Nevertheless it must be admitted that in process of time the representations of Gautama Buddha developed certain peculiar varieties of form as well as differences in attitude. These differences, indeed, constitute a highly interesting topic of inquiry, and perhaps deserve more attention than they have hitherto received in any treatise with which I am acquainted.

Without going minutely into every point, we may begin by noting a few general characteristics common to all the Buddha's images.

In the first place, they all represent Gautama as clothed—not naked. In this respect they present a pleasant contrast to the images of Jaina saints; for, as

---

[1] See 'Brāhmanism and Hindūism,' p. 214.

already pointed out, Gautama discountenanced all extremes of bodily mortification, and disapproved the practice of going about nude, according to the custom of Hindū devotees. In the Dharma-pada it is said, 'Not nakedness, not matted hair, not dirt, not fasting, nor lying on the ground, nor smearing with ashes, nor sitting motionless can purify a mortal who has not overcome desires.'

Gautama's robe was drawn gracefully over his shoulders like a toga, but probably the right shoulder was always left bare on formal occasions. The Piṭakas give no clear information as to this point. In Indian statues the robe is sometimes represented as fitting so closely to the body that the figure seems garmentless[1]; its presence being merely denoted by a line running diagonally over the left shoulder across the breast, and under the right arm. This line frequently looks so like a cord that some have mistaken it for the thread to which, as a Kshatriya, Buddha was entitled[2]. In some ancient images no trace of the line is left, but they are not really nude. Most Indian images have the right shoulder bare (even in the case of nuns). Of course in colder climates both shoulders are covered. Even in Southern countries some have both shoulders covered, or the right partially so.

In contradistinction to the clothed images of the Buddha, all the representations of his great opponent

---

[1] A good example of this tight-fitting robe is afforded by the ancient statue of the Buddha, mentioned at p. 467, note.

[2] When Gautama renounced his family and caste, he doubtless discarded the cord, just as a true Sannyāsī is required to do (p. 78).

and rival Deva-datta (see pp. 52, 405) make the latter unclothed, like a Jaina ascetic, or only partially clothed up to the waist. Deva-datta is also represented as shorter in stature than the Buddha.

Other characteristics generally to be observed in the earlier images of Gautama Buddha are:—the impassive tranquil features, typical of complete conquest over the passions, and of perfect repose; the absence of all decoration and ornament; the long pendulous ears, which occasionally reach to the shoulders [1]; the circle or small globe or lotus [2], or auspicious mark of some kind, on the palm or palms of the supinated hands (as well as often on the soles of the feet), and the short knobby hair, often carved so as to resemble a close-fitting curly wig.

It must not be forgotten that Gautama signalized his renunciation of the world by cutting off his hair with a sword, and the resulting stumps are said to have turned into permament knobs or short curls [3].

In images brought from Burma and Siam a curious horn-like protuberance on the crown of the head—either tapering to a point, or rounded off at the ex-

[1] In the Jaina statues, the lobes of the ears, so far as I have observed, always touch the shoulders.

[2] Some think that this represents the wheel of the Ćakra-vartī emperor, or the wheel of the law, or the cycle of causes, or the continual revolution of births, deaths, and re-births. Dr. Mitra maintains that a lotus, and not a wheel, is always intended, though the lotus is often so badly carved that it may pass for any circular ornament.

[3] Dr. Rajendralāla Mitra considers that curly locks were given to Gautama Buddha because the possession of curls is believed to be an auspicious sign. Some have actually inferred from the curl-like knobs, that Buddha was a negro!

tremity—is noticeable. Often, too, sculptures found in India show the rounded form of this excrescence.

Some think that it represents an ascetic's mass of hair coiled up in a top-knot on the crown of the head, as in images of the god Śiva. Others regard it as the rough outline of what ought to be an Ushṇīsha or peculiar crown-like head-dress, such as may be seen in many later images of the Buddha. Some legends declare that the Buddha was born with this Ushṇīsha, which was indicative of his future supremacy.

Others, again, maintain that this protuberance (sometimes lengthened out so as to be as high as the head itself) was a peculiar growth of the skull, and one of the marks of a supreme Buddha indicative of supernatural intelligence ; just as in other images (especially those brought from Ceylon) five flames—in shape like the fingers of a hand—are represented issuing from the crown of the head (see p. 453), to typify the Buddha's diffusion of light and knowledge throughout the world.

It is said that this outgrowth of the Buddha's skull has been preserved as a sacred relic in a town of Afghānistān near Jalālābād.

In many representations of the Buddha, a Nimbus or aureola of glory encircles the head (see p. 478), and in some images rays of light are represented as emerging from his whole body. An image with a halo of this kind surrounding the entire figure was seen by me in a temple near Kandy in Ceylon (see p. 453).

In Nepāl many images represent Buddha holding his alms-bowl, but these are not common in other places.

With regard to the size of the images, they vary

from diminutive examples, two or three inches long, to colossal statues twelve, eighteen, twenty, thirty, forty, or even seventy feet high. They are generally carved in stone or marble, but sometimes in metal, sometimes in wood, and occasionally moulded in clay.

Much difference of opinion prevails as to the Buddha's actual stature. When I asked the opinion of Buddhist teachers in Ceylon, they all agreed in assigning to the founder of their religion a majestic bodily frame, not only gifting him with the possession of the thirty-two distinguishing marks of a perfect man and supreme Buddha (see p. 20), but with great height and imposing presence. A common idea is that the eighteen-feet statues represent life-size. According to other legends the Buddha's stature reached to twenty cubits. In China, the mythical history of Buddha gives him a height of only sixteen feet [1]. His arms are by some said to have been so long, that he was able to touch his knees with his hands without stooping, and if we are to take the supposed impress of his foot on Adam's Peak and in Siam as the measure of his stature, he must have been the most gigantic giant that ever lived. Even one of the most enlightened natives of Ceylon, the late Mr. James d'Alwis—a convert to Christianity—told me, in explanation of the abnormal size of the eye-tooth at Kandy, that he was convinced that all human beings were taller in Buddha's time, and that Gautama was taller than his fellow-men of those days, and was about eight feet high. It was his

[1] See Dr. Edkins' 'Chinese Buddhism' (p. 256).

SCULPTURE FOUND BY SIR A. CUNNINGHAM AT SĀRNĀTH, NEAR BENARES,

Illustrating the four principal events in Gautama Buddha's life—his birth from his mother's side, his attainment of Buddhahood under the tree, his teaching at Benares, and his passing away in complete Nirvāṇa. (Date of the sculpture, about 400 A.D.)

[*To face page* 477.

opinion that as sin increases in the world, so men's stature decreases. Probably the Buddha was tall, even for the North-west of India, where the average of a man's stature is about five feet eight or nine inches.

As to the attitudes of Gautama's images, they may be classed under the three heads of sedent, erect, and recumbent. I use the word 'sedent' for what ought to be called a squatting position, with the legs folded under the body. Images which represent a figure sitting in European fashion are rare.

Four principal images represent the four principal events in Buddha's life, as shown in the Sārnāth sculpture engraved on the opposite page (compare p. 387).

The first sedent attitude may be called the 'Meditative.' The example below is described at p. xxx. 15.

This represents the Buddha seated, in meditation,

on a raised seat under the sacred tree, with the two hands supinated, one over the other.

The second sedent attitude may be called the 'Witness-attitude.' It is perhaps the most esteemed of all, and is represented in a good sculpture delineated below (from Sir A. Cunningham's photograph, see p.

xxx. 17). This represents Gautama at the moment of achieving Buddhahood after his long course of meditation, seated on a lion-throne (siṉhāsana) with an ornamental back, having two lions carved below (compare p. 394). His legs are folded in the usual Indian fashion, the feet being turned upwards, while the right hand hangs over the right leg and points to the earth, and the left hand is supinated on the left foot. He

has an aureola round his head and a mark—perhaps the caste-mark of a Kshatriya—on his forehead, and an umbrella over the sacred tree. This attitude is well shown in the Sārnāth sculpture (facing p. 477).

The tradition is that at the moment of his enlightenment Gautama was taunted by the evil being Māra with being unable to give any proof or sign of his Buddhahood. Thereupon Gautama pointed, not to heaven as a Brāhman might have done, but to the earth beneath his feet, calling it to witness. Then a six-fold earthquake and other miraculous phenomena followed [1].

At this time, too, the evil being Māra sent his enchanting daughters (p. 34) to seduce the Buddha. This is shown in the engraving facing p. 477.

The incident of calling the earth to witness is thus mentioned by Hiouen Thsang:—

> In the Vihāra, was found a beautiful figure of Buddha in a sitting position, the right foot uppermost, the left hand resting, the right hand hanging down. He was sitting facing the east, and as dignified in appearance as when alive. The signs and marks of a Buddha were perfectly drawn. The loving expression of his face was like life. Now it happened that a Śramaṇa, who was passing the night in the Vihāra, had a dream, in which he saw a Brāhman who said:—
>
> 'I am Maitreya Bodhi-sattva. Fearing that the mind of no artist could conceive the beauty of the sacred features, I myself have come to delineate the figure of Buddha. His right hand hangs down, in token that when he was about to reach Buddhahood the evil Māra came to tempt him, saying, "Who will bear witness for you?" Then Tathāgata dropped his hand and pointed to the ground, saying, "Here is my witness." On this an earth-spirit leapt forth to bear witness.' (Beal's Records, ii. 121, abridged.)

This 'Witness-attitude' is also shown in the annexed

---

[1] See Lalita-vistara (Calc. ed.), pp. 402, 403, 449, ll. 6–14.

engraving from a photograph of one of the only statues that remained in the exterior niches of the ancient Buddha-Gayā temple before its restoration.

The two seal-like circles on each side contain the usual 'Ye dharmā' formula (see p. 104 and p. xxx. 18).

The third sedent pose or position may be called the 'Serpent-canopied.' This is commemorative of the legend that Gautama, when seated in meditation after his attainment of Buddhahood, was sheltered from a violent storm by the expanded hood of the Nāga, or serpent-demon Mućalinda (see p. 39), while the coils of the snake were wound round his body, or gathered under him to form a seat. Similarly the ascetic form of Śiva is often represented under a serpent-canopy.

Only one example of this has been found at Buddha-Gayā. Such images, however, are common in the south, and their prevalence there is not difficult to account for. Indeed, the connexion of Buddhism with the serpent-worship of southern countries and with the Nāgas of Hindū mythology (see p. 220 of these Lectures), was one inevitable result of its readiness to graft popular superstitions on its own doctrines [1].

I procured a good specimen of the 'Serpent-canopied' Buddha during my stay in Ceylon. It is made of heavy brass, and curiously enough represents Buddha with an aquiline nose. It has the five rays of light before alluded to (see pp. 453, 475) issuing from the crown of his head. See the frontispiece opposite title-page.

In some images an umbrella alone, and in some, as at p. 478, both an umbrella and tree form the canopy.

The fourth sedent posture may be called the 'Argumentative' (Tarka) attitude (as shown in the engraving opposite p. 477). It represents Gautama with the thumb and finger of the right hand touching the fingers of the left, and apparently going through the heads of his doctrine [2], and enforcing it, as he usually did, by reiterations. This is sometimes called the 'Teaching' attitude.

Often the 'Ye dharmā' formula (see p. 104) is carved either under or at the side of images in this attitude.

---

[1] See my remarks on the worship of serpents in 'Brāhmanism and Hindūism,' p. 319; and Fergusson's great work, 'Tree and Serpent Worship.'

[2] There is a striking parallel in a well-known picture by Bernardino Luini (of the Milan school) of 'Christ disputing with the Doctors' to be seen in our National Gallery.

The fifth may be called the 'Preaching' attitude. It is often erect. The Buddha has one finger raised in a didactic manner. Monks in the present day often read the Law and preach in the same manner.

The sixth attitude also—as a rule—comes under the erect class, and is often scarcely to be distinguished from the last. It may be called the 'Benedictive' attitude (Āśirvāda). See the engraving opposite p. 477.

It represents the Buddha in the act of pronouncing a benediction, the right hand being raised. This attitude is sometimes sedent. Even to this day Buddhist monks bless laymen in a similar attitude. Occasionally the figure with the hand upraised has a crown, and an ornamental head-dress; but it may be taken for granted that all images of the Buddha which represent him with a crown of any kind *after his attainment of Buddhahood*, are comparatively modern and incorrect.

On the other hand, it is clear that even ancient sculptures, when they represent him as a prince, may correctly give him decorations and a head-dress.

The seventh attitude may be called the 'Mendicant.' This also is a standing figure, holding a round alms-bowl in one hand, and sometimes screening it with the other (compare p. 40). Examples of this attitude are rare. There are no real mendicants in Buddhism. No monk ever begs, he only receives alms.

The eighth and last attitude is recumbent, and this is perhaps as important as the second, though not so common (see the uppermost figure opposite to p. 477). It represents the moribund Gautama lying down on his right side, with his head turned towards the north, and his right cheek resting on his right hand, about to pass away in the final consummation of Pari-nirvāṇa (see pp. 50, 140). In many representations of this attitude, the usual five rays of light often mentioned before are made to issue from the crown of the head. A colossal image of this kind was seen by me in a temple near Colombo, and there is a good example of it in the Indian Institute at Oxford[1]. In some carvings of the dying Buddha a few attendants are represented, who hold umbrella-like canopies over the recumbent figure, or bow down reverentially before it. It has been asserted that this scene—as commemorative of the grand consummation of the Buddha's career through countless existences—is held in as much reverence by Buddhists as the crucifixion is by Christians.

The representation of the Buddha in the act of being born is found in sculptures and bas-reliefs, but is never found as a separate image. It represents him springing out of the side of his mother (note, p. 180). This birth-scene is occasionally carved on temples. It is shown in the lower part of the engraving (opposite page 477). The god Brahmā is seen receiving the new-born child, while Indra stands on his right and the mother's sister (i.e. nurse, p. 24) is on her left.

Some representations of the Buddha, or of certain forms of the Buddha—such as Amitābha—show a sedent figure emerging from a lotus-blossom, or seated on a pedestal formed of lotus-leaves, this flower symbolizing perfection.

---

[1] Procured for me by Mr. Burrows, of the Ceylon Civil Service.

It must not be forgotten that in every country the images of the Buddha are generally moulded according to the type of countenance prevalent in each country. Hence the contour and expression of face differ in Ceylon, Burma, Siam, Tibet, Mongolia, China, and Japan, although as a rule the features are calm, mild, meditative, and passionless.

In Burma the people are merry; hence the images sometimes have a twinkle in the eye and smiling lips.

In China, again, examples sometimes occur of images which do not exhibit Buddha as the ideal of a man who has conquered his passions, but rather with the figure and features of a self-indulgent libertine[1]; while others again portray him with a grim aspect.

We now pass on to the representations of other Buddhas, Bodhi-sattvas, saints, gods and goddesses.

Often two other images are associated with that of Gautama Buddha himself.

And, first of all, his image was joined with the other two persons of the earliest Triad (see p. 175), viz. Dharma (the Law) and Saṅgha (the Monkhood). A sculpture, in a broken and imperfect condition, representing this earliest Triad, and dating from the ninth to the tenth century, was found at Buddha-Gayā. The image of Buddha, under an umbrella-like tree, is in the centre; that of the Saṅgha is on his right, with a full-blown

---

[1] See especially an image in the British Museum. In China Bas-relief images of Buddha are sometimes inserted by Buddhist priests in large mussel-shells while the animal is living, and are covered by it with a coating of mother of pearl. This they call a miracle. An example is in the Indian Institute, presented by Mrs. Newman Smith.

lotus (p. 177, note 2), and having one leg hanging down, while that of Dharma (a female) is on his left with a half-blown lotus. A drawing of this (from Sir A. Cunningham's photograph) is given below:—

In Nepāl the image of Dharma is always that of a sedent female, who is supposed to be an embodiment of supreme wisdom (prajñā pāramitā), and sometimes has four arms (see note, p. 178).

Next come the images of the Buddhas who preceded Gautama, especially Kāśyapa Buddha, Kanaka-muni, and Kraku-ććhanda. It is often mentioned that the images of one or other of these three, as of the Bodhi-sattvas, are set up side by side with that of Gautama.

Then, of course, there are the images of the five Dhyāni-Buddhas. Perhaps the commonest of these is that of Amitābha (see p. 203), but images of Akshobhya and Ratna-sambhava are by no means rare.

Then as to the Bodhi-sattvas, of whom Maitreya is the first and the only one worshipped by Buddhists of all countries (see p. 182), Fā-hien records that he saw in Northern India a wooden image of Maitreya Bodhi-sattva eighty cubits high, which on fast days emitted a brilliant light. Offerings were constantly presented to it by the kings of surrounding countries (Legge, 23).

Hiouen Thsang (Beal, i. 134) also describes this image of Maitreya as very dazzling, and says it was the work of the Arhat Madhyāntika, a disciple of Ānanda. He saw another image of Maitreya made of silver at Buddha-Gayā, and another made of sandal-wood in Western India. The latter also gave out a bright light. Probably these images were covered with some kind of gilding.

In the present day the images of Maitreya often represent him with both hands raised, the fingers forming the lotus-shaped Mudrā, the body yellow or gilded, and the hair short and curly.

Passing next to the images of the triad of mythical Bodhi-sattvas, Mañju-śrī, Avalokiteśvara, and Vajrapāṇi (p. 195), we may gather from what has been already stated (p. 196), that the interaction of Buddhism and Hindūism affected both the mythology and imagery of both systems. Yet it does not appear that the images of the Bodhi-sattva Mañju-śrī were ever unnaturally distorted. They are quite as human and pleasant in appearance as those of Gautama and Maitreya. In general Mañju-śrī is represented in a sedent attitude, with his left hand holding a lotus, and his right holding the sword of wisdom, with a shining blade to dissipate the darkness of ignorance (see p. 201). His body ought to be yellow.

It was not till the introduction of the worship of Avalokiteśvara that the followers of Buddha thought of endowing the figures of deified saints with an extra number of heads and arms.

The process of Avalokiteśvara's (Padma-pāṇi's) creation and the formation of his numerous heads by the Dhyāni-Buddha Amitābha, is thus described (Schlagintweit, p. 84, abridged):—

Once upon a time Amitābha, after giving himself up to earnest meditation, caused a red ray of light to issue from his right eye, which brought Padma-pāṇi Bodhi-sattva into existence; while from his left eye burst forth a blue ray of light, which becoming incarnate in the two wives of King Srong Tsan (see p. 271), had power to enlighten the minds of human beings. Amitābha then blessed Padma-pāṇi Bodhi-sattva by laying his hands upon him, so that by virtue of this benediction, he brought forth the prayer 'Om maṇi padme Hūm.' Padma-pāṇi then made a solemn vow to rescue all the beings in hell from their pains, saying to himself:—'If I fail, may my head split into a thousand pieces!' After remaining absorbed in contemplation for some time, he proceeded to the various hells, expecting to find that the inhabitants, through the efficacy of his meditations, had ascended to the higher worlds. And this indeed he found they had done. But no sooner was their release accomplished than all the hells again became as full as ever, the places of the out-going tenants being supplied by an equal number of new-comers. This so astounded the unhappy Bodhi-sattva that his head instantly split into a thousand pieces. Then Amitābha, deeply moved by his son's misfortune, hastened to his assistance, and formed the thousand pieces into ten heads.

Schlagintweit states, and I have myself observed, that Avalokiteśvara's eleven heads are generally represented as forming a pyramid, and are ranged in four rows. Each series of heads has a particular complexion. The three faces resting on the neck are white, the three above yellow, the next three red, the tenth blue, and the eleventh—that is, the head of his father Amitābha at the top of all [1]—is red. In Japanese images the heads are much smaller, and are arranged like a crown, the centre of which is formed by two entire figures, the lower one sitting, the other standing above it. Ten small heads are combined with these two figures.

The number of Avalokiteśvara's hands ought to amount to a thousand, and he is called 'a thousand-eyed,' as having the eye of wisdom on each palm. Of course all these thousand arms and eyes cannot be represented in images. Still there is an idol in the British Museum which represents him with about forty arms, two of which have the hands joined in an attitude of worship.

A remarkable description of an image of Avalokiteśvara seen by Sarat Chandra Dās (so recently as 1882) in the great temple at Lhāssa occurs in his 'Narrative' (which I here abridge):—

Next to the image of Buddha, the most conspicuous figure was that of Chanrassig (i.e. the eleven-faced Avalokiteśvara). The origin of this is ascribed to King Sron Tsan Gampo (p. 271 of this volume). Once the king heard a voice from heaven, saying that if he constructed an image of Avalokiteśvara of the size of his own person, all his desires would be fulfilled.

Thereupon he proceeded to do so, and the materials he used were a branch of the sacred Bodhi-tree, a portion of the Vajrāsana, some soil from an oceanic island, some sand from the river Nairañjana, some pith of Gośīrsha sandal-wood, a portion of the soil of the eight sacred

---

[1] The sculptured figures of Padma-pāṇi observed by me in the caves of Elorā represent him with Amitābha in his head-dress.

places of ancient India, and many other rare articles pounded together and made into paste, with the milk of a red cow and a she-goat. This paste the king touched with his head, and prayed to the all-knowing Buddhas and the host of Bodhi-sattvas, that by the merit of making that image, there might be god-speed to the great work he had undertaken—namely, the diffusion of Buddhism in Tibet.

The gods, Buddhas, saints, etc. filled the aerial space to listen to his prayer.

The king then ordered the Nepālese artist to hasten the completion of the image, and with a view of heightening its sanctity, obtained a sandal-wood image of Avalokiteśvara from Ceylon and inserted it inside, together with the relics of the seven past Buddhas. When the work was finished, the artist said:—

'Sire, I cannot say that I have made this image, it has passed into self-grown existence.' Then a current of lightning flashed forth from its feet. Afterwards, the souls of the king and his queen are said to have been absorbed into it, in consequence of which this image is called 'the five-absorbed self-sprung.'

It is recorded in another tradition that a wonder-working image of Avalokiteśvara was set up in a monastery near Kabul, and another in Magadha near the Ganges. Any worshipper who approached these idols in devotion and faith were favoured with a personal vision of the saint. The statues opened, and the Bodhi-sattva emerged in bright rays of light (compare Koeppen, i. p. 499).

Originally, and still in Tibet, Avalokiteśvara (otherwise called Padma-pāṇi) had only male attributes; but in China this deity (as we have already mentioned at p. 200) is represented as a woman, called Kwan-yin (in Japan Kwan-non), with a thousand arms and a thousand eyes. She has her principal seat in the island of Poo-too, on the coast of China, which is a place of pilgrimage.

There are two images of Kwan-yin in the British Museum, one with sixteen arms and the other with eight.

Images of the third mythical Bodhi-sattva—the fierce Vajra-pāṇi, 'holding a thunderbolt in one hand'—like one form of Śiva—are almost as common as those of the merciful and mild Avalokiteśvara. He has been described in a previous Lecture (p. 201).

In the Pitt-Rivers collection at Oxford there is an image of this Bodhi-sattva engaged in combating the power of evil. It is remarkable that the figures of three monkeys are carved underneath, one stopping his ears with his hands, another stopping his eyes, and another his mouth, to symbolize the effort to prevent the entrance of evil desires through the three most important organs of sense.

With regard to the images of female deities we may observe that Tārā, the wife or Śakti of Amogha-siddha (p. 216), is represented as a green sedent figure; her right hand on her knee, her left holding a lotus.

A standing image of the goddess Paṭṭinī (p. 217 of this volume) may be seen in the British Museum.

In a temple which I visited near Dārjīling I saw the image of the Padma-sambhava or 'lotus-born' form of Buddha occupying the centre of the altar, with the images of Gautama Buddha and of Buddha Āyushmat, or the 'Buddha of Life,' on each side.

Sir R. Temple (Journal, p. 212) relates how in a chamber of a Sikkim monastery there were three figures, the central of which, with a fair complexion, was Amitābha, that on its right Gautama Buddha, and on its left Gorakh-nāth (see p. 193 of this volume).

In the monastery of Galdan (p. 441) Mr. Sarat Chandra Dās saw the golden image of Tsong Khapa (with his golden chain and his tooth and his block-prints), along with the images of Amitābha, Gautama, Maitreya, Bhairava (the awful defender of Buddhism), Yama 'the lord of death,' and his terrific messengers.

In the great Cho Khang at Lhāssa (see p. 459) he saw images of Avalokiteśvara, Mañju-srī, Maitreya, Kuvera, Padma-sambhava, with an immense number of others, and especially one of the terrific goddess Paldan (or Pandan) who is feared all over Tibet, Mongolia, and China, as the greatest guardian deity of the Dalai and Tashi Lāmas and of the Buddhist Dharma. He found her shrine infested with mice, who are believed to be metamorphosed monks.

At Sera (p. 442) he saw images of the Buddha in his character of 'demon-vanquisher,' along with Maitreya (in silver), Avalokiteśvara, the six-armed Bhairava, the goddess Kālī, Dolkar (= Tārā, p. 271), the Tāntrik Vajra-vārāhī, the sixteen Sthaviras (pp. 48, 255), and a great variety of others.

At Radeng (p. 273) he saw a golden image of Mila-raspa (p. 384).

In the monastery of Sam ye (p. 448) he saw images of the Indian Paṇḍits who brought Buddhism into Tibet, with a vast number of other images.

At Tashi Lunpo he saw golden images of Buddha and Maitreya, besides images of 1000 other Buddhas (p. 189), and the four guardians of the quarters (p. 206).

At Yarlung he saw an image of Vairoćana Buddha, besides images of the sixteen Sthaviras, and a gigantic image of the king of the Nāgas, and a terrific representation of the demon Rāvaṇa (of the Rāmāyaṇa).

At Mindolling he saw fresco paintings of the six classes of beings (p. 122) inhabiting the six corresponding worlds. Of course delineations of the Jātakas (p. 111) and pictures of all kinds were common in monasteries and temples everywhere.

The two wonder-working images brought from Nepāl and China have been already mentioned (p. 271).

As an illustration of the monstrous superstition and idolatry prevalent in modern Buddhist countries, I venture, in conclusion, to quote, with abridgment, the following description of an idol seen by Miss Bird in Japan (see her 'Unbeaten Tracks in Japan,' published by Mr. Murray):—

In one shrine is a large idol spotted all over with pellets of paper, and hundreds of these may be seen sticking to the wire-netting which protects him. A worshipper writes his petition on paper, or, better still, has it written for him by the priest, chews it to a pulp and spits it at the divinity. If, having been well aimed, it passes through the wire and sticks, it is a good omen, if it lodges in the netting the prayer has probably been unheard.

On the left there is a shrine with a screen, to which innumerable prayers have been tied. On the right sits one of Buddha's original sixteen disciples (see p. 47 of these Lectures). A Koolie with a swelled knee applied it to the knee of the idol, while one with inflamed eyelids rubbed his eyelids on it!

LECTURE XVII.

Sacred Objects.

NEXT to the subject of images and idols comes that of certain sacred objects which Buddhists of all Schools —whether adherents of the Hīna-yāna or Mahā-yāna systems—hold in veneration; for example, relics, relic-receptacles or Stūpas, foot-prints, trees, utensils, bells, symbols, and animals.

The narratives of the Chinese travellers, frequently mentioned before, teem with descriptions of such objects. Take, for instance, Fā-hien's account of the district of Nagāra, near Peshawar in Northern India (Legge, 34–40), in which several sacred objects are stated to exist—such as a fragment of Buddha's skull, one of his teeth, portions of his hair and nails, his alms-bowl, his staff (contained in a wooden tube, so heavy that even a thousand men could not lift it), his robe, and the impression of his shadow. This was at the beginning of the fifth century of our era.

Fā-hien's statements are confirmed by Sung-Yun, the next Chinese traveller mentioned before (p. 161 of this volume [1]), who started on his journey rather more than a century after Fā-hien.

We then visited the Ki-Ka-lam temple near Nagāra. This contains the yellow robe (Kashāya) of Buddha in thirteen pieces. Here also is

---

[1] Observe that Sang Yun, as there given, is more correctly spelt Sung Yun.

the staff of Buddha, in a wooden case covered with gold-leaf. The weight of this staff is sometimes so heavy that a hundred men cannot raise it, and at other times it is so light that one man can lift it. In the city of Na-kie (Nagarahāra) is a tooth of Buddha and also some of his hair, both of which are contained in precious caskets. Morning and evening religious offerings are made to them.

We next arrive at the cave of Go-pāla, where is the shadow of Buddha. To anyone entering the cavern, and looking for a long time (or, from a long distance) at the western side of it opposite the door, the figure, with its characteristic marks, appears; on going nearer, it gradually grows fainter and then disappears. On touching the place where it was, there is nothing but the bare wall. Gradually retreating, the figure begins to come in view again, and foremost is conspicuous that peculiar mark between the eyebrows (ūrṇa), which is so rare among men.

Before the cave is a square stone, on which is a trace of Buddha's foot (Beal's Translation, p. cvii, abridged).

Hiouen Thsang, the third traveller, confirms the statements of his predecessors in regard to the relics in this district, and adds as follows:—

There is another little Stūpa, made of the seven precious substances, in which is deposited the *eye-ball* of the Buddha, large as an Āmra fruit, and bright and clear throughout. It is deposited in a sealed-up casket (Beal, i. 96).

It is easy to perceive from the above extracts that the worship of certain sacred objects connected with the founder of Buddhism had become even in Fā-hien's time a marked feature of Buddhism. In fact, the number of such objects increased so rapidly that before long it became usual to classify them under three heads as follow[1]:—

(1) Śārīrika (or Śarīra-dhātu or simply Śārīra), objects

---

[1] Compare Hardy's 'Monachism,' p. 212.

which once formed part of the Buddha's body, such as a bone, a tooth, a hair, a nail.

(2) Pāribhogika, 'objects possessed or used by the Buddha,' such as his seat, alms-bowl, drinking-vessel (kumbha), staff, vestments, and even his spittoon. Under this division is placed the Bodhi-tree.

(3) Uddeśika, objects worshipped as in some way commemorative of the Buddha or of some event or incident in his life.

It would be difficult to decide under which of these categories the *sacred books* containing the Buddha's Law are to be placed, and yet they are deeply revered, and at the present day almost deified, as if they were intelligent and omniscient beings. They are wrapped in costly cloth or silk, and their names are mentioned with the addition of honorific personal titles. Occasionally such sacred books are placed on a kind of rude altar, near the road-side, that passers-by may place offerings of money upon them[1].

Without attempting, therefore, to follow any particular classification, we proceed to notice some of the chief objects in the order of their importance, beginning with relics.

Relics.

Adoration of relics constitutes an important point of difference between Buddhism and Brāhmanism; for Brāhmanism and its offspring Hindūism are wholly opposed to the practice of preserving the ashes, bones,

---

[1] See Hardy's 'Eastern Monachism,' p. 192.

hair, or teeth of deceased persons, however much such individuals may have been revered during life.

I remarked in the course of my travels through India that articles used by great religious teachers—as, for example, robes, wooden shoes, and seats—are sometimes preserved and venerated after their death. All articles of this kind, however, must, of course, be removed from the body before actual decease; for it is well known that, in the minds of Hindūs, ideas of impurity are inseparably connected with death, and contamination is supposed to result from contact with the corpses of even a man's dearest relatives. Nor is the mortal frame ever held in veneration by the Hindūs as it was by the ancient Egyptians, and as it generally is in Christian countries.

Even the living body is regarded as a mass of corruption, a thing to be held in contempt, and a constant impediment to sanctity of life. How much more then ought every part of a dead body to be got rid of without delay! Hence in the present day a corpse is burnt, and its ashes are generally scattered on the surface of sacred rivers or of the sea.

It is true that the bodies of great Hindū ascetics and devotees are exempted from this rule. They are usually buried—not burnt. Not, however, because the mere corporeal frame is held in greater veneration, but because the bodies of the most eminent saints are supposed to lie undecomposed in a kind of trance, or state of intense ecstatic meditation (samādhi).

The Buddhist, too, is a thorough Hindū in contemning the living body; but when the corpse is burnt, he does not scatter the ashes on rivers. He takes measures to preserve them.

We know that according to the teaching of Brāhmanism the burning of a corpse is followed by religious ceremonies called Śrāddhas[1]. The greater the number of Śrāddhas which a living man is able to perform in behalf of his deceased relatives, the greater is the benefit which accrues to their souls; and if the dead man's soul happens to be in one of the hells, the sooner it is released from its purgatorial pains.

A true Buddhist, on the other hand, considers all such Śrāddhas as useless; although it is certainly a fact that in the end the more developed Buddhism of the North invented similar ceremonies, called Bardo (see pp. 293, 334).

True Buddhism, in short, has only one way of honouring ancestors, and only one method of keeping alive the memory of those perfected saints whose whole personality has become extinct, and whose transition into other forms of life has finally ceased.

The calcined ashes, or certain unconsumed portions of the body—such as fragments of bone or hair or nails or teeth—are deposited in relic-shrines.

Of course the most sacred of all Buddhist relics are those of the Buddha himself. It is said that after the cremation of his corpse the chief remains consisted of four teeth, the two cheek-bones, and fragments of the skull. But it is believed that, even before his death, portions of his hair and nails were preserved and placed

---

[1] See my 'Brāhmanism and Hindūism,' p. 303.

under Dāgabas (Stūpas). One legend relates that when Gautama had decided on abandoning all worldly associations, his first act was to cut off the mass of his hair, with its ornament (ćūḍā-maṇi), and that these were taken up by the god Indra to the Trayastriṉśa heaven, and there placed under a Dāgaba and worshipped by the gods.

Fā-hien, in a passage already alluded to, says that in the country of Nagāra there is a particular spot where Buddha shaved off his hair and clipt his nails, and, having done so, proceeded to erect a lofty mound or Stūpa to enshrine them, as well as to be a model for all future Stūpas (p. 504 of this volume).

Hiouen Thsang relates a tradition that when the two travelling merchants Trapusha and Bhallika (see p. 40) were converted, the Buddha gave them at their own request some of his own hair and nail-parings, besides his alms-bowl, staff, and a portion of his clothing, and bade them deposit each article in Stūpas or Dāgabas. The two merchants, it is narrated, went home to their own country and acquired an enormous stock of religious merit by being the first to erect a Stūpa for the reception of personal memorials of the great Buddha. According to a tradition the two merchants were from Burma, and the shrine which was erected to receive eight of his hairs afterwards developed into the great Rangoon Dāgaba (Pagoda). It may be inferred from this legend (as Dr. Oldenberg has already remarked) that the care of the Buddha's relics, and the institution of ceremonies in their honour, were in the first instance left to the devotion of religiously minded Buddhist laymen.

'What are we to do,' Ānanda asks of the Master, when his end is drawing near [1], 'with the body of the Perfect One?' 'Let not the honours due to the body of the Perfect One trouble you, Ānanda. Seek ye rather perfection for yourselves. There are, Ānanda, wise men among the nobles, the Brāhmans, and the citizens, who believe in the Perfect One; they will honour the body of the Perfect One.'

Hiouen Thsang (Beal, ii. 40) also states that when certain Indian Rājas, eight in number, heard of the Buddha's death, they collected armies and marched to Kusi-nārā (p. 424) to seize portions of the relics; but the prince of Kusi-nārā refused to give them up. In the end the matter was settled amicably, and the relics were divided, so that each of the eight princes might take a share. Then all departed to their own homes, and each prince built a Stūpa over his own portion of the relics. The gods also took their portions.

Fā-hien (chap. xxiii) alludes to the building of the eight Stūpas, and adds that king Aśoka destroyed them, and in their place built 84,000 others—one for the conservation of each atom of the elements of the Buddha's body; the belief being that the bodies of all human beings consist of that number of elementary particles (see p. 423). The eight-fold division is described in 'Buddhist Suttas,' pp. 133–136 (S. B. E. vol. xi).

It appears probable that the earliest relics of his burnt body held in honour were his teeth; and of these again the most celebrated seem to have been his

[1] 'Mahā-p.' p. 51. 'Milinda Pañha,' p. 177. 'It is certainly noteworthy,' says Oldenberg, 'that as the care for Buddha's remains is not represented as belonging to the disciples, so the Vinaya texts are nearly silent as to the last honours of the deceased monks. To arrange for their cremation was probably committed to the laity.'

four eye-teeth. One of the four is said to have been appropriated by the gods and another by the Nāgas, while the third was taken to Gāndhāra in the north-west, and the fourth to Kaliṅga in the south-east.

The first two eye-teeth have only mythical histories, and little is recorded of the third, but the fourth has gone through a series of terrestrial adventures, which have been much written about and would fill several volumes. One of the immediate followers of Gautama is said to have gained possession of it on the occasion of the eight-fold distribution of the great sage's relics (p. 499), and to have conveyed it to a place afterwards called Danta-pura, 'tooth-city[1],' the capital of Kaliṅga (Orissa), where it is believed to have remained undisturbed for about 800 years. After that period it was seized, at the instigation of some Brāhmans, by a powerful Hindū king who reigned at Pāṭaliputra. Its vicissitudes and adventures for centuries afterwards were very varied. It was conveyed surreptitiously to Ceylon about the year 311 of our era by a princess of Kaliṅga, who concealed it in her hair. There it remained till 1315, when it was carried back to Southern India. After a time it was taken back to Kandy in Ceylon. Next it was seized by the Portuguese and carried off to Goa. Thence it was transported to Pegu, and finally the precious tooth-relic (dāṭhā-dhātu), or at least some imitation of it, was restored to the good people of

[1] Subsequently called Purī, and noted for the worship of Jagan-nāth or Kṛishṇa, who became the successor of Buddha as an object of worship (see p. 166 of this volume).

Kandy, where it is still preserved by them as a veritable Palladium, with every possible precaution against further outrage, although under the protecting ægis of our government its security ought not any longer to be matter of anxiety.

Every native of Ceylon (Laṅkā), whether Buddhist or Hindū, seems to feel that the welfare of his country depends on its careful conservation. At any rate the Sinhalese have placed their tooth-temple—called Dalada Māligāwa—in the loveliest part of their beautiful island (see p. 454), amid richly wooded hills, from which may be obtained some of the most enchanting views in the world. The eye-tooth is in appearance like a piece of discoloured ivory about two inches[1] long, and one inch across in the thickest part. Indeed, all the supposed relics of the Buddha's body, and the dress and implements he used, are of such a size as to make his worshippers believe that his stature far exceeded that of ordinary men.

The tooth is enclosed in nine bell-shaped, jewelled golden cases, one within the other, each locked by a key, and each key consigned to the custody of a separate official. The interior cases increase in costliness till the most highly jewelled of all is reached, and within this on a golden lotus lies the relic. When I visited the tooth-temple in 1877, the cases were kept within iron bars in a dimly-lighted shrine—redolent with flower-offerings which exhaled an overpowering

[1] Hardy's 'Eastern Monachism,' p. 224. The size of the tooth does not seem very preposterous, on the assumption of the truth of the tradition that Gautama attained to the stature of twenty cubits.

perfume—and in the very centre of the buildings of the temple. When the Prince of Wales visited Kandy in 1876, all the officials assembled to unlock the cases and exhibit the treasured relic.

A detailed account of the tooth is given in a book called Dalada-vaṉsa or Dāṭhā-vaṉsa, said to have been written originally in ancient Sinhalese (Elu) about the year 310 of our era, and translated into the sacred Pāli about the year 1200. This book has been rendered into English by the late Sir Coomāra Swāmy. The tooth is also described in many other Pāli and Sinhalese books, including the Mahā-vaṉsa.

And here it may be remarked that one feature of the Buddha's relics was that they gave forth on special occasions celestial light, and had the power of working miracles. Sometimes a reverent circumambulation of the shrine which contained the relics was believed to be sufficiently efficacious in stimulating their miraculous powers. Sometimes they were taken out and exhibited. The following extract from Fā-hien reminds one of what takes place at Kandy in the present day:—

In the city of He-lo (the present Hiḍḍa, west of Peshawar) there is the flat-bone of Buddha's skull, deposited in a Vihāra adorned all over with gold-leaf and the seven sacred substances. The king of the country revering the bone, and anxious lest it should be stolen, has selected eight individuals representing great families, and committed to each a seal with which he should seal the shrine and guard the relic. At early dawn these men come, and after each has inspected his seal, they open the door. This done they wash their hands with scented water, and bring out the bone, which they place on a lofty platform, where it is supported on a pedestal of the seven precious substances. The king every morning makes his offerings and performs his worship. The chiefs of the Vaiśyas also make their offerings.

Then they replace the bone in the Vihāra, under a Stūpa of the seven precious substances (p. 528 of this volume) more than five cubits high (Legge, pp. 36–38, abridged).

Fā-hien records a similar exhibition of the Buddha's alms-bowl in the country near Peshawar:—

When it is mid-day they bring out the bowl and make offerings to it. It may contain about two pecks, and it has a bright lustre. When poor people throw into it a few flowers, it becomes full. If the rich throw in myriads of flowers, they are not able to fill it.

He states that the Buddha's robe was also brought out to be worshipped:—

When there is a drought the people collect in crowds, bring out the robe, pay worship to it and make offerings, on which there is immediately a great rain from the sky (Legge, pp. 35, 39, abridged).

The relics of all great saints in Buddhist countries were revered in a similar manner. At the same time it ought to be noted that the periodical exhibition of relics, before the eyes of worshippers, was not a usual occurrence (as it is in Roman Catholic countries). Indeed, as a general rule, the custom seems to have been to shield the ashes and remains of revered dead bodies from observation and liability to be touched. Hence they were commonly sealed up hermetically, as it were, in the interior of receptacles which effectually concealed them from view and protected them from disturbance.

And this leads us to advert to the form and character of Buddhist relic-receptacles.

It is probable that at a very early period, and even before the Buddha's time, the Hindūs were accustomed to raise heaps or tumuli over the ashes of kings, great men, saints and sages, just as even to this day among the Sikhs of the Panjāb, the ashes of great men are so honoured. Some think that the hemispherical dome-like form of the tumulus was intended to represent a bubble—the most transitory of all material objects. In all likelihood the dome of the Sāñchī Stūpa—which is thought to be as old as the time of Buddha—was constructed in memory of some great man.

Such heaps were at first generally called Ćaityas, and afterwards Stūpas (from the Sanskṛit roots ći and styai, meaning 'to heap together'); but Ćaitya ultimately denoted a relic-structure in an assembly-hall (see p. 450), while the word Stūpa denoted one in the open air. Then inside the Ćaitya or Stūpa (Pāli Thūpa, corrupted into Tope) there was a casket—made of silver, gold, stone, earthenware, etc.—in which were deposited the ashes, fragments of bone, or the teeth or nails of the deceased. And this relic-casket was called in Sanskṛit Dhātu-garbha, or in Pāli Dāgaba (corrupted into Dagoba and afterwards into Pagoda)—that is, a repository of the elementary particles of which all bodies are composed.

Then in time the word Dāgaba (Pagoda) denoted the monument as well as the relic-casket. Moreover Ćaityas and Stūpas were often mere pyramidal structures, enshrining images or marking important events (see p. 390), but not containing relics. Among the Hindūs Ćaitya often denotes the sacred village-tree planted on a mound.

The process by which the simple Ćaitya or mound developed into more elaborate structures is remarkable. First came erections of stone or brick, generally bell-shaped or domed like bee-hives. These again ex-

VOTIVE STŪPA, RECENTLY FOUND AT BUDDHA-GAYĀ.

(Date about ninth or tenth century of our era.)

[*To face page* 505.

panded into elongated pyramidal structures, springing from cylindrical or octagonal or hexagonal bases, and ornamented with images of Gautama, and resting on plinth-like foundations, the summits tapering into finials consisting of three, or seven, or nine, or eleven, or even fifteen tiers of umbrella-shaped ornaments (see note, p. 393).

Then, again, in time, these elaborate Dāgabas expanded into vast Pagodas of enormous height, as, for example, the Rangoon Pagoda (see p. 456) and that at Anurādhapura in Ceylon.

It is doubtful whether in early Buddhism Ćaityas and Stūpas were ever empty monuments or cenotaphs. Probably all of them contained ashes, fragments of bone, teeth, or hair, though in some cases the most careful examination has failed to discover the vessel in which they were deposited. If made of fragile materials, it rapidly crumbled into dust. But Stūpas, even without relics, were themselves objects of reverence.

In the later period of Buddhism the practice of carving, or moulding mere memorial or votive Stūpas, and dedicating them at sacred spots became common. The examples of this kind of Stūpa which I saw unearthed at Buddha-Gayā have been described (p. 397).

The engraving opposite to this page is a copy of one of these votive Stūpas which I procured for the Indian Institute through Mr. Beglar.

At Mandalay there is a large Pagoda with about 620 smaller ones round it (in rows of six or seven deep). Each small Pagoda enshrines a tablet—exposed to view—on which some portion of the Law is engraved.

Many small Pagodas are simply canopies of brick or some solid material erected over images.

Outside the Buddhist convent near Dārjīling, when I visited it in 1884, a monk was roughly moulding a number of small votive Stūpas in clay, with which he was probably mixing the powdered bones of some deceased Lāma. Here is a copy of one exactly the size of the original:—

If broken open, a terra-cotta seal, inscribed with some sacred formula, would probably be found inside.

Of course most of the Buddha's chief disciples, such as Sāriputta, Maudgalyāyana, Kāśyapa, Ānanda, Upāli, each had Stūpas erected over their relics.

Sacred Foot-prints.

Next in importance to the worship of relics is that of foot-prints (Sanskṛit Śrī-pada or Śrī-pāda). Everywhere throughout Buddhist countries the supposed impressions of the Buddha's feet are as much honoured as those of the god Vishṇu are by Vaishṇavas.

When Fā-hien reached Gṛidhra-kūṭa (see pp. 404, 406), he is said to have used words to the following effect: 'I, Fā-hien, was born when I could not meet with Buddha, and now I only see the foot-prints which he has left' (Legge, 83).

It is well known that the practice of bowing down and honouring the feet is a thoroughly Asiatic custom. The idea seems to be derived from a kind of *a fortiori* argument. If the feet, as the lowest member of the body, are honoured, how much more is homage rendered to the whole man. Hence children honour their parents, not by kissing their faces, but by prostrating themselves at their feet and touching them reverentially. Another reason for venerating the feet is well expressed in one of our hymns:—

> O let me see Thy foot-marks,
> And in them plant my own;

and in Longfellow's

> Foot-prints on the sands of time;
> Foot-prints which perhaps another,
> Sailing o'er life's solemn main,
> A forlorn and shipwrecked brother,
> Seeing may take life again.

This shows that even Europeans are familiar with the idea. There is a Roman Catholic church at Vienna which possesses a celebrated image of Christ on the Cross. On one occasion I visited this church and observed several worshippers kissing the feet of the image, while others—too short in stature to reach it with their lips—touched its feet with their fingers and then kissed their fingers. A similar honour is paid to the images of St. Peter at Rome, and indeed to that Apostle's living representatives. The alleged foot-prints of Christ are not numerous, but they exist in certain holy places[1].

Every sentiment in the East is exaggerated, and it need not therefore be matter of wonder if a veneration for foot-prints has led to an excessive multiplication of these symbols, and to an excess of superstitious worship paid to them by Hindūs of various sects in every part of India. No true Vaishṇava will leave his house in the morning without marking his forehead with the symbol of Vishṇu's feet. In travelling from one place to another I often came across what appeared to be an empty shrine, but on a close inspection I found that it contained two foot-prints on a little raised altar made of stone. These are called Pādukā 'shoes,' but are really the supposed impressions of the soles of the feet of the person to whom the shrines are dedicated. In 1876 I visited the celebrated Vishṇu-pad temple at Gayā. Crowds were worshipping the foot-mark impressed on the bare stone, but concealed by offerings, and surrounded by a silver fence under a silver canopy (see 'Brāhmanism and Hindūism,' p. 309).

It is true that Buddhists never imitate the practice

[1] Mr. Lesley, in his 'Lectures on the Origin and Destiny of Man,' states that there are two foot-prints sculptured on the summit of Mount Olivet, and worshipped by pilgrims as the marks left when Christ sprang into the sky at His ascension. There is another alleged foot-print of Christ in the Mosque of Omar, and two foot-prints at Poitiers in France. There are two foot-prints of Ishmael in the temple at Mecca. This is mentioned by Mr. Alabaster (p. 262).

of the worshippers of Vishṇu by marking their foreheads with the supposed impressions of the Buddha's feet, but they will nevertheless make long and toilsome pilgrimages to bow down before what they believe to be the impression of his foot on a rock.

The Jainas, who are the only Hindū representatives of the Buddhistic system left in India, are quite as ardent foot-print worshippers. In 1884 I ascended Mount Pārasnāth (Pārśva-nāth) in Bengal at the same time with crowds of Jaina pilgrims who, like myself, toiled up the hill to visit the numerous Jaina temples scattered over the uneven surface at the summit, some five thousand feet above the plain. Our objects were very different. Theirs was the acquisition of merit, mine was the acquirement of knowledge. Lepers lined the rough pathway, and much additional merit was held to accrue to the pilgrims by distributing alms among them. I found that nearly every shrine at the summit consisted of a little domed canopy of marble, covering two foot-prints of some one of the twenty-four Jaina saints (especially Pārśva-nāth) impressed on a marble altar. The soles of the supposed foot-prints were either white or black and marked with small gilded circles.

Groups of worshippers bowed down before the shrines and deposited offerings of money, rice, almonds, raisins, and spices on the foot-marks. No sooner did they quit one shrine for the next, than a troop of frolicking monkeys promptly took their place and scampered off with the edible portion of the objects offered.

It is impossible to state positively when either

Buddhism or Jainism first introduced foot-print worship, but the practice must have begun very early.

With regard to this point General Sir A. Cunningham, in his account of the Bharhut Stūpa—a Stūpa which dates from the second century B. C.—says:—

Foot-prints of Buddha were most probably an object of reverence from a very early period—certainly before the building of the Bharhut Stūpa—as they are represented in two separate sculptures there. In the first sculpture the foot-prints are placed on a throne or altar, canopied by an umbrella, hung with garlands. A royal personage is kneeling before the altar, and reverently touching the foot-prints with his hands. The second example is in the bas-relief representing the visit of Ajāta-śatru to Buddha. Here, as in all other Bharhut sculptures, Buddha does not appear in person, his presence being marked by his two foot-prints. The wheel symbol is duly marked on both (p. 112, abridged).

The General justly remarks that perhaps the worship of the Buddha's foot-prints may have sprung up in imitation of the homage alleged to have been paid by Mahā-Kāśyapa and 500 monks to his feet, which, it is said, were exposed to view when his body was lying on the funeral pile. The legend states that while the monks were in the act of bowing down in adoration before the feet, the funeral pile ignited spontaneously.

On one of the gate-pillars of the ancient Sāñchī Stūpa there is a sculpture of a foot-print marked with the wheel (Ćakra, p. 522) symbol, which the late Mr. Fergusson ascribed to the early part of the first century of the Christian era.

There are also sculptured representations of the Buddha's foot-prints at Amarāvatī, supposed to date from the second or third century of the Christian era. These representations are often carved on so-called altars or else placed before altars.

But of all foot-prints, that on Adam's Peak (the highest mountain in Ceylon, more than 7000 feet above the sea), supposed to have been left by the Buddha when he ascended thence to heaven, is the most celebrated.

According to Fā-hien (Legge, p. 102), when Buddha was in Ceylon he planted one foot on the north of the royal city and the other on Sumana-Kūṭa (Adam's Peak), fifteen yojanas, or about a hundred miles, distant.

This fancied impression of the Buddha's foot (believed by Christians to be that of St. Thomas, by Muhammadans to be that of Adam, and by Hindūs to be that of the god Śiva) is merely a shapeless hollow in the rock, five feet seven inches long by two feet seven inches broad, which would give the Buddha a stature of about thirty-five feet. It is said to have been discovered by a hunter at the beginning of the century before Christ, and, although very difficult of access, is annually visited by about 100,000 Buddhist pilgrims. Near it, on the summit of the mountain, is a small temple dedicated to Saman (p. 217).

In a shrine near the tooth-temple at Kandy, I saw a so-called facsimile of this foot-print. Those who are physically incapable of toiling up the mountain to bow down before the sacred impression on the rock, gain nearly as much merit by worshipping its copy. The shrine was filled with fragrant flowers recently deposited on the facsimile.

Other foot-prints in various places throughout India, Burma, Siam, Tibet, Mongolia, and China, are from two to five feet long. A tradition is mentioned by Fā-hien (Legge, 29) that, when Buddha visited Northern India, he came to the country of Woo-chang or Udyāna, and there he left a print of his foot, which appears long or short according to the ideas of the beholders.

Another legend states that Buddha left the print of his left foot on Adam's Peak, and then, in one stride, strode across to Siam, where he left the impression of his right foot.

The Siamese hold their foot-print in as much reverence as the Sinhalese hold theirs. It is called Phra Bat, and, according to Mr. Alabaster, its appearance is like that of the foot-print on Adam's Peak. Nothing is to be seen but a hole in the rock, about five feet long by two broad. A temple is built over it, and every precaution taken to protect it from over-zealous worshippers. Mr. Alabaster thus describes his visit to this sacred spot:—

The grating which usually covers the foot-print was removed to enable us to see the bottom, but the temple was so dark that we could not see much of it. We moved aside some of the offerings lying on it, but could see nothing of the pattern except the five marks of the toe-nails—five grooves in the rock—which some declare to have been made with chisels. On inquiry we were told that the other marks were long ago destroyed by an accidental fire. Likeness to a foot there is none. Yet to this holy foot-print year after year crowds of Siamese flock with varied offerings, and even the most enlightened amongst them—the late King for instance—have observed and encouraged the practice. ('Wheel of the Law,' p. 284, abridged.)

The soles of the Buddha's feet are represented as quite flat, and all the toes of equal length. Each sole possesses, as we have seen (p. 20), one hundred and eight auspicious marks (maṅgala-lakkhaṇa), and of these the principal is generally the wheel (Ćakra), while around it are grouped representations of animals, inhabitants of various worlds, and symbols of different kinds. In all probability the idea is that all things are subject to the Buddha or belong to him; they are therefore metaphorically placed under his feet. (Compare the metaphor in Psalm viii. 6–8.)

The one hundred and eight marks vary in various specimens. A good typical example (brought from Burma) of the impression of one foot may be seen in the British Museum. The sole is divided into compartments, each compartment containing a mark. There are five conch-shells, one in each of the five toes, this symbol being highly esteemed by Buddhists as well as by Hindūs.

Among the one hundred and eight auspicious marks on the Siamese foot-print are the following:—A spear, trident (tri-ratna), book, elephant-goad, Indra's elephant, dragon (makara), ocean, golden ship, water with lotuses, conch-shell, four-faced Brahmā, umbrella, king of Nāgas, king of horses, of tigers, of birds, sun, moon, ten mountains, peacock, flag of victory, deer, fish, water-jar. The wheel (Ćakra) does not occur in Mr. Alabaster's list ('Wheel of the Law,' p. 290), but the two feet of the Amarāvatī Stūpa, described by Mr. Fergusson, have a wheel in the centre of the soles. Above is the Tri-ratna emblem with a Svastika symbol on each side.

There are other Svastika marks, and others on the toes (see p. 523).

The Skanda-Purāṇa and Bhāgavata-Purāṇa give similar lists of marks on the sole of Vishṇu's foot.

Sacred Trees.

We now pass on to a brief consideration of sacred trees. Most persons are aware that the homage offered to trees and plants is not confined to Buddhism. It existed very early in Brāhmanism and is still common everywhere throughout India (see my 'Brāhmanism and Hindūism,' p. 330).

In point of fact various forms of tree-worship prevail at the present moment in almost every part of the world where superstition and ignorance are ruling influences. Nor can we really condemn, as either unnatural or unreasonable, the feeling of veneration with which trees are generally regarded, bearing in mind the grateful shade and shelter which they afford, the beauty of their foliage, their importance as purifiers of the atmosphere, and the hundreds of useful purposes to which their wood, leaves, and fruit are applicable. According to Dr. E. B. Tylor ('Primitive Culture,' ii. 223), the North American Indians of the Far West often hang offerings on the trees to propitiate the spirits and procure good weather and good hunting. He adds that Mr. Darwin describes the South Americans as doing much the same.

In Persia and other Eastern Countries trees may often be met with, the branches of which have been recently hung with offerings of cloth, rags, and even garments.

In India the notion of trees being inhabited by deities or semi-divine beings or spirits is to this day very common, and we have already noted (p. 112) that during the period of Gautama's Bodhi-sattvaship, in the course of which he had to undergo countless births in preparation for his Buddhahood, he was born forty-three times as a tree-god.

In Siam, according to Mr. Alabaster, offerings are commonly made in the present day to the spirits or deities inhabiting trees. People hang various votive objects on the branches, or place them on a stand or altar beneath any particular tree whose deity they wish to propitiate. Moreover they are very averse to the cutting down of any trees of any kind, lest the tree-gods should be angry.

'Some years ago,' says Mr. Alabaster, 'when I employed my spare energy in showing the Siamese how to make roads in the, till then, roadless suburbs of Bangkok, I had to cut my lines through villages, temple-groves, orchards, plantations, and patches of jungle. For the "wicked" duty of cutting down the trees, a gang of the lowest criminals was placed at my disposal.' But he adds that the removal of any specially holy building or tree was interdicted by the Government.

We have already seen that, according to the theory of later Buddhism, every Buddha is supposed to have his own special tree under which he sat and meditated, and in the end attained supreme knowledge (see p. 136). For example, there is the Pippala (also called Aśvattha, *Ficus Religiosa*) sacred fig-tree of Gautama Buddha, the Vaṭa or Banyan-tree (*Ficus Indica*) of Kāśyapa Buddha, the Uḍumbara (*Ficus Glomerata*) of Kanaka-muni; the Śirīsha (*Acacia Serisa*) of Kraku-Ććhanda; the Śāla (*Shorea Robusta*) of Viśva-bhū; the Puṇḍarīka (*White*

Lotus) of Śikhin[1]; the Pāṭali (*Bignonia Suaveolens*) of Vipaśyin.

These six Buddhas with Gautama are sometimes held to be the seven principal Buddhas, and, according to some authorities, the tree of the future Buddha (Maitreya) will be the Iron-wood tree (Sideroxylon)[2]. Specimens of some of these trees are to be found growing in the area of the Buddha-Gayā temple, and several are represented in the sculptures of the Stūpa of Bharhut (of the second century B.C.). On one of the pillars of that Stūpa elephants are carved in the act of worshipping both the Pīpal-tree and the Banyan-tree. In fact it must be borne in mind that Gautama Buddha is said to have meditated under both of these trees, and is therefore connected with both (see p. 39).

It might have been expected, too, that the Śāl-tree would have ranked next in sacredness to the Pīpal and Banyan; for according to one legend, Māyā gave birth to Gautama while standing under a Śāl-tree, and according to another legend, Gautama died on a couch placed between two Śāl-trees (pp. 23, 50). This tree, however, appears to be more honoured in connexion with the Buddha Viśva-bhū (p. 136, note 1).

There are other trees which were held in veneration by Indian Buddhists:—for example, the Mango (Āmra) and the Jambu, and the Aśoka. The first of these appears frequently in sculptures, and is known by the shape of its fruit.

---

[1] Or according to some the Śālmali or Silk-cotton tree (Sīmal).

[2] Spence Hardy's 'Eastern Monachism,' p. 215.

Two other trees under which the Buddha is said to have meditated after his attainment of Buddhahood—namely, the Mućalinda-tree[1] and the Rājāyatana-tree—are not identified.

But among all trees revered by all Buddhists of all nationalities, the Aśvattha or Pippala (Pīpal), under which Gautama achieved Buddhahood and perfect knowledge, takes the precedence. In some Buddhist countries the climate prevents its introduction, but if it can by any means be made to grow, it is everywhere planted close to Buddhist temples, monasteries and Dāgabas, and in many cases is the product of a seed brought from the supposed original tree at Buddha-Gayā.

A tradition relates that Gautama during his lifetime directed Ānanda to break off a branch from that original tree and to plant it in the garden of the Vihāra, or monastery, at Śrāvastī—Gautama's favourite place of residence—'He who worships it,' said Gautama, 'will receive the same reward as if he worshipped me[2].'

This is a mere legend resting on no historical basis; but the tradition which makes Gautama choose a seat under the sacred Pippala or Aśvattha as the spot where the first stirrings of a divine afflatus and the first whisperings of divine communications—symbolized by the mysterious quivering and rustling of its leaves—

---

[1] I conjecture that the Mućalinda-tree may have been the Sandal, for it is described in Sanskṛit literature as infested by snakes. The fact of a serpent having emerged from the roots of this tree and protected the Buddha instead of injuring him, may account for the sacred character of the sandal-wood statue (see p. 408).

[2] Hardy's 'Eastern Monachism,' p. 212.

were likely to make themselves felt, points to a probable fact—a fact quite in harmony with what we have already noted in regard to his early Brāhmanical education and ideas. We read in the Kaṭha Upanishad (VI. 1) that the root of the Aśvattha-tree was identified with the Supreme Being, Brahman. In a passage of the Muṇḍaka Upanishad (III. 1. 1) and in a Mantra of the Ṛig-veda (I. 164. 20) the same idea is alluded to. It is true that Gautama afterwards repudiated the possibility of any divine inspiration coming from any external source whatever, yet it is probable that when he first seated himself under the sacred fig-tree, which is even now regarded by the Hindūs as a manifestation of the god Brahmā, he expected supernatural communications of some kind [1].

The history of the original sacred Pippala (Aśvattha) tree, or as it is commonly called the Bodhi-tree (Bo-tree) of Gautama Buddha at Buddha-Gayā, has already been sketched in a previous Lecture (see pp. 392–394).

Hiouen Thsang's description of the tree, as he saw it in the seventh century, has also been given (see p. 399). Fā-hien, who saw it at Buddha-Gayā in the fifth century, calls it the Patra-tree. The following is an abridgement of what he says about it:—

The Bodhi-sattva advanced to the Patra-tree, placed the Kuśa grass at the foot of it, and sat down with his face to the east. Then King

---

[1] I noticed a fine specimen of this tree growing in the courtyard of the temple of the god Brahmā at Pokhar, near Ājmere, visited by me in 1884. Near it were two Banyan trees, a Nīm tree, and Aśoka tree. Brahmā's other temple at Idar was not visited by me.

Māra sent three beautiful damsels to tempt him. The Bodhi-sattva put his toes down to the ground, and the young maidens were changed into old grandmothers. Buddha, after attaining perfect wisdom, contemplated the tree for seven days (Legge, p. 88).

Fā-hien also saw the offspring of the original Bodhi-tree growing in Ceylon (Legge, p. 103).

It is recorded that soon after Mahinda, son of Aśoka, arrived in Ceylon (about 250 B.C.) for the purpose of propagating Buddhism, his sister, who had become a Buddhist Nun, also arrived there, and brought with her from King Aśoka a branch of the sacred Bodhi-tree of Buddha-Gayā. This was planted at Anurādha-pura, and the zealous Buddhists of Ceylon fully believe that the identical tree exists there still.

An interesting account of the state of this tree or its descendant, about thirty years ago, is given in Sir Emerson Tennant's 'Ceylon' (vol. ii. p. 613). I here give an abridged extract:—

The Bo-tree of Anurādha-pura is in all probability the oldest historical tree in the world. Its conservancy has been an object of solicitude to successive dynasties, and the story of its vicissitudes has been preserved in a series of continuous chronicles.

It would almost seem to verify the prophecy pronounced when it was planted, that it would flourish and be green for ever.

The degree of sanctity with which this extraordinary tree has been invested by Buddhists, may be compared to the feeling of veneration with which Christians regard the attested wood of the Cross.

The other Bo-trees which are found in the vicinity of every temple in Ceylon are said to be all derived from the parent-tree at Anurādha-pura, but they have been propagated by seeds; the priesthood adhering in this respect to the precedent recorded in the Mahā-vaṉśa (when Mahinda himself, taking up a fruit as it fell, gave it to the king to plant), and objecting religiously to lop it with any weapon.

In the fifth century Fā-hien found the Bo-tree at Anurādha-pura in vigorous health, and its guardians displaying towards it the same vigilant tenderness which they exhibit at the present day.

The author of the Mahā-vaṉsa, who wrote between the years 459 and 478 of our era, after relating the ceremonial which had been observed nearly eight hundred years before, at the planting of the venerated tree by Mahinda, concludes by saying:—'Thus this monarch of the forest, endowed with miraculous powers, has stood for ages in Laṅkā, promoting the spiritual welfare of its inhabitants and the propagation of true religion.'

When Buddhism became thoroughly mixed up with Hindūism the Kalpa-tree or divine tree of Indra's paradise was often introduced. It is supposed to have its terrestrial counterpart in some sacred spots on earth, and there to grant all desires, the worshipper having merely to stretch out his hand and take the gifts suspended from its branches[1]. In one sculpture it is represented pouring out coins on the ground. This kind of wishing-tree is believed to present, among other things, any food that its worshippers may ask for, and to present it ready-cooked, if cooking is needed.

The miraculous tree which developed out of the Buddha's tooth-cleaning twig, when thrown by him on the ground, has been already described (see p. 419, and compare 'Brāhmanism and Hindūism,' p. 337).

Sacred Symbols.

Some of the sacred objects already described may be regarded as symbols. Of those which are more

---

[1] Compare my translation of 'Śakuntalā,' pp. 90, 91 (fifth edition). The Christmas-tree with its suspended gifts offers a curious and interesting analogy. The wonderful tree described by Messrs. Huc and Gabet as seen by them (vol. ii. p. 53, Hazlett's translation) can only be regarded as an example of a remarkably clever hoax.

strictly symbols the *Tri-ratna* 'three-jewel' emblem comes first. It is three-pointed, and the three points are simply emblematical of the Buddha, the Law, and the Monastic Order. It is often used as an ornament. Good examples may be seen in some of the Bharhut sculptures (see Sir A. Cunningham's work). The central point is often the least elevated.

The use of this triple symbol is another proof of the connexion between Buddhism and Hindūism. Both delight in triads and in symbolizing triads [1], but the Buddhist 'three-jewel' symbol should not be confused with the Hindū Tri-śūla, which is Śiva's trident used as a weapon in his warfare with the demons. The Tri-ratna is merely the analogue of the Tri-śūla, as it is also of the triple horizontal mark on the forehead of Śaivas, and of the Tri-puṇḍra or triple frontal mark of the Tengalai sect of Rāmānuja Vaishṇavas. The two outer marks of the latter stand for Vishṇu's two feet and the middle for his consort Lakshmī [2].

Sir A. Cunningham was the first to show that the three fetish-like figures of Jagannāth (Kṛishṇa) and his sister and brother, at Purī in Orissa, were derived from three of the combined emblems of the Buddhist Tri-ratna (compare p. 166 of this volume).

Next to the Tri-ratna comes the *Ćakra* or wheel. This symbolizes the Buddhist doctrine that the origin

[1] Mr. R. Sewell has written an interesting article on 'Early Buddhist Symbolism,' in which he connects certain symbols with solar ideas derived from the West. Mr. Frederic Pincott thinks that the triple symbol stands for the ancient Y of the 'Ye dharmā' formula.

[2] See my 'Modern India,' p. 193, published by Messrs. Trübner and Co., and 'Brāhmanism and Hindūism,' p. 127.

of life and of the universe (p. 119) are unknowable—the doctrine of a circle of causes and effects without beginning and without end. The wheel also typifies the rolling of this doctrine over the whole surface of the world (pp. 410, 423). It is perhaps one of the most important symbols of Buddhist philosophy. It is often represented as either supporting the Tri-ratna or supported by it, or the latter may be inserted in it.

Observe that the Ćakra or wheel is equally a Vaishṇava symbol, but in the hand of Vishṇu or of Kṛishṇa it is a circular weapon, hurled at a demon-foe.

Another symbol is the *Lotus-flower*. Its constant use as an emblem, seems to result from the wheel-like form of the flower—the petals taking the place of spokes, and thus typifying the doctrine of perpetual cycles of existence—or from the perfection typified by the regularity of these petals, or from the idea that its expanded flower, reposing on a calm mirror-like lake, is a fit emblem of Nirvāṇa.

The Wheel, the Tri-ratna, and the Lotus are so important, as symbols of Buddhism, that they are combined in the vignette on the title-page of this volume.

Another symbol is the *Svastika* mark, consisting of two lines crossing each other, the termination of each arm of the cross being usually bent round in the same direction[1]. Much controversy has been devoted to the origin and meaning of this symbol, which simply symbolizes good luck, and equally belongs to Hindūism.

[1] The Jaugada inscription has two Svastikas, the arms in each of which are bent in opposite directions.

Long ago I propounded a theory that it might represent the four arms of Lakshmī. I now think it a mere curtailed form of the Wheel, consisting of four spokes with a portion of the periphery of the circle. In my opinion, the four spokes may represent the four groups of worlds (i.e. the lower worlds and three groups of heavens, p. 213) circling in an eternal cycle. Sir A. Cunningham considers this symbol to be a monogram or interlacing of the letters of the auspicious words *su asti* (*svasti*) in the Aśoka characters.

Another symbol is the *Throne* or seat of Buddha—a favourite emblem in many sculptures. In Cunningham's 'Stūpa of Bharhut' the throne of each Buddha is often represented under his Bodhi-tree (but without any image), and the thrones of the last four Buddhas are joined together in a single bas-relief. Sometimes the throne is covered by an umbrella with garlands, or the Buddha's bowl may rest on it. Sometimes two foot-prints are on a foot-stool under the throne.

Another venerated symbol is the *Stūpa* (see p. 505). It is often an object of adoration in itself.

I need scarcely revert to the *Umbrella* symbol (see p. 393). In Eastern countries it typifies supremacy. If a king is present no one else ought to carry an umbrella.

The *Śaṅkha* or *Conch-shell* is a very auspicious symbol, especially if the convolutions turn to the right in the Nandy-āvarta form, as on the Buddha's foot (see p. 513).

The Tibetan symbol of the '*Flying horse*' (Lung-ta) —able to transport a man round the world in one day—has been mentioned before; also the *Norbu* gem (see pp. 381, 528).

Sacred Animals.

It may be truly said that all animals are more or less venerated—though not actually worshipped—under the Buddhist system. How can it be otherwise when every Buddhist believes that the Buddha himself was incarnated in various animals during the period of his Bodhi-sattvaship (see p. 111)?

In the same way the Hindūs believe that the god Vishṇu was incarnated in animals, such as a fish, a tortoise, and a boar.

Buddhism in this as in other respects is like Brāhmanism and Hindūism. The feeling of reverence for animals rests on the doctrine of metempsychosis. It is difficult for either a Hindū or a Buddhist to draw a line of demarcation between gods, men, and animals, when the same living being may exist as a god, a man, or an animal. It is on this account that in India animals appear to live on terms of the greatest friendship and mutual confidence with human beings.

Everywhere in India animals dispute possession of the earth with man. Birds build their nests and lay their eggs in the fields, untroubled by fears or misgivings, before the very eyes of every passer-by, and within the reach of every village school-boy. Animals rove over the soil as if they were the landlords. Bulls walk about independently in the streets, and jostle you on the pavements; monkeys domesticate themselves jauntily on the roof of your house; parrots peer inquisitively from the eaves of your bedroom into the mysteries of your toilet; crows make themselves at home on your window-sill, and carry off impudently any portable article of jewellery that takes their fancy on your dressing-table; sparrows hop about impertinently and take the bread off your table-cloth; a solitary mongoose emerges every morning from a hole in your verandah, and expects a share in your breakfast; swarms of insects claim a portion of your mid-day meal, and levy a tax on the choicest delicacies at your dinner table; bats career triumphantly about your head as you light yourself to your bedroom; and at certain seasons snakes domicile themselves unpleasantly in the folds of your cast-off garments. (Quoted from my 'Brāhmanism and Hindūism.')

Perhaps the most sacred animal in the estimation of all Buddhists is the elephant. This will be easily understood by recalling what has been said in a previous Lecture (see pp. 23, 24). In one of the Bharhut sculptures the white elephant is seen descending to enter the side of Gautama's mother Māyā ('Stūpa of Bharhut,' p. 84). The elephant, says Sir A. Cunningham, is a favourite subject for delineation. It is represented in almost every possible position, as standing, walking, running, sitting down, eating, drinking, throwing water over its own back, and lastly, kneeling down in reverence before the holy Bodhi-tree.

Probably the next sacred animal to the elephant is the deer. The Buddha was born eleven times as a deer (p. 111), and he delivered his first sermon in a deer-park (p. 42). The 'goose' (Haṉsa, sometimes called 'a duck' or 'a swan') is also very sacred. With regard to other animals, Sir A. Cunningham remarks:—

The animals represented in the Bharhut sculptures are of two classes, the natural and the fabulous. The latter, however, are limited to three varieties, an elephant with a fish-tail, a crocodile with a fish-tail, and a winged horse; while the former comprises no less than fourteen quadrupeds, six birds, one snake, one fish, one insect, one crocodile, two tortoises, one lizard, and one frog. The quadrupeds include the lion, elephant, horse, rhinoceros, wild boar, bull, deer, wolf, monkey, cat, dog, sheep, hare, and squirrel. The birds comprise the cock, parrot, peacock, goose, wild duck, and quail. The snakes and fishes appear to be of only one kind. The solitary insect is a flesh-fly (p. 41, etc.).

In Burma people feed sacred fish, and save their lives in seasons when they would perish through the drying up of rivers and ponds (see p. 364).

Dr. Eitel, in his Lectures (p. 136), points out that even pigs are held sacred, though not worshipped, by Northern Buddhists. We must not forget that the Buddha in two of his births was a pig (p. 112), that he died of eating pork, and that in sculptures of the Tāntrik goddess Vajra-vārāhī—adopted by Northern Buddhists—a row of seven pigs is carved underneath her three-headed figure, one head being that of a pig.

Miscellaneous Objects.

Among these may be reckoned *bells* of various kinds. The prayer-bells common in Tibet, which are held in the hand and used during the chanting of prayers, have been already described (p. 323).

In Burma bells abound everywhere. They are of all sizes, and often of immense weight, but are not used in the same way as in Tibet. Nor are they ever rung in peals or with a clapper. Their use is not to call people to religious services. It is no part of the business of monks or priests to summon the laity to any service. Every man worships on his own account, and for himself, and by himself, and no so-called priest reminds him of his religious duties, or is responsible if he neglects them.

The real use of bells in Burmese temples is to draw the attention of the deities and spirits (Naths) to the act of worship, and so secure the due registering of prayer-merit. When a man has finished his repetitions, he strikes the bell with a piece of wood or other sacred implement lying near, and the more noise he makes the better. Mr. Scott informs us that every large pagoda has dozens of bells of all sizes, hanging outside, and one or two inside the central shrine. They are constantly dedicated by religious people, and thus multiplied *ad infinitum.*

The form of dedication is inscribed on every bell, and is in the Pāli language, though instances of the vernacular occur.

The following is a portion of a remarkable inscription in the vernacular (Shway Yoe, i. 243, abridged):—

This bell was moulded with great care and much expense, and is humbly offered by Moung San Yah and his wife, who seek refuge in the boundless mercy of the pitiful Buddha, in the majesty of the eternal law, and in the examples of the venerable assembly. They humbly strive to gain merit for themselves. May the good Naths look smilingly on them. May the Naths who dwell in the air and the earth defend their two fat bullocks—which plough the fields—from evil creatures. May the guardian Naths of the house and of the city keep Chit Oo, their son, and little Mah Mee, their darling daughter, from harm.

The weight of the bell is generally added to the dedication.

There is a fine Burmese bell in the Indian section of the South Kensington Museum. It has a long Pāli inscription, a portion of the translation of which I here give:—

'Without charity you cannot attain to Nirvāṇa'—so it is written in the Pāli Texts.

I, the giver of this bell, was staying in the sweet-smelling town of Ma-oo—of which I collect the taxes for the king—and with me was my wife—my life's breath—like to the pollen of a lily, from whom I will not be separated in all the existences which are to come, and out of which we hope soon to escape. We adore Buddha, that we may embark in the golden raft of the Noble Path, which will lead us to the final plunge into Nirvāṇa. We two, brother and sister (that is, husband and wife), have given this bell as an offering. The exact weight of the bell is 2500 kyats. We took our own weight in gold and silver and bright copper and other metal, and mixed them well together, in the year 1209 (1847 A.D.).

Now I will record all the alms I gave and what I erected within the sacred enclosure. I gave a sacred flag-staff (see p. 380 of these Lectures), the price of which, with all expenses in putting up, was 500 rupees. At the foot of it I built four small pagodas. Outside I built a monastery and a rest-house. Such are all the offerings. May I be freed from the Four states of Punishment, from the Three Great Calamities (war, famine, and plague), from the Eight Evil Places, from the Five Enemies, from unfortunate times and seasons, and from bad people. May I escape all these when I die.

All the merits I have gained, may they be shared with my parents, teachers, and all my relations; with kings, queens, nobles, and all people in the thirty-one places of habitation throughout the universe. (See p. 121 of these Lectures.)

Under the head of miscellaneous objects, we may note the seven precious minerals or substances to which allusion has frequently been made. They are gold, silver, pearl, sapphire or ruby, cat's eye, diamond, and coral (Childers); but they vary, and some authorities substitute lapis lazuli for pearl. In Hindūism there are nine precious substances (nava-ratna).

We may also enumerate here the seven treasures belonging to every universal monarch. These are:—1. a wheel which, being set in motion by the monarch, rolls before him to establish the Law in his dominions; 2. an elephant; 3. a flying horse (see p. 523); 4. a jewel which on the darkest night illuminates the earth for seven miles round (p. 381); 5. a good queen or wife; 6. a good minister or servant, who has the power of discovering hidden treasures; 7. a good general (compare Alabaster's 'Wheel of the Law,' p. 81).

Supplementary Remarks on the Connexion of Buddhism with Jainism [1].

Having during the progress of the foregoing Lectures, incidentally mentioned the subject of Jainism, I ought not to conclude them without explaining some of the chief points of difference between the system of the Jainas (conveniently contracted into Jains) and that of the Buddhists. The Jains in India, according to their own reckoning, number 1,222,000; but this is incorrect, for by the last Census they only number half a million. A great authority (Sir William Wilson Hunter) confirms this. (See his 'Gazetteer' and 'Indian Empire.')

Most scholars in the present day are of opinion that the Jaina Teacher Vardhamāna Mahā-vīra (Nātaputta) and Gautama Buddha were contemporaries, and that Jains were an independent sceptical sect, probably a little antecedent to the Buddhists, and were their rivals. At any rate it seems certain that the Nigaṇṭhas [2] or

[1] The expression Jainism corresponds to Śaivism, just as Jaina does to Śaiva. Consistency would require Bauddhism and Bauddha for Buddhism and Buddhist, but I fear the latter expressions are too firmly established.

[2] Nigaṇṭha (also spelt Nigganṭha) is from the Sanskṛit Nir-grantha, 'having no ties or worldly associations.'

Dig-ambara Jains, that is, a sect of naked ascetics, existed before the Buddha's time, and that the Tripiṭaka alludes to them.

Probably Vardhamāna Mahā-vīra (usually called Mahā-vīra) was merely a reformer of a system previously founded by a teacher named Pārśva-nātha. Not much is known of the latter, though he is greatly honoured by the Jains. His images are 'serpent-canopied' like those of Buddha (p. 480). His pupils are called Pāsāvaććijja (for Pārśvāpatyīya, 'belonging to the descendants of Pārśva'). They were only bound by four vows, whereas Mahā-vīra's teaching imposed five vows.

We have seen that Gautama Buddha, in the fifth century B.C., came to the conclusion that bodily austerities were useless as a means of obtaining liberation. His main idea seems to have been that liberation from the painful cycle of continued re-births, that is, from Saṃsāra, was to be obtained by means of knowledge (Bodhi), evolved out of the inner consciousness through meditation (dhyāna) and intuition; whereas, in contradistinction to this Buddhist idea, the main idea of the Jain teacher Mahā-vīra seems to have been that liberation was to be obtained through subjugation of the passions and through mortification of the body (tapas). The term Jina, 'conqueror,' is used in both systems, but Gautama Buddha was a Jina or conqueror through profound abstract meditation, whereas Mahā-vīra was a Jina through severe bodily austerity.

In fact, the Jains, like all other ascetics, were impressed with the idea that it was necessary to maintain a defensive warfare against the assault of evil passions, by keeping under the body and subduing it. They had also a notion that a sense of shame implied sin, so that if there were no sin in the world there would be no shame. Hence they argued rather illogically that to get rid of clothes was to get rid of sin; and every ascetic who aimed at sinlessness was enjoined to walk about naked, with the air or sky (Dig) as his sole covering (Dig-ambara).

In the Kalpa-sūtra of the Jains we read that Mahā-vīra himself began his career by wearing clothes for one year and one month, and after that he walked about naked. Now Gautama Buddha was an opponent of Jain asceticism, and it seems to me probable that one of the chief points on which he laid stress was that of decent clothing. In the Dhamma-pada (141) occurs the sentiment that 'Nakedness cannot purify a mortal who has not overcome desires.' And again, in the Sekhiyā Dhammā we have 'properly clad' 'must a monk itinerate.' (See p. 473 of these Lectures.)

It is recorded in the Vinaya (Mahā-vagga I. 6. 7–9) that Upaka, a man of the Ājīvaka sect of naked ascetics, founded by Gosāla (said to have been a pupil of Mahā-vīra), met the Buddha just after his enlightenment, and noticing his bright countenance, asked him who had been his teacher? He replied, 'Having gained all knowledge, I am myself the highest teacher.' Thereupon the naked ascetic shook his head and went another road.

Clearly these naked Nigaṇṭhas, disciples of the Jain Teacher Mahā-vīra, were no friends of the Buddha. It seems to me even possible that Gautama's great rival, Deva-datta (see pp. 405, 406), may have belonged to a Dig-ambara sect who opposed the Buddha on questions of stricter asceticism, especially in the matter of clothing; for in ancient sculptures Deva-datta is generally represented naked or nearly so, and is usually in close proximity to his cousin Gautama Buddha, who, in marked contrast to the other, is always clothed. Evidently the question of dress was a crucial one, and in process of time a party seems to have arisen, even among the Dig-ambara Jains, opposed to strict asceticism in this particular.

This party ultimately formed themselves into a separate sect, calling themselves Śvetāmbaras, that is, 'clothed in white garments.' It is well known that in early Buddhism two similar parties arose, the strict and the lax. But the two Buddhist parties were ultimately reunited. The second council is supposed to have settled the controversy.

Dr. Jacobi has shown that the separation of the two Jain sects must have taken place (according to the traditions of both parties) some time before the first century of our era.

It appears probable that the strict Dig-ambaras preceded the more lax Śvetāmbaras, though each sect claims to be the oldest. The two Jain sects have remained separate to the present day, though in all essential points of doctrine and discipline they agree.

When I was last in India, in 1884, I ascended the two hills, Pārasnāth (for Pārśva-nāth) and Ābū—both of them most sacred places in the estimation of the Jains, and covered with their temples. My ascent of the former has been already described (p. 509). I also visited Delhi, Jaypur, Ājmere, and some other chief Jain stations. Jaypur is the stronghold of the Dig-ambara Jains, and two intelligent Dig-ambara Paṇḍits, named Phaṭe Lāl and Syojī Lāl, visited me there. We conversed for a long time in Sanskṛit, and I asked them many questions about their religion, and the points in which they differed from the Śvetāmbara sect.

Three chief differences were stated to be: First, the Śvetāmbaras object to entirely nude images of any of the twenty-four Jinas or Tīrthaṃ-karas accepted by both sects. Hence all Śvetāmbara statues ought to have some appearance of a line round the middle of the body, representing a strip of cloth. In one respect the images of the Jinas differ from those of the Buddhas. They have a jewel-like mark on the breast. This is especially conspicuous in Pārśva-nāth. They are also of different colours, and have symbols (generally animals, such as a deer, tortoise, pig) connected with them.

Secondly, the Śvetāmbaras admit women into their order of ascetics just as Buddhists have their Bhikkhunīs, or nuns; whereas the Dig-ambaras, for obvious reasons, do not admit women.

Thirdly, the Śvetāmbaras have distinct sacred books of their own, which they call Aṅgas, 'limbs of the Law,' eleven in number, besides others, making 45 Āgamas, 11 Aṅgas, 12 Upāṅgas, 10 Pāinnas (Prakīrṇaka), 4 Mūlas, 6 Ćhedas, 1 Anuyoga-dvāra, and 1 Nandi. Dr. Bühler places the composition of the Aṅgas in the third century

B.C. Dr. Jacobi places them at the end of the fourth or beginning of the third century. They are written in Jain Prākṛit (sometimes called Ardha-Māgadhī, a later form than Pāli), with Sanskṛit commentaries. The Digambaras substitute, for the Aṅgas, later works, also written in more modern Prākṛit (probably in the fifth or sixth century after Christ), and maintain that the Śvetāmbara Canon is spurious. Both sects have valuable Sanskṛit works in their sacred literature.

I now add a few characteristics of both sects of Jains as distinguishing them from Buddhists.

I need scarcely notice the fact that the Jains of the present day keep up Caste. The two Jain Paṇḍits who came to me at Jaypur were Brāhmans, and wore the Brāhmanical thread. I believe this to be a mere modern innovation, which does not properly belong to the Jain system.

More important are the following points :—The Jain saints, or prophets, are called by a peculiar name Tīrthaṃ-kara, 'ford-makers,' i.e. making a ford across the troubled river of constant births or transmigrations (Saṃsāra) to the Elysium of Nirvāṇa; whereas the name Tīrthaṃ-kara with the Buddhists means a 'heretical teacher.' Then there are twenty-four Jain Tīrthaṃ-karas, whereas there are twenty-five Buddhas. Of the twenty-four Jain saints, the twenty-third and twenty-fourth—Pārśva-nāth (pp. 509, 529) and Mahāvīra—are the only historical personages. The others, beginning with Ṛishabha, are mythical.

Next, the Jains have no Stūpas or Dāgabas (p. 504) for preserving the relics of their saints.

Still more important is the point that the Jains believe in separate individual souls (Jīva), whereas the Buddhists deny the existence of souls. Souls, according to the Jains, may exist in stocks, stones, lumps of earth, drops of water, particles of fire. In Buddhism there is, as we have seen, no true metempsychosis, but rather a connected series of metamorphoses, and this stops at animals; whereas the metempsychosis of Jainism extends to inorganic matter.

With regard to the moral code two or three points may be noticed. The Jaina 'three jewels' are Right-belief, Right-knowledge, and Right-conduct, whereas the Buddhist Tri-ratna consists in the well-known Triad—the Buddha, the Law, and the Monkhood.

Then as to the five chief Moral Prohibitions—the fifth with Jains is: 'have no worldly attachments;' whereas with Buddhists it is: 'drink no strong drink.' I believe the Buddhists to have been the first to introduce total abstinence from strong drinks into India. The Jains, too, lay even more stress than the Buddhists on the first prohibition:—Kill no living creature. They strain water before drinking, sweep the ground with a silken brush before sitting down on it, never eat in the dark, often wear muslin before their mouths to catch minute insects, and even object to eating fruits containing seed.

Another interesting difference is that Jainism makes Dharma and Adharma, good and evil, or rather merit and demerit, two out of its six real substances—its fundamental and eternal principles (Astikāya)—the other four being matter (pudgala), soul (jīva), space and time. The Jains reject the Buddhist theory of the five Skandhas (see p. 109).

Lastly, the prayer-formula of the Jains differs from the well-known 'three-refuge' formula of the Buddhists ('I go for refuge to the Buddha, the Law, and the order of Monks') thus: 'Reverence to the Arhats, to the Siddhas, to the Aćāryas, to the Upādhyāyas, to all the Sādhus' (Namo Arihantāṇaṃ namo Siddhāṇaṃ namo Ayariyāṇaṃ namo Uvajjhāyāṇaṃ namo loe sabba-sāhūṇaṃ).

Time will not permit me to notice minor differences, such as the Jain rule that the hair should be painfully torn off, instead of cut off, etc.

Certainly Jainism, when viewed from the stand-point of Christianity, is even a colder system than Buddhism, and has even less claim to be called a religion. Yet no system can show a greater number of temples. Every Jain who is noted for his piety builds a small temple. He never repairs the temples of others. At Pālitāna in Kāthiāwār, there is a whole city of Jain temples. Nor is it at all necessary that every temple built to hold a Jain saint should possess either priests or worshippers. What is aimed at is the acquisition of merit by the performance of pious acts.

I must conclude by expressing my opinion that Indian Jainism is gradually drifting back into the current of Brāhmanism, which everywhere surrounds it and attracts it. Jainism, like Buddhism, came out from Brāhmanism, and into Brāhmanism it is destined to return.

LECTURE XVIII.

Buddhism contrasted with Christianity.

In the previous Lectures I have incidentally contrasted the principal doctrines of Buddhism with those of Christianity.

It will be my aim in this concluding Lecture to draw attention more directly and more in detail to the main points of divergence between two systems, which in their moral teaching have so many points of contact, that a superficial study of either is apt to lead to very confused ideas in regard to their comparative excellence and their resemblance to each other.

And first of all I must remind those who heard my earlier Lectures of the grand fundamental distinction which they were intended to establish—namely, that Christianity is a religion, whereas Buddhism, at least in its earliest and truest form, is no religion at all, but a mere system of morality and philosophy founded on a pessimistic theory of life.

Here, however, it may be objected that, before we exclude Buddhism from all title to be called a religion, we ought to define what we mean by the term 'religion.'

Of course, it will be generally acknowledged that mere morality need not imply religion, though—taking the converse—it is most undeniably true that religion must of necessity imply morality.

Unquestionably there have been great philosophers in ancient times who have lived strictly moral lives without acknowledging any religious creed at all. Many excellent men, too, exist among us in the present day, who resent being called irreligious, and yet hold no definite religious doctrines, and decline to accept any system which commits them to absolute belief in anything except an eternal Energy or Force.

Clearly the definition of the word 'religion' is beset with difficulties, and its etymology is too uncertain to help us in explaining it[1]. We shall, however, be justified if we affirm that every system claiming to be a religion in the proper sense of the word must postulate the eternal existence of one living and true God of infinite power, wisdom, and love, the Creator, Designer, and Preserver of all things visible and invisible.

It must also take for granted the immortality of man's soul or spirit, and the reality of a future state and of an unseen world. It must also postulate in man an innate sense of dependence on a personal God—a sense of reverence and love for Him, springing from a belief in His justice, holiness, wisdom, power, and love, and intensified by a deep consciousness of weakness, and a yearning to be delivered from the presence, tyranny, and penalty of sin.

---

[1] Cicero (De natura deorum) derives *religion* from relego, and explains it as a diligent practice of prayer and worship. Others have derived it from religo, and hold that it means 'binding to God.'

Then, starting from these assumptions, it must satisfy four requisites.

First, it must reveal the Creator in His nature and attributes to His creature, man.

Secondly, it must reveal man to himself. It must impart to him a knowledge of his own nature and history—what he is; why he was created; whither he is tending; and whether he is at present in a state of decadence downwards from a higher condition, or of development upwards from a lower.

Thirdly, it must reveal some method by which the finite creature may communicate with the infinite Creator—some plan by which he may gain access to Him and become united with Him, and be saved by Him from the consequences of his own sinful acts.

Fourthly, such a system must prove its title to be called a religion by its regenerating effect on man's nature; by its influence on his thoughts, desires, passions, and feelings; by its power of subduing all his evil tendencies; by its ability to transform his character and assimilate him to the God it reveals.

It is clear, then, that tried by such a criterion as this, early Buddhism could not claim to be a religion. It failed to satisfy these conditions. It refused to admit the existence of a personal Creator, or of man's dependence on a higher Power. It denied any eternal soul or Ego in man. It acknowledged no external, supernatural revelation. It had no priesthood—no real clergy; no real prayer; no real worship. It had no true idea of sin, or of the need of pardon (p. 124), and it condemned man to suffer the consequences of his own sinful acts without hope of help from any Saviour or Redeemer, and indeed from any being but himself.

The late Bishop of Calcutta once said to me, that being in an outlying part of his diocese, where Buddhism prevailed, he asked an apparently pious Buddhist, whom he happened to observe praying in a temple, what he had just been praying for? He replied, 'I have been praying for nothing.' 'But,' urged the Bishop, 'to whom have you been praying?' The man answered, 'I have been praying to nobody.' 'What!' said the astonished Bishop, 'praying for nothing to nobody?' And no doubt this anecdote gives an accurate idea of the so-called prayer of a true Buddhist. This man had not really been praying for anything. He had been merely making use of some form of words to which an efficacy, like that of sowing fruitful seed in a field, was supposed to belong. He had not been praying in any Christian sense.

Here, however, an objector might remind me that according to my own showing, various developments of Buddhism modified and even contradicted the original creed, and that what has been here said about prayer, is only strictly applicable to early Buddhism as originally taught in the most ancient texts.

I grant this—I grant that expressions of reverence for the Buddha, the Law, and the Monkhood, developed into expressions of wants and needs, and that these expressions, gradually led on to the offering of actual prayers to deified Buddhas and Bodhi-sattvas.

I admit that we ought to judge of Buddhism as a whole. We ought to give full consideration to its later developments, and the gradual sliding of its atheism and agnosticism into theism and polytheism. We are bound to acknowledge that Buddhism, as it extended to other countries, *did* acquire the character of a theistic religious system, which, though false, had in it some points of contact with Christianity.

Nevertheless, admitting all this, and taking into account all that can be said in favour of Buddhism as a religious system, it will be easy to show how impossible it is to bridge over the yawning chasm which separates it from the true religion.

It is, indeed, one of the strange phenomena of the present day, that even educated people who call themselves Christians, are apt to fall into raptures over the precepts of Buddhism [1], attracted by the bright gems which its admirers delight in culling out of its moral code, and in displaying ostentatiously, while keeping out of sight all its dark spots, all its trivialities and senseless repetitions [2]; not to speak of all those evi-

---

[1] Here is an extract from a book called 'The Mystery of the Ages,' published in 1887:—'Buddhism is the Christianity of the East, and, as such, even in better conservation than is Christianity, the Buddhism of the West.'

[2] As instances of the trivialities I give the following from the Ćulla-vagga (Sacred Books of the East, vol. xx. v, 31, p. 146; v, 9. 5, p. 87):—

'Now at that time the Bhikkhus hung up their bowls on pins in the walls, or on hooks. The pins or hooks falling down, the bowls were broken. They told this matter to the Blessed One. "You are not, O Bhikkhus, to hang your bowls up. Whosoever does so, shall be guilty of a dukkata" (offence). Now at that time the Bhikkhus put their bowls down on a bed, or a chair; and sitting down thoughtlessly they upset them, and the bowls were broken. They

dences of deep corruption beneath a whited surface, all

---

told this matter to the Blessed One. "You are not, O Bhikkhus, to put your bowls on a bed, or on a chair. Whosoever does so, shall be guilty of a dukkata" (offence). Now at that time the Bhikkhus kept their bowls on their laps; and rising up thoughtlessly they upset them, and the bowls were broken. They told this matter to the Blessed One. "You are not, O Bhikkhus, to keep your bowls on your laps. Whosoever does so, shall be guilty of a dukkata" (offence). Now at that time the Bhikkhus put their bowls down on a sunshade; and the sunshade being lifted up by a whirlwind, the bowls rolled over and were broken. They told this matter to the Blessed One. "You are not, O Bhikkhus, to put your bowls down on a sunshade. Whosoever does so, shall be guilty of a dukkata." Now at that time the Bhikkhus, when they were holding the bowls in their hands, opened the door. The door springing back, the bowls were broken. They told this matter to the Blessed One. "You are not, O Bhikkhus, to open the door with your bowls in your hands. Whosoever does so, shall be guilty of a dukkata." Now at that time the Bhikkhus did not use tooth-sticks, and their mouths got a bad odour. They told this matter to the Blessed One. "There are these five disadvantages, O Bhikkhus, in not using tooth-sticks—it is bad for the eyes—the mouth becomes bad-smelling—the passages by which the flavours of the food pass are not pure—bile and phlegm get into the food—and the food does not taste well to him who does not use them. These are the five disadvantages, O Bhikkhus, in not using tooth-sticks." "There are five advantages, O Bhikkhus" (etc., the converse of the last). "I allow you, O Bhikkhus, tooth-sticks." Now at that time the Ćhabbaggiya Bhikkhus used long tooth-sticks; and even struck the Sāmaṇeras with them. They told this matter to the Blessed One. "You are not, O Bhikkhus, to use too long tooth-sticks. Whosoever does so, shall be guilty of a dukkata. I allow you, O Bhikkhus, tooth-sticks up to eight finger-breadths in length. And Sāmaṇeras are not to be struck with them. Whosoever does so, shall be guilty of a dukkata." Now at that time a certain Bhikkhu, when using too short a tooth-stick got it stuck in his throat. They told this matter to the Blessed One. "You are not, O Bhikkhus, to use too short a tooth-stick. Whosoever does so, shall be guilty of a dukkata. I allow you, O Bhikkhus, tooth-sticks four finger-breadths long at the least."'

those significant precepts and prohibitions in its books of discipline, which indeed no Christian could soil his lips by uttering [1].

It has even been asserted that much of the teaching in the Sermon on the Mount, and in other parts of the Gospel narratives, is based on previously current moral teaching, which Buddhism was the first to introduce to the world, 500 years before Christ [2]. But this is not all. The admirers of Buddhism maintain that the Buddha was not a mere teacher of the truths of morality, but of many other sublime truths. He has been justly called, say they, 'the Light of Asia,' though they condescendingly admit that Christianity as a later development is more adapted to become the religion of the world.

Let us then inquire, for a moment, what claim Gautama Buddha has to this title—'the Light of Asia?'

Now, in the first place those who give him this name forget that his doctrines only spread over Eastern Asia, and that either Confucius, or Zoroaster, or Muhammad might equally be called 'the Light of Asia.'

---

[1] Although this Lecture was written and in type before the publication of the Bishop of Colombo's article in the July (1888) number of the 'Nineteenth Century,' I need not say that I wish here, as the Bishop has done, to draw attention to the collection of 'moral horrors' existing in some parts of the Pārājika books—the disgusting detail of every conceivable form of revolting vice, supposed to be perpetrated or perpetrable by monks.

[2] Dr. Kellogg, in his excellent work, 'the Light of Asia and the Light of the World,' well criticizes Professor Seydel's Buddhist-Christian Harmony, as well as the Professor's views on this point expressed in his work entitled 'Das Evangelium von Jesu in Seinen Verhältnissen zu Buddha-Sage und Buddha-Lehre.' Leipzig, 1880.

But was the Buddha, in any true sense, a Light to any part of the world?

It is certainly true that the main idea implied by Buddhism is intellectual enlightenment. Buddhism, before all things, means enlightenment of mind, resulting from intense self-concentration and introspection, from intense abstract meditation, combined with the exercise of a man's own reasoning faculties and intuitions.

Of what nature, then, was the so-called Light of Knowledge that radiated from the Buddha? Was it the knowledge of his own utter weakness, of his original depravity of heart, or of the origin of sin? No; the Buddha's light was in these respects profound darkness. He confessed himself, in regard to such momentous questions, a downright Agnostic. The primary origin of evil—the first evil act—was to him an inexplicable mystery.

Was it, then, a knowledge of the goodness, justice, holiness, and omnipotence of a personal Creator? Was it a knowledge of the Fatherhood of God? No; the Buddha's light was in these respects also mere and sheer darkness. In these respects, too, he acknowledged himself a thorough Agnostic. He admitted that he knew of no being higher than himself.

What, then, was the light that broke upon the Buddha? What was this enlightenment which has been so much written about and extolled? All that he claimed to have discovered was the origin of suffering and the remedy of suffering. All the light of knowledge to which he attained came to this:—that suffering arises from indulging desires, especially the desire for continuity of life; that suffering is inseparable from life; that all life is suffering; and that suffering is to be got rid of by the suppression of desires, and by the extinction of personal existence.

Here, then, is the first great contrast. When the Buddha said to his converts, 'Come (ehi), be my disciple,' he bade them expect to get rid of suffering, he told them to stamp out suffering by stamping out desires (see pp. 43, 44). When the Christ said to His disciples, 'Come, follow Me,' He bade them expect suffering. He told them to glory in their sufferings—nay, to expect the perfection of their characters through suffering.

It is certainly noteworthy that both Christianity and Buddhism agree in asserting that all creation groaneth and travaileth in pain, in suffering, in tribulation. But mark the vast, the vital distinction in the teaching of each. The one taught men to be patient under affliction, and to aim at the glorification of the suffering body, the other taught men to be intolerant of affliction, and to aim at the utter annihilation of the suffering body.

What says our Bible? We Christians, it says, are members of Christ's Body—of His flesh and of His bones—of that Divine Body which was once a suffering Body, a cross-bearing Body, and is now a glorified Body, an ever-living, life-giving Body. Hence it teaches us to honour and revere the human body; nay, almost to deify the human body.

A Buddhist, on the other hand, treats every kind

of body with contempt, and repudiates as a simple impossibility, all idea of being a member of the Buddha's body. How could a Buddhist be a member of a body which was burnt to ashes—which was calcined,—which became extinct at the moment when the Buddha's whole personality became extinguished also?

But, say the admirers of Buddhism, at least you will admit that the Buddha told men to avoid sin, and to aim at purity and holiness of life? Nothing of the kind. The Buddha had no idea of sin as an offence against God, no idea of true holiness (see p. 124). What he said was—Get rid of the demerit of evil actions and accumulate a stock of merit by good actions.

And let me remark here that this determination to store up merit—like capital at a bank—is one of those inveterate propensities of human nature, one of those irrepressible and deep-seated tendencies in humanity which nothing but the divine force imparted by Christianity can ever eradicate. It is for ever cropping up in the heart of man, as much in the West as in the East, as much in the North as in the South; for ever re-asserting itself like a pestilent weed, or like tares amidst the wheat, for ever blighting the fruit of those good instincts which underlie man's nature everywhere.

Only the other day I met an intelligent Sikh from the Panjāb, and asked him about his religion. He replied, 'I am no idolater; I believe in One God, and I repeat my prayers, called "Jap-jee," every morning and evening. These prayers occupy six pages of print, but I can get through them in little more than ten minutes.' He seemed to pride himself on this rapid recitation as a work of increased merit.

I said, 'What else does your religion require of you?' He replied, 'I have made one pilgrimage to a holy well near Amritsar. Eighty-five steps lead down to it. I descended and bathed in the sacred pool. Then I ascended one step and repeated my Jap-jee with great rapidity. Then I descended again to the pool and bathed again, and ascended to the second step and repeated my prayers a second time. Then I descended a third time, and ascended to the third step and repeated my Jap-jee a third time, and so on for the whole eighty-five steps, eighty-five bathings and eighty-five repetitions of the same prayers. It took me exactly fourteen hours, from 5 p.m. one evening to 7 a.m. next morning, and I fasted all the time.'

I asked, 'What good did you expect to get by going through this task?' He replied, 'I hope I have laid up an abundant store of merit, which will last me for a long time.'

This, let me tell you, is a genuine Hindū notion. It is of the very essence of Brāhmanism, of Hindūism, of Zoroastrianism, of Confucianism, of Muhammadanism. It is even more of the essence of Buddhism. For, of all systems, Buddhism is the one which lays most stress on the accumulation of merit by good actions, as the sole counterpoise to the mighty force generated by the accumulation of demerit through evil actions in present and previous forms of life.

Nor did the Buddha ever claim to be a *deliverer from guilt*, *a purger from the taint of past pollution*. He *never pretended to set any one free from the penalty*, power, and presence of sin—from the bondage of sinful acts and besetting vices. He never professed to furnish any cure for the leprosy of man's corrupt nature—any medicine for a dying sinner[1]. On the contrary, by his doctrine of Karma he bound a man hand and foot to the inevitable consequences of his own evil actions with chains of adamant. He said, in effect, to every one of his disciples, 'You are in slavery to a tyrant of your own setting up; your own deeds, words, and thoughts in your present and former states of being, are your own avengers through a countless series of existences.

> "Your acts your angels are for good or ill,
> Your fatal shadows that walk by you still."

'If you have been a murderer, a thief, a liar, impure, a drunkard, you must pay the penalty in your next birth—perhaps as a sufferer in one of the hells[2], per-

---

[1] It is true that in the Lalita-vistara Buddha is described in terms which appear to assimilate his character to the Christian conception of a Saviour; but how could any man, however good and great, have any claim to be called either a Saviour or Redeemer, who only revealed to his fellow-men such a method of getting rid of pain and suffering, through their own works and merits, as must lead them in the end to extinction of all personal existence? The very essence of Christ's character as a Saviour is His divine power of transferring His own perfect merits to imperfect men, and leading them from death to eternal life, not to eternal extinction of life.

[2] In regard to the Buddhist doctrine of terrific purgatorial torments in some of the numerous Hells see p. 120 of this volume.

haps in the body of a wild beast, perhaps in that of some unclean animal or loathsome vermin, perhaps as a demon or evil spirit. Yes, your doom is sealed. Not in the heavens, O man, not in the midst of the sea, not if thou hidest thyself in the clefts of the mountains, wilt thou find a place where thou canst escape the force of thine own evil actions[1]. Thy only hope of salvation is in thyself. Neither god nor man can save thee, and I am wholly powerless to set thee free.'

And now, contrast the few brief words of Christ in his first recorded sermon[2]. 'The Spirit of the Lord is upon Me, because He hath anointed Me to preach good tidings to the poor; He hath sent Me to proclaim liberty to the captives, and recovering of sight to the blind, and the opening of the prison to them that are bound.'

Yes, in Christ alone there is deliverance from the bondage of former transgressions, from the prison-house of former sins; a total cancelling of the past; a complete blotting-out of the handwriting that is against us; an entire washing away of every guilty stain; the opening of a clear course for every man to start afresh; the free gift of pardon and of life to every criminal, to every sinner—even the most heinous and inveterate.

Still, I seem to hear some admirers of Buddhism

[1] See Dhamma-pada, 127.

[2] I have not followed the exact words in our authorized translation of St. Luke iv. 18, because they must be taken with Isaiah.

say: We admit the force of these contrasts, but surely you will allow that in the moral law of Buddha we find precepts identically the same as those of Christianity—precepts which tell a man not to love the world, not to love money, not to hate his enemies, not to do unrighteous acts, not to commit impurities, to overcome evil by good, and to do to others as we would be done by?

Well, I admit all this. Nay, I admit even more than this; for many Buddhist precepts command total abstinence in cases where Christianity demands only temperance and moderation. The great contrast, as I have already explained, between the moral precepts of Buddhism and Christianity, is not so much in the letter of the precepts, as in the power brought to bear in their application.

Buddhism, I repeat, says: Act righteously through your own efforts, and for the final getting rid of all suffering, of all individuality, of all life in yourselves. Christianity says: Be righteous through a power implanted in you from above, through the power of a life-giving principle, freely given to you, and always abiding in you. The Buddha said to his followers: 'Take nothing from me, trust to yourselves alone.' Christ said: 'Take all from Me; trust not to yourselves. I give unto you eternal life, I give unto you the bread of heaven, I give unto you living water.' Not that these priceless gifts involve any passive condition of inaction. On the contrary, they stir the soul of the recipient with a living energy. They stimulate him to noble deeds, and self-sacrificing efforts. They compel him to act as the worthy, grateful, and appreciative possessor of so inestimable a treasure.

Still, I seem to hear some one say: We acknowledge this; we admit the truth of what you have stated; nevertheless, for all that, you must allow that Buddhism conferred a great benefit on India by encouraging freedom of thought and by setting at liberty its teeming population, before entangled in the meshes of ceremonial observances and Brahmanical priestcraft.

Yes, I grant this; nay, I grant even more than this. I admit that Buddhism conferred many other benefits on the millions inhabiting the most populous part of Asia. It introduced education and culture; it encouraged literature and art; it promoted physical, moral, and intellectual progress up to a certain point; it proclaimed peace, good will, and brotherhood among men; it deprecated war between nation and nation; it avowed sympathy with social liberty and freedom; it gave back much independence to women; it preached purity in thought, word, and deed (though only for the accumulation of merit); it taught self-denial without self-torture; it inculcated generosity, charity, tolerance, love, self-sacrifice, and benevolence, even towards the inferior animals; it advocated respect for life and compassion towards all creatures; it forbade avarice and the hoarding of money; and from its declaration that a man's future depended on his present acts and condition, it did good service for a time in preventing stagnation, stimulating exertion, promoting good works of all kinds, and elevating the character of humanity.

Then again, when it spread to outlying countries it

assumed the character of a religion; it taught the existence of unseen worlds; it permitted the offering of prayers to Maitreya and other supposed personal saviours; it inculcated faith and trust in these celestial beings, which operated as good motives in the hearts of many, while the hope of being born in higher conditions of life, and the desire to acquire merit by reverential acts, led to the development of devotional services, which had much in common with those performed in Christian countries. Nay, it must even be admitted that many Buddhists in the present day are deeply imbued with religious feelings, and in no part of the world are the outward manifestations of religion—such as temples and sacred objects of all kinds—so conspicuous as in modern Buddhist countries.

But if, after making all these concessions, I am told that, on my own showing, Buddhism was a kind of introduction to Christianity, or that Christianity is a kind of development of Buddhism, I must ask you to bear with me a little longer, while I point out certain other contrasts, which ought to make it clear to every reasonable man, how vast, how profound, how impassable is the gulf separating the true religion from the false philosophy, and from the later religious systems developed out of it.

And first, observe that Buddhism has never claimed to be an exclusive system. It has never aimed at taking the place of other religions. On the contrary it tolerates all, and a Buddhist considers that he may be at the same time a Hindū, a Confucianist, a Tāoist, a Shintoist, and even, strange to say, a Christian.

A Christian, on the other hand, holds as a cardinal doctrine of his religion, that there is only one Name under heaven given among men, whereby any human being can be saved. To be at the same time a believer in Christ and a believer in Buddha implies an utter contradiction in terms.

Then it need scarcely be repeated here that Christ is before all things a majestic example of a great historic personality. Any really historical, matter-of-fact account of the life of Buddha, like that of the life of Christ by the four Evangelists, may be looked for in vain through all the Buddhist scriptures. The Buddha's biography is mixed up with such monstrous legends, absurd figments, and extravagant fables, that to attempt the sifting out of any really historical element worthy of being compared with the pregnant simplicity—the dignified brevity of the biography of Christ, would be an idle task.

Still we may note two or three obvious points of comparison and contrast.

And perhaps the most important is, that Christ constantly insisted on the fact that He was God-sent, whereas the Buddha always described himself as self sent. How indeed could the Buddha have said 'the great I AM hath sent me unto you[1]' when he had no belief in the eternal existence of any Ego at all? Not even in the reality of his own individuality.

All that he affirmed of himself was that he came into the world to be a teacher of perfect wisdom, by

[1] Exodus iii. 14.

a force derived from his own acts. By that force alone he had passed through innumerable bodies of gods, demi-gods, demons, men, and animals, until he reached one out of numerous heavens, and thence by his own will descended upon earth and entered the side of his mother in the form of a white elephant (see pp. 23, 477). Let those who speak of his 'virgin-mother' bear this in mind.

Christ, on the other hand, made known to his disciples, that He was with His Father from everlasting, 'Before Abraham was, I am.' Then in the fulness of time, He was *sent* into the world by His Father, and was born of a pure virgin, through the power of the Holy Spirit, in the likeness and fashion of men.

Next let us note a vast contrast in the fact that Christ was sent from heaven to be born on earth in a poor and humble station, to be reared in a cottage, to be trained to toilsome labour as a working-man; whereas the Buddha came down to be born on earth in a rich and princely family; to be brought up amid luxurious surroundings, and finally to go forth as a mendicant-monk, depending upon others for his daily food and doing nothing for his own support.

Then, again, Christ as He grew up showed no signs of earthly majesty in his external form, whereas the Buddha is described as marked with certain mystic symbols of universal monarchy on his feet and on his hands, and taller and more stately in frame and figure than ordinary human beings (see pp. 476, 501).

Then, when each entered on his ministry as a teacher, Christ was despised and rejected by kings and princes, and followed by poor and ignorant fishermen, by common people, publicans, and sinners; Buddha was honoured by kings and princes, and followed by rich men and learned disciples.

Then Christ had all the treasures of knowledge hidden in Himself, and made known to His disciples that He was Himself the Way, and the Truth,—Himself their Wisdom, Righteousness, Sanctification, and Redemption. Buddha declared that all enlightenment and wisdom were to be attained by his disciples, not through him, but through themselves and their own intuitions; and that, too, only after long and painful discipline in countless successive bodily existences.

Then in regard to the miracles which both the Bible and the Tripiṭaka describe as attestations of the truth of the teaching of each, contrast the simple and dignified statement that 'the blind receive their sight, the lame walk, the lepers are cleansed, the deaf hear, the dead are raised up, and the poor have the gospel preached unto them[1],' with the following description of the Buddha's miracles in the Mahā-vagga (I. 20, 24)[2]: 'At the command of the Blessed One the five hundred pieces of fire-wood could not be split and were split, the fires could not be lit up and were lit up, could not be extinguished and were extinguished. Besides he created five hundred vessels with fire. Thus the number of these miracles amounts to three thousand five hundred.'

Then, although each made use of missionary agency,

---

[1] St. Matthew xi. 5.

[2] Sacred Books of the East, xiii. 133.

the one sent forth his high-born learned monks as missionaries to the world at the commencement of his own career, giving them no divine commission; the other waited till the close of His own ministry, and then said to His low-born, unlearned disciples, 'As My Father hath sent Me, even so send I you' (St. John xx. 21).

Then, when we come to compare the death of each, the contrast reaches its climax; for Christ was put to death violently by wicked men, and died in agony an atoning death, suffering for the sins of the world at the age of thirty-three, leaving behind in Jerusalem about one hundred and twenty disciples after a short ministry of three years. Whereas the Buddha died peacefully among his friends, suffering from an attack of indigestion at the age of eighty, leaving behind many thousands of disciples after forty-five years of teaching and preaching.

And what happened after the death of each? Christ, the Holy One, saw no corruption, but rose again in His present glorified body, and is alive for evermore—nay, has life in Himself ever flowing in life-giving streams towards His people. The Buddha is dead and gone for ever; his body, according to the testimony of his own disciples, was burnt more than 400 years before the Advent of Christ, and its ashes were distributed everywhere as relics.

Even according to the Buddha's own declaration, he now lives only in the doctrine which he left behind him for the guidance of his followers.

And here again, in regard to the doctrine left behind by each, a vast distinction is to be noted. For the doctrine delivered by Christ to His disciples is to spread by degrees everywhere until it prevails eternally. Whereas the doctrine left by Buddha, though it advanced rapidly by leaps and bounds, is, according to his own admission, to fade away by degrees, till at the end of 5000 years it has disappeared altogether from the earth, and another Buddha must descend to restore it. (Compare Postscript at end of Preface, p. xiv.)

Then that other Buddha must be followed by countless succeeding Buddhas in succeeding ages, whereas there is only one Christ, who can have no successor, for He is alive for ever and for ever present with His people: 'Lo, I am with you alway, even unto the end of the world.'

Then observe that, although the Buddha's doctrine was ultimately written down by his disciples in certain collections of books, in the same manner as the doctrine of Christ, a fundamental difference of character—nay, a vast and impassable gulf of difference—separates the Sacred Books of each, the Bible of the Christian and the Bible of the Buddhist.

The characteristic of the Christian's Bible is that it claims to be a supernatural revelation, yet it attaches no mystical talismanic virtue to the mere sound of its words. On the other hand, the characteristic of the Buddhist Bible is that it utterly repudiates all claim to be a supernatural revelation; yet the very sound of its words is believed to possess a meritorious efficacy capable of elevating any one who hears it to heavenly abodes in future existences. In illustration I may advert to a legend current in Ceylon, that once on a time 500 bats lived in a cave where two monks daily recited the Buddha's Law. These bats gained such merit by simply hearing the sound of the words, that, when they died, they were all re-born as men, and ultimately as gods.

Then as to the words themselves, contrast the severely simple and dignified style of the Bible narrative, its brevity, perspicuity, vigour, and sublimity, its trueness to nature and inimitable pathos, with the feeble utterances, the tedious diffuseness, and I might almost say 'the inane twaddle' and childish repetitions of the greater portion of the Tripiṭaka (see note 2, p. 541).

But again, I am sure to hear the admirers of Buddhism say: Is it not the case that the doctrine of Buddha, like the doctrine of Christ, has self-sacrifice as its key-note? Well, be it so. I admit that the Buddha taught a kind of self-sacrifice. I admit that he related of himself that, on a particular occasion in one of his previous births [1], he plucked out his own eyes, and, that on another, he cut off his own head as a sacrifice for the good of others; and that again, on a third occasion, he cut his own body to pieces to redeem a dove from a hawk [2]. Yet note the vast distinction between the self-sacrifice taught by the two systems. Christianity demands the suppression of selfishness; Buddhism demands the suppression of self, with the one object of extinguishing all consciousness of self. In

---

[1] It is necessary to point out that these acts of self-sacrifice took place in former states of existence, for when a man becomes a Buddha he has no need to gain merit by self-sacrifice.

[2] See p. 130.

the one, the true self is elevated and intensified. In the other, the true self is annihilated by the practice of a false form of non-selfishness, which has for its real object, not the good of others, but the annihilation of the Ego, the utter extinction of the illusion of personal individuality.

Furthermore, observe the following contrasts in the doctrines which each bequeathed to his followers :—

According to Christianity :—Fight and overcome the world.

According to Buddhism :—Shun the world, and withdraw from it.

According to Christianity :—Expect a new earth when the present earth is destroyed ; a world renewed and perfected ; a purified world in which righteousness is to dwell for ever.

According to Buddhism :—Expect a never-ending succession of evil worlds for ever coming into existence, developing, decaying, perishing, and reviving, and all equally full of everlasting misery, disappointment, illusion, change, and transmutation.

According to Christianity, bodily existence is subject to only one transformation.

According to Buddhism, bodily existence is continued in six conditions, through countless bodies of men, animals, demons, ghosts, and dwellers in various hells and heavens ; and that, too, without any progressive development, but in a constant jumble of metamorphoses and transmutations (see p. 122).

Christianity teaches that a life in heaven can never be followed by a fall to a lower state.

Buddhism teaches that a life in a higher heaven may be succeeded by a life in a lower heaven, or even by a life on earth or in one of the hells.

According to Christianity, the body of man may be the abode of the Holy Spirit of God.

According to Buddhism, the body whether of men or of higher beings can never be the abode of anything but evil.

According to Christianity:—Present your bodies as living sacrifices, holy, acceptable to God, and expect a change to glorified bodies hereafter.

According to Buddhism :—Look to final deliverance from all bodily life, present and to come, as the greatest of all blessings, highest of all boons, and loftiest of all aims.

According to Christianity, a man's body can never be changed into the body of a beast, or bird, or insect, or loathsome vermin.

According to Buddhism, a man, and even a god, may become an animal of any kind, and even the most loathsome vermin may again become a man or a god.

According to Christianity :—Stray not from God's ways ; offend not against His holy laws.

According to Buddhism :—Stray not from the eightfold path of the perfect man, and offend not against yourself and the law of the perfect man.

According to Christianity :—Work the works of God while it is day.

According to Buddhism :—Beware of action, as causing re-birth, and aim at inaction, indifference, and apathy, as the highest of all states.

Then note other contrasts.

According to the Christian Bible:—Regulate and sanctify the heart, desires, and affections.

According to the Buddhist:—Suppress and destroy them utterly, if you wish for true sanctification.

Christianity teaches that in the highest form of life, love is intensified.

Buddhism teaches that in the highest state of existence, all love is extinguished.

According to Christianity:—Go and earn your own bread, support yourself and your family. Marriage, it says, is honourable and undefiled, and married life is a field on which holiness may grow and be developed. Nay, more—Christ Himself honoured a wedding with His presence, and took up little children in His arms and blessed them.

Buddhism, on the other hand, says:—Avoid married life; shun it as if it were 'a burning pit of live coals' (p. 88); or, having entered on it, abandon wife, children, and home, and go about as celibate monks, engaging in nothing but in meditation and recitation of the Buddha's Law—that is to say—*if you aim at the highest degree of sanctification.*

And then comes the important contrast that in the one system we have a teaching gratifying to the pride of man, and flattering to his intellect; while in the other we have a teaching humbling to his pride, and distasteful to his intellect. For Christianity tells us that we must become as little children, and that when we have done all that we can, we are still unprofitable servants. Whereas Buddhism teaches that every man is saved by his own works and by his own merits only.

Fitly, indeed, do the rags worn by the monks of true Buddhism symbolize the miserable patchwork of its own self-righteousness.

Not that Christianity ignores the necessity for good works; on the contrary, no other system insists on a lofty morality so strongly; but never as the meritorious instrument of salvation[1]—only as a thank-offering, only as the outcome and evidence of faith.

Lastly, we must advert again to the most momentous—the most essential of all the distinctions which separate Christianity from Buddhism[2]. Christianity regards personal life as the most sacred of all possessions. Life, it seems to say, is no dream, no illusion. 'Life is real, life is earnest.' Life is the most precious of all God's gifts. Nay, it affirms of God Himself that He is the highest Example of intense Life—of intense personality, the great 'I AM that I AM,' and teaches us that we are to thirst for a continuance of personal life as a gift from Him; nay, more, that we are to thirst for the living God Himself and for conformity

---

[1] A Buddhist writer in a magazine, published in Ceylon, has lately taken me to task for asserting that Christianity denies the all-sufficiency of good works as an instrument of salvation. The writer has much to learn as to the true character of our Bible, in which no text has full force without its context, and no part can be taken to establish a doctrine without a comparison with other parts, and without the balancing of apparent contradictions. The Old Testament must not be read without the New, nor St. James without St. Paul.

[2] This Lecture was written before I had seen Bishop Titcomb's excellent little book on Buddhism. Some of my contrasts are nearly identical with his.

to His likeness; while Buddhism sets forth as the highest of all aims the utter extinction of the illusion of personal identity—the utter annihilation of the Ego—of all existence in any form whatever, and proclaims as the only true creed the ultimate resolution of everything into nothing, of every entity into pure nonentity.

What shall I do to inherit eternal life?—says the Christian. What shall I do to inherit eternal extinction of life?—says the Buddhist.

It seems a mere absurdity to have to ask in concluding these Lectures:—Whom shall we choose as our Guide, our Hope, our Salvation, 'the Light of Asia,' or 'the Light of the World?' the Buddha or the Christ? It seems a mere mockery to put this final question to rational and thoughtful men in the nineteenth century: Which Book shall we clasp to our hearts in our last hour—the Book that tells us of the dead, the extinct, the death-giving Buddha, or the Book that reveals to us the living, the eternal, the life-giving Christ?

POSTSCRIPT.

Since the printing of my concluding Lecture, it has occurred to me that I ought to make a few remarks in regard to a very prevalent error—the error that Buddhism still numbers more adherents than any other religion of the world. For these remarks the reader is referred to the Postscript at the end of the Preface (p. xiv).

INDEX.

Observe—In the following Index the numbers indicate the pages. When more than one page is referred to the numbers are separated by semicolons. A unit or single number separated from a preceding number by a comma indicates that the reference is to a foot-note.